1993

A HERITAGE OF KINGS

STUDIES IN ORIENTAL CULTURE, NUMBER 21
COLUMBIA UNIVERSITY

A
HERITAGE
OF
KINGS

One Man's Monarchy
in the Confucian World

JaHyun Kim Haboush

Columbia University Press
New York
1988

The author and publisher gratefully acknowledge the generous support
toward publication given them by the National Endowment for the
Humanities and the University of Illinois Research Board.

Columbia University Press
New York   Guildford, Surrey
Copyright © 1988 Columbia University Press
All rights reserved

Library of Congress Cataloging-in-Publication Data

Haboush, JaHyun Kim.
A heritage of kings.

(Studies in Oriental culture ; no. 21)
Bibliography: p.
Includes index.
1. Yŏngjo, King of Korea, 1694–1776. 2. Confucianism
and states—Korea. I. Title. II. Series.
DS913.392.Y66H33   1988   951.9′02′0924   87-31972
ISBN 0-231-06656-2

Book Design by Jennifer Dossin
Printed in the United States of America
Hardback editions of Columbia University Press Books are Smyth-sewn
and are printed on permanent and durable acid-free paper.

TO BILL

CONTENTS

ACKNOWLEDGMENTS

In the course of completing this work, I have benefited enormously from discussions, suggestions, criticisms, comments and other assistance from many friends and colleagues here and abroad. My first thanks go to Professor Gari Ledyard of Columbia University. From the time it was conceived to its conclusion, this work was enriched by his enthusiastic encouragement and erudition. I also owe special thanks to Professor Wm. Theodore de Bary of Columbia University who, despite the fact that my work is essentially outside of his main area of interest, supported my inquiry. I am also particularly indebted to Professor Edward Wagner of Harvard University who always responded to my urgent inquiries. I would also like to express my appreciation and gratitude to Professors Irene Bloom of Columbia University, Patricia Ebrey of the University of Illinois at Urbana-Champaign, John Meskill of Barnard College, James Palais of the University of Washington, and Pei-yi Wu of Queens College, all of whom read the whole or parts of this manuscript at various points and offered many useful comments and suggestions. I am also especially indebted to an anonymous reader whose suggestions for revision I have largely followed. Professors Koh Byong-ik and Lee Mangap, both formerly of Seoul National University, and the late Professor Chong Pyonguk of Seoul National University helped while I was conducting research in Seoul. I also received invaluable assistance

xi

Acknowledgments

from Mr. Yi Sangun of the Kyujanggak Library at Seoul National University, Mr. Paik Lin of the Harvard Yenching Library, and Mr. Eugene Chai, Miss Amy Lee and Mr. Kennenth Harlin of the C. V. Starr East Asian Library at Columbia University, and would like to express my gratitude to them all. Finally, I would like to thank the Social Science Research Council which financed the research necessary to the completion of this project and the National Endowment for the Humanities and the University of Illinois Research Board, both of which gave support toward the publication of this book.

EXPLANATORY NOTE

In referring to age, I have adhered to the traditional Korean method of counting (*se*). That is, one is said to be one year old at birth and a year is added on each lunar new year. Thus, one is the same age throughout the year and does not gain a year on one's birthday. For readability, I have remained with standard usage, saying that someone is so many years old rather than so many *se*, but the reader should remember to subtract at least one year to convert to the Western equivalent. For date and year, I have converted the lunar calendar into the Western calendar. Thus, the thirteenth day of the intercalary fifth month, the *imo* year is rendered July 4, 1762.

Royal personages are referred to by the names they are best known by in contemporary Korea. Members of the royal family were routinely given and designated by titles that changed with their station at any given time. As a title symbolized a new status, the old title was discarded. This process went on after death. Yŏngjo, the protagonist of this book, was no exception. Like any upper-class male, he had a formal name (*myŏng*), Kŭm; a style name (*cha*), Kwangsuk; and a courtesy name (*ho*), Yangsŏnghŏn. But no one called him by any of these names. Rather, he was referred to as Yŏninggun (Prince Yŏning), the title given to him in 1699 when he was six. In 1721, he was appointed heir apparent to his brother and was referred to as *Seje* (Brother Heir Apparent).

Explanatory Note

While he was on the throne, he had no title except the several honorific designations used in reference to the king. Upon his death in 1776, he was given the temple name, Yŏngjong. In 1889, his descendants honored him further by changing this name to Yŏngjo, a more exalted name. Thus, referring to him as Yŏngjo is definitely anachronistic. But that is the name by which he is known. No one would recognize other designations. For the same reason, I have chosen to refer to his son as Prince Sado, the name Yŏngjo conferred upon his son soon after he put him to death in 1762. I have applied the same principle to other members of the royal family, including ladies. For persons who were not members of the royal family, I have used their formal names (*myŏng*).

A HERITAGE OF KINGS

INTRODUCTION

This book is a study of the Confucian kingship as it was understood and practiced by Yŏngjo, the twenty-first king of Yi Korea (1392–1910), who ruled from 1724 to 1776. The Confucian kingship, guided and formed as it was by the ideal of the sage king, was an exceedingly demanding one. The ruler was an ordinary mortal, not a divine being, yet his virtue had to be such that his mandate was premised upon it. Not only was he expected to perfect himself; he was also burdened with effecting perfect order in his realm. This, or the lack thereof, was seen as the index of his virtue. The practice of sage kingship, however, was another matter. Like other political ideologies, it was used in the context of institutional, political, and social realities. In China, where our ideas of rulership have been significantly clarified by such illuminating works as those by Professor Jonathan Spence on the Emperor K'ang-hsi and Professor Harold Kahn on the Emperor Ch'ien-lung, the emperor was enshrined in a nearly mythic aura. As the Son of Heaven, the Chinese emperor was the mediator between Heaven and the civilized world. The monarchical institution also developed in such a way as to enhance the awesomeness of imperial authority. The bureaucracy grew vast and, by the Sung dynasty (960–1279), it came to be staffed by professional, rather than aristocratic, bureaucrats selected by the civil service examination. From the Ming dynasty (1368–1644), the throne acquired a nearly unchallengeable power. In this context, the emperor could with impunity avail himself of the rhetoric of the sage king to buttress the imperial image.

The Yi monarchy shared with China the concept and rhetoric of the sage king, but it employed it in a very different situation. Neither was the Korean king the Son of Heaven as the Chinese

1

emperor was nor did he rule a huge country known and seen as the central kingdom. The institutional structure in which he ruled sharply impinged upon his freedom of action. The bureaucracy was rather small and was dominated by aristocratic bureaucrats who vied with the throne for power. Seasoned practitioners of Confucian rhetoric themselves, the bureaucrats could compete with the throne in their use of the rhetoric of moral rule. Thus, a Yi king who wished to establish monarchical authority and power using the ideal of the sage king, as Yŏngjo did, had to submit to the rigors this ideal demanded.

Yŏngjo's pursuit of sage kingship was predicated on his belief that the rhetoric and ideas of the sage king would render him with effective means with which to deal with the demands of his court and society. The effectiveness of his pursuit, first of all, depended on whether he could persuade his bureaucrats and subjects of the seriousness of his intent. In this respect, Yŏngjo seems to have succeeded. He pursued his ideal with single-minded commitment. His relentless construction of an image as a sage king during his fifty-two-year reign, the longest Yi reign, led to bureaucratic capitulation to his moral superiority. His continued display of concern for his people seems to have earned gratitude and appreciation. His excursions into the streets in the later years of his life were greeted with spontaneous cheers, a rare phenomenon in Yi Korea.

Perhaps more importantly, Yŏngjo's pursuit can be evaluated by how effectively he was able to use the rhetoric and the concepts of the sage king in dealing with the specific social and political problems of his day. Eighteenth-century Korea, over which he presided, is generally regarded as having been peaceful and prosperous. Yi society had resolved much of the conflict resulting from the adoption of the Neo-Confucian social and political system. The ensuing changes, coupled with the relative economic prosperity, however, resulted in pressing needs for certain reforms. The government had successfully overcome the trauma of the Manchu conquest of China. This, in the Korean view, was a barbarian usurpation of the very center of civilization. Korea emerged with a new sense of mission as the sole custodian of the one true civilization. This led to a sense of insecurity which was expressed by an extreme concern with orthodoxy in the seventeenth century. By Yŏngjo's time this gave way to a freer and more diverse intellectual atmosphere. Yet the political ethos of Yŏngjo's court was anything but tolerant. Factional battles, once fought over such issues as the definition of civilization and the role of the Yi monarchy in the changed world order, had successively become more intense. Yŏngjo's two predecessors had used factional politics, pitting factions against each other in their bids for royal power. Fifty years of violent factionalism, in which hundreds or thousands of officials and scholars had been executed and purged, left the scholar-bureaucrat community torn and acrimonious. The memory of this bloodshed and bitter struggle during the reign of Kyŏngjong, his predecessor and brother, instilled in Yŏngjo a strong desire to avoid such an outcome. The rebellion of 1728, which broke out in the fifth year of his reign, further convinced him of the need to enact certain reforms to ease the conditions of life for the general population and to contain the factionalism which he saw as the immediate cause for the rebellion.

Yŏngjo astutely sought and utilized the appropriate rhetoric and thematic content in Confucian rule in his attempts to effect the policies he thought necessary. In putting through the military tax reform, for instance, he used the rhetoric of the ruler-father, while in his effort to curb factionalism, he evoked the theme of grand harmony. In some areas, such as the adoption of the military tax reform, his method was effective, if only as a result of sheer determination. In other areas it was less so. His containment policy toward factionalism did completely stop the bloodshed within the court circle. Embedded in the political and social realities of several generations and rooted in human emotions, however, factional animosities could not be appeased by royal appeals to utopian ideals of harmony. In addition, Yŏngjo had to contend with charges of regicide. The rebellion of 1728 was carried out under this slogan, perhaps by those who had lost power by his enthronement. Even after 1728, there were repeated intimations of rebellion rationalized by this charge. Thus, if court officials shed no blood, many rebels did. Yŏngjo, it seemed, had to pay the price somewhere. And in his private life, in his relationship with his only son and heir, Prince Sado, Yŏngjo paid most dearly. It was as if the conflicts and difficulties of Yŏngjo, a mortal man seeking to fulfill the ideals of the sage king in a complex reality, were crystallized in his troubled relationship to his son.

My first chapter is devoted to a discussion of the Yi monarchical structure and the political culture of the Yi court. This is intended to provide the background in which Yŏngjo's pursuit of sagehood unfolded. The second chapter examines Yŏngjo's technique of image building. He had inherited a throne whose moral authority and, to an extent, power had been severely depleted by his two immediate predecessors' indiscriminate use of royal prerogative. But this throne also accorded him the various roles of a Confucian ruler—carrier of the dynastic mission, chief priest, and civilizer. The ritual and rhetoric of this throne, which demanded of its occupant that he fulfill these roles, were also the tools with which he could cultivate his image. He sought to restore monarchical authority by submitting to the moral demands imposed on a Confucian ruler. Thus, he toiled lifelong in his quest for sage kingship, and this quest was his quest for authority. But how did this quest reflect his commitment to Confucian rule? How Yŏngjo sought to fulfill his role as a Confucian ruler and what he accomplished were determined by how he, as a man, estimated his society and how he was perceived. In this sense, the manner in which Yŏngjo sought sagehood illuminates his mentality and that of his era.

The subject of the third chapter is Yŏngjo's use of the rhetoric of Confucian rule in the execution of social policies. Deeply troubled by the 1728 rebellion, he had set out, so to speak, to win the hearts of the people. Thus, his politics of patriarchy. But with this, he also successfully enacted certain reform measures, most notably the military tax reform, which would benefit the general populace. The question of the military tax, from which the upper class had been exempt, had long been a vexing issue for the Yi government. Because of bureaucratic opposition to reform, it had remained unresolved. How Yŏngjo overcame this opposition reveals the way in which he turned rhetoric into practical politics.

Yŏngjo's use of the utopian rhetoric of grand harmony in his interactions with the politics of his court is the subject of the fourth chapter. Pursued in the context of his invidious and fractious court, the execution of his policy of grand harmony demanded that Yŏngjo compromise his image as a flawlessly moral ruler. When this image came into conflict with his policy of grand harmony, he had to adjust his role to his method of rule. These changes, how Yŏngjo effected them, and how he, as man and monarch, changed with them are the focus of the chapter.

The impact of Yŏngjo's public role on his private life is examined in the fifth chapter. More generally, it is an attempt to highlight the dual character of the Confucian ruler, as public figure and private man. For Yŏngjo, this duality is poignantly expressed in his troubled relationship with his son. Yŏngjo's conflicting drives for absolute legitimacy and a perfect moral image were paralleled by his conflicting expectations of his son, Prince Sado. He wanted his son to be at once a private son—the avenger of his humiliations—and a public heir, a future sage king. Constrained by his position, Yŏngjo imposed these demands through the rhetoric of filial piety. Faced with these impossible demands, Sado responded through various attempts to escape from his role. In the end, Yŏngjo had to resort to a tragic and cruel act, which severely violated the tenets of Confucian humanism. This incident perhaps best illustrates the conflict faced by Yŏngjo in his personal life and in his rule, and the tensions of the society whose demands he so valiantly strove to meet.

This work concludes with four appendices. Their content is for the most part self-evident. The last one is devoted to a historiographical discussion of several key sources. These sources include the *Sillok*, the *Records of Royal Secretariat* (*Sŭngjŏngwŏn ilgi*), the *Changhŏn Seja tonggung ilgi* (Record of Prince Sado's Tutorial Office), *Yi Kwanghyŏn's Diary* (*Yi Kwanghyŏn ilgi*), and *A Journal Written in Leisure* (*Hanjungnok*) by Lady Hong.

CHAPTER 1

Confucian Kingship and Royal Authority in the Yi Monarchy

Great Heaven was moved with
   indignation,
and charged my deceased father
   Wan
reverentially to display its majesty;
but he died before the work was
   completed . . .
I, who am a little child,
early and late am filled with
   apprehension.
I have received a charge
from my deceased father Wan.

—*Book of Documents*

THE IDEAL OF THE SAGE KING

One of the keys to understanding the Confucian world view is the perception that Heaven is rational, that the universe is moral, that human reason is a sufficient instrument to fathom the divine, and that man can reproduce on earth the moral order immanent in the universe. The Confucian kingship was conceived in this framework. It sought divine ordination, but the ordination was conditional, not absolute, and subject to human appraisal.

The Mandate of Heaven (*Ch'ŏnmyŏng*) was conferred upon "the sincere, intelligent and perspicacious among men"[1] to establish this moral order. The sage kings of the antiquity, Yao and Shun, who were chosen exclusively on the basis of their virtue, embodied this kingship. The sage king was an ordinary man but for his virtue; but this virtue rendered him omnipotent. The king, by sheer force of his moral charisma, was to tap the goodness of man. With unfailing discernment, he was to choose men of virtue to help him to rule. With concern and compassion, he was to provide his people with livelihoods. With undivided dedication to public welfare, he was to be an impartial ruler, fair and just to each and all of his people. By his shining example, he was to lead men into a perfect order in which they lived in harmony with themselves and the moral universe.[2]

While Yao and Shun were but the ideal figures of a mythical era, and historical sovereigns inherited the throne by birth rather than by their own virtue, the fundamental concept of kingship did not change. The mandate might be given to a ruling house and a rightful heir might inherit this mandate but he could keep it only so long as he proved himself to be worthy of the task. If he were to fail to do so, if he could not "cause the people to have pleasure,"[3] and if he "be not benevolent,"[4] he could not prevent his throne from passing from him. It is the people through whom Heaven speaks: "Heaven sees as my people see; Heaven hears as my people hear."[5] If the kind of popular sovereignty implicit in the Confucian idea of the mandate was in fact used by conquerors and founders of dynasties to justify their claims to rule, in so using it these sovereigns nevertheless had to accept royal accountability to the divine order and to the people for their welfare.[6]

The ideal of a sage king modeled on Yao and Shun acquired further importance in Neo-Confucian political theory. The Neo-Confucians of eleventh- and twelfth-century Sung China articulated a vision of the moral universe in which the state of the human mind was directly linked to the universal moral order. Man, every thinking man that is, had a responsibility to exert himself for his moral perfection, to pursue sagehood and to uphold the moral order. It was an ongoing task demanded of him. This process, as is well known, was explicitly laid out in the eight steps of the *Great Learning (Ta-hsüeh)*; the first five steps were devoted to the intellectual, spiritual, and moral development and cultivation of self, while the last three concerned one's duty to family, the state, and the world. This seems to clearly reflect the Neo-Confucian view of man both as an individual and a social being.

While Neo-Confucianism was eventually accepted as state orthodoxy, its role in Sung government seems to have been, in the words
of Professor James T. C. Liu, "little more than a political gesture."[7] Neo-Confucianism was conceived by and primarily intended for potential and actual scholar-officials. By the Sung (960–
1279) period, an imperial bureaucratic system staffed with those
who were chosen by a meritocratic civil service examination had
long been in effect and officials were drawn from a large educated
populace. Serving in the imperial bureaucracy as professionals,
scholar-officials faced a situation in which they were mere servants of the state rendering requisite service. The vastness of the
bureaucracy and its inevitable routinization of work must have
made scholar-officials keenly aware of the limits of individual
ability. The preeminence accorded to man's pursuit of moral perfection in Neo-Confucianism and specifically in the *Great Learning*
in a way reaffirmed man's worth as a moral being as well as the
vital role he played in the total scheme of the moral universe.
Constant disturbances in the moral order were viewed as clear
signs of man's fallibility. Rather than despair and feel helpless,
Neo-Confucians stressed the urgency of individual effort. That man
was fallible was all the more reason why he should strive harder
for sagehood, incessantly if necessary. Being moral was not a matter of attaining a result but rather of maintaining a certain state
of mind and attitude. If this was a difficult task, it was not an
impossible one. After all, man was perfectible and he was rational. And in this way, by attending to his own cultivation, he
could at least do his share to uphold the moral order even if he
could not and did not have a chance to make a visible difference
in the workings of government.

As for the ruler, naturally, expectations were higher. As his sphere
of influence was the widest, his cultivation of self correspondingly
was more crucial. As the ultimate source of national well-being
as well as of the harmony between the moral order in the universe
and the ethical and social order in the kingdom, the rectification
of the imperial mind acquired a central importance. Thus the
statement by Fan Tsu-yü, an eleventh-century Sung scholar: "Order and disorder in the world all depend on the heart-and-mind
of the ruler. If his heart-and-mind are correct, then the myriad

affairs of the court will not be incorrect."[8] Hence, the rectification of the imperial mind emerged as a task that called for the concerted efforts of all concerned, the ruler as well as all his officials.[9] Leaving aside evaluations of relative imperial effort, even with maximal effort the attainment of sage kingship remained elusive. For a sage king was not only burdened with the fulfillment of his own virtue but also with the restoration of the moral order. And the inherently imperfect nature of human society constantly impinged upon the ideal kingship. Human fallibility at this apex of the political order thus had to be confronted with ever-increasing zeal. Hence the note of urgency in Chu Hsi's celebrated memorial of 1188 to the Emperor Hsiao-tsung: "None of these six points can be neglected, but they all have their root in Your Majesty's mind-and-heart. . . .Therefore this root of empire is also the most urgent of all urgent needs and cannot be put off even for a little while."[10]

But there was more than one way to confront human fallibility. The ideal of the sage king was pursued in the reality of a monarchy at a given time. How it interacted with the politics of each reign was a complicated matter closely related to such factors as the mentality of the age, the balance of power between the monarchy and the bureaucracy and institutional and social structures. One of the more direct ways of achieving some measure of recognition for sagacity seems to have been the proclamation of this status by the ruler.

Rather than worry about whether he was a sage king, a monarch could use the rhetoric and ritual available to him to pose as one. If this were done successfully, any blame for imperfection and imbalance in the society would fall upon the ministers who, in a Confucian monarchy, were responsible for transmitting and effecting the ruler's intentions. But this led to an inconsistency, for a sage king should naturally appoint only able and virtuous officials. After all, the sage king, by definition, should bring perfect order. What the self-proclaimed sage king could do was either to gloss over the problems of his reign as insignificant or to present himself, rather in the mold of Confucius, as a sage whose personal virtue did not attain public fulfillment because of the deficiencies of his era. But then if he was a sage and a king should

10

he not be a sage king? And if so, shouldn't his officials be transformed by his moral force? How could the notion of an unappreciated sage be applied to the most powerful man in the realm?

Unchallengeable monarchical power went a long way toward circumventing this logical discrepancy. In China, apparently such power took root in the Ming dynasty (1368–1644)[11] and became so deeply entrenched by the reigns of Emperors Yung-cheng (r. 1722–1736) and Ch'ien-lung (r. 1736–1795), the Ch'ing dynasty (1644–1912) contemporaries of Yŏngjo (r. 1724–1776) of Yi Korea (1392–1910), that to question the moral or intellectual prowess of the emperor was simply not permissible.[12] Thus the monarch could maintain an image of infallibility as a ruler and a sage.[13]

ROYAL AUTHORITY IN YI KOREA

The Confucian Kingship

The authority of the Yi king was first and foremost based on the rhetoric of the ideal Confucian kingship. This was clearly stated in the founder's coronation edict of 1392. It proclaimed that, due to his ancestors' virtue, Heaven had conferred the mandate upon the Yi house, and it appealed to officials for their help in discharging the awesome responsibilities of governing in accordance with Heaven's will, promising the people that the ruler, though unworthy and deficient in virtue, would toil for their benefit and share their joys and sorrows.[14]

If the Confucian rhetoric in Yi T'aejo's (r. 1392–1398) edict sounds familiar, and was to be repeated again and again in successive Yi kings' edicts, it nevertheless marked a new beginning for Korea. Written by Chŏng Tojŏn, the chief ideologue of the founding group, it was a clear statement of the vision under which the new dynasty was born—the creation of a new Confucian moral order. While the Yi dynasty was founded soon after the founding of the Ming dynasty, and was certainly aided by the change of power in China as the old Koryŏ regime (918–1392) had been compromised by long years of subjugation to the Yüan dynasty (1279–1368), the Korean dynastic founding differed from its Chinese counterpart

11

on several crucial points. Unlike the Ming dynasty, which had succeeded through civil war, the Yi dynasty was the result of a bloodless coup.[15] Unlike the Confucian intellectuals behind Chu Yüan-chang's rise, intellectuals who, looking back on the failure of the Sung dynasty, harbored grave doubts about the ability of the Confucian bureaucracy to rule successfully,[16] the Yi Neo-Confucian founders, with no past failures to contend with, were driven by a commitment to forge a new Confucian social order which would be a complete break from the old Buddhist Koryŏ society. With this sense of mission, they engineered and carried out the change. The founding of the Yi dynasty was thus more than anything else a Confucian revolution.[17]

One of the first issues the founding group addressed was how to promote meritocracy in the context of a hereditary monarchy. The resulting political structure at the beginning of the dynasty was a Prime Minister–centered bureaucracy in which royal authority flowed from the almost entirely symbolic status of the king, while most decision making and administrative power was delegated to the Prime Minister. Devised by Chŏng Tojŏn, it was consonant with his vision of the Confucian polity, a vision that took the division between symbolic and real authority as an essential ingredient of success. That is, the legitimacy of the monarchy was based on the mandate of the Yi royal house, while the efficiency and stability of the system was maintained by the executive power of the State Council (*Ŭijŏngbu*) led by the Prime Minister.[18] In placing power in the hands of ministers who would be chosen by merit and experience, Chŏng was hoping to insure the efficacy of the system against two obvious problems: royal autocracy and the vagaries of individual kings who would inherit the throne through birth.

At the same time, Chŏng emphasized the hierarchical structure of the bureaucracy lest it disintegrate. Junior officials were not allowed to challenge their seniors in public. And while he sanctioned the censors' right to voice criticism of the throne and their fellow officials, he cautioned against excessive censorial power as he thought it would result in the paralysis of the government.[19]

In order to staff the bureaucracy on the basis of meritocracy a wide pool of talent trained in Confucian ideals of public service

12

was needed. A public school system was promoted and the civil service examination was opened to a wider spectrum of candidates.[20]

Relentless social engineering by the ruling group initiated a Confucianization of Korean society.[21] A wide dissemination of Confucian values and mores through education and ritual and a corresponding institutional development accelerated the process. Family structure was thoroughly reorganized. The uxorilocal marriages of the Koryŏ period became patrilineal units. The importance of patrilineality seems to have been occasioned, at least in part, by upper-class adoption of the rituals specified in Chu Hsi's *Family Ritual (Chu Tzu chia-li)* as regular features of life. These rituals, especially the mourning and ancestral rites, assume a patrilineal five mourning grade (*obok*) family unit.[22] The government also sanctioned patrilineality by requiring that, in the census registers, all freemen, especially yangban, specify the names and posts of four generations of ancestors in the father's line but only two generations in the mother's line. This was a departure from Koryŏ practice in which the mother's line was given equal weight.[23] In this broad context, many associated changes occurred. Consanguineous marriages, for instance, were replaced by exogamy.

These changes, however, were not completed for several centuries. Uxorilocal marriages seem to have been rather common well into the sixteenth century.[24] Daughters continued to receive property and acted as heirs in ritual performances. But sometime in the seventeenth century, there was a marked decline in daughter's shares of inheritance[25] accompanied by a sharp increase in the practice of adopting male heirs from the same clan.[26] Patrilineality seems to have taken root at about this time. Genealogies rapidly proliferated[27] as well as local gentry associations (*hyang-an*) with rosters of membership.[28] Likewise, Confucian social ethics based on the five relations (*oryun*) were widely propagated and became the ideal norm for familial and social relationships. Embraced by the upper class, Confucian mores and ethics trickled down to the lower strata of society aided by such practices as community compacts (*hyangyak*).[29]

The Confucianization of the Yi court also proceeded in the context of the political and social situation of each period. The first century of the Yi dynasty was fraught with succession struggles. King T'aejong (r. 1400–1418) came to the throne after eliminating several of his brothers. Chŏng Tojŏn, who supported T'aejo's younger son, was killed by T'aejong in 1398. King Sejo (r. 1455–1468) usurped the throne from his young nephew, Tanjong (r. 1452–1455). Unwilling to be subjected to the ideological restraints of Confucian rule and jealous of royal power, these strong-willed kings insisted on a more direct control of state affairs. This resulted in changes alternating between a bureaucracy centered around the Prime Minister and one centered around the monarch.[30] Succession struggles and the unstable political situation of the early Yi had produced a large number of merit subjects (*kongsin*) who had assisted various monarchs' rises to power. It seems that almost each reign produced several tens of merit subjects, and sometimes more. They were rewarded with special hereditary status and generous financial remuneration in the form of heritable land and slaves.[31] They also dominated high civil and military posts.[32]

Meanwhile a century of Confucian education produced its share of committed adherents. Once they entered bureaucracy, they called for reforms in government structure and policy to conform to their vision of Confucian government. For the first half of the sixteenth century, the Yi court was enveloped in major ideological disputes and political upheavals. Merit subjects and a more ideologically oriented group clashed repeatedly, with several kings actively taking part in the fray.[33] The pendulum swung wildly, and many in both camps were killed. King Yŏnsan (r. 1494–1506), for instance, before he was dethroned in 1506, went so far as to demolish most of the institutions that he saw as ideological strongholds of the bureaucracy, such as the National Academy, the Royal Lecture, and the Censorate.[34] The Confucian tide, however, seems to have been irresistible and, by the mid-sixteenth century, the ideologically committed group emerged triumphant. Their arrival had an indelible impact on the ethos of the court. What had once been a mechanism of rule came to be a value system to which the ruling group, including the monarch himself, had to submit.

By the mid-sixteenth century, with the Confucianization of the court a certain balance between the monarchical and bureaucratic roles seems to have been achieved. Alternations between a Prime Minister–centered bureaucracy and a monarch-centered one eventually evolved into a system in which the State Council had a great deal of decision-making power, subject to royal approval. The king and the high-ranking ministers deliberated on policies of import. Thus, the Yi court struck a certain compromise and left room for royal initiatives and influence. The degree of utilization of this avenue varied according to individual kings' inclinations.

That a more balanced distribution of power between the monarch and the bureaucracy came to be preferred, but premised on royal virtue, can be seen in the political theory of the scholars of the sixteenth century. Yi Yulgok, commonly considered as one of the two most renowned Yi Neo-Confucian scholars, for instance, endorsed an activist king. While Yi did not undervalue the role of ministers, he viewed their role as basically that of assisting the king, who had the final responsibility and duty to effect good government. In fact, he thought that unbalanced dominance of the throne by ministers, which he acknowledged to have been the case in the Yi regime from time to time, was detrimental to the effectiveness of rule.[35] At the same time, he strongly advocated that the Kingly Way (*wangdo*) be pursued by the king in earnest. Taking the sage kings of antiquity as models, the ideal kingship of Yi Yulgok incorporated much of the Neo-Confucian theory of self-cultivation of the monarch as the foundation of national well-being.[36]

This ideological check on the throne by the bureaucracy, which was an integral part of the evolving political structure, would not easily have been possible without consolidation of the power bases of the bureaucrats. True, Yi monarchs were subjected to intense Confucian education, and they probably internalized the Confucian value system. Still, without bureaucratic pressure, they might have more readily deviated from the norm when it suited them. This reinforcement was made possible, at least in part, by a monopoly of power within a small elite. Departing from the sort of meritocracy endorsed by Chŏng Tojŏn—the selection of officials through an examination system open to commoners, all of whom had access to education through a public school system—the indigenous social structure, which emphasized a rigid class distinction, remained unchallenged.[37] The hereditary elite,[38] commonly referred to as the yangban, enjoyed legal and social privileges. And the power elite constituted the upper echelon of the yangban. Even the political upheavals of the early sixteenth century do not seem to have broken the power of this small group.[39] True, adhering to the Confucian ideal of meritocracy, the government service examination, especially the *munkwa*, the final civil examination, emerged as the channel to officialdom. Nor was there a legal prohibition against commoners taking examinations. In practice, however, candidates were in large measure yangban and those who passed the *munkwa* and entered the bureaucracy were mainly drawn from a small group.

Thus, unlike in China, where the government service examination evolved into an effective means of dispersing power to a wider group, in Korea it functioned more as a mechanism with which to legitimize a relatively small group. Edward Wagner's analysis of 14,600 *munkwa* passers during the Yi dynasty reveals that twenty-one leading clans produced 40 percent of the total number of *munkwa* degree holders through the dynasty, and that thirty-six clans produced 53 percent.[40] While there was some mobility for members of lesser, or even occasionally unknown, clans,[41] it is noticeable that those holding high office almost always had equally illustrious ancestors. The most cursory examination of biographical dictionaries or genealogies confirms this impression.[42] While power obviously shifted from group to group at various times, and clans were also subdivided, there seems to have been a remarkable concentration and perpetuation of power within a small number of clans. The exclusivity of the official class went beyond paternal lines as well. In 1414, very early in the Yi dynasty, a law was enacted discriminating against concubines' children, including those fathered by the yangban, however great and powerful. They were barred from taking higher government examinations, and hence were disqualified from all but the most lowly functionary positions in the government.[43] Considering marriage practices among the power elite, which seem to have generally favored unions among families of equal social status, the bureaucrats were likely to have had illustrious paternal and maternal family backgrounds. At any rate, the king's hereditary

16

claim to the throne was paralleled by similar claims to public office by his officials, though more muted and indirect.

This meant that the bureaucracy could effectively vie with the throne for power.[44] This was not new to Korea. Intense rivalry between monarchical and bureaucratic power had characterized the Korean polity at least from the Silla unification in 668.[45] With the Confucianization of the court in the sixteenth century, however, the contest was, at least rhetorically, for moral superiority. Each side had to seek a raison d'être under the standard of Confucianism. While bureaucratic loyalty to the ruler was still emphasized, their counsel, as moral advisers to the king, gained in strength and intensity. The ruler often found that he had to attain authority as a latter-day sage king. Thus, each monarch faced a fundamentally difficult task—to be a virtuous king by bureaucratic standards while cultivating his own power.

The bureaucrats seem to have preserved a fair measure of ideological independence from the state, and this might have been related to the emergence of private academies. In the early Yi dynasty, a public school system was instituted. Four district schools (*sahak*) were established in the capital and country schools (*hyanggyo*) in the provinces. The Royal College (*Sŏnggyun'gwan*), with a quota of two hundred students, served as a tertiary university.[46] From the early sixteenth century, private academies (*sŏwŏn*) began to appear. For a while, the government actively supported these academies, chartering them and granting them land and tax exemption status. They rapidly grew in number. Eighty-eight were founded by 1600, and by 1700 there were more than six hundred private academies,[47] a number that exceeded the number in China.[48] They emerged as centers of learning and scholarship and, in prestige, they soon replaced the public schools which deteriorated in quality. By at least the mid-seventeenth century, most of the yangban seem to have been educated in private academies.[49] This probably meant that, rather than being indoctrinated in a state-centered Confucian ideology, the bureaucrats were schooled in more independent Confucian ideals.[50] At any rate, by the time they entered the bureaucracy, they were well prepared to engage in the rhetoric of Confucian rule by virtue.

In addition, the relative smallness of the Yi bureaucracy must have influenced how the monarch and the officials related to each other. There were only about five hundred civil officials in the central bureaucracy.[51] In addition, there were about one thousand provincial officials, as well as the military bureaucracy.[52] But, for the most part, military personnel were excluded from the decision-making process. Officials with whom the king deliberated on policy matters and with whom he had frequent contact numbered less than about fifty. These included the high-ranking ministers of the State Council, the ministers of the six bureaus, special counselors who also functioned as royal tutors, censors who participated in the Royal Lecture, royal secretaries and historians. Some of these, such as the three highest-ranking ministers of the State Council, consulted with the king almost daily. The king probably knew most, if not all, of his officials by name. And with those with whom he worked frequently, he probably developed a close relationship. Some were his tutors before his accession, and this often was the basis of a special relationship. Moreover, given the exclusivity of the power elite and the small number of officials, the king probably often knew the fathers, grandfathers, or other close relatives of his officials. Conversely, older officials often would have served in previous reigns, which gave them an aura of added authority. This situation stood in marked contrast to that of the Chinese court in which the august emperor, whose power was nearly impregnable, presided over a vast bureaucracy whose members, in contrast to their Korean counterparts, were much more diverse in regional origin and were far less likely to have had powerful family connections. The almost oligarchic nature of the Korean government probably made it far more difficult for a Korean king to resist bureaucratic pressure.

The Yi monarchical institution also reflected royal vulnerability. Yi kings did not have an "ideologically uncommitted group" at their disposal like those that the Ming[53] or Ch'ing emperors[54] used to countervail the bureaucracy. The eunuchs were at most agents of the truly powerful, never emerging as an independent force. Members of the royal clan up to four generations from the reigning monarch were forbidden from holding any office accompanied by actual power.[55] Freed from this restriction by genealogical distance, many members of the Chŏnju Yi, the royal clan, took the examination and had successful official careers.[56] But they probably served more as bureaucrats than as members of the royal family. Clan solidarity counted for something, but the Chŏnju Yi could at most function as a neutralizing force.

In the absence of meaningful power blocs outside the bureaucracy, royal distaff relatives often gained influence. Yet even this group tended to claim their power and prestige on the basis of their credentials as scholar-officials rather than their relationship to the monarch. Moreover, during periods when they were powerful, power usually came at the expense of the throne.

The Confucianization of the court in the sixteenth century also brought about changes within the bureaucracy. The strict hierarchy within the bureaucracy, in which the executive branch had enjoyed supreme power and privilege, was also revised. Early in Sŏngjong's reign (r. 1469–1494), the right of junior officials to publicly voice views different from their superiors' came to be acknowledged.[57] More crucially, the censorial voice, which had a shaky start,[58] gained force. Much of the political upheaval in the first half of the sixteenth century was concerned with the workings of the bureaucracy—the selection methods, functions, and power of the executive versus the admonitory and advisory offices.[59] The triumph of a younger and more ideologically committed group resulted in the inviolability of the censorial voice, referred to as the conscience of the nation. The Censorate, with surveillance and remonstrance functions for fellow officials and the monarch, emerged as a powerful and independent institution, constituting a force in a tripartite structure shared by the throne and an executive branch headed by the State Council.

The censors, given immunity from punishment for their criticism, exercised their right with impunity. This brought about various changes in the workings of the government, one of the more obvious being further limitations on the king's freedom of action. His minutest action was now subjected to scrutiny. The Confucian concept of the impartial ruler was brought to a new height. As an impartial ruler, he was perforce to maintain an absolutely open court. That is, he was not allowed to transact any business in secret. He was always accompanied by royal secretaries and historians in public functions, and everything that went on was recorded and was open to official view. All official memorials and communications to the throne went through the Royal Secretariat (*Sŭngjŏngwŏn*), as did royal answers, and they were also open to view. Secret tête-à-têtes with one or more officials were strictly forbidden. This had been in force from the inception of the dynasty, but now it was an ironclad rule. From the seventeenth century on, there were only two deviations from the rule in Yi history. One was Hyojong's (r. 1649–1659) solitary audience (*toktae*) with Song Siyŏl in 1659,[60] the content of which has been reported.[61] Another one was King Sukchong's (r. 1674–1720) secret audience with Yi Imyŏng in 1717;[62] for his refusal to let the content of their conversation be known, Sukchong was severely criticized.[63] Except for women and servants, this system rendered it impossible for a king to cultivate a coterie of loyal supporters devoted exclusively to his personal interests. Restricted by institutions, hampered by convention, and bound by ideology, the Yi kings often found themselves pawns in the grip of bureaucratic rhetoric.

From the mid-Yi, factionalism became a factor in Yi politics. The traditional date for the emergence of the first recognizable factions, the Tongin (Easterners) and the Sŏin (Westerners), is put at 1575. Factional history evolved through such issues as those arising from Hideyoshi's invasion of Korea in the 1590s, the fall of the Ming dynasty in 1644, and the succession struggles of various kings. Such questions as what kind of role factionalism played in the politics, how alliances were formed, and how rigid these structures were in each period remain to be investigated. Given the smallness of the power elite and the perpetuation of power within the group, however, factional issues tended to inflame the court, and the factional groups seem to have become rigidified in time. This seems to have happened by the late seventeenth or early eighteenth century. Individual kings responded differenty. Some, notably Sukchong, tried to foster royal power through a divide-and-rule tactic.[64] Yŏngjo, on the other hand, eschewed factional politics and attempted a containment policy. Though this was necessary—further alienation of any group would have threatened the stability of the government—factional enmities ran too deep to be easily appeased. Confronted with bureaucrats who had long since consolidated their power bases, and faced with fac-

20

tional clamors to which he could not respond, Yŏngjo could find no alternative but to seek an image that placed him above the fray. And so Yŏngjo sought to project an image as a sage king.

The idea of moral rule that pervaded Yŏngjo's court[65] and that Yŏngjo attempted to abide by was essentially an echo of that articulated by Yi Yulgok in the sixteenth century:

> The study of the Way is to make goodness clear through the investigation [of things] and the extension [of knowledge] and to cultivate one's self through sincerity [of thought] and rectification [of mind]. When [they are] contained in one's person, [they] become the virtue of Heaven and when [they are] carried out in government [they] become the Kingly Way.[66]

Civilization and Nation

Unlike the Chinese emperor, the Son of Heaven (*T'ien-tzu*), who enjoyed a special status as the unequivocal mediator between Heaven and the civilized world, the Yi king had a relatively modest claim. He may indeed have received the Mandate of Heaven to rule Korea. But the Confucian world view, by which his mandate was justified, also placed China at the center of the world order.[67] The Yi adoption of Confucianism, *a fortiori*, led to the acceptance of this Confucian world order in which Korea was placed in a peripheral and subservient position to the central kingdom. Thus, the investiture (*komyŏng*) of the Korean ruler by the Son of Heaven came to acquire both symbolic and real importance.

It symbolized the tributary status of Yi Korea to China. As a recognition of the Chinese emperor's unique authority, the Korean king referred himself as *sin/ch'en*, the term a subject used of himself to his ruler, in his communications to the Chinese emperor. Investiture also symbolized peace and good will between the two countries, and mutual protection against foreign invasions. Most importantly, it symbolized a definite and secure place for the Yi monarchy in the hierarchy of an orderly universe.

If this carried unmistakably compromising implications for the sovereignty of the Yi Korean state, it also affirmed Yi membership in Confucian civilization. The conflict between the political

21

and cultural identities of Yi Korea, apparent in this imperial investiture, was partly resolved through Yi perceptions which placed the political questions of Yi statehood in a larger cultural context. The founding of the Yi state was based on commitment to the Confucian ideal, and the founders took their inspiration for the Yi polity from the classical model. The present Chinese model, though certainly not perfect, deserved a certain respect. As a direct inheritor of Confucian tradition, the Ming dynasty occupied a superior status in the Confucian cosmos. Hence, Ming leadership was willingly accepted by Koreans who looked to Ming China for guidance in their search for a place in this hierarchy. The early Yi emulation of things Chinese, such as the use of the Ming reign year and the adoption of the Ming criminal codes and Ming court dress, the latter two being carried out voluntarily, indicated Korean eagerness to conform to the norms of civilization.

Yi statehood continued to be defined by cultural identity. In the Confucian world view, only China was civilized, relegating all other countries to varying degrees of barbarism. As a way to transcend this, Koreans regarded Confucian norms as universal standards by which a society was adjudged to be either civilized or barbarous. And Yi Korea was to become a member of the civilized world, even better than China, through excelling by this standard. This attitude can be clearly detected in the *Songs of Flying Dragons,* (*Yongbi ŏch'ŏn'ga*) the autopanegyric songs of the Yi royal house composed under royal commission in the fifteenth century after the Korean alphabet was developed. This celebrated piece praises the Yi ancestors' virtues and justifies their founding of the dynasty with their receipt of the Mandate of Heaven. What is noticeable here is that the Yi ancestors were more virtuous, more valiant, more modest, more generous, and more trusting than their Chinese counterparts.[68] Eulogizing the royal ancestors strictly in terms of Confucian virtues connotes commitment to a universal standard, while praise of Yi ancestors and comparisons unflattering to the Chinese emperors indicate a Korean aspiration to excel by this standard.

This is not to say that Yi Koreans ignored their nativistic tradition. On the contrary, the Yi monarchy saw itself as the inheritor and custodian of Korean tradition. Even the Yi adoption of

Confucianism was projected as a rediscovery of the native tradition that an ancient sage Kija (Chi Tzu) had initiated and which had since been lost.[69] That the *Songs of Flying Dragons* was the result of the development of Korean script and that it was written in that script indicate a desire for a separate cultural identity. Nor were Yi Koreans unaware of the differences and possible conflicts between the particulars of Korean custom and the general norms of Confucianism, especially in accommodating Confucian rituals. Nevertheless, the trend was definitely toward universal values and norms, though certain concessions to indigenous mores were made as inevitable consequences of time and place.[70]

What can be described as the Korean sense of cultural competition with China in the fifteenth century—that they adhered to the basic tenets of Confucian spirit more closely than the Chinese[71]—took a more ideological turn in the following century, when Yi Koreans became the defenders of the authentic Confucian tradition. This resulted from the Korean commitment to Chu Hsi orthodoxy. The Korean scholars saw popularity of the Wang Yang-ming school in Ming China as a grave deviation from the truth. The canonization of Wang Yang-ming in the Confucian temple in 1584, for instance, elicited a great hue and cry from Korean adherents of the Chu Hsi school.[72]

Still, the existence of the Ming dynasty was a comforting affair. Not only did it give Yi Koreans a sense of security in knowing that the world order was intact, it literally provided them with military security. When the Japanese invaded Korea in the 1590s, Ming China sent a large and badly needed military contingent[73] and saved the Yi dynasty from the brink of destruction. This produced an overwhelming sense of gratitude among Koreans which effectively overshadowed any reserve toward the Ming dynasty. From a Korean point of view, the Chinese had translated a common heritage into action at great cost. What had been a spiritual bond between two Confucian countries was now sealed in blood.

Thus, the demise of the Ming dynasty in 1644 was truly a traumatic event for Yi Korea. The replacement of a Chinese ruling house by the barbarian Manchus in the central kingdom disturbed their sense of the Confucian world order. This was tantamount to the disintegration of civilization, and thus it threatened the Korean cultural identity. This was accompanied by a sense of anxiety over the survival of the Yi monarchy, which might be challenged by the rise of a pro-Ch'ing group. Though this did not happen, the political and intellectual repercussions of dealing with this event lasted almost a century.

King Kwanghae (r. 1608–1623), who witnessed the beginning of hostilities between Ming China and the Manchus, adopted an evenhanded policy. He repeatedly affirmed Korean loyalty to the Ming while trying to appease the Manchus. But his less than total allegiance to the Ming and the possibility that he intended double-dealing[74] led to his downfall. He was dethroned, having been accused of betraying the "Court of Heaven" (*Ch'ŏnjo*), forgetting gratitude and reducing Korea, the country of righteousness and propriety, to barbarism.[75] The succeeding regime, led by Injo (r. 1623–1649) who was enthroned by a fervent pro-Ming group, ignored all Manchu overtures for peaceful settlement. This prompted military invasions in 1627 and then in 1636. The second one was led by Abahai himself, later Ch'ing T'ai-tsung, and it resulted in Korean capitulation.[76] Hyojong (r. 1649–1659), who, as a prince, spent many years as a hostage in Mukden, for ten years on the throne harbored a burning desire to attack the Manchus and to restore a rightful Chinese dynasty, possibly joining forces with Chinese Ming loyalists. Ming resistance movements in China, however, seemed to be on the wane and Hyŏnjong's (r. 1659–1674) court had to face the very real possibility of continued Ch'ing existence. Intense debate was followed by political repercussions that lasted through the reign of Sukchong, his successor.[77] Korean hopes were temporarily rekindled by Wu San-kuei's rebellion in 1673, but the conquest of Taiwan by the Ch'ing court in 1683[78] put an end to dreams of restoration.

What emerged from the Korean recognition of Ch'ing China as a permanent, not temporary, reality was the perception that Korea was now the only bastion of Confucian civilization and that, as the sole carrier of the civilized tradition which was lost in China, the Yi monarchy had to be guarded with an even greater zeal. Shared by the entire political and intellectual elite, this new sense of mission probably effectively eliminated the possibility of the rise of a pro-Ch'ing group. On the question of how best to fulfill this mission and the respective roles the king and the bureaucracy should play in it, however, there were differing opinions.

One group essentially saw civilization as the entire span of human experience, at least from the era of the sage kings. Viewing civilization as constantly evolving, those who held this outlook gave sufficient scope to Yi Korea's role as the perpetuator of civilization. Yun Hyu, a representative of this school, for instance, held that one should only keep the spirit of previous sages such as Confucius or Chu Hsi but should not remain bound by their precepts or doctrines.[79] Song Siyŏl, a powerful spokesman of the other school, however, maintained a more rigid position. Regarding Chu Hsi philosophy as the peak of human achievement and Chu Hsi orthodoxy as the essence of civilization, he held to the view that the best way to perpetuate civilization was to adhere to Chu Hsi orthodoxy as closely as possible.[80] He charged Yun Hyu with heterodoxy, a threat to Yi Confucian culture. The entire scholarly establishment seems to have become embroiled in the issue of what orthodoxy should be.[81] These two camps also had different opinions of monarchical authority. Song Siyŏl, viewing scholar-officials as the rightful heirs to Chu Hsi philosophy, saw them as guardians of this tradition by whom the king's credentials should be evaluated. Yun Hyu, on the other hand, took a royal supremacist view—the king's authority should not be called into question and whatever moral counseling and advice officials might offer him should be offered in this context.[82]

The contest between these groups, the Sŏin and the Namin, developed into intense factional conflicts.[83] This political turmoil can be described as a process of adjustment to what Koreans believed to be the new role of the Yi monarchy as the sole custodian of civilization. In this sense, the Yi state was now equated with civilization. Correspondingly, the Yi king now represented Confucian civilization as well as the nation. This in a way compensated for the loss of investiture by the rightful Son of Heaven.

But the Yi king continued to receive investiture from the illegitimate Son of Heaven, the Ch'ing emperor. Despite the Koreans' contemptuous view of the Ch'ing dynasty as barbarian usurpers, it still was the powerful *de facto* ruler of China, and the Yi dynasty was its tributary state. Since the Korean capitulation in 1637, the

Yi court had to transfer to the Ch'ing all the rituals that it once performed to the Ming.[84] The contradiction in this was obvious— the Yi monarchy needed Ch'ing investiture for its survival, but its survival was perceived as the preservation of a civilization of which the Manchus were the antithesis.

The contradiction became more acute as Ch'ing China not only prospered materially but, under able rulers such as Emperors K'ang-hsi (r. 1661–1722), Yung-cheng, and Ch'ien-lung, also flowered culturally, in a recognizably Confucian manner at that. Those who went to China on ambassadorial missions were quite impressed by Ch'ing achievements.[85] Though the Korean perception of the Manchus as illegitimate usurpers did not change, and though the rhetoric of the Yi court on civilization and the Yi role in it ranged somewhere between that expressed by Yun Hyu and that expressed by Song Siyŏl, it was no longer possible to write the Manchus off as completely worthless barbarians.[86] This conflict was never successfully resolved. For Yŏngjo, an eighteenth-century monarch, it became a progressively more intricate task to draw symbols of authority from the past and present Chinas.

History and Tradition

Confucian rule was rule by historical examples. From the sage kings of mythical era through the ruling figures of ancient states down to more recent monarchs, statesmen, and philosophers, supposedly historical figures were held up as examples by which the sovereign should enact virtuous rule: they were none other than moral principle at work. Principle, which was universal, constant, and immanent in all things, was clearly manifest in historical events and persons. Historical examples fell into two groups—moral and hence worthy of emulation, and immoral and hence suitable only for avoidance. As flesh-and-blood variations on a theme, they provided accessible and invaluable lessons.

The primacy of historical examples may be explained by the Confucian belief in the close relationship between knowledge and action and between inner state and outer behavior. Since knowledge was linked to action, historical knowledge helped one to make better decisions and enact correct policies on contemporary affairs. Moreover, the learning process was not just a one-way process, from the inner to the outer realm. One could also arrive at the right state of mind by emulating correct behavior.[87] The emulation of certain behavior that embodied principle, for instance, was thought to help one to understand principle, even if one could not grasp principle immediately.

Historical models were also useful in checking the excesses and flaws of the occupants of the throne who were often, unfortunately too often, fallible. Yi bureaucrats in fact resorted to history with impunity in their contest for power with the king. By the same token, the king could use history for his advantage, selecting pertinent examples, offering his own interpretations, and appealing to the authority of past sages and kings. In fact, the monarchical bureaucratic intercourse, be it friendly or confrontational, whether in a study session or a policymaking occasion, was so strewn with historical analogies, allusions, and debates that one is often reminded of a seminar on history.

Historical-minded as they were, Yi Confucians did not have what we presently call a sense of history. In fact, the universalistic Confucian view precluded an organic and autonomous view of history. True, Confucians took pains to record in the minutest detail every event that they thought was significant. But for them, the primary value of recorded events lay in that they offered yet further illustrations of how principle operated; they were not especially valued for their inherent and independent worth. In dealing with contemporary problems, the particulars of a case also had to be placed in the context of universalistic moral schemata. Application, thus, led to problems of interpretation. The ruling body had to attend to problems that were rooted in the specific circumstances of time and place, and solutions might call for courses of action that did not neatly fall into acceptable categories. Nonetheless, history was to be evaluated and judged so that lessons could be derived from it.[88]

The same cannot be said of tradition. In the Confucian view, Confucian tradition, seen as the accumulation of past struggles of humanity against barbarism, was not perceived in a morally neutral context. Civilization was seen as the transmission of right or legitimate tradition. This view did not intrinsically obstruct change;

a new system of thought with its accompanying changes in mores and customs could be termed the recovery or restoration of a right or legitimate tradition. Neo-Confucianism was propagated under this rhetoric in China. Its adoption as state ideology by the Yi founders was also described as the recovery of a civilized tradition, in this case, the one started by Kija.[89] Individual reformers also often appealed to the authority of the classical era or its texts in order to bypass the imperfect present.[90] It was also true that tradition was not seen as something fixed, but as something continuously evolving, which therefore should be constantly renewed. But change and renewal were sought, in most instances, within the limits of the spirit of correct tradition.

Informed by this sense of correct tradition, the importance of the morality of one's forebears and the central role of filial piety in Confucian culture accorded the ancestral tradition the foremost veneration. This was true of ordinary families, but it was particularly true of the ancestral tradition of the royal family. Since the mandate of a ruling house was posited on the claim that it possessed moral superiority, and since it was believed that its mandate lasted only as long as successive rulers renewed their virtue, tradition set by royal ancestors had to be justified as morally superior. Otherwise, the raison d'être of the monarchy itself would be undermined. Thus, the ancestral tradition in a Confucian monarchy acquired almost unchallengeable authority. His legitimacy being directly linked to the sacredness of this tradition, the occupant of the throne could scarcely challenge its authority. This resulted in the politics of filial piety and an extreme caution in reversing a predecessor's policies. The ancestral tradition, however, was not always an unmixed blessing for a ruler. At times, the need to establish his own legitimacy could come into conflict with the demands of filial piety. For Yŏngjo, who came to the throne after many decades of intense factional politics and labored under the suspicion that he had murdered his immediate predecessor, this was particularly true. For him who had twenty forebears to serve, the ancestral tradition was simultaneously a source of authority, and a predicament.

CHAPTER 2

Yŏngjo's Reign: Images of Sagehood

O chestnut-tree, great-rooted blossomer,
Are you the leaf, the blossom or the bole?
O body swayed to music, O
  brightening glance,
How can we know the dancer from
  the dance?

—William Butler Yeats

In a Confucian monarchy, a coronation was seldom a jubilant event. Conducted as it was in the palace precinct where the recently deceased monarch lay in state, the conventions of filial piety made it impossible that it be joyous. Rather, the solemnity of the occasion was emphasized—a new ruler was inheriting the mandate of the royal house with the attendant responsibility to govern in accordance with Heaven's will, bringing peace and order to his domain and welfare to his people. Thus, when Yŏngjo acceded to the throne on October 6, 1724, the gravity of the ceremony gave little indication that anything was amiss. Everyone behaved with excruciating propriety. The bureaucrats, in humble prostration, begged the heir apparent to ascend the throne. The heir apparent, citing his unworthiness to accept such an awesome responsibility, refused for the entire morning. Only after repeated pleas from the ministers of the State Council and repeated urgings by the two queen dowagers to whom he owed filial obedience did Yŏngjo agree to perform the ceremony.

At noon, the entire bureaucracy, clad in court attire, was lined up in its appointed place in the lower part of the courtyard facing Injŏng Hall. A throne was placed in the center of the elevated platform in the courtyard. The heir apparent, having changed from a costume of deep mourning into ceremonial robes, emerged from the temporary hut in which he was to stay for the duration of the mourning period. Led by ceremonial officials, Yŏngjo first entered the funeral chamber in which the coffin of the deceased king was laid and announced to him his receipt of the royal mantle, and burned incense. Then he was led to Injŏng Hall through its east gate and to the throne. As soon as Yŏngjo seated himself, the bureaucracy bowed four times in unison and shouted, "Long live the king!" The new king then got up from the throne and walked through the main chamber of Injŏng Hall to the east gate, retracing his steps to his temporary hut. There he changed back into mourning clothes.

Soon afterward, the accession edict was promulgated at Injŏng Gate. In a familiar Confucian rhetoric, it referred to the new king's grief over the sudden death of his predecessor, his older brother Kyŏngjong (r. 1720–1724). Coming after only four years of his reign, death had cruelly thwarted his chance to effect a rule almost as perfect as that of the sage kings of antiquity. The new king then declared his profound anxiety over his responsibility in inheriting the ancestral mission to govern his people and professed that, despite his insufficient virtue and ability, he would do his very best to carry out his duty. He pledged that he would toil and rest along with his people to be able to share their joys and sorrows and pronounced that the government should above all else display benevolence, though it also should seek to reform corrupt practices. He announced that he would begin his reign by reducing the penalities of the guilty and by offering provisions to the needy and gifts to every official. The edict ended with an appeal for help and cooperation from all for the years to come.[1]

The sobriety of this ceremony, however, belied the tension of the court over which Yŏngjo would preside. The Soron bureaucrats must have attended with heavy hearts. Under Kyŏngjong, they had opposed Yŏngjo's appointment as heir apparent. In what came to be known as the purge of 1721–22 (*sinim sahwa*), the Soron bureaucracy had banished and executed many members of the Noron, its rival faction which had supported Yŏngjo. Some of the more extreme members of the Soron had, before his accession, even plotted for this newly enthroned king's life. In 1721, Yŏngjo had even found it necessary to flee his residence at night to seek protection at the residence of Queen Inwŏn, his stepmother.[2] But it was not the profound anxiety that the officials in attendance must have felt that made this ceremony so odd. What was strangest about the ceremony and what most acutely expressed the intense factional strife in the bureaucratic community was the total absence of Noron officials. This was a product of the struggles that had raged through the Yi court of the last several reigns, particularly those of Yŏngjo's father Sukchong and his older brother Kyŏngjong.

Indeed, the fifty years from the beginning of Sukchong's reign in 1674 until the end of Kyŏngjong's in 1724 constituted one of the worst periods of political conflict in Yi history. Intent on restoring royal authority and power, which he saw as having been diminished, Sukchong adopted a divide-and-conquer policy toward the scholar-official community and played faction against faction, deepening already formidable animosities. The purge of the Noron in 1721–22 during Kyŏngjong's reign,[3] though its effect would so plague Yŏngjo's reign, was but a continuation of severe factional strife that had been set in motion decades earlier.

If Yŏngjo's coronation edict seemed merely a reiteration of Confucian rhetoric, it also indicated how he was going to rule—he would rule with the rhetoric of sagacious kingship. Coming to the throne at the age of thirty-one, and having witnessed and even been a victim of the volatile politics of his father's and brother's courts, Yŏngjo was aware that the magnitude of the rift and the rancor in the scholar-official community had reached an extreme and that to push it any further by adopting his predecessors' factional politics might even endanger the Yi polity itself. The power bases of the scholar-bureaucrat class had long since been firmly entrenched and, ferocious as Sukchong's attack on the bureaucratic community might have been, it necessarily was directed at individuals, not at the structure. Kyŏngjong, who had attempted to assert himself with his father's techniques but had none of his father's political instincts, nullified any progress his father might have made in enhancing royal power. Their political legacy dictated that the successor to this throne find a new approach, something that would enable him to unify his contentious court and to restore the authority and power of the throne. Thus the rhetoric of moral kingship.

Yŏngjo also had personal reasons to seek moral authority. For a ruler so formidably burdened, Yŏngjo had rather weak credentials. His mother was a low-born secondary consort, a fact held in disapprobation. He had come to his position through a series of accidents—Kyŏngjong had left no heir and Yŏngjo was the only surviving son of Sukchong.[4] True, the Yi royal succession did not conform to rigid primogeniture and the majority of kings were not first-born sons, but sons by concubines were a different matter. Though the Yi practice of severe discrimination against them was somewhat milder in the case of royal children, their succession to the throne had hitherto been largely avoided, when possible. Several kings born of concubines acceded and did not fare well. Kyŏngjong was one example. Kwanghae (r. 1608–1623), another, had been deposed.

Unsatisfactory qualifications concerning his mother, however, paled in significance compared to the shadow cast on Yŏngjo by charges of regicide. Very soon after Kyŏngjong died, rumors circulated implicating Yŏngjo in his brother's death: Kyŏngjong died from eating pickled crab, presumably poisoned and sent to him by Yŏngjo. This accusation seems to have originated with the extremist Soron who had tried to eliminate Yŏngjo, and it strains credulity. Kyŏngjong had been in feeble mental and physical health for a long time. Yi Chae, who served as Kyŏngjong's tutor when Kyŏngjong was the crown prince, mentions that Kyŏngjong experienced a gradual mental deterioration and that, by 1710, ten years prior to his accession, he was not at all well.[5] Min Chinwŏn echoes Yi's statements and also refers to Kyŏngjong's impotence.[6] Even if these two, both Noron, might have exaggerated, the Soron never disputed the feebleness of Kyŏngjong's health.

No matter. The existence of the charge alone was serious enough.

Not only did it undermine the king's legitimacy since, if true, this amounted to usurpation, but it also expressed the invidious and fractious atmosphere of the court. That those who harbored deep resentment and hostility were numerous and extended far beyond the confines of the court was soon to become palpable with the outbreak of rebellion in 1728, the fourth year of Yŏngjo's reign. The rebellion was carried out nominally to restore a legitimate ruler to the throne, Yŏngjo presumably being illegitimate because of his alleged fratricide. This event was to exert a decisive influence on the course of Yŏngjo's rule but, even as he was embarking on his reign he was made aware that he had to establish his moral credentials.

Thus, from the beginning, Yŏngjo pinned his hopes for a successful reign on the restoration of the throne's moral authority. It was not just a question of dispelling doubts on his personal credentials but, more importantly, of replenishing the status of kingship. In his perception, both the achievement of political stability and his own survival as a functioning monarch required that the prestige of the throne be reinforced and that this be done by acquiring moral authority. Coming to the throne in the 333d year of the Yi dynasty he could entertain only the smallest hope for institutional change or for challenges to entrenched bureaucratic bases of power. One of the few tenets that the bureaucracy could not challenge was the ideal of the sage king upon which the Yi monarchy was premised. Yŏngjo could seek to achieve recognition as a sage king. And he sought just such recognition out of a belief that moral authority and power were inseparably linked, and hence, to attain authority was the only way for him to restore royal power.

RESTORATION

Yŏngjo had no difficulty in finding the theme for his rule. There were historical examples of "restoration" (*chunghŭng*): a reprise in the waning years of a dynasty, recapturing the vitality of its golden years and temporarily arresting the inevitable decline— an inevitability guaranteed by the cyclical view of history. But the "restorations" of Chinese history had always come after major rebellions.[7] Yŏngjo's succession was superficially a normal one following some eighty years of peace undisturbed by uprisings. To proclaim that his reign would be a "restoration" under the circumstances would have been tantamount to a public announcement that preceding reigns, especially those of his father and his brother, were deficient. This unfilial declaration, unacceptable for a Confucian monarch, was even more so for Yŏngjo with his loyalty to his brother under a cloud as it was.

Thus Yŏngjo invoked only the spirit of restoration,[8] seeking in it an impetus appropriate to his time. The scion of a three-hundred-year-old dynasty, he would have seemed presumptuous in offering a future that would exceed the brilliant moments of this past. True, his nation was not much moved by that great fear, that hunger for order, that foretold dynastic downfall, but there did exist an unmistakable unease and a palpable yearning for the order and stability of old. Hence, restoration. In this Yŏngjo could find a role. Bearer of tradition, restorer of glory, these images would do for rule.

Yŏngjo did not define his role as that of a perpetuator of dynastic power; rather he cast himself as a carrier of tradition, the spiritual foundation of dynastic authority. This was the dynastic tradition that had begun with commitment to the Confucian vision of moral rule and that had boasted such brilliant moments as the reign of King Sejong (r. 1418–1450), revered as a latter-day sage king. This was the tradition that, after the demise of the Ming dynasty in China, had been charged with a sense of mission as the last bastion of Confucian civilization. Other aspects of the monarchy might have been compromised and even tainted, but this tradition was beyond challenge, indisputable and resplendent in its authority. In invoking the spirit of restoration, Yŏngjo was confirming his commitment to this vision of moral rule and declaring that he was going to establish for himself an independent place within this tradition.

Yŏngjo's pursuit of moral authority was closely interwoven with his use of the rhetoric and the ritual of the Confucian monarchy which he inherited with the throne. For him, this was not a mat-

34

ter of choice but of necessity. The historical weight that pressed Yŏngjo to invoke the theme of restoration also dictated how he should seek to realize it. Clearly, for the twenty-first monarch of the Yi dynasty, innovation lay not in changing the ideology or the institutions but rather in how he handled them.

The lynchpin of this ideology and these institutions was the Confucian concept of kingship. Thus, the system bore down with its myriad demands upon the ruler-sage. This Confucian ruler had at once to be chief priest of his people, dynastic instrument to his forebears, civilizer, upholder of the classics, exemplar and father to his people. If this seems a crushing burden, it was also a formidable arsenal. For it was precisely in these emblems and symbols that authority lay. And by putting them to proper use the monarch ruled.

But for Yŏngjo to avail himself of the rhetoric and rituals in such a way to be able to successfully fashion an image as a moral ruler was no simple matter. The bureaucrats with their own power bases and with their own claim to the Confucian heritage did not allow him the exclusive use of the rhetoric of ideal sagacity. Thus, Yŏngjo could assert sagacity only by scrupulous adherence to the letter and spirit of the Neo-Confucian rhetoric of the pursuit of sagehood, a rhetoric that stressed continuous striving and sincere commitment. Regardless of his own convictions and satisfactions in this pursuit he had to do it in such a way that the bureaucracy had to admit to being convinced of his striving and commitment. Thus he had to behave as though he was absolutely sincere in this quest and he had to do so all of his life. In this respect, Yŏngjo's performance was a tour de force. His relentless construction of an image as a moral ruler brought him recognition in his lifetime, while his predecessors had been so honored only in the grave. But in this process of mythmaking, Yŏngjo became the captive of his own creation.

SUPREME HIEROPHANT

The ritual observances assigned to a Confucian monarch, which symbolized his status as the intermediary between Heaven and his people[9] and the carrier of a dynastic mandate, were, perhaps, the most unqualified proof of royal prestige. Admittedly, a Yi monarch was not the Son of Heaven, as a Chinese emperor was, nor was he entitled to perform such sacrifices as the *feng* and *shan* sacrifices to Heaven and Earth.[10] Nevertheless, he represented Koreans to Heaven, nature, and the civilized world; he was the living symbol of Yi dynastic continuity, and he performed rituals and sacrifices unique to these roles.

Befitting its Confucian ethos, the Yi monarchy devoted a great deal of attention to systematizing rituals into different categories, with protocols prescribed in minute detail. Rituals were roughly divided into five categories; auspicious or sacrificial rites (*killye or cherye*); mourning rites (*hyungnye*); guest rites (concerning diplomatic embassies) (*pinnye*); military rites (*kunnye*); and rites of happiness (i.e., weddings) (*karye*).[11]

Of these, perhaps the most significant and regularly observed rituals were sacrificial rites. There were three grades of sacrifices: great offerings (*taesa*); medium offerings (*chungsa*); and lesser offerings (*sosa*). The great offerings included regular sacrifices to the Yi Ancestral Temple (*Chongmyo*) conducted five times a year; spring and autumn sacrifices at Yŏngnyŏngjŏn, in which the tablets of the four ancestors of the Yi founder, short-reigned kings and some princes were laid; and sacrifices to the Altar of Land and Grain (*sajik*), conducted thrice a year. The medium offerings were sacrifices to various gods of nature such as the gods of wind, clouds, thunder, rain, mountains and hills, and the sea and streams; sacrifices to protectors of agriculture and weaving, sacrifices to Confucius, his disciples, and other worthies, both Korean and Chinese, at the Confucian temple (*Munmyo*); and sacrifices to the founders of previous Korean dynasties. The lesser offerings were sacrifices to various gods associated with horses and equestrianism, the star of agriculture, the star of longevity, spirits of high mountains and big rivers, the god of winter, and gods of war, and sacrifices to spirits of those who died in epidemics and those who did not receive other offerings. They were all conducted at designated times.[12]

The grades of these rituals corresponded with the ranks held by those who were expected to perform and participate in the ceremony, as well as with the elaborateness of the preparations and provisions for it—the costumes, the sacrificial offerings, the utensils used, the music and dance, as well as the actual protocols of the ceremony. At the great offerings, for instance, the monarch was supposed to be the first officer of the ceremony. The offerings consisted of the uncooked heads of three kinds of animals, usually an ox, a goat, and a pig, and various kinds of fruits, grains, wine, and cakes.[13] The medium and lesser offerings were proportionately less elaborate.

Aside from these regular offerings, there were other sacrifices—more frequent sacrifices to recent ancestors, sacrifices to certain folk heroes, and prayers for rain when drought persisted. These were not necessarily less demanding. Those connected with the king's immediate ancestors, in particular, were extremely elaborate, but they were categorized differently, each with its own ritual protocol.

Not all of these rituals required the king's personal presence. Considering their extensiveness, this was simply impractical. Even in the case of the great offerings in which the monarch's participation was expected, he often delegated high-ranking officials to stand in for him. This practice was accepted without much ado and ritual protocols made the necessary provisions. In those cases when the king personally performed the ceremony, the preparations became somewhat more intricate.[14]

Yet, whoever might perform the ceremony, they were deputies of the king, offering sacrifices on his behalf. It was the monarch alone who presided, in theory and spirit, over these rituals. Thus, these rituals were for the monarch—the chief operator—an extraordinary oppportunity; revered symbols, political emblems, and cultural archetypes to be employed, manipulated, and invested with monarchical hopes to enhance the prestige of the throne, to enlarge royal authority, and to inspirit the monarch's image.[15]

By Yŏngjo's time, however, history and precedent had set the tone for much ritual activity. If auspicious and festive ceremonies, such as ancestral worship or the king's symbolic spring plowing, were routinized and—despite the attendant pomp—depleted of much meaning, rogative ceremonies, like those associated with natural calamities, still weighed heavily on the monarch. If drought continued, for instance, despite a ruler's prayers, he implicitly bore the blame. If it led to famine, he was ultimately responsible.

Yŏngjo seems to have had a sure grasp of the subtler aspects of ritual—the potential for gain or loss. He knew that in order to utilize ritual to the fullest, he had to suppress banality and monotony. He did this through constant and conspicuous personal attention. Hemmed in by the institutionalization and routinization of monarchical activity, the sovereign's personal behavior was one of the throne's few variables and it was observed with intense curiosity.

Yŏngjo did not merely wish to emphasize auspicious or commemorative rituals and to imbue them with meaning; he also wished to lower the stakes in rogative ones by displaying his sincerity (*sŏng*). In a society where motives and intentions were at least as important as results, this was an effective tactic. Action might accomplish his purposes, but his expressions of remorse and reverence would earn him his reputation for humanity (*in*) and virtue (*tŏk*). Thus Yŏngjo's success in employing ritual required meeting the demands it imposed upon him. Whether Yŏngjo attended these rituals in cold calculation, or whether he was as involved with them as his actions suggest, so long as the barometer of his success was the public response to his "sincerity," he could not escape at least feigning that quality. In the end, what were his expectations of these rites, if not sincere?

Nowhere was the sincerity of his expectations more apparent than in the acts of penance to which Yŏngjo resorted—probably more often than any other Yi monarch. These may have been fitting gestures in times of disaster or in response to ominous portents. There were established ways in which a monarch could appease the wrath of Heaven as it was implicitly expressed by natural calamities. He could release prisoners,[16] attend sacrifices in person,[17] and issue decrees of self-reproach in which he begged for advice from all concerned.[18] Yŏngjo did all of these things. In a drought of 1753, for example, he prayed for rain in person three

times. But this was not all. On June 30, he refused to retire for
the night. In official attire he burned incense and prayed till dawn.[19]
If he could not reverse or stop nature, he at least could offer penance. Yŏngjo consistently made a point of declaring abstinence
on the appearance of ominous portents such as thunder, an eclipse,
or other natural signs.[20]

As might be expected, these activities did not always produce
the desired result. Drought might continue and famine might
spread. Penance was fine, but he had to find a way to appease the
populace. In addition to relief programs, Yŏngjo always demon-
strated sympathy for the afflicted. Depending on the seriousness
of the situation, he either announced abstinence from regular food[21]
or, more effectively, he would make an emotional display before
a crowd. On June 14, 1761, for instance, during a particularly bad
famine, Yŏngjo went out to meet a crowd of people suffering from
lack of food. His voice breaking with emotion, he cried: "The misery is just too much to bear. I simply wouldn't be able to swallow
my food!" On the spot, he announced a reduction of taxes and an
immediate dispatch of relief grain to the capital region and to the
three southern provinces.[22]

While Yŏngjo was sensitive to the signs of Heaven and nature,
he did not neglect to use the symbols of history and tradition.
Korea's ambiguous position in the world hierarchy also found its
ritual correlative. Consistent with their new sense of mission as
heirs to the civilized tradition that had been represented by the
Ming dynasty in China, Koreans searched for ways to ritualize
this status.

The first discussion of sacrifices to the Ming house occurred in
1704, the first sexagesima of the end of the Ming dynasty in 1644.
Not surprisingly, the Yi appropriation of the Ming heritage contained an element of monarchical bureaucratic rivalry. The bureaucrats pressed their own claim to this heritage, while King
Sukchong wished to establish a ritual link between the Ming house
and the Yi house.[23] Both sides conceded to each other's claim to
a certain extent. A shrine to Emperors Wan-li and Ch'ung-chen
was erected at Hwayang in Ch'ungch'ŏng Province, the hometown

of Song Siyŏl, the founder of the Noron faction. Called *Mandong-myo*, this shrine served as a symbol of the scholar-bureaucrats' link to the Ming tradition.

As for Yi royal house rituals, matters were somewhat more complicated. Sacrificial rites performed by the Yi royal house to previous ruling houses connoted its status as their descendant house, and since the Ming house, despite the Yi devotion to it, was an alien dynasty, the question had to be dealt with with extreme delicacy. This posed no problem in performing the sexagesima sacrifice to Emperor Ch'ung-chen as this was viewed as a one-time commemoration. It was performed in the grand manner in accordance with the prescriptions for great offerings, with Suk-chong as the first ceremonial officer. The eulogy was full of laments over the collapse of civilization in China and resolution to carry on the tradition in Korea.[24] But when it came to the erection of a permanent altar to Emperor Wan-li, as was Sukchong's wish, the question of ancestry had to be somehow circumvented. This was possible because Wan-li was the one who had sent troops to assist Korea during the Japanese invasion and the expressed purpose of the construction of the altar dedicated to him, to be called *Taebodan*, the Altar of Great Gratitude, was to ritualize Korean gratitude for this. Nevertheless, the connotation of ancestry was present both in the design of the altar and the ritual protocols of the sacrificial offerings. The height of the Altar of Great Gratitude was one *ch'ŏk* higher than that of the Yi ancestral altar, following the proportions of the Ming ancestral altar, while the width was that of the Yi altar. The sacrifices, to be offered in the spring and the autumn, were categorized as great offerings.[25]

Yŏngjo, however, wanted to press on in establishing the role of the Yi royal house as symbolic heir to the Ming. Yŏngjo seems to have believed that, since the Ming dynasty was defunct, the ritual appropriation of the Ming as a spiritual ancestor would not compromise the sovereignty of the Yi royal house; rather it would render prestige to the Yi house by reminding the scholar-bureaucrats of its role as the inheritor of the Ming mantle. Yŏngjo's campaign to achieve this status began rather early. In 1727, the third year of his reign, for instance, he managed to extend the taboo on the use of his dynastic ancestors' personal names to include those of the Ming emperors.[26] But in 1749, his effort to include Emperors Hung-wu and Ch'ung-chen, the first and last rulers of the Ming dynasty, in sacrifices at the Altar of Great Gratitude, which would unmistakably affirm this status, met considerable bureaucratic resistance. The bureaucratic community, ever alert to potential gains and losses of prestige and power in court politics, did not fail to see the true intent of the king and it responded to the king's suggestion with considerable caution. Thus, it took substantial maneuvering by Yŏngjo to bring it about.

Rather than tackling the issue all at once, the question of offering a sacrifice to the Emperor Ch'ung-chen was broached first and was adopted relatively easily. The rationale given for this adoption, however, was still the same as that involving the Emperor Wan-li—namely, that Ch'ung-chen had wished to send troops to Korea during the Manchu invasion, though this was not realized due to the Korean capitulation to the Manchus. This logic, coupled with Yŏngjo's assertion that his father Sukchong surely would have included Ch'ung-chen had he known of Ch'ung-chen's intention, made it difficult for the bureaucracy to oppose this measure.[27]

Within a week of this adoption, however, the subject of including the founder of the Ming dynasty, the Emperor Hung-wu, in the sacrifice was brought up. The reason Yŏngjo gave was that Emperor Hung-wu had conferred the name Chosŏn on the Yi dynasty as heirs to the Kija Chosŏn, the alleged ancient Korean state founded by Kija, the legendary Confucian civilizer of the Korean people; the Koreans were indebted to Hung-wu for this generous recognition and bestowal. This was introducing a new idea. Yŏngjo buttressed his argument with a reference to the Korean role as the carrier of civilization: "the Central Plains exude the stenches of barbarians and our Green Hills are alone."[28] This did not, however, persuade the bureaucrats. They went to the heart of the matter, the connotation of ancestry. They pointed out that sacrifices at the Altar of Great Gratitude were for military assistance and that the measure the king was proposing, repaying the kindness of the Emperor Hung-wu, was an act appropriate to dealing with

41

one's parents or ancestors but not with one's superiors or rulers. At this point, Yŏngjo had to acknowledge this implication and tried to defend the proposal on this basis. He said:

> Incense and paper money for the imperial house has long since been extinguished. That is why we want to sacrifice to the three emperors at the altar. If there were to be a restoration [of the Ming dynasty] in the Central Plain, then of course our country should not sacrifice to them. If incense and paper money had not stopped and if we were still to sacrifice to the three emperors, then it would be a sacrilege.[29]

This argument, however, only strengthened official reservations. Realizing this, Yŏngjo took a different tack. The following is the *Sillok* account of how he got his way:

> About nine o'clock that night, sitting in front of the inner palace gate, the king summoned high-ranking officials. When they arrived, he said: "I was too disturbed to go to bed, so I came out here. And the Late Majesty came upon me and reached me." Then he asked a royal secretary to read aloud four poems supposedly written by Sukchong. The third poem read:

> > *The lofty emperor conferred upon us the name, Chosŏn;*
> > *Who could reproduce the dragons and snakes of*
> > *his brush?*
> > *For three hundred years, we have been in his debt.*
> > *How could we repay his heavenly sagacious kindness?*

The fourth poem read:

> > *To uphold the Way in a solitary castle by the*
> > *aura of the moon year upon year,*
> > *Each year unable to renew the Court of Heaven.*
> > *Alas! Sad! The sixth sexagesima of the sin year*
> > (the founding of the Ming dynasty in 1368)
> > *draws near,*
> > *Yet no one recommends sacrificial vessels.*

Thereupon the king threw himself prostrate on the ground, his hands on his chest, and cried for a long time. Then he said:

"I am neither a loyal nor a filial man. You ministers are also wrong. The word 'repay' in the Late Majesty's poem refers to Great Gratitude while 'sacrificial utensils' means his wish to offer sacrifice. Yet until I heard these poems, I did not realize that he cherished such a wish. How unfilial I am! Then earlier today we compared and measured the merits and virtues of the Emperors Hung-wu and Ch'ung-chen and debated whether or how much we were indebted to them. I tremble with fear when I think what I have done. This was really a disloyal act. In discussing the question of whether Emperor Hung-wu should be included in sacrifices at the Altar of Great Gratitude, all of you expressed deep reservations. [This is] forgetting and rejecting three hundred years' graciousness of the [Ming] imperial court. Can you say that this was not wrong? My mind is already made up. Please speak your opinion."

Prime Minister Kim Chaero replied: "Since the Late Majesty's word 'repay' already indicated his wish, Your Majesty's duty now lies in complying with it. The matter should be decided accordingly." The Minister of the Left Cho Hyŏnmyŏng said: "When Your Majesty speaks the four words [not filial and not loyal], your humble servants deserve ten thousand deaths. With Your Majesty's intention already firm, how dare your humble servants further discuss it?"[30]

Once the official resistance was overcome, the rest was a routine affair. The Altar of Great Gratitude was enlarged to accommodate the inclusion of the first and last emperors of the Ming dynasty along with other necessary changes and preparations. Yŏngjo paid a great deal of attention to each step so that everything would be ready in time for the spring sacrifice. In approaching the occasion, he carried out the ritual duties demanded of him to the letter. He examined the sacrificial offerings and utensils and after performing the preparatory ceremony on the day before the grand ceremony, he stayed the night at a temporary hut. On May 26, 1749, the first sacrifice to the three Ming emperors was performed with Yŏngjo as the first officer.[31] The descendant role of the Yi royal house, which was felt to enhance the prestige of the Yi house, was thus ritually confirmed.

Yŏngjo acquired this status for the Yi royal house despite bureaucratic resistance. Unlike his brother and his father before him he did this without threats and without naked coercion. Whatever one may think of the theatrics and the emotional tensions he used to manipulate his bureaucrats, he had, by unearthing his father's poems and by the terms in which he argued his position, built a carefully crafted case rigorously attuned to the strictest demands of Confucian rhetoric. The presentation and the timing simply left his officials with no defense.

Yŏngjo's use of Ming symbols continued throughout his reign. Whenever the occasion allowed, he sought to reaffirm his special relationship to the Ming. His conduct during the second sexagesima of Emperor Ch'ung-chen's death is a good illustration of how he used what would have been a routine public function to further his own image. The ceremony was scheduled for April 20, 1764. Three weeks before that, he arrived at the site to oversee the preparations. On April 15, he rehearsed the ceremony and announced that, in memory of the Ming emperor, he would abstain from medicine until the ceremony was over. For the next few days, he discoursed to everyone including the heir apparent on the indebtedness of the Yi royal house to the Ming. On the 17th, he moved into a temporary hut adjoining the altar. On the 19th, he performed the preparatory sacrifice of bowing. In the afternoon, he refused food. Pressed by officials of the Medical Bureau, he broke into sobs and replied that he just could not bring himself to take food when he thought of the tragic end (suicide) of Emperor Ch'ung-chen on Wan-shou Hill. Then, punning twice on the character for Ming, he wrote "the sun and the moon of the imperial house are the great brightness of our eastern kingdom"[32] and ordered that it be copied and distributed throughout the country. On the 20th, the sacrificial ceremony was performed in all solemnity and pomp.[33]

Yŏngjo was not content with just these public activities, however. He sought other ways to express his personal attachment to the Ming emperors. Soon after his accession, he sanctioned the publication of Emperor Hung-wu's calligraphy and collected works.[34] The calligraphy of Emperors Wan-li and Ch'ung-chen received similar treatment.[35] Numerous works on the Ming or by Ming writers were published.[36] He also held an audience for descendants of Ming refugees living in Korea, showering them with gifts.[37]

With these activities, Yŏngjo was doing all he could to link his dynastic mission directly to the Ming dynasty. He was thus seeking enhanced recognition as the bearer of the civilized tradition that it stood for. Hence, glorification of the Ming conferred on him a unique status in which no living man stood between him and the sources of civilization.

Clearly, Yŏngjo's unqualified reverence for the Ming was contingent on the fact that the object of his adulation belonged to history. These emperors of a bygone China could be deified with no implications of Korean servitude to the Ming. But since Koreans' piety for the Ming corresponded to their contempt for the Ch'ing, their activities in honor of this China of the past often came into conflict with the China of the present. The Korean choice of calendrical designation was a case in point.

Calendrical designation expressed in terms of Chinese imperial reign titles was a symbolic acknowledgment of the cosmic role of the Chinese imperial house. As Koreans had not accepted Ch'ing status, they continued to use the reign titles of Emperor Ch'ung-chen, the last Ming ruler, in calendrical designation except in some documents, especially those sent to the Ch'ing court. The Ch'ing court kept a watchful eye on this practice. In 1730, the Ch'ing government discovered the offending reign title on the identification plaques (*mapa'e*) Koreans were required to carry.[38] It sent a letter of inquiry to the Yi court demanding further details. Yŏngjo was forced to send the Ch'ing government an official apology, and on the following day he ordered that the Ch'ing reign year be used on identification plaques.[39]

Yŏngjo was aware of the full ramifications of the Ch'ing presence for the Yi royal house—Ch'ing power reinforced the security of the Yi monarchy while it did not render moral prestige to the Korean throne, as indicated by Yŏngjo's conduct in dealings with the Ch'ing. In observing necessary rituals connected with the Ch'ing, for instance, he was solemn and exact but displayed no emotion. The embassies of 1735 and 1736 that announced Emperor Yung-cheng's death, Emperor Ch'ien-lung's accession, and his mother's elevation to empress, were greeted in this fashion. In appropriate attire, Yŏngjo mourned Emperor Yung-cheng,[40] promulgated an amnesty for Emperor Ch'ien-lung's accession,[41] and offered congratulations to be delivered to the empress.[42] He also welcomed, visited, and sent off Ch'ing envoys with the proper decorum. Other Yi kings would have done more or less the same thing but Yŏngjo was punctilious. Yet as soon as each of these envoys had departed, he made some gesture to express his profound respect for the Ming.[43]

Even where less formal matters were concerned, Yŏngjo still wished to establish to his officials that the use of the symbols of prestige and power associated with the Ming and Ch'ing was a prerogative of the throne. He made this point, for instance, with Ming reign titles. In 1730, he decreed that Ming reign titles should be used at sacrifices to folk heroes of Chinese origin,[44] but when officials made suggestions of a similar nature in 1746 and 1747, he rejected them.[45] There are numerous incidents of this type.[46] The message was clear: he was the inheritor of the Ming mantle and the right to use its symbols was his.

Yŏngjo's reluctance to share Ming symbols with the officials was paralleled by an equal reluctance to allow them to disparage Ch'ing "barbarism." In 1748, Yŏngjo received a report from the winter mission which had just returned suggesting that the Ch'ing court suffered from a terrible lack of discipline and order. He deplored the situation but did not want to accept similar sentiments expressed by one of his royal secretaries. The following is their exchange:

Yŏngjo's Reign: Images of Sagehood

YI HYŎNGMAN: Law and discipline have already broken down and the state still hopes to be sustained? Since barbarians do not have propriety and righteousness, they have only discipline and order to rely upon. If one judges things by the example of the barbarian Yüan, once discipline and order disappear, the country would just collapse.

KING: The royal secretary might talk about conditions in another country. But the lack of discipline and order in our country is just as lamentable.[47]

The peculiar relationship between the Yi monarchy and Chinese regimes, which forced Yŏngjo to seek prestige from a past dynasty while practical support could come only from a present one, was not sure ground for the bases of royal authority. He took every opportunity China offered, but Yŏngjo still paid considerably more attention to the symbols of an independent and internal legitimacy for Korea that reached back through native dynasties to a primordial founder who stood outside the Chinese line. There were established ritual practices to confirm this heritage, the most obvious being the sacrifices to founders of the previous dynasties. Categorized as medium offerings, they were performed at *Samsŏngsa*, a shrine dedicated to Tan'gun, the mythical progenitor of the Korean people; *Sungnyŏngjŏn*, the shrine of Tan'gun and King Tongmyŏng, the founder of Koguryŏ; *Sunginjŏn*, the shrine of Kija, the reputed civilizer of Korea; *Sungdŏkchŏn*, the shrine dedicated to the founder of Silla; *Sungnyŏlchŏn*, the shrine of King Onjo, the founder of Paekche; and *Sungŭijŏn*, the shrine dedicated to the founder of Koryŏ, T'aejo, and several other Koryŏ kings.[48]

Symbols of Korean history and civilization, plentiful and uncompromised, were a fertile resource for the assertion of royal authority. But they had different merits and meanings and the question of course was how to use them to make the point one wished to make. Yŏngjo's campaign to establish Korea's noble origins commenced with his rejection of the slightest suggestion of Korean barbarism. For example, in 1740, he was so incensed by a passage in the *Ta-hsüeh yen-i pu* (Supplement to the Extension of the Great Learning) referring to Korea as a barbarian nation that

47

he immediately ordered a ritual expungement of the offending passage.[49] Then, Yŏngjo began with the symbols of antiquity. The tombs and shrines of Tan'gun and Kija, for instance, were renovated and maintained with great care.[50] But his main interest lay in affirming the role of the Yi monarchy as the inheritor of the legitimate tradition in Korea, and thus he paid particular attention to the Silla and Koryŏ dynasties through which legitimacy was considered to have been transmitted. With Silla, he basically limited his attention to its first and last rulers. In 1732, he sent a high-ranking minister to attend a sacrifice to the founder,[51] and in 1748, he appointed five attendants for the care of the tomb of King Kyŏngsun, the last ruler.[52] This placed Kyŏngsun on equal footing with the Koryŏ kings. In 1757, Yŏngjo went further, sending a royal secretary as his personal emissary to sacrifice to him.[53]

Yŏngjo expended even greater efforts for Koryŏ, the immediate predecessor of the Yi dynasty. As early as 1727, he proposed extending the taboo on using the personal names of kings from Yi kings to the Koryŏ kings. His officials objected, but a compromise was struck—the taboo would apply to Koryŏ T'aejo, the dynastic founder.[54] Beyond the normal maintenance of royal tombs and regular sacrifices,[55] he visited Kaesŏng, the Koryŏ capital, in 1728[56] and wrote a sacrificial eulogy to the Koryŏ founder.[57] He unsuccessfully sought descendants of the Koryŏ royal house to confer honors upon them,[58] then, instead, conferred positions on descendants of loyal Koryŏ ministers such as Kim Chu and Chŏng Mongju.[59] Perhaps his most significant act in this program was the inclusion of *An Outline of Koryŏ History (Yŏsa chegang)* in the Royal Lecture session.[60] When he selected the book, he was aware that it did not follow precedent but insisted on it, saying that he wanted to do so out of respect for the brilliant accomplishments of the Koryŏ founder.[61]

Then there were other symbols that Yŏngjo put to use. Foremost among them were sacrifices at the Confucian temple, but other historical figures that Yŏngjo deemed useful were also honored. He ordered sacrifices to Chu-ko Liang of Shu-Han and Wen T'ien-hsiang of Sung to honor their loyalty to their lords, to Chinese generals who participated in fighting against the Japanese during

48

the Japanese invasion of Korea,[62] and to Kuan Yū. Kuan Yū was a general of Shu-Han, whose martial bravery is well known through *The Romance of the Three Kingdoms (San-kuo chih yen-i).* Though Chinese in origin, he had been adopted as a martial guardian in the wake of the Japanese invasions and a highly nationalistic cult was formed around him. Yŏngjo frequently visited the Kuan Yū shrine *(Kwanjemyo)* and sacrificed to its fierce protector.[63]

The most important sacrificial rites of the Yi monarchy were of course those offered to the Yi royal ancestors; these were the nucleus and substance of dynastic ritual. Their function in a Confucian monarchy need not be elaborated. Suffice it to say that these rites were the symbolic expression of the present monarch's right to rule as the direct descendant of a royal house possessing the mandate. They fell into two groups. The first affirmed the dynastic mission, while the second had more to do with familial obligations. Rites of the first group were more formal in nature and included sacrifices to the Altar of Land and Grain,[64] the Yi Ancestral Temple, and Yŏngnyŏngjŏn, which were classified as the great offerings,[65] as well as ritualistic reports of certain significant events at the ancestral temple. Those of the second group were gestures of remembrance to individual kings in the form of visits and sacrifices at their tombs and shrines. Together, they demanded a formidable amount of time and attention of the monarch, particularly as the dynasty wore on. Later kings such as Yŏngjo had twenty or more forebears to serve.

Far from regarding them as burdensome chores, Yŏngjo seemed to welcome these observances as opportunities to display his devotion. Unlike his brother Kyŏngjong who had often left ceremonial duties to others, Yŏngjo eagerly carried them out, seeking ways to do more than was expected of him. His frequent personal inspection of sacrificial animals and utensils fell into this category.[66] Also, in the course of his reign he visited the tombs of all previous kings except those of Kings Yŏnsan and Kwanghae, who had been dethroned.[67]

The dynastic founder always occupied a special place in the royal ancestral pantheon, and Yŏngjo displayed particular reverence to him. The following incident typifies his behavior. At the beginning of 1768, the sixth sexagesima of the death of T'aejo, the dynastic founder, Yŏngjo announced that the playing of music would be prohibited at court for the entire year. Then, lest this prohibition be interpreted as applying nationwide, he sent down the edict: "We instructed the prohibition of music. But scholars and the common people are not bound by it. Especially in playing music at home in service of one's parents, there is no prohibition." Nevertheless, some officials obviously thought the measure rather excessive. A censor, Kang Chihwan, made this view known to the king, saying that there was neither a prescription for it in the ritual texts nor had there been a precedent for it. Yŏngjo was irate. He charged Kang with insolence and meted out punishment.[68]

There were other useful ancestors as well. Yŏngjo selected several of them for special treatment, apparently with hopes of enhancing his prestige through identification. The kings he chose were Sŏnjo (r. 1567–1608), Injo (r. 1623–1649), and Hyojong (r. 1649–1659). They all held special places in the Yi imagination. Sŏnjo ruled during the Japanese invasion, while Injo witnessed the change of dynasties, from Ming to Ch'ing, in China; and Hyojong who, as a prince, had been taken to Manchuria as a hostage, was known for his anti-Ch'ing stance. But Yŏngjo selected them for a different reason. Like him, they all had come to the throne as adults, quite unexpectedly, and to stress this he departed from the traditional rites. He conferred posthumous honors on Sŏnjo's and Injo's fathers, who had not been reigning monarchs,[69] he placed the records of Injo's and Hyojong's days as princes in the royal archive,[70] and he paid special visits to Sŏnjo's and Injo's residences as princes.[71]

But it was Hyojong, who had most sterling credentials, whom Yŏngjo singled out for his model qualities, and in the years that followed he tried, indirectly, to assert that he resembled him. In 1737, he placed a commemorative plaque before Hyojong's residence as a prince, which required passing horsemen to dismount in respect.[72] In 1740, he conferred another posthumous title, *Myŏngŭi chŏngdŏk* (Bright Righteousness and Correct Virtue), on Hyojong's already lengthy title,[73] and in 1746 he made a generous gift to Hyojong's son-in-law who had survived to the venerable

50

age of ninety-four. Finally, in 1751, lest the resemblance go un-
noticed, Yŏngjo, his voice aquiver with emotion, announced:

> His Late Majesty Hyojong and I both came to inherit the great
> line quite by chance. Hyojong was one of three brothers, but
> [his older brother] Crown Prince Sohyŏn passed away early
> as did Prince Inp'yŏng. There were also three of us, but my
> royal brother became the guest of Heaven and [my younger
> brother] Yŏnnyŏng also died young. Indeed, there are many
> things about me which resemble Hyojong.[74]

Distant ancestors were fine for metaphoric significance, but more
recent ones offered the opportunity to display a more human
quality—filial affection. Not that rituals dedicated to immediate
predecessors lacked symbolic content, but these close relatives were
expected to elicit grief. Here too Yŏngjo excelled. His reign, like
previous reigns, opened in mourning for the late king. Yŏngjo was
impressive as a mourner. Dressed in hempen clothes, his hair
dishevelled, he mourned his predecessor as a father, as royal custom demanded.[75]

This also meant that Yŏngjo had to serve his brother's consorts
as a son. As Sukchong's son, Yŏngjo had filial obligations to him
as well. Thus, he had altogether eight people to serve in this manner—Sukchong and his two deceased consorts, Queen In'gyŏng
and Queen Inhyŏn, and his surviving widow, Queen Inwŏn;
Kyŏngjong, his deceased consort Queen Tanŭi, and his surviving
widow, Queen Sŏnŭi; and finally, his own deceased mother. Even
for Yŏngjo, this should have been quite enough. Nonetheless, he
could not do enough in their honor. While most of his numerous
visits and sacrifices at their tombs and shrines do not require
comment, some of his activities still seem distinctive. In 1729 and
1772 respectively, Yŏngjo placed his father's and grandfather's
tablets in the eternal sanctuary (*sesil*) of the ancestral temple.[76]
This was an honor reserved for great kings,[77] and it required special effort on Yŏngjo's part.

The first sexagesima of the death of Queen Inhyŏn in 1761 was
commemorated with deep solemnity. She was regarded as a paragon of feminine virtue and Yŏngjo was said to have had, in his

childhood, a special affection for his stepmother. A biography reports that when Yŏngjo was five years old, he gathered flowers in the palace garden and made wine from them, offering it to Queen Inhyŏn when she was ill. The queen was supposedly deeply touched by this.[78] At the beginning of 1761, on the occasion of her sexagesima, Yŏngjo declared a moratorium on the construction of pleasure pavilions and the playing of music.[79] When Queen Sŏnŭi, Kyŏngjong's widow, died in 1730, his observance of the mourning ritual was exemplary. He peformed a sacrifice in pouring rain despite official pleas that he designate a stand-in[80] and, regardless of weather, he did not miss a single offering to the very end of the mourning period.

But it was his attention to Queen Inwŏn, his surviving stepmother, that added a chapter to the canons of filial piety even in his Confucian kingdom. In addition to daily greetings, he heaped honors on her. For instance, he offered a total of nine two-character honorary titles (*chonho*) to her—*Hŏnnyŏl* (Exemplary Fortitude); *Kwangsŏn* (Brilliant Manifestation); *Hyŏnik* (Magnificent Succor); *Kangsŏng* (Serene Sagacity); Chŏngdŏk (Immaculate Virtue); *Such'ang* (Longevous Auspiciousness); *Yŏngbok* (Unending Fortune); *Yunghwa* (Noble Influence); and *Hwijŏng* (Exalted Serenity)—eight of them while she was still alive.[81] She had already received two—*Hyesun* (Gracious Decorum), from Sukchong; and *Chagyŏng* (Affectionate Reverence), from Kyŏngjong—and the additional eight made her the queen with the longest honorary title by far. He also celebrated her birthdays and personal holidays in grandiose style, embellished by poems of his own composition. The following is the poem he offered on her sixtieth birthday:

> *Oh, Magnificent span!*
> *Oh, Brilliant duration!*
> *The sexagesima is complete.*
> *Behold! A new beginning*
> *Has brought to our court*
> *A blessed festivity.*
> *Oh, New beginning!*
> *Reverentially, we wish*

The mother of our nation,
Long joys!
Long pleasures!
The loving influence,
everywhere manifest,
Is a multitude of blessings
Like springtimes.
For four decades,
We were honored to serve Thee.
On this happy occasion,
Bountiful felicities!
Joy overflows even the ancestral shrines.
This great joy at court is
equalled beyond.
Your humble servant, with
all officialdom,
With the sincerity
Of ever increasing devotion and love,
Respectfully offer Thee:
Congratulations as high as
a mountain![82]

Queen Inwŏn was reputed to have said that Yŏngjo was like her own son.[83] They did have a close relationship. It was to her residence that Yŏngjo had fled when he felt his life threatened one night during Kyŏngjong's reign in 1721 and she, invoking Sukchong, exhorted the Soron ministers to preserve the dynasty by protecting Yŏngjo.[84] When Inwŏn died in 1757, Yŏngjo wailed and fasted for days.[85] And characteristically, he wrote an affectionate and grief-filled biography of her,[86] as well as a number of commemorative pieces over time.[87]

ATTENDANT AT THE MATERNAL SHRINE

If Yŏngjo's filial piety shone brilliantly at times it was also known to burn. While his ritual ministrations kept his court constrained

53

to praise, his reverence for his mother imposed no such limit. Lady Ch'oe (Ch'oe Sukpin) had not been queen, and Yi custom maintained a rigid distinction between primary and secondary consorts, even if their issue reigned ascendant. A secondary consort was, in principle, a concubine forever barred from the royal pantheon.[88] On the other hand, no king who had not firmly established his filial piety could effectively claim sage status. To meet the demands of propriety he had to ritually treat his mother in a purely private way. Nonetheless, if Yŏngjo were to sin, his sagehood would best be served by sins of excess. Not only virtue was at stake; enhancing his mother's status enhanced, although indirectly, his aura of legitimacy. Thus, propelled by his quest for authority, and perhaps by fleeting glimpses of a certain official smugness over this maternal origins, he sought to honor his mother. But his officials, the possessors of a punctilious expertise in the minutiae of such matters, kept an unrelenting surveillance lest some tradition-quaking honor fall upon the "private parent" (*sach'in*).

In time, Yŏngjo would show how marked he was by his mother's status, but at first he was discreet. He rejected a proposal for a grander title for Lady Ch'oe, declined a larger tombstone for her, and postponed enlargement of her shrine,[89] though this did not forestall censorial laments over its eventual expense.[90] But, if Yŏngjo visited her shrine more frequently than any other, his commemorations were humbly private. He seemed satisfied with his only gesture, the officially acceptable conferral of a posthumous post on his maternal grandfather.[91]

But, in 1739, assured by fifteen years of rule, Yŏngjo let his grief burst through. This occurred during one of his visits to his mother's tomb. The day before the scheduled visit, dissatisfied with the protocols that the Board of Rites had drawn up, he censured two officials who were directly responsible for them. The *Sillok* explains the measure: "The king respectfully served his private parent, but he suspected that the officials were unwilling to comply with his desire. Thus, on each occasion sudden clashes erupted, inevitably followed by a distressing royal declamation."[92] But obviously neither what the *Sillok* refers to as a "distressing royal declamation"—that the officials in the Board of Rites did not understand propriety—nor royal punishment of them led to the desired change, and further collisions were on the way. This occurred after the ceremony at the site:

> The king was leaving his private parent's tomb for the palace. He was about to mount the palaquin but instead he summoned the Minister of Military Affairs, Kim Sŏngŭng. Breaking into sobs, he said: "Since the *sin* year [1731], this was the first time I came to pay respect [to my mother]. For those ten years, my heart has been filled with sadness. When children fall down, they automatically call out for their mother. This is human nature. At the time of divination, if there is no person offering earth, how can there be a divination? I have sent down orders but the bureaus in charge ignored them. True, the ruler is not allowed to have private [concerns], but it is wrong to lose trust [in him]. The elite scholars of today are just too cold-hearted. These 'elite scholars' must also have parents. They could not have fallen from Heaven or sprung from Earth."[93]

Then Yŏngjo put the Minister of Rites on probation. Upon learning that a certain Song Ikhwi was in charge of the military escort, he had him beaten, and dismissed him from his post. But Song Ikhwi had nothing to do with the offending protocols.

He was, in fact, the nephew of Song Inmyŏng, Minister of the Right, who had approved the protocols as they were with no specification that they were to be a "a most reverential ceremony" (*kŭkhaeng*), and it is just this that laid Yŏngjo's feelings bare. For Song Inmyŏng enjoyed a very special relationship to Yŏngjo and was one of several ministers who were the king's closest supporters. It was apparent to the court that the monarch was punishing Song through his nephew for having approved the protocols. Song admitted as much by pleading for his nephew, prostrate outside the palace gate. The *Sillok* goes so far as to dryly remark that the allegation "seems true enough in this case."[94]

The incident developed into a full-fledged confrontation. The beating of Song Ikhwi elicited censorial protests that the propriety governing the relationship between the ruler and his officials had been violated. Yŏngjo withdrew from his officials. He refused to hold daily meetings with the officials of the Medical Bureau and from his private quarters he sent down one declamation after another, one more aggrieved and bitter in tone than the previous one. The officials claimed that they were concerned with the propriety of royal behavior, Yŏngjo lamented, but what they were concerned with was only propriety toward them, certainly not with propriety toward his mother. But "the way of Yao and Shun simply lay in being filial and brotherly," and it was the officials' refusal to allow him to properly express his filiality, the most important tenet of royal sagacity, that led him to excessive measures. "How could they, having driven their ruler to that state, have the temerity to face the ruler and call themselves his subjects? Until the heads of these arrogant men are all posted on poles, I will not see another official."[95]

But he did see them in several days. Cajoled by a group of high-ranking officials that included his close confidant, Cho Hyŏnmyŏng, who professed their deep distress at this royal displeasure, Yŏngjo unburdened himself. First he mentioned that Emperor Wen-ti of the Han dynasty had been the son of a secondary consort. He conceded that, unlike in China, Korean family law was very strict. He certainly had no intention of violating this law, which would bring disgrace rather than honor to his mother. But for him to perform a proper ceremony at his mother's tomb was entirely within the limits of Korean custom. He was deeply hurt by the officials' begrudging him this small wish and angered by their insolent insistence in such minor matters.[96]

If Yŏngjo was frustrated it was not without reason. He was confronted with one of the sternest prohibitions in Yi law. As Yŏngjo remarked, it was markedly different from Chinese practice. True, China had its share of ritual controversies. The father of Emperor Ying-tsung of the Sung and that of Emperor Chia-ching of the Ming had not been reigning emperors. Since their sons became ritual sons of their imperial predecessors, how to honor the emperors' biological fathers became the object of heated controversy. But when it came to the mothers, there was no problem. An enthroned

56

son could confer upon his mother the position of empress irrespective of her previous station. Indeed, Yŏngjo had cited the historical example of Wen-ti of Han to his bureaucrats. But if history could gall, then what of his contemporary, Emperor Ch'ien-lung? He had elevated his mother to empress from a position inferior even to that of Lady Ch'oe[97] and Yŏngjo had sent his congratulations just three years before.

Nonetheless, Yŏngjo's pleas would be ignored. His officials confessed their deep pain and distress and they offered their apologies and resignations. Yet, buttressed by tradition, they would not yield one jot in their right to limit the king's behavior. A week after Yŏngjo's confrontation with his officials, we find him still fuming over what he believed to have been an official reference to the distinction between the children of primary and secondary consorts.[98] It seemed that Yŏngjo's fifteen-year discretion would have to continue.

But the blow at Song Inmyŏng was only the opening salvo in a campaign that would continue to his death. For what drove Yŏngjo was more than frustration, more than an irritating example from the middle kingdom. What must have driven him, earnest hierophant that he was, was that his discreet observances ritualized his mother's status as a mere concubine. Because of this he could view official admonitions as mere taunts.

He may have been accustomed to such taunts. Officials, all born of primary wives (*chŏk*), might have taken a rather condescending view in dealing with princes whose parentage would not have qualified them for membership in officialdom. In youth, when his father's treatment of him tended toward the lavish, officials had been quick to lecture Sukchong on frugality and modesty. Sukchong actually decried official "contempt" for his two younger sons, Yŏngjo and Prince Yonnyŏng.[99] But other kings had been born of concubines. If Yŏngjo was particularly sensitive, it could have stemmed, at least in part, from other rumors about his mother.

In fact the rumor was that she had been a *musuri*, the lowest type of slave, at Queen Inhyŏn's quarters. This was definitely a matter of oral legend,[100] but one unofficial account of how she came to Sukchong's attention tends to confirm it. She was observed by Sukchong while she was performing a secret birthday ceremony for Queen Inhyŏn in the palace after the queen's departure.[101] Queen Inhyŏn had been deposed in 1689, and until her restoration in 1694, she had been forced to live in private quarters, and most of her more significant attendants had accompanied her. Only Queen Inhyŏn's more lowly or insignificant attendants would have remained at the palace. A more revealing indication, however, is Yŏngjo's extreme sensitivity to any reference to the words "slaves" or "lowly servants" in connection with his mother. In the episode that I discussed, in a moment of extreme anger, he charged that an official reference to the word "slave" could only be interpreted as an intentional insult directed at him.[102]

In any case, Lady Ch'oe first appears in the *Sillok* in 1693 when Sukchong made her a lady of the fourth rank.[103] It was only after she bore him three sons, two of whom died in infancy, that she achieved first rank.[104]

If she really had been a *musuri*, she certainly did quite well for herself. Not only had she achieved first rank and mothered a king, but she would go on to become a lady of high virtue. She acquired this reputation by informing Sukchong of Lady Chang's (Chang Hŭibin) practice of black magic, which had supposedly contributed to Queen Inhyŏn's death in 1701. Lady Chang had been the cause of Inhyŏn's deposal in 1689, but after five years she lost her grip on the king and hence her queenship as well. In 1694, Queen Inhyŏn was restored to her former position as well as her husband's affection. Lady Chang is alleged to have become vindictive toward her rival and to have resorted to black magic against her. Both the *Sillok*[105] and Min Chinwŏn, Queen Inhyŏn's brother,[106] substantiate Lady Ch'oe's role in directing Sukchong's attention to Lady Chang's activity. But all in all, she must have never been fully accepted in Sukchong's court. Both Sukchong's extreme sensitivity to the official treatment of Yŏngjo and Yŏngjo's caution in honoring her suggest it.

Lady Ch'oe did not live to enjoy her greatest glory. She died in 1718 at the age of forty-nine at her private residence, in accordance with Yi custom which forbade secondary consorts from dying in the palace compound.[107] This was before her only surviving son became heir apparent. Yŏngjo failed his first test of filial piety. A son was born to him in 1719, though sexual abstinence was prescribed for the mourning period. Even Sukchong, not known for austerity, disapproved.[108]

But on the throne Yŏngjo made amends. If anything, he was obsessed with his mother's status. As his authority grew, he used it to confer honors upon her, progressively transforming her from the private parent she had been for the first fifteen years of his reign into a more public parent, a parent more appropriate to the king he wished to be.

He began, soon after the confrontation of 1739 which had ended in stalemate, to slowly elevate her status, at first cautiously, but later with increasing force. In February of 1744, he conferred posthumous honors on three generations of Lady Ch'oe's ancestors, and neutralized the effect by doing the same for another of Sukchong's concubines.[109] Then he began in earnest. In April, he named his mother's shrine *Yuksang* (the parent who reared him) and demanded and received improved sacrificial protocols.[110] In 1753, the twenty-ninth year of his reign, Yŏngjo requested that, in commemoration of the sexagesima of his mother's receipt of rank in 1693, an honorary title be offered to her. "I already have received sixteen characters in titles but I have not been able to offer even one character to my mother," he pleaded. Yŏngjo indeed had an impressive string of four four-character titles: *Chihaeng sundŏk* (Perfect Action, Purest Virtue); *Yŏngmo ŭiyŏl* (Glorius Plan, Resolute Valor); *Changŭi hongnon* (Manifest Righteousness, Profound Principle); and *Kwangin tonhŭi* (Shining Principle, True Blessing). On the same day, Lady Ch'oe was given a two-character title, *Hwagyŏng* (Harmonious Reverence), and her shrine and tomb were also elevated one rank.[111] After performing the first ceremony at her shrine in accordance with her elevated status,[112] Yŏngjo happily announced: "Now, I have no more regrets!"[113] Toward the end of the same year, he ingeniously did away with the term "private" in referring to her. Rather than the offending "private parent," she was to be referred to as the "loving parent" (*chach'in*), closer to "loving majesty" (*chajŏn*) as queen mothers were called but as she could never be called.[114] And after 1754, he visited her shrine on New Year's Day after his formal ritual duties.[115] She was now a public figure whom all could recognize as such.

Lady Ch'oe's elevation corresponded to an increase in Yŏngjo's authority. His officials still disapproved, but they had become increasingly fearful of the king. This would have satisfied Sukchong, who delighted in victory regardless of the means, but it did not satisfy his son. Yŏngjo desperately wanted authority, but abhorred any suggestion that he might be authoritarian or arbitrary. As the authority he wanted could come only through moral perfection, success required more than fearful surrender. It required official admiration and approval. Consequently, the elevation of Lady Ch'oe alone did not satisfy him. He waited in vain for the homage from his officials for this filial act.

His officials could not claim ignorance. He had communicated his desires quite clearly. His officials must have known, for in 1746, when he expressed his preference for a temple name, Yŏngjong, he had chosen the name of Emperor Ying-tsung (Korean: Yŏngjong) of the Sung dynasty, saying that he resembled him greatly.[116] But Ying-tsung's father had not been emperor and his short four-year reign was chiefly known for a great ritual controversy which had ended by forbidding Ying-tsung from honoring his father.

But Yŏngjo's officials responded with cold-eyed silence. He retaliated with increasing arbitrariness, frequently dismissing officials or taking other punitive measures for imagined insults to Lady Ch'oe. Just to give one example, in 1767, when Han Ingmo, Minister of the Left, citing the cold weather and the king's frail health, urged that Yŏngjo return quickly to the palace after a ceremony to his mother, he angrily retorted: "You ministers have parents too. How can you not understand my yearning [for my mother]?" He then dismissed Han from his post, though he reinstated him two days later.[117]

Yŏngjo's high-handed manner, however, was not limited to maternal matters. A septuagenarian, he had been on the throne for more than forty years. He clearly exhibited the scars of long years of frustrated endeavor. Dismayed that the status of moral ruler that he had so earnestly sought might be slipping away, he pressed to attain it immediately. In his obsession, he could no longer tolerate what he saw as challenges to his perfection. Official dissent or criticism would prompt him, after severely punishing the offending official, to leave the palace grounds and lock himself in Ch'angŭi Palace, his residence as a prince. He would then refuse admittance to officials until he was satisfied with their pleas that he return.

In these returns to his old residence, Yŏngjo, displeased with the present, sought the reassurance of being courted back by his officials. He had constructed an imaginary world of perfect harmony in which officials revered a sage king ruling over the content masses. If reality would not support his vision, he would act to force others to verify it. Yet at times his actions further shattered it. He would prod his officials with absurd tests of loyalty. In 1770, for instance, he asked his officials whether they remembered the birthday of his deceased stepmother, Queen Inwŏn. When an attendant was unable to reply, the king was so offended that he made him a commoner on the spot. When the Prime Minister fearfully voiced an objection, Yŏngjo dismissed him and set off for his old residence.[118]

But, of course, Yŏngjo was engaged in a futile exercise. By the last years of his reign, his officials were willing and fearful participants in his world. They raised no dissent and paid proper homage. They would describe his reign as that of a sage king like Yao or Shun. Now it was Yŏngjo who remained a captive of his past. In 1773, while an official was reading to him Lu Chung-lien's biography from the *Shih-chi* (Records of the Grand Historian),[119] Yŏngjo suddenly rose from his bed, pounded the floor with his fists and flew into a screaming tantrum when he thought he heard the phrase, "and his mother was a slave" (*erh mu pei yeh*). But the reader had omitted the phrase. In fact, he was reading from a text in which the phrase in question had been blotted out with ink. The bureaucracy, knowing the king's sensitivity on the topic, did not want to take any chances.[120] But obviously Yŏngjo knew that the phrase was there. He had failed to come to terms with his past, however awesome his authority. Here no command would do to set his heart at ease.

In the fifty-first year of his reign, however, he nearly found peace. In 1775, a grand celebration was held in honor of his eighty-first birthday. Yŏngjo wanted to make this occasion grand for his mother as well. He announced that he would receive the first series of congratulations at Lady Ch'oe's shrine. Through a misunderstanding, a congratulatory oration from the students at Sŏnggyun'gwan, the Royal College, was omitted and Yŏngjo, in a rage, accused the students of disapproving of his receiving honors at the shrine. After the usual flurry of activities—a retreat to Ch'angŭi Palace, ministerial explanations and apologies—it ended on a happy note with considerable honor for Lady Ch'oe.[121] The next celebration, marking the beginning of his fifty-second year on the throne, went much better. Lady Ch'oe was honored with no mishap.[122]

The process reached its culmination with Yŏngjo's successor. In January 1776, Yŏngjo appointed his grandson prince regent. On March 14 of that year, Yŏngjo received two more four-character titles. In the interim, he had received titles on two occasions. *Ch'ech'ŏn kŏn'guk* (Substance of Heaven, Establishment of the Ultimate) and *Sŏnggong sinhwa* (Sagacious Merit, Divine Influence) in 1756; and *Taesŏng kwangun* (Great Accomplishment, Wide Movement) and *Kaet'ae kiyŏng* (Great Opening, Permanent Foundation) in 1772.[123] His title was now forty characters long. But the characters chosen this time were extraordinary. They were *Yomyŏng Sunch'ŏl* (Brilliance of Yao, Wisdom of Shun) and *Kŏn'gon konnyŏng* (Strength of Heaven, Peace of Earth). This was the first time a Yi king had received a title containing the characters Yao and Shun,[124] and even Yŏngjo expressed surprise at them. But the officials assured him that the new title correctly reflected his reign.[125] On the same day, the new prince regent, who would become Chŏngjo, placed a jade seal and gold plate engraved with an additional honorary title in Lady Ch'oe's shrine. Lady Ch'oe by now had three two-character titles. *Hwagyŏng* (Harmonious Reverence); *Hwidŏk* (Magnificent Virtue); and *Ansun* (Tranquil Purity). The ritual paralleled one for the founder of the dynasty and another for Yŏngjo's deceased first wife, Queen Chŏngsŏng, all performed on the same day.[126] Celebrated in such company, she was now a "public" figure and so honored. But there was a limit. She could never be a *chajŏn*—a queen mother. On March 20 of that year, when he withdrew to Ch'angŭi Palace for the last time,[127] none could say that Yŏngjo was not brooding over it.

GREAT DIDACT

The Confucian classics reigned supreme as sacred scriptures to guide the spirit and morality of the state.[128] Thus, a Confucian monarch, who was supposed to transform his subjects through his moral influence, should exemplify the ideals and values expressed in the classics. The institution of the Royal Lecture (*Kyŏngyŏn*) or Classics Mat Lecture (*Ching-yen*), in which scholars lectured to the king, was designed to assist the ruler to achieve this goal. The ascendance of this institution paralleled the rise of Neo-Confucianism, with its stress on rectification of the royal mind as the foundation of good government. And Neo-Confucian scholars, with their knowledge of the classics and their duty to counsel their ruler, emerged as his teachers.[129]

In Korea, the Royal Lecture was first instituted in 1116, but was discontinued in 1146 until it was revived in the mid-fourteenth century under Neo-Confucian influence. It was an integral part of the monarchical institution from the beginning of the Yi dynasty. Some of the earlier strong-willed kings, however, viewing it as bureaucratic indoctrination, seldom attended.[130] The Royal Lecture was briefly abolished by King Yŏnsan (r. 1494–1506) shortly before his dethronement, but after it was restored by King Chungjong (r. 1506–1544), it remained unchallenged through the dynasty.[131] Of course, some kings neglected the Royal Lecture but they did so at their own expense.

The ruler's role in the Royal Lecture was potentially dual. He was a student, but so were his teachers as far as the classics were concerned. Thus, he could compete in scholarship and effort with his teachers. This required that he be a diligent and conscientious student. But, if he could surpass his teachers, then he could claim a role as arbiter.[132] When Yŏngjo ascended the throne, he was very much a student. As his reign wore on, he became more and more the arbiter. He consolidated his authority and power, and by the end of his reign, Yŏngjo lectured to his officials, writing tome upon tome of lessons and confessions.

Though Yŏngjo's role in the Royal Lecture changed drastically over the total span of his lengthy reign, the transformation was actually gradual and continuous. While Yŏngjo appears to have been conscious of the changes, he did not impose them by fiat. Rather he was aware that each change had to be painstakingly earned and he spared no effort to do so.

The Yi Royal Lecture sessions were of two types, the *kyŏngyŏn* and the *sodae*. Of the two the *kyŏngyŏn* was much more formal in nature. Ideally, it was to be held three times a day if possible— morning (*chogang*), afternoon (*chugang*), and evening (*sŏkkang*). Compared to Chinese practice, which had evolved into three sessions a month by the late Ming,[133] this was a heavy load. The morning lecture was viewed as the most important, and certain high-ranking officials were required to attend. Either one of the three directors of the Office of the Royal Lecture, who were concurrently ministers of the State Council, or one of the three deputy directors, who simultaneously served as ministers of boards, officiated. Lower-ranking officials from the Office of the Royal Lecture were also required to assist in the proceedings. The afternoon and evening lectures were review sessions, and consequently a smaller group of lower-ranking officials attended.[134] The *kyŏngyŏn* was, in theory, obligatory except on those days when the king was to carry out certain important state functions. On these occasions, the Royal Secretariat would inform the king of his duty. Otherwise, the Royal Secretariat would send him a memo each day inquiring after the king's plans for the *kyŏngyŏn* of the following day. The king would then answer indicating which sessions would be held. He reserved the right to decide that there would be none. When the king did so, he was expected to specify his reasons, but he did not always do so.

In contrast, the *sodae* was rather informal. It was held only when the king explicitly asked for it, and the highest-ranking officials whose attendance was required were those of the third rank. There was also a monthly plenary session (*hoegang*), which was held with the entire staff of the Royal Lecture in attendance.

By all accounts, Yŏngjo's attendance ranked very high. The frequency of sessions was an incomparable improvement over his predecessor Kyŏngjong, who had held a total of just three lecture sessions (one *kyŏngyŏn* and two *sodae*) during his entire four-year reign. Conscientious though a ruler might be, his extensive ritual and administrative duties would have made it impossible to hold lecture sessions daily. Anything more than five sessions a month must have been regarded as a good performance. To take a random example, Yŏngjo held eight lectures, one *sodae* and seven *kyŏngyŏn*, in the third month of 1725. In the following month, there were seven *kyŏngyŏn*.

When Yŏngjo cancelled a session, the reasons varied, but with few exceptions they involved conflicting obligations. For instance, of the twenty-two days in the third month on which there were no *kyŏngyŏn*, ten days were devoted to such ritual ceremonies as a commemoration of the deceased queen or sacrifices to the Ming emperor, four days were spent attending ceremonies designating Prince Hyojang heir apparent, three days were spent welcoming, entertaining, and seeing off Ch'ing envoys, one day was spent administering criminal cases, and the remaining four cancellations were for miscellaneous administrative or personal reasons. In the following month, of the twenty-three days on which Yŏngjo did not have *kyŏngyŏn*, seven were occupied with ritual duties while the remaining sixteen cancellations were occasioned by either administrative obligations or poor health.[135]

Since Yŏngjo knew that he could not maintain the ideal of daily lectures, he expressed his "sincere" commitment to learning through skillful timing of sessions. For instance, he might call for a *sodae* on a day when it was least expected, as he did on the day of commemoration for the deceased Queen Changgyŏng in April, 1725.[136] Or he might hold more than one session a day, perhaps two or even three,[137] which, in spite of the statutory ideal, was a practice rather unusual in other reigns. Yŏngjo must have hoped that this would be perceived as eagerness, even impatience, to return to his books and discussions whenever possible; indeed, it was clearly effective as such. In recording a lecture that Yŏngjo held in 1728 between the trials of principals of the rebellion that had just been subjugated, the *Sillok*, which is not necessarily generous toward the king, comments: "The king is diligent in his study. When he ascended the throne, he never missed even one of the three daily sessions until [the late king's] funeral. Now as soon as the rebellion is brought under control, he holds the lecture. This is truly model behavior for later kings."[138]

Perhaps the most impressive aspect of Yŏngjo's performance in the Royal Lecture was the list of books he read and the number of times he read them. Since the curriculum of the Yi Royal Lecture was based on Chu Hsi orthodoxy, it went through few changes during the five hundred years of the dynasty, though there were additions and deletions in the course of time. The *kyŏngyŏn* sessions were largely reserved for the study of the Confucian classics, especially the Five Classics and the Four Books, while the *sodae* sessions were devoted to discussions of more recent philosophical and historical works, both Korean and Chinese.[139] Since the curriculum was fairly fixed, Yŏngjo did not have much choice in what he read, but he read everything he was supposed to, often many times over. One might attribute this to the length of Yŏngjo's reign, but a comparison of his reading matter to that of his father Sukchong, whose reign was only six years shorter, makes it clear that it was diligence, not time, that made him one of the most well-read of Yi kings. A comparison of Yŏngjo's and Sukchong's respective performances is appended.[140]

Though what Sukchong studied was not inconsiderable and his performance was not below average,[141] he did not reread a book even once. In contrast, not only did Yŏngjo study a far greater number of books, he also restudied many several times. For instance, he read the *Doctrine of the Mean (Chung-yung)* and the *Great Learning (Ta-hsüeh)* as many as eight times. This was a unique record unmatched by any other king of the Yi dynasty. Even Sejong (r. 1418–1450), who is regarded as the most sagacious of Yi kings, did not rededicate himself to these fundamental texts.[142]

A king's conduct in the Royal Lecture consisted of at least two distinct, though related, components. First of all, the monarch was confronting his eternal rivals, the officials. The Royal Lecture, particularly the *kyŏngyŏn*, was scarcely designed to avert confrontation. The king's "tutors" were none other than the officials with whom he conducted state affairs, and this, of course, tended to make the lecture sessions into an extension of the day's political debates, particularly as there was no rule against discussing current affairs. Usually the officials of the Office of the Royal Lecture would read the designated text by turns, but the discussion would then proceed in a rather unstructured manner. As the study of the classics or history was to assist the king in achieving wisdom and benevolence, either the king or his officials could bring up whatever they felt was relevant. It might be a theoretical or moral principle, but it might also be a practical matter over which they had argued just a few minutes before. It might be brought up through a subtle analogy to the text, but it could just as well be introduced quite bluntly.

If the king was a rival to his officials, in the Royal Lecture he was also their student. The primacy of the ministerial obligation—to assist the ruler to attain moral virtue—was quintessentially expressed by the Royal Lecture. In this setting, the king's ministers were clearly his mentors. They imparted learning and wisdom to the student-king. Grave teacher-officials unflinchingly espoused the fundamentals of good rule. They continuously expounded upon the necessity of rectifying the royal mind, the source of national well-being. In sum, these sessions were, either by implication, analogy, or allusion, an unending series of admonitions and exhortations of which the focus was the monarch's deficient virtue.

In the beginning, for all his concern for authority, Yŏngjo was almost an ideal student. He was all ears, an attentive and humble student eager for any enlightenment his teachers might offer. He was never defensive about his lack of virtue. If the teacher-officials, in deference to their sovereign, merely hinted at such a lack, Yŏngjo elaborated on it frequently and at length. He would confess and lament; he would plead for help and for guidance. His self-deprecation knew no bounds in discourse with such illustrious scholars as Chŏng Chedu.[143]

Yŏngjo's striking deference, however, was no concession. On the contrary, it was one with his quest for moral charisma. The Royal Lecture was a competition over who better understood the spirit of sagehood, since none of the participants could pose as a sage himself. Under the circumstances, Yŏngjo's self-deprecation came closer to the ideal being vied for than the more self-assured tone of his teachers. By the time the officials recognized this, Yŏngjo was already well ahead in the game. In his role as student, as in his other roles, Yŏngjo emerged the victor by accepting the rigors and demands of his role to such an extent that his officials could only counsel restraint in his efforts.

In his long career in the Royal Lecture, Yŏngjo may have risen above the need to approach his lecturers in all humility, but he never eschewed his posture as a seeker who was woefully inadequate in comparison to the great sages of the past, unceasing in his quest for greater wisdom and virtue. Gradually the group of people toward whom he was willing to maintain this attitude of deference became smaller and smaller, as he metamorphosed from student to arbiter, until it contained no one but the ideal figures of the past. He announced the phases of his metamorphosis by the historical figures to whom he obliquely compared himself and the manner in which he did it.

In a lecture session of 1728, Yŏngjo, in deep abnegation, confessed shame that his governance still could not be compared to that of Han and T'ang times.[144] By 1736, he expressed superiority over the widely admired emperors T'ang T'ai-tsung and Shih-tsung of the Later Chou. On August 1, he had the following conversation with a royal secretary in a *sodae:*

> YŎNGJO: On these terribly hot days, I think of [resting in] a grass-covered room, but my mind cannot relax. [If] I stop the lecture for one day, then I jump up with a start and say to myself, "How can I abandon one day's effort?" Though T'ang T'ai-tsung was very intelligent, he began in diligence but ended in indolence. I always try to bear this in mind.
>
> KIM SANGSAENG: Your Majesty is not free from a tendency

to want too much too soon, and this may contrarily harm the way of protecting and guarding [virtue]. It is better to be concerned with steady and ceaseless effort.

YŎNGJO: [If one] cares about one's comfort, then it is easy to fall into indolence. This is what an ape thinks of and what a horse once loosened [from harness] will become. Sheer idleness. Then indolence [will lead] to dissoluteness.[145]

In a *sodae* on August 7:

YŎNGJO: As for the personal campaign of Shih-tsung of the Later Chou, when [it was] finished, [he was] finished. This was caused by his self-satisfaction. This example should serve as a warning.

KIM SANGSAENG: Your Majesty's instruction is true indeed. Chou Shih-tsung was preeminent but for five years. From ancient time, all sage rulers must have guarded themselves against arrogance. Because once it germinates, then the virtuous charge [i.e., rule] does not progress, and the channel for [official] expression (*ŏllo*) gets blocked. The way of Yao and Shun simply lies in a sage not regarding himself a sage. Your humble servant hopes that Your Majesty will avoid this pitfall.

YŎNGJO: Those who are self-satisfied, of course, regress. Sages always thought themselves deficient. How much more [this should be] with ordinary people. Lord Yi [Kwang-jwa] also cautioned me to guard myself against arrogance. I surely hope I won't be like that. [But] there is no affair that the ruler of men conducts by himself. [If all of us approach state affairs with] Yao and Shun's sagacity, then though eight Yüan dynasties might rise, there will be eight triumphs [over them]. But the ruler and officials are bound by mutual responsibility. If one man alone achieves [sagacity], how is it possible that he would be able to act upon it?[146]

The implication in his last remark is startling. Yŏngjo was no longer deferential to his officials. No longer sagacious teachers guiding a deficient monarch, they were now deficient officials obstructing him from effecting the sagacity of Yao and Shun. Yŏngjo pronounced this sentiment more explicitly in 1742, this time using an analogy of Confucius and Mencius. Irate over continuing factional scuffles among officials, he threatened abdication:

> Formerly, Confucius and Mencius had not attained [the position of ruler] to propagate the Way, and [made their ideas] known in the *Book of Odes* and the *Book of Documents*. While I have attained the position of ruler, like them, I have no means to effect the Way.[147]

Clearly, by 1742 Yŏngjo's expertise on the texts as well as his ability to use them to his advantage became so proficient that attending officials in the lecture, who, unlike the king, changed rather frequently, were no match for him. How he handled official advice that he pay more attention to the official counsel in a session in October of that year is a good illustration. In discussing a passage from the *Classic of the Mind (Hsin-ching)* concerning Sung Jen-tsung, a tutor indicated, as an example for Yŏngjo to follow, the Sung emperor's acknowledgment that he was able to avoid mistakes by listening to his minister Tu Yen. Yŏngjo's evaluation of Sung Jen-tsung was less favorable: Sung Jen-tsung needed his minister's instruction because he was lacking in self-restraint in the first place. But Yŏngjo admitted his sense of shame for his own lack of self-restraint, which was indeed worse than Jen-tsung's. Another tutor hurriedly assured him that he had no cause for shame, and that in fact he was needlessly belittling himself while his subjects were entertaining hopes that his sagacity would approach that of Yao and Shun. This prompted a confession of his "lack of self-restraint":

> But I have this disease. Rain and sunshine, cold and hot are the ways of Heaven and Earth, yet still they make me anxious from dawn till night. Right now, the autumn air is still crisp and it is certainly not yet cold, but I am already worrying about whether my people are cold or not. One [drop

of] rain, and I fear for flood, one [minute] of sunshine, and I am terrified of drought. Either when I walk one step or when I eat one spoonful of food, all my thoughts are of my people's conditions, and so, my mind is always in a flurry. This is different from the natural concern [that the ruler should display toward the people] on hunting trips. This is but a disease which stems from the lack of self-restraint.

The officials in attendance prostrated themselves, and one of them said: "Your Majesty's concern for the people is indeed profound. Your humble servants cannot but admire it."[148]

That Yŏngjo had the upper hand over his officials in the Royal Lecture seems to have been common knowledge at the court for sometime. One *Sillok* entry in 1738 comments that "while the king's understanding [of the classics] is superb and he is eager to gain more knowledge from his tutors, the tutors are not equipped to offer much."[149] Four years later, its criticism of the officials became sharper. They only talked "in platitudes" and offered "pleasantries" which did not benefit royal study in the least.[150] The time had come when the king had achieved all he could as a student; there was no point in continuing.

But even in halting the lectures for a time, Yŏngjo achieved a characteristic tour de force. In the fourth month of 1746 he attended one *soade* and nineteen *kyŏngyŏn*, including two sessions a day for nine days.[151] But in the following month, there were only six sessions,[152] and afterwards there were hardly any. Though there were *kyŏngyŏn* in 1747,[153] it was by now an unusual event. The appointment of Prince Sado as regent in 1749, the twenty-fifth year of his reign, provided Yŏngjo with a legitimate excuse for eliminating the lectures entirely. The prince's lecture sessions were now stressed.[154] Two months after Sado's appointment, Yŏngjo ordered that the Royal Secretariat stop sending him a daily memo inquiring about the Royal Lecture. Unless otherwise instructed, it was to assume that no lecture would be held.[155]

From 1749 to the middle of 1756, there was no *kyŏngyŏn*. But Yŏngjo was not idle; he was preparing for something. For the text he chose for the infrequent *sodae* of this period was *A Royal Self-*

Reflection (Ŏje chasŏng p'yŏn), which Yŏngjo wrote in 1746. It consisted of two sections, the first devoted to the principles of sage kingship and a reflection upon them, and the second a compendium of the virtuous acts of historical rulers.[156] In sum, it was a selection of Yŏngjo's ideals of good government in theory and practice. In using this text for the Royal Lecture, he, in effect, announced his elevation to the status of arbiter. His opinions and views now stood beside those of the greatest scholars of the past. No longer was he a mere receiver of wisdom; he was a contributor to the accumulated wisdom that would enlighten the present and enrich the future. Yŏngjo cautiously introduced *A Royal Self-Reflection* in a *sodae* for the first time in 1750.[157] After a gap of five years, it became the text for all the *sodae* held from late 1755 to early 1756. Something obviously was in the air.

When, after a seven-year suspension, Yŏngjo reopened the *kyŏngyŏn* on June 3, 1756, the thirty-second year of his reign, he was the lecturer. His text was the *Doctrine of the Mean*. He began by observing:

> Mater Chu was sixty *se*, when he wrote the preface to the *Doctrine of the Mean*, and I am now past sixty [sixty-three], and yet I have not mastered it. Isn't it shameful?

Throughout the session, he remained in total control, interpreting the text himself. The official-teachers were completely upstaged. They offered their observations, but these were merely evaluated and judged by Yŏngjo.[158]

The next eight or nine years were devoted to amending the situation that Yŏngjo had described as "shameful." His goal was clear—he wished to establish his credentials as a scholar and authority equal to Chu Hsi himself. Previously, as a student, he had acquired the necessary erudition. Now it was time for investigation and analysis. In the past, he had read extensively; now he concentrated more narrowly on the central Neo-Confucian texts, especially the *Great Learning* and the *Doctrine of the Mean*. In the twenty-eight-month period beginning in June 1756, Yŏngjo read the *Great Learning* eight times and the *Doctrine of the Mean* seven times. The other texts he covered included the remaining two of the Four Books, the *Analects,* and *Mencius,* as well as the *Book of Odes* and the *Book of Documents.* A heavy Neo-Confucian orientation is also reflected in the philosophical and historical texts chosen for the *sodae* of this period.

All of these books espoused the rectification of the mind and correctness of conduct as ways to become a moral person and to effect sagacious rule. Clearly Yŏngjo wanted to establish, if only through the frequency with which he consulted the texts, that he had not only penetrated into the fundamental spirit of sage rule but had, in fact, attained it. In this period, Yŏngjo's fervent activity in striving for the ideal might have been spurred by his all too real difficulties with his son, Prince Sado, whom he put to death in 1762.[159] At any rate, by 1765 he seems to have felt that a regular study of the classics had nothing more to offer, for on January 6 of that year, he attended his last regular *kyŏngyŏn.*[160]

Now Yŏngjo, a septuagenarian, played the sage and demanded that he be recognized as one. To communicate his sagacity, he wrote. Royal writing was certainly an effective means of adding substance to his actions. Personally composed edicts carried great weight, while a poem of remembrance on a commemorative occasion tended to substantiate the mourner's grief. From the beginning this medium had appealed to Yŏngjo and he had frequently taken up the brush. In 1757, he wrote the *Royal Mirror of the Past and Present (Ŏje kogŭm yŏndae kwigam).* Like *A Royal Self-Reflection* of 1746, this was an instructional piece making use of historical examples.

Yŏngjo's writings of the 1760s were on similar themes. *Royal Questions and Answers on Cautioning the World (Ŏje kyŏngse mundap)* (1762); *Continuation to the Royal Questions and Answers on Cautioning the World (Ŏje kyŏngse mundap songnok)* (1763); *A Royal Discourse on Cautioning the World (Ŏje kyŏngse p'yŏn)* (1764); and *A Royal Study on the Sources of Good Conduct (Ŏje paekhaengwŏn)* (1765)[161] are all admonitions on wise rule. Unlike the earlier works in which Yŏngjo had substantiated his points with historical precedents, these pieces are forthright expositions of his views. They are more general, dwelling on philosophical principles. It seems that Yŏngjo, having garnered sufficient expertise, felt that there was no longer any need to call upon other texts. He was the authority and he needed no other support.

The gradual change in topic from historical events and their lessons to Yŏngjo's personal vision of Confucian ideals continued until his writings had become a virtual chronicle of his own development as a sage. He himself, and his agonies and tribulations in quest of sagehood, became the ultimate lessons. There are at least two thousand different works under his authorship in the Yi royal family library, Changsŏgak, most of them written during the last ten years of his life (1767–1776), with a heavy concentration in the 1770s.[162] This suggests that, in the last five or six years of his life, he must have written something almost daily.

These works are mostly short poems or essays, seldom more than two or three leaves. Scores of pieces bear the same or closely similar titles. Identical themes would be developed in different genres. A sampling of the titles gives a fairly accurate impression of the range of his oeuvre: "A Royal Lament" *(Ŏje kanggae);* "On Steadfastly Holding in the Royal Mind" *(Ŏje kosusim* or *Ŏje koyŏsim); "A Record of Royal Emotions and Longings on Observing Those Who Labor at Ninety and a Hundred" *(Ŏje kŭn'gyŏn paekse su chikchiin ch'umo kihoe);* "On the Royal Longing for the Great Shun" *(Ŏje mo Tae Sun);* "A Royal Appraisal of the Great Yao" *(Ŏje ch'ing Che Yo);* "A Royal Inquiry Into His Own Mind" *(Ŏje munyŏsim);* "Royal Agonies of a Long Night" *(Ŏje minyajang);* "A Royal Laugh at My Generation" *(Ŏje so ilse);* "A Royal Laugh at Oneself" *(Oje chaso);* "Morning and Night, My Heart Is Only with the People" *(Ŏje sungya simyujaemin);* "On Royal Suffering" *(Ŏje simmin);* "On Royal Daily Tribulations" *(Ŏje ilmin* or *Ŏje ilganggae);* "Royal Self-Awakening" *(Ŏje chasŏng)* and "Royal Questions and Answers for Himself" *(Ŏje chamun chadap).*

In these chronicles of his minutest emotions, Yŏngjo presented the ongoing saga of his battle with human frailty in the maintenance of sagehood. His writings dwelt on his imperfections, but this was merely evidence of the intensity of the fray. Every stepping-stone on his journey through sagehood was commemorated. His sagehood was institutionalized and made a matter of public record.

This torrent of virtue, which had orginated in Yŏngjo's confrontation with his officials, now proceeded of its own momentum. The officials, who had been dominant when it all began, now played only a minor role as bystanders. They could do nothing but accept and praise his accomplishments. But their acceptance was conditioned by their fear of royal wrath, not Yŏngjo's moral authority. The *Sillok* entry of December 28, 1775 has the following postscript:

> At the time, from the highest ministers of the State Council down to the lowest functionaries, all were nothing but supernumeraries merely occupying offices. The ministers would come in and do nothing but sing the praises of the king's accomplishments and his sagacious virtues. Besides that, they would sit around exchanging small talk. When they retired from the court at the end of the day, they would exchange knowing smiles at each other.[163]

This then was how it ended. Yŏngjo had sought an elusive sagehood to command; now dominance held sagehood in its sway.

GRAND EXEMPLAR

It is a fundamental tenet of Confucian ethics that no man may demand of his fellows what he would not accept for himself. What, then, of the ruler? He was responsible for the sins of an entire nation, and it was he who was expected to cure the ills and excesses of his people.[164] What of his sins, his ills and excesses? If he wished to rule wisely and well, each of his prescriptions and injunctions fell just as heavily on him.

Of course, moral suasion was not the only instrument of rule. In Ch'ing China, imperial power had acquired a certain autonomous sway. And Sukchong, ever willful, had used royal prerogatives when gentler tactics had proven inconclusive.

But Yŏngjo believed that royal power flowed from moral authority. Uncertain of his power and eternally in quest of an elusive absolute legitimacy, he sought cosmological support, or at least an effective image of sublime enforcement.

Indeed, his contemporaries understood this in Yŏngjo. His hagiographical biographer recalled, perhaps with the force of hindsight, that a palace guard had dreamt, on the night of Yŏngjo's birth at Ch'angdŏk Palace, that a white dragon perched on Pogyŏng Hall at the palace.[165] An auspicious omen this certainly was, foretelling the future greatness of the newborn. A dragon dream, however, with all of its accepted symbolism, had become a mere de rigueur accoutrement of the birth of a future king, especially one who was not born as the natural heir, and thus such a dream was not something to be reassured by. Yŏngjo, at any rate, was not. He further sought cosmic power in a struggle to perfect his conduct and to project a superhuman strength in his comportment. Thus Yŏngjo became his rule; he was the grand exemplar in whose acts its lineaments were read.

When Yŏngjo took the throne, he had appealed to restoration as his guiding principle. This implied that his society, from the royal house to the meanest slave, had turned degenerate, and deviated from Confucian norms. Customs and mores had to be rectified. Sumptuary laws, which governed the material life of every inhabitant of the society, should be reinforced.

Sumptuary laws reaffirmed the Yi social hierarchy, which was in turn believed to mirror the cosmic order. They regulated one's abode, clothing, headgear, and mode of transport according to social status. Though they were effective tools for maintaining social distinctions, they were also rationalized as the mark of a civilized society in which a person, living within his limits and privileges, would not fall into excess. Economic considerations also played an important role. The Confucian economic view, based on an agrarian social vision, was that natural resources and products had definite upper limits and so, sumptuary laws, especially their delimiting features, were considered necessary. The moral implication was also very strong. To consume no more than one was allotted was to acknowledge and consider others' needs and, in this sense, frugal living was a kind of moral duty.

Sumptuary laws, like many ritual protocols and legal codes, were established during Sejong's reign. For instance, the size of a housing lot was set at 1,170 *p'yŏng*[166] for royal children by the legal consort, 975 *p'yŏng* for royal children by secondary consorts, 585 *p'yŏng* for officials of the first and second rank, 390 *p'yŏng* for those of the third and fourth rank, 312 *p'yŏng* for those of the fourth and fifth rank, 156 *p'yŏng* for those of seventh and below as well as other yangban, and 78 *p'yŏng* for commoners.[167] The size of the house was regulated at 60 square *kan*,[168] with a 10-square *kan* reception chamber, for royal sons by the legal consort; at 50 square *kan*, with an 8-square *kan* reception chamber, for other royal children; at 40 square *kan*, with a 6-square *kan* reception chamber, for officials of the second rank and up; at 30 square *kan*, with a 5-square *kan* reception chamber, for officials of the third rank and below and other yangban; and at 10 square *kan*, with a 3-square *kan* reception chamber, for commoners. Other construction and decoration details were specified as well.[169] This fifteenth-century regulation was periodically modified. In later periods, officials could build a house as big as 99 square *kan*.[170]

Sumptuary laws on public attire at the court remained more constant. Modeled on Ming court dress,[171] it became, after the demise of the Ming in China, a symbol of the Korean role as the perpetuator of civilization. This was still true in eighteenth-century Korea.[172]

If Yi society does not seem to have changed greatly in its material life, especially in the matter of clothing, each age also had its fads and fashions. Deviations inevitably occurred, and enforcement of the rules was not always successful. Yŏngjo was not one to take such matters lightly. He evaluated each problem for real and symbolic meaning, the possibility of successful regulation, and, especially, the moral questions involved. He rebuked deviations of a symbolic nature, but he severely castigated excesses characterized by conspicuous consumption. This he regarded as selfish and immoral and tending to lead the country to material penury and spiritual degeneration.

One of the deviations concerning clothing was color. The Yi king, unable to share yellow with the Son of Heaven, had to make do with red,[173] but red had come to be shared by the officials of

Yŏngjo's court though it should have been the exclusive royal color. The king attempted to change this but, when enforcement proved difficult, he did not pursue it except by occasionally making disparaging remarks on the indiscriminate official use of red.[174] He adopted the same attitude of mild censure toward popular chromatic perversion—a persistent predilection for white, although blue, the color of the east, should have been worn in the Eastern Kingdom.[175]

When it came to ostentatious display, however, Yŏngjo was far less tolerant. Richly patterned Chinese silk, imported through a border black market, had been gaining popularity in the upper class. When repeated exhortation proved ineffectual, Yŏngjo in 1746 proscribed importation of the offending fabric with a stern punishment for violators.[176] But soon fickle fashion sought out, instead, unpatterned silk from China. In 1748, Yŏngjo prohibited the importation and use of this material as well, and punished those officials who were found to have violated the ban.[177]

Still more corrupt, in Yŏngjo's view, were the elaborate coiffures, which were sometimes as much as a foot high and incorporated ornaments and jewels, that were de rigueur in his time.[178] For, aside from sheer ostentation, these styles, in their use of hairpieces, remunerated those who cut their hair, a practice forbidden by Confucian norms. After numerous discussions, Yŏngjo, in 1763, decided to allow the style, provided that no hairpieces were used.[179]

In his attempts to rectify customs and mores, Yŏngjo displayed a similar practical bent. Confucian moralist that he was, he certainly did not neglect to shore up public morality and to discourage what he considered to be corrupt Buddhist practices. He published morality books, forbade Buddhist monks from presiding at funerals, and barred nuns from the capital.[180] But he expended his undivided energy on the campaign for abstinence from alcohol.

Viewing alcohol as a cause of loose moral conduct as well as a tremendous drain on valuable grain resources, Yŏngjo pursued a temperance campaign with conviction and persistence. He repeatedly promulgated royal edicts expounding upon the wastefulness and harmful consequences of brewing and drinking wine.[181]

When moral suasion alone did not produce the desired result, he resorted to legal and punitive measures. In November 1755, a prohibition on brewing wine was announced. Then, in January 1757, he imposed heavy penalties on violators—officials were to have their names expunged from the official register, while commoners were to be enslaved for life. Yi society did seem to have had its share of thirsty souls and, to the dismay of Yŏngjo who had hoped that penalties would function effectively as a deterrant, seven hundred violators were arrested within a year. Unwilling to punish them according to the law, he freed them and lightened the penalties.[182]

Lest his release of the criminals be interpreted as permissiveness, he declared that the first violator of the new law would be executed.[183] Within weeks, a violator was caught and Yŏngjo was now bound by his own decision. To uphold the law, he held an open, if somewhat impromptu, trial of the accused before the execution. The following is the *Sillok* description of this trial.

> The king went to Honghwa Gate. One Yu Segyo, accused of having violated the wine law, was brought in. A big crowd of city inhabitants gathered. It was expected that the head of the accused would be displayed on a pike as a warning. The king ordered that the tribunal officials examine the wine jar. They all said it was wine. Next, he asked that it be shown to commoners. They all said it was wine. He then addressed his ministers: "The accused say it is vinegar and others say it is wine. You lords examine it closely." The Minister of the Left, Kim Sangno, said: "At first, it looked like wine, but when I dipped a piece of paper and smelled it, it was more like vinegar." The king went inside and ordered a eunuch to bring the wine jar. After a while, the king returned and said: "Since a man's life is of uttermost importance, I have tasted it myself. It was indeed vinegar." He ordered the accused freed and those who arrested him relieved of their posts.[184]

Whether Yŏngjo and his officials were aware of the relationship between wine and vinegar or whether they had quite uncommon taste in wine must remain a topic of speculation.

79

If, on this occasion, Yŏngjo's justice had been leavened with the yeast of mercy, it probably was because the accused was a hapless commoner. The king most likely, if belatedly, realized that the fact that he was arrested was proof that he had neither the power nor the financial means to cover up or smooth over his illicit activity. Yŏngjo often deplored the inequity between the wealthy and powerful and the poor and powerless in application of the law.[185] He certainly did not want to make this luckless peasant a victim of his ordinances. In fact, his austerity campaign was, in the main, directed at the official-scholar class which not only should set a model for the general populace but also had the financial means to indulge in luxury. Thus, it is not surprising that he was sterner toward officials in applying his temperance law. The *Sillok* records instances in which he dismissed officials from their posts upon discovery of their concealed indulgence.[186] In 1767, under popular pressure, he allowed that wine could be used for ritual libation[187] but his zeal for temperance remained unabated. In 1770, he added beating to the penalties for brewing in quantity.[188]

These austerity measures could not have been greeted enthusiastically. But Yŏngjo attempted to overcome resistance by making the royal family the first and most eager participants in the program. Ever the zealous guardian of his own moral credibility, he scrupulously cultivated an impression that the royal family lived in frugal discipline. Indeed, one of his first acts upon accession was to decrease his son's allowance. When Hyojang was invested as a prince in 1724, the king ordered that his annual allowance be two thousand taels of silver and one hundred *sŏk* of rice, instead of his legal entitlement of double that amount.[189] Then, in 1729, he enforced the payment of taxes of all lands held by the royal family except for legally exempt plots.[190]

Naturally, the royal family was inclined to occasionally overstep the bounds of its privileges, but he maintained vigilance lest this occur. His strict injunction[191] against selecting ladies-in-waiting from among commoners is one example.[192] And when, in 1746, the Prime Minister, Kim Chaero, suggested that perhaps the royal family was immoderate in its spending, not only did the king receive the ministerial admonition "with delight;"[193] he went on to codify standards of royal consumption by publishing the *T'akchi chŏngnye* (Rules and Regulations of the Board of Taxation) in 1749. In twelve volumes, prepared by Pak Munsu, Minister of Taxation, and his assistants, this manual prescribes, in minutest detail, both the quantity and kind of food, clothing, regional specialties, and all else that the royal family might use in daily life, as well as rules for scheduling marriages, funerals, and related ceremonies.[194]

Thus, Yŏngjo assigned to his clan an exemplary role in the austerity policies he instituted. In 1747, when he banned patterned silk, royal family members were not allowed to wear it even at ceremonies at the Altar of Land and Grain.[195] When, in 1761, he proscribed the use of excessive and luxurious articles, he decided to implement the ban at his grandson's wedding, and the grand heir had to make do with, among other inconveniences, gilded rather than gold objects.[196]

These examples beg comparison to Sukchong's approach, for he equated power with prerogative, and authority with grandeur. He had sought impressive display, battling his ministers for greater richness at his son Yŏngjo's wedding.[197] For Yŏngjo, though, command was but the product of a moral force. Therefore, in rigor and austerity what he truly sought was dominance—a heavenly transcendant power over his officials and his nation.

Hence Yŏngjo's personal austerity. He wished to be a living exemplar of his own policies. He refused elaborate decor or extensive renovation of his residence even when it seemed necessary.[198] He took pains to let it be known that he kept to a simple diet.[199] He customarily wore only thin clothing which offered scant protection against the cold. This elicited the concern of his royal secretaries, to whom he would respond by saying that he was used to wearing thin clothing, having never indulged in luxury.[200] These remarks are rather typical:

All my life, I have worn thin clothes and eaten simple food. Her Majesty the Queen Mother constantly worries about this. And Yŏngbin [Lady Yi] has warned me saying, "I was able to render only the most meager services. [Your Majesty] will suffer illnesses in old age." But that I have no illness now is the effect of light food and light clothes. Ordinary people spend their entire energy in heavy clothing and heavy meals. I hear that many scholar-officials' families wear furs and leathers and eat delicacies of which I don't even know the names. Isn't this indulgence and luxury too extreme?[201]

No wonder then that his officials confessed shame at the sight of the king in a plain cotton bedcloth reading in his unadorned bedchamber.[202]

For all his frugal habits, however, Yŏngjo was not above falling into excess himself. He is known to have succumbed to the temptations of alcohol. Intimations of his drinking and excessive sexual activities appeared in 1754,[203] and on one occasion in 1755, he got roaring drunk in public.[204] This was a trying time for him, during which he endured continuing factional animosities and persistent rumors of regicide. He once said, "a man is not made of wood or stone,"[205] and it seems that he too could falter. But he compensated for his lapses.

He compensated by fasting. Yŏngjo fasted to do penance in time of natural calamity and he fasted for sheer self-castigation. He sometimes fasted because his deficient virtue had failed to inspire his people to a purer morality,[206] because his faults had brought on some natural calamity, because the thought of his people's suffering left him with no appetite, or for whatever reason he felt was appropriate for the occasion. In the end, what Yŏngjo fasted for was authority. And as time passed he grew ever more obsessive in pursuit of that unmaculated recognition that seemed to elude him.

But cold and starvation did at last produce a sign. In January of 1764, he delightedly displayed his right arm to his officials. Certain marks had formed there. His ministers saw nine dragons,[207] heavenly writ upon his flesh. Thus Yŏngjo found at last the mark of Heaven on his rule.

CHAPTER 3

Yŏngjo's Rule:
Politics of Patriarchy

Heaven sees as my people see;
Heaven hears as my people hear.

—*Book of Documents*

Yŏngjo's tireless construction of his moral image was predicated on his belief that power flowed from moral authority. Gratifying though it may have been to be praised for his sagacity, Yŏngjo might not have pursued it with such single-mindedness had he not thought it useful to his rule. His main goal in his various roles as high priest, scholar, and exemplar seems to have been to establish his moral superiority over his officials so that he could use the advantages thus attained in the execution of practical policies. He had a country to rule and people's livelihoods to worry about.

This is not to say that the bureaucracy stood in the way of his discharging his responsibility. In fact, the bureaucracy, both in rhetoric and practice, was the medium through which monarchical policies were transmitted and effected. As the ruling elite, the scholar-officials had as much at stake as the king in maintaining peace and order in the society in which they occupied a privileged position. Many of them, dedicated Confucian statesmen schooled in the ideology and art of Confucian government, devoted their lives to the cause of public welfare.

On the whole, however, given their belief in the rationality of the social hierarchy and their vested interest in preserving their status, these bureaucrats could not be very responsive to demands for those social reforms, which they saw as a threat to their privilege. In this, their views and interests could diverge from those of the monarch. His primary interest lay in strengthening the state, and sometimes this required instituting reforms and policies at the expense of the bureaucratic ruling class.

Nothing was more urgent, in his estimate, than a reform of the military tax system. The yangban were exempt from the military tax and this resulted in the depletion of the state treasury and an increased burden on commoners. This was a clear-cut case in which monarchical and bureaucratic interests ran counter to each other. As important as it was for the king to change the tax system, it was equally important for the bureaucratic community to keep it the way it was, and their resistance to the reform reflected this. This was the reason why Sukchong, even with his authoritarian approach, was unable to bring about the change in spite of several attempts.

How the monarch and the bureaucrats defined the problem of the military tax and how they defended their respective positions reflect the ways in which they employed Confucian rhetoric in approaching certain social issues. The problem of the military tax was not merely that the yangban were exempt from the tax but also that the tax-exempt group was increasing both in absolute number and as a proportion of the population. The exact composition of this group and how this increase occurred are not very well understood. But the increase in the yangban population and various tax evasion practices are cited as major reasons for the increase in the tax-exempt population. There are many uncertainties and questions concerning the increase in the yangban population but it appears that it was closely related to the spread of the Confucian way of life and with it education and the practice of ritual. The power of the ruling elite does not seem to have been greatly challenged by this phenomenon. It is not clear whether the ruling elite felt a sense of affinity to those yangban who were separated from them by position and prestige. But when their own interests were lumped together with those of these yangban, they defended class interests.

But these interests had to be defended in the context of Confucian rhetoric. The ruling elite sought their defense in their role as the custodians of Confucian custom and ritual and as a paradigm for the people. Yi Chongsŏng, a minister of the State Council, articulated this view in his memorial opposing the reform. The bureaucrats and yangban, as the leaders of the people, were burdened with carrying out the Confucian way of life. They pursued scholarship and they performed family and ancestral rites. This incurred high costs. Moreover, forbidden from engaging in other professions such as farming, commerce, and artisans' trades, many were reduced to relative poverty. It was the responsibility of the Confucian state to protect this class.[1] This argument expressed the hierarchical aspect of Confucianism.

On the other hand, it was in the interests of the throne to evoke a more egalitarian aspect of Confucianism. Though the state needed the yangban class and sanctioned its privileges, when its interests worked against those of the state, the king was forced to move beyond class in search of a rhetoric that would favor the welfare of the entire population. Thus, the two strands of Confucianism, the hierarchical and egalitarian, came into conflict.

This conflict seems to have been rather pervasive in Korean society. In a larger context, it might be ascribed to both the imposition of a meritocratic Sung Neo-Confucianism on the rigid Korean social structure as well as the way Neo-Confucianism was assimilated into and interacted with the indigenous system. This was evidently an exceedingly complex phenomenon. On social issues, however, one's stance was related to one's sphere of influence, responsibility, and interests. The throne had to be accountable for the whole population. The bureaucrats also frequently endorsed the more egalitarian approach when it was demanded by their position as the governing and national elite. But in areas in which this approach came into a direct conflict with their interests, they opted for the hierarchical solution. The military tax reform was a clear instance in which the egalitarian approach of the throne and the hierarchical approach of the bureaucracy came to a clash. Given the Yi political structure and the decision-making process, however, it was not possible for the throne to enact a reform measure without the approval or at least the acquiescence of the bureaucracy. Thus, for Yŏngjo to succeed in a military tax reform was not just a matter of devising a solution or finding a rhetoric but of using them in such a way as to render bureaucratic opposition impossible.

Yŏngjo overcame this opposition, at least in part, by generating popular support. Of course, rulers in both the East and the West who faced similar situations often allied themselves with the less privileged in order to override the powerful, and they had to resort to a variety of tactics in order to achieve this. Yŏngjo attained his goal through an ingenious use of the Confucian rhetoric of the ruler-patriarch.

The concept of the ruler as the father of his people was a familiar idea. The notion that the royal mandate depended on winning the people's hearts had long been accepted as the theoretical basis for the legitimation of Confucian monarchs. As a father would for his children, sovereigns were to toil to insure the livelihoods of their people, to make them content, and to please them as much as they would please themselves.[2] Unchallengeable though this idea remained, it was subsumed in the Yi bureaucratic structure which provided few channels for the throne to have direct contact with the people. This was done by the bureaucrats, royal delegates to the people, while the king remained within the palace walls. The Yi kings depended on officials for reports on contemporary problems, and this obviously endowed the officials with considerable power. Yŏngjo did not acquiesce to this role. He turned the rhetoric of ruler-father into the politics of patriarchy. He sought ways to contact his people in order to cultivate his image as a concerned "ruler-father" and used popular support to break bureaucratic opposition in instituting the military tax reform. In this, as his rhetoric was masterfully applied in the arena of practical politics, his belief that power flowed from moral authority seems to have been realized.

GOVERNMENT POLICY AND EIGHTEENTH-CENTURY YI SOCIETY

Yŏngjo pursued the politics of patriarchy out of a deeply felt sense of necessity. The society that Yŏngjo's court ruled displayed formidable confusion. This social order, modeled on the Confucian ideal of an agrarian society, was predicated upon a division between a relatively small governing class, the officials, and a population consisting largely of peasants and slaves. By the eighteenth century, this model no longer reflected reality and was inconsistent with the social and economic forces at work.

The exact division among the social classes in the early Yi is not known because of an absence of records.[3] The earliest extant records date from 1630. Studies based on household registers in various areas put the percentage of yangban, the hereditary upper class, somewhere at 9 to 16 percent of the population in the late seventeenth century. The population of the Taegu district in Kyŏngsang Province, the southwestern region, in 1690 breaks down into 9.2 percent yangban, 53 percent commoners, and 37.8 percent slaves.[4] The Kŭmhwa district in Kangwŏn Province, the central western area, in 1672 was composed of 14.2 percent yangban, 75 percent commoners, and 10.8 percent slaves,[5] while records made in 1663 on the western fringes of Seoul city show that yangban households comprised 16.6 percent, commoners 30 percent, and slaves more than half of the total population.[6]

Through the eighteenth century and later, this composition underwent changes. In Kyŏngsang Province where census registers are available, yangban increasingly occupied a greater proportion of the population. The percentage of yangban in the Taegu district almost doubled every sixty years to 18.7 percent in 1727, 37.5 percent in 1789, and 70.2 percent in 1858. The commoner population remained rather constant during the eighteenth century—it was 54.6 percent in 1727 and 57.8 percent in 1789—until it fell to 28.2 percent in 1858, while slaves were reduced to 26.7 percent of the population in 1727, 4.7 percent in 1789, and virtually disappeared, at 1.6 percent, in 1858.[7] A similar trend is discernible in the other areas of the same province. Further studies on the Ulsan district,[8] the Sangju district,[9] and the Tansŏng district[10] all tend to confirm that, by the mid-eighteenth century, the yangban constituted about 30 percent, commoners about 50 percent, and slaves about 20 percent of the population.

Since these studies are confined to several districts in Kyŏngsang

Province, one should be cautious in generalizing. Kyŏngsang Province was in many ways atypical. This region enjoyed a relatively prosperous economy.[11] The province was a stronghold of what is known as the Yŏngnam school of Confucian scholarship (*Yŏngnam hakp'a*), the scholarly rival of the Kiho school (*Kiho hakp'a*) which consisted mainly of the power elite from the capital region.[12] The independent outlook of this province can be seen in the concentration of private academies, which numbered about 240, by far the largest number in one province.[13]

Nevertheless, this upward social mobility appears to have been rather widespread. One gets a strong impression that the yangban population was visibly increasing in the eighteenth century. Even conceding that a fair portion of this increase resulted from population growth within the class,[14] not all of the increase can be accounted for in this way. True, documentary evidence is lacking, but one encounters numerous anecdotes and references to the increasing number of new yangban.[15] This phenomenon apparently was a complicated process resulting from the interaction of various factors such as the economy, government policies, general aspirations and the way in which these were channeled, educational opportunities, the concept of family, local practice and the method of upgrading one's status and keeping records, etc. It seems that Yi Koreans, who undoubtedly had a strong class consciousness, actively sought ways to move up the social ladder. With the increasing importance of patrilineage, people seem to have emulated those attributes of the upper class, particularly its manners and way of life, that were associated with higher social status. The fact that Yi society, though stratified, permitted associations between classes through such practices as community compacts, probably made it possible for the manners and mores of the upper class to trickle down to lower strata. The practice of Chu Hsi's *Family Ritual*, for instance, was the prerogative of the yangban, but people from the lower strata also seem to have adopted these rituals, if in somewhat diluted form. The religious component of ancestor worship must also have played a role in this. At any rate, in 1709, the government found it necessary to limit the practice of mourning rituals among commoners.

In most instances, economic wealth appears to have been the decisive factor in this social mobility. Not only did people move up but they also moved down the social scale, though apparently more moved up. In general, a greater proportion of the yangban owned a larger share of choice lands in comparison to persons below them on the social scale, but a considerable number of them were impoverished.[16] This is believed to have eventually led to loss of privilege.[17] At the same time, a fair number of commoners succeeded in amassing land. Improvements in agricultural technology and the rise of commercial farming also contributed to the emergence of well-to-do farmers,[18] and the government accordingly created a legal channel through which they might upgrade their social status, namely the purchase of special titles bearing certain yangban privileges. This practice, which began in 1593 during the Imjin Wars as a means of supplementing the state treasury, continued.[19] In 1690, for instance, the government sold these titles to 20,000 persons. Apparently many well-to-do peasants took advantage of this opportunity. A fair portion of those who gained yangban privileges in the Sangju district in Kyŏngsang Province, for instance, fall into this category.[20] There are also indications that some forged genealogies and, by bribing local clerks, falsely attained yangban status.[21]

This increase in the number of yangban seems to be related also to the spread of literacy. The state responded to the growth of the literati population by administering more examinations and passing a larger number of people. The Yi government examinations consisted of two exams, the *munkwa* (civil examinations) and the *mukwa* (military examinations). As the civil bureaucracy emerged all-powerful, the competition focused on the civil examination. The civil examination system was quite complex. The preliminary level consisted of the *saengwŏn-si* (classics licentiate examination) and the *chinsa-si* (literary licentiate examination). The next stage was the *munkwa* examination, a three-part examination culminating in the palace examination. A full round of examinations was administered every third year. To those taking the *saengwŏn* and *chinsa* examinations, one hundred *saengwŏn* degrees and one hundred *chinsa* degrees were awarded and those who received them were afterwards addressed by these respective titles. Either degree permitted a candidate to sit for the *munkwa* examination, which only thirty-three people passed. These thirty-three *munkwa* degree holders were to receive official posts.[22]

While this was the basic structure, the examination system also contained certain irregularities and loopholes. Besides the regular examination, there were irregular examinations, which were held when the king wished to celebrate some felicitous occasion.[23] In fact, the irregular *munkwa* examination was more flexible than the regular *munkwa* examination concerning the candidates' qualifications and the number of people it selected.[24] In addition, there was a group of people referred to as *yuhak* (student scholar), who could bypass the preliminary examinations. It is not clear who was entitled to call himself a *yuhak*, but they were yangban. At any rate, the number of *yuhak* increased and they steadily replaced *saengwŏn* and *chinsa* as the major group of successful candidates for the *munkwa*. They constituted 24.4 percent of candidates from 1495 to 1591, 33.8 percent from 1592 to 1724, 68.0 percent from 1725 to 1800, and 82.1 percent from 1801 to 1894. A consequence of this process was that those who passed the *saengwŏn* and *chinsa* examinations had progressively smaller chances of passing the *munkwa*, decreasing from 75.6 percent to 66.2 percent to 32.0 percent to 17.9 percent for the periods noted.

Nevertheless, due to an increasing administration of irregular examinations, the total number of *saengwŏn* and *chinsa* increased. This number converted to an annual average was 56.6 from 1392 to 1494, 80.4 from 1495 to 1591, 102.2 from 1592 to 1724, 95.5 from 1725 to 1800, and 141 from 1801 to 1894. The geographical distribution of *saengwŏn* and *chinsa* gradually shifted away from a concentration in the capital area. Those from Seoul, who had constituted almost half of the total number until 1725, were reduced to about 38 percent in the eighteenth century.[25]

The number of *munkwa* degree holders also increased through a still more frequent administration of irregular *munkwa*. Their average number per year was fifteen during the early Yi, and about thirty or more in the seventeenth century, reaching more than sixty in the mid-nineteenth century.[26] Since the *munkwa* degree was the most prestigious one, it was proportionately harder for an outsider to penetrate. According to Professor Edward Wagner's study, 750 clans were represented among the passers, but 21 clans produced 40 percent of the degree holders, while 560 clans produced 10 percent.[27] Thus, while a small number of powerful families dominated the *munkwa* degrees, minor clans were not completely shut out. The geographical distribution of successful candidates seems to have been quite equitable. Candidates from the northern provinces, commonly regarded as being remote from the seat of power, constituted 10 percent of the total number for most of the duration of the Yi dynasty, but about 20 percent beginning in the late eighteenth century.[28]

Providing channels to upgrade social status and passing more candidates in both the preliminary and the final examinations seem to have been a government response to economic and social changes.

Admittedly, using examination degrees to confer honors rather than strictly adhering to their original purpose of staffing the bureaucracy had its pitfalls. Despite the increasing number of degree holders, available posts in the government remained nearly fixed. One could argue that, by producing a far greater number of degree holders than could be absorbed into the bureaucracy, the state was creating a large group of malcontents whose expectations remained frustrated. This question seems to be particularly germane in Yi society where power was perpetuated within a small group. The Yi government was not oblivious to this danger, yet it must have decided that the benefit exceeded the potential danger. And in many ways, this view was justified. Since examination degrees in no way guaranteed governmental posts, candidates might not have entertained exaggerated expectations. To obtain one or more degrees enhanced a person's standing in his community; it was an honor worth pursuing. Owing their honors to the government, degree holders played the role of intermediary between the state and the local community and acted as guardians of Confucian mores.

Often, a central concern of governments presiding over traditional heirarchical societies was to strike a balance between responding to social change and maintaining hierarchical order. Changes somehow had to be absorbed and proportioned into the system. If one takes longevity as a measure of success, the Yi government seems to have succeeded. The Yi dynasty lasted more than five hundred years, displaying a remarkable degree of internal stability. The way in which the Yi government achieved this seems to have been to allow general upward social mobility, especially in the enlargement of the lower strata of the yangban class, while safeguarding power within a small number of powerful families. In fact, the increase of yangban seems to have resulted in an increasing number of layers at the bottom of this class.[29]

Yŏngjo's government did not deviate from this general pattern. During his reign, the number of yangban increased at least in some parts of the country and *saengwŏn* and *chinsa* degrees were conferred on a greater number of newcomers, while power was preserved within a small group. In fact, one hardly encounters anyone in the upper echelon of the bureaucracy who did not have equally illustrious ancestors. Faced with this broad picture, it is difficult, or even futile, to see what kind of roles individuals played in shaping these changes.

It is clear, however, that Yŏngjo was acutely aware of a need to make certain concessions, however small, to those groups who were visibly discriminated against or who displayed extreme discontent, lest their resentment explode. At times he also expressed a certain dissatisfaction with the continued concentration of power and position in a small group, as this obviously hindered royal freedom of action. A wider dissemination of honor, and hopefully power, would strengthen the throne by gaining the support of newly favored groups. At the same time, he also knew that he could neither alienate the power elite nor challenge it in any substantial manner. He resolved these conflicting demands mainly by resorting to rather sporadic and symbolic acts which established his concern for the less privileged but left the power structure intact.

Once in 1747, the twenty-third year of his reign, for instance, he found fault with the examination committee's choice of top candidates in a preliminary examination. The two top candidates were descendants of illustrious ministers. He reordered the ranking, and put an unknown person from Kaesŏng on top and selected several others who had similarly undistinguished familial connections. Accusing the examiners of having engaged in corrupt nepotism and having violated the rule of awarding a certain number of examination degrees to candidates from the countryside, he dismissed them from their official posts. Yet, a few days later, Yŏngjo was chided by his officials, including Cho Hyŏnmyŏng, whom he held in high esteem. Cho reminded the king that the present Korean social structure did not permit exchanges in position between children of high ministers and those of commoners. Short of demolishing the entire structure, one had to adhere to the restrictions imposed by the system. He warned that tampering with accepted practices would lead to undesirable confusion. Yŏngjo was deeply disappointed, not merely in that the officials' opinions differed from his but also in the fact that those who expressed them were persons he frequently turned to for support. Their withholding of support clearly defined the limits of his actions in this area.[30] This stance on the part of Yŏngjo might have contributed to the increase in number of *saengwŏn* and *chinsa* with undistinguished rural backgrounds. His encounter with his officials on this occasion, however, suggests that his attempt was more a frustrated outburst than it was the beginning of a well-planned policy.

It was not only those of undistinguished background that Yŏngjo supported. During the later half of Yŏngjo's reign, the number of royal clansmen, Chŏnju Yi, who passed the *munkwa* reached an unprecedented peak. Though the Chŏnju Yi clan produced the largest number of *munkwa* passers during the Yi dynasty, the average of five per year during the second half of Yŏngjo's reign surpassed the yearly average during Kojong's reign (r. 1863–1907) when *munkwa* degree holders almost doubled in number.[31] It is unlikely that this was coincidental. It is more likely that Yŏngjo, who by this time had consolidated his power, brought in his clansmen. During this period, Yŏngjo was hoping to subdue factionalism, and he probably looked to them for support to countervail other powerful bureaucrats. Whether he received it is not clear, but Chŏnju Yi officials might have functioned as a neutralizing influence. At any rate, his authority and power were hardly challenged in his later years.

Yŏngjo took a more deliberate and cautious approach to questions concerning children born of concubines. Since the enactment of discriminatory laws against them in the early Yi, this issue, especially where it concerned yangban children by concubines, had emerged as one of thorniest social problems. Yangban children of concubines had a very ambiguous status. They were neither permitted to inherit the family line nor to sit for the *munkwa* examination. Thus, they could only aspire to minor positions as functionaries. Given the considerable practice of concubinage, especially among the well-to-do, it was quite common for yangban to father children in this way. This probably left them somewhat sympathetic to the plight of these individuals. At the same time, the bureaucrats, all children by legal wives, were not willing to share their privileges with their less-fortunate half-brothers. Periodically, one scholar-official or another criticized the wastefulness of this practice, and the government also from time to time relaxed its rules, but no substantial changes were made. As the yangban population grew, however, the number of people ambiguous in this sense also grew, and they became quite vocal in their attempts to eliminate the discriminatory practices imposed on them.

They made an appeal to Yŏngjo at the beginning of his reign. On the day after the state funeral for Kyŏngjong, on the way to a postfuneral ritual, the royal carriage was blocked by a large group of men of this status who tried to deliver a joint memorial to the throne. The memorial bore the signatures of 260 people headed by a *chinsa*, Chŏng Chin'gyo. It was an eloquently written petition analyzing the historical origins of this "unjust" practice and discussing the social waste and personal affliction in which it resulted.[32]

For a long time, Yŏngjo did little in response. Even what he did after a long silence was quite minor. In 1740, he made a gesture of personal concern to a small group,[33] and, in 1742, created some technical positions in the government for this group.[34] Even when, in 1745, Yi Chujin, the Minister of Personnel, argued on behalf of children by concubines, he merely opened the discussion. When Prime Minister Kim Chaero made an expected objection, Yŏngjo dropped the issue.[35] Then, suddenly, one day in 1772 after almost fifty years on the throne, which endowed him with requisite power, he ordered that children of concubines should not be prevented from taking positions as "pure officials" (*ch'ŏnggwan*). On the same day, three such persons were appointed to the Censorate.[36] This was quite a feat. Censorate posts were usually reserved for those young officials with immaculate reputations who were on the way to high executive posts. They were certainly not positions granted to persons with such dubious credentials as sons of concubines. This was the first time that this kind of appointment was made. I could not find any evidence that this was repeated with any regularity. Yŏngjo did not tackle the discriminatory laws in any fundamental way; this would have been too difficult. It was only in 1894 that this law, along with all the other constraints concerning the social class system, was abolished. Still, this appointment was a symbolic act that gave hope to a large group, and was the tentative beginning of a more accommodating government policy.

Yŏngjo's approach to the penal codes provides another example of how he handled the demands of his society. One of his more frequent complaints was that the criminal laws were not applied equitably between the powerful and wealthy, on the one hand, and the powerless and the poor, on the other.[37] Aside from being conscientious in administering criminal cases, there was not much he could do about it. But he could eliminate, without opposition, some of the more cruel penal codes. After all, this posed no threat to anyone. Thus, in 1725, he forbade torture by pressing the knees with a heavy board[38] and ended the practice of posthumously convicting of additional crimes those already executed for serious crimes.[39] He proscribed binding the legs and twisting a sharp weapon between them (1732),[40] branding the body with a hot iron

(1733),[41] and branding criminals on the face (1740).[42] He substantially modified the laws banishing an entire family (1744)[43] and forbade the reckless beating of criminals (1770).[44]

THE MILITARY TAX SYSTEM

Symbolic politics, though it played a significant role in Yŏngjo's adoption of the military tax reform, was not in itself sufficient to solve the problem. Real changes were needed. The inadequacies of the military tax system had long been felt. The Yi government began to debate possible reform measures as early as Hyojong's (r. 1649–1659) reign, but could not reach any consensus. What prevented reform was, for the most part, contention between monarchical and bureaucratic power. The former preferred an increase in the tax base that would include the yangban class, while the latter insisted instead on a curtailment of military forces.[45] The problem, however, was much more complex and intimately related to the way in which the tax system evolved and how it affected taxpayers.

During the early Yi dynasty, there was a system of national conscription. With the exception of those with aging parents to support[46] and certain categories of slaves, every man between the ages of sixteen and sixty was responsible for some form of military service.[47] The military organization did go through changes, but in 1457 its structure was essentially fixed in the Five Commanderies (*Owi*). Each commandary consisted of special units, mainly composed of royal family members and descendants of officials, and large units of commoners and slaves.[48] Though there were exceptions,[49] positions in the special units, which carried a salary, were used by officials as interim positions between posts. The rest of the army received no salary. Instead, two civilians were financially responsible for one man in active service.[50] They fulfilled this obligation by paying him one *p'il* of cloth per month.[51] Maintaining the system required that only a fraction of those eligible be on active duty at any given time. The duration of service as well as the selection of those on active duty seem to have depended on the unit, the status, and probably, to some extent, willingness to serve of conscripts.[52]

As always, very few liked active military duty. It was really a matter of tremendous inconvenience for farmers who had to tend their fields. Consequently, the practice of paying a rather high price to engage a substitute emerged.[53] This was alleged to have spread to the special units as well, where well-off would-be officials paid others to stand in for them in training sessions and on active duty. With the passage of time, the military consisted, for the most part, of people who were interested in financial remuneration rather than military training. The Confucians at court could only lament such a development.[54]

The inadequacy of this system was painfully revealed in the Imjin Wars and the government had to seek an alternative. In 1593, Sŏnjo recruited soldiers by offering a salary as an emergency measure to create a professional unit. It was supposedly suggested by a Ming general, Lo Hsiang-chih, and a Korean minister, Yu Sŏngnyong. This was called the Military Training Corps (*Hullyŏn togam*) and it became a permanent division in the following year,[55] remaining the elite core of the military until 1882.[56]

With the introduction of the Military Training Corps, the military system went through fundamental changes. Military conscription was for the most part eliminated and it was replaced with a tax[57] of two *p'il* of cloth per month.[58] Also gone with the conscript system was the pretense that military duty fell equally on all classes. Only those who had formerly belonged to ordinary units in the Five Commanderies were obliged to pay the military taxes. Having designated commoners and certain categories of slaves as military taxpayers, they were distinguished from officials and yangban. A situation of this type had been developing informally, and the legal change of 1595 could be described as the legalization of an already existing phenomenon. If this restructuring cleared away some of the old confusions, it was soon beset by other complications.

Between 1624 and 1626, four other military corps had appeared for different reasons and serving different functions. Two of them, the General Defense Unit (*Ch'onggyech'ŏng*) based in Kyŏnggi

Province, and the Royal Castle Defense Unit (*Suŏch'ŏng*), mainly an engineering and construction division, were apparently more like a militia. The other two, the Royal Commandery Division (*Ŏyŏngch'ŏng*) and the Palace Defense Unit (*Kŭmwiyŏng*), were more or less combat troops, but their composition was mixed, including both professional soldiers and those who chose to serve rather than pay taxes.[59] This partial return to the conscript system was motivated by financial considerations. The government could not meet the expense of maintaining a large professional army. But the experience of the Manchu invasion and the strong anti-Ch'ing sentiment, especially during Hyojong's reign, resulted in royal insistence on maintaining a large army.

These five units, which made up the Five Military Corps (*Ogunyŏng*), were distinguished from the earlier Five Commanderies in that they were, at least in their financial management, completely desynchronized on a national level. There was no office that oversaw military tax collection and distributed it to the various military corps. Instead, each military corps specified the number of people and revenues it required from each province, with little coordination with other corps. Coupled with poor statistics on the number of eligible taxpayers in each province, this often led to immense inequities in the tax levied per person. In other words, each province had to meet the demands of five different military corps which in turn based their levies on internal need rather than any realistic estimate of the number of taxpayers.[60] Local governments, which were responsible for collecting the military tax, were in general not terribly distinguished for their efficiency or honesty, and the situation soon degenerated.

Movement between social classes and various tax loopholes exacerbated the situation. The impression one might get from general upward social mobility—that peasants were experiencing an improvement in economic status—seems misleading. True, some obviously did move upward, benefiting from advances in agricultural technology. Better irrigation and planting methods raised crop yields. The new practice of transplanting rice made it possible to double-crop rice and barley in one field. The introduction of new crops such as sweet potatoes, a widespread cultivation of cotton, and the unprecedented spread of commercial farming of vegetables and tobacco brought higher incomes for some peasants.[61] A certain number of them seem to have achieved a measure of economic freedom and possibly enhanced social status. The economic status of those who remained commoners, however, seems to have deteriorated rather than improved.

A study of landholdings in the southern provinces shows that in 1720, a majority of commoners held less than 25 *pu* of land,[62] which is considered the subsistence level for the period, and that average landholdings had decreased over time.[63] That total registered arable land did not increase substantially from the late sixteenth century onward, while the population did, was an obvious factor.[64] What made the situation more acute, however, was the increase in tax-exempt land[65]—government estates and portions of palace estates—and the trend toward concentration of ownership. The palace estates, individually owned by members of the royal family, which had expanded its landholdings enormously since the seventeenth century, are usually taken as examples of the emergence of large estates,[66] but the trend toward concentration went much deeper than this. Many great families and other yangban, though not all, also increased their holdings. A study of a 1720 land survey reveals that the pattern was "latifundia-minifundia," that is, large holdings grew larger while small holdings were divided even further, and that land distribution was extremely uneven. A small group of persons owned most of the fertile land, leaving the peasants with very little, often less than was necessary for subsistence.[67]

Tax loopholes were partly responsible for this phenomenon. As a way to avoid heavy military taxes, many commoners sought refuge under powerful landlords. Some of them went to yangban landlords who were exempted from the military tax. Others hid under local or central government agencies whose estates were given a totally tax-exempt status to enable them to meet their expenses on their own. The most frequently cited loophole was a practice in which commoners, on paper, annexed their land to the estates owned by these private or public landlords while, in reality, still maintaining control over it. They had to pay the landlord some fixed sum for this protection, but presumably it was considerably less than what they had to pay in military tax. Though illegal, this practice was widespread. Local and other officials overlooked legal technicalities either out of negligence, greed, or even fear of the powerful.[68] The exact number of tax evaders cannot be easily determined, but the government estimated that the number of those who received protection under central government agencies was 10,358 in 1699.[69]

This led to an undesirable decrease in state revenues, the further enrichment of the wealthy, and a proportionate increase in the burden on the rest of the population. Realizing the magnitude of the problem, successive governments sought a solution, but with little effect. Unlike Hyojong who insisted on maintaining a large professional army, Hyŏnjong (r. 1659–1674) was rather willing to try to gradually shift from a professional army to a conscript system.[70] The outcome was, however, not a saving but an increase in the number of conscripted soldiers with no substantial decrease in the professional army.[71]

By Sukchong's accession in 1674, the shortage of revenues was of a stupendous proportion and in 1676, the Board of Military Affairs brought the matter to the young king's attention. Its members suggested that unless an alternative could be found, the eligible age for conscription and taxation would have to be lowered to eleven. This was promptly dismissed as highly impractical.[72] Instead, a reform measure, the household tax (*hop'o*), was discussed in earnest as a possible solution. The household tax referred to a system of levying taxes based on family size. Large, medium, and small families were to pay from three to one *p'il* of cloth respectively regardless of social class. This reform, which would have increased revenues both by broadening the tax base and by sealing obvious tax loopholes, was exactly what Hyojong had failed to implement.

Spurred by Sukchong's active interest and his strong personality, and promoted by Yun Hyu, a reform-minded scholar-official of the Namin faction, prospects for adoption seemed promising. But the bureaucrats won the intense debate, which lasted from late December 1677 to the end of January 1678. Yun Hyu's lone voice was stifled and the king had to defer to the overwhelming majority who denounced the reform as dangerous to the morale of the yangban class.[73] Soon Sukchong's court was engulfed in the inflammatory factional issues which led to the fall of the Namin faction and the rise of the Sŏin faction in 1680. With the change, the question of military tax reform reemerged in 1681.

This time, the debate was more protracted and acrimonious as Sukchong, more in command, insisted longer. It resulted in a tentative agreement on a compromise measure. The household tax would be implemented in the northern provinces on an experimental basis.[74] Even this was not tolerated for long. In early 1682, Sukchong's court became a battleground. Despite repeated bureaucratic condemnations, Sukchong defended the partial adoption as a "good law" which would benefit the people enormously. A forceful endorsement of the household tax by the Minister of the Military Affairs, Yi Samyŏng, further divided the bureaucratic community. The Prime Minister, Kim Suhang, supported the reform, but the Ministers of the Left and the Right opposed it. The State Council was paralyzed and Sukchong failed to get the official support necessary for reform. The king was forced to drop the discussion altogether.[75]

The rest of the Sukchong's reign was punctuated by repetitions of this same pattern. The officials were not unaware of the urgency of the situation but they remained recalcitrant on the idea of the household tax. Alternative measures, not very new ones at that, were pursued, bringing little improvement. An attempt at reduction of the professional corps in 1682[76] and a drive to track down tax evaders in 1699[77] failed. Local officials refused to cooperate with and even obstructed the central government's efforts to discover tax evaders.[78] Even a committee set up by Sukchong to make a comprehensive analysis of the situation failed to break new ground. The only progress made by this committee was a standardization in the length of cloth used to pay the tax.[79]

When Sukchong's final attempt to adopt the household tax was thwarted in 1711,[80] he initiated a search for a substitute plan. It was decided that the first step should be to make a systematic investigation into various loopholes and to take strong provisions against them. It took two years to complete the investigation.[81] In 1714, a variation of the household tax—one *p'il* of cloth levied equally on the entire population of taxable age—was considered but again there was no follow-up.[82]

The problem of the military tax, which Sukchong, with his forceful personality, could not resolve, only intensified during Kyŏngjong's reign. In 1721, Yi Kŏnmyŏng endorsed a practical and acceptable measure, reducing the tax to one *p'il* and supplementing the difference from other sources.[83] But his execution in the anti-Noron purges of 1722 put an end to the experiment.

MILITARY TAX REFORM AND YŎNGJO'S POLITICS OF PATRIARCHY

By the time Yŏngjo ascended the throne in 1724, the situation had reached a desperate point. A report from the governor of Ch'ungch'ŏng Province in 1723 claimed that, in his province, each commoner was burdened with four times the amount of tax he should legally have been obliged to pay.[84] Upon accession, Yŏngjo assigned a high priority to the problem of the military tax and expressed a determination to solve it. Active debate ensued. As always, the proposals included the household tax, a head tax, a return to the Five Commanderies, the abolition of two military corps, a reduction of the payment in cloth, and a tax based on the amount of land one owned.[85]

The 1728 rebellion further strengthened his resolve. While the rebellion seems to have been conducted mainly by extremist members of the Soron who used allegations of regicide as their rallying cry, without some measure of popular support it would have been far more difficult to stage. This uprising, which threatened his mandate and legitimacy, was a traumatic experience for Yŏngjo.[86] It led to his obsessive aversion to factional politics and a compulsive need to convince the people of his concern. The reform of the military tax system was one of the more urgent tasks that he felt he had to accomplish.

Yŏngjo, however, was under no illusion that the solution would be quick or easy. As a first step, he embarked on a thorough examination and analysis of the situation, ranging from the taxable population to loopholes and tax evaders. In 1734, he formed an investigation committee, appointing eight high-ranking officials and sending them separately to eight provinces to supervise the project in cooperation with provincial officials.[87] In order to synchronize and channel these findings, in 1742, he formally reinstated the Agency for the Investigation of the Military Service (*Yangyŏk sajŏngch'ŏng*) which Sukchong had established in 1703. Then he appointed Cho Hyŏnmyŏng, one of his most trusted officials, to combine the findings and to write an analytic report based upon them.[88] Lest the undertaking be hampered by dubious dealings by local officials, he sent secret censors to the eight provinces in 1745.[89] The result of this effort was the completion, in 1748, of the *Yangyŏk silch'ong* (Facts and Statistics of the Military Service), a report in ten volumes.

The findings revealed a situation even worse than had been suspected. The uneven geographical distribution of the tax burden, the astonishing discrepancy between the amounts levied, and the small number of actual taxpayers all made it patently clear that corrective measures were necessary.[90] Yŏngjo had facts with which he could attempt to persuade his bureaucracy. Another advantage Yŏngjo accrued from making these preparations was that he gained supporters for the reform among those who became convinced of its necessity. They were Cho Hyŏnmyŏng, Pak Munsu, Song Inmyŏng, Hong Kyehŭi, and a few others. They were small in number, a handful, but they were powerful officials who commanded a great deal of respect.

Yŏngjo, however, knew that neither the shocking statistics nor the support of a few officials would suffice to win over the bureaucracy. He was aware of the problems his predecessors had encountered. As a counterveiling measure, he looked toward popular support. It was here that he relied on the Confucian concept of the ruler-father for, using it as a justification, he had in fact been cultivating direct contacts with the populace for a long time.

One is tempted to say that it was his politics of patriarchy that distinguished Yŏngjo's reign from others. At least, in making contact with the people, he was transcending accepted norms. For despite the rhetoric of ruler-father, the hierarchical structure of a Confucian monarchy made little provision for direct contact between the ruler and the ruled. The Yi kings, unlike Chinese emperors, had even foregone ritualistic inspection tours. The emperor's inspection tours in China were one of the more easily recognizable institutionalized devices with which the ruler might express his concern for the people. These tours first appear in the *Book of Documents* in which the sage king Shun tours the four corners of his kingdom.[91] They became an imperial tradition which lasted to the Ch'ing dynasty. Whether these tours were a source of pride for the ruler as they were for Emperor K'ang-hsi who, in his final valediction, boasted of the modest expenditure he incurred on his numerous and extensive tours,[92] or whether they were a technique for aggrandizing an image, as they were for Emperor Ch'ien-lung who shamelessly used filial piety toward his mother, who accompanied him, to rationalize his proclivities for pomp,[93] these inspection tours were prompted by the ideal of a "concerned" ruler, one who displayed his solicitude by personally inquiring into the people's living conditions and listening to their problems and complaints.

For whatever reason, Yi kings did not emulate this custom. In fact, compared to their Chinese counterparts, the Yi kings lived a rather sedentary life. They lived in one palace compound throughout the year—there were no hunting trips or military expeditions. The monotony was broken only by trips to ancestral tombs. Even Sukchong and Yŏngjo, both vigorous and having long reigns, aside from visits to tombs, made but one trip each—to Onyang, a famous hot spring resort some forty miles south of Seoul. Royal isolation in a way strengthened the bureaucratic role as a link between the throne and the world beyond the palace walls.

Yŏngjo, however, was not a complete stranger to the outside world. He had not been born an heir to the throne. It was Yi custom that the royal princes other than the crown prince take a separate residence outside the palace when they reached eighteen years of age. Accordingly, Yŏngjo lived for nine years, from 1712 to 1721, when he was designated the heir apparent, in his prince's residence, Ch'angŭi Palace, located in the central part of Seoul.[94] Having spent his young adult years, from eighteen to twenty-seven years of age, outside the palace, he might have developed a certain affinity for the people and a corresponding insight into how, so to speak, to win their hearts.

The first thing Yŏngjo did was to try to win popular faith in the throne by making certain that the royal house not abuse its power. He understood that commoners, with good reason, entertained such suspicions and that, unless the royal house refrain from any practice that might be construed as extortion of the powerless, any rapport between him and his people was impossible. Thus Yŏngjo painstakingly compensated his populace for any damage inflicted by the royal house. His frequent processions to the tombs, for instance, could damage fields and crops and impose heavy expenses on those along the route. Though Yi kings were traditionally careful in this respect, Yŏngjo was notably meticulous in insuring that any damage done on these occasions be fully offset.[95]

Yŏngjo was equally determined that his family should abstain from any overt use of power in dealings with commoners. In 1746, the royal house purchased land from commoners to provide revenues for the upkeep of Lady Ch'oe's shrine and tomb. When he discovered that the transaction had been carried out against the wishes of the former owners, he ordered that the land be returned with no delay.[96] Nor were his son and grandson exempt from these policies. Just before Prince Sado died in 1762, it was discovered that he had commandeered numerous items from merchants. Yŏngjo fully repaid the debts his son had incurred.[97] A similar incident occurred in 1771 involving his grandson. This time, the sum was rather small and the merchants denied that they had been taken advantage of. Yŏngjo threatened to punish them unless they answered truthfully.[98] He did not want them to harbor silent resentment.

More importantly, Yŏngjo wanted to persuade the people of his personal concern for their well-being and thus to gain their support. For this, he needed opportunities for direct contact. At first, however, he had few opportunities for it except on occasions like tomb visits. The first recorded instance of his approaching the populace directly took place in 1725. Returning from a tomb, he abruptly halted the procession and spoke to passersby. He asked them about local officials, farming problems, and their lives in general.[99] He did the same thing in a provincial city. Hearing complaints of high taxes, he ordered a substantial reduction on the spot.[100]

Despite its rewards, Yŏngjo found this type of contact too limited. Especially if he were to use popular opinion as a countervailing force against the anticipated bureaucratic opposition in instituting the military tax reform—and he was sure that he would need to resort to it—a more formal channel had to be found. Suddenly one day in September 1749, about nine months before he tackled the military tax reform in earnest, Yŏngjo announced to his officials that he had written a set of ritual regulations which he referred to as the ceremony of expressing sympathy to the people (*hyulmin ui*). It was ostensibly based on *Yang-cheng t'u-chieh* (Diagrams and Explanations on the Cultivation of Correctness) by Chiao Hung, a famous Ming scholar.[101] Claiming that he was inspired by the section in *Yang-cheng t'u-chieh* that deals with the reign of King Wen of Chou, Yŏngjo explained his motivation in wishing to institute this ceremony:

> It has been many years since I took the throne, but [because of] my lack of virtue, I have not been able to reach my people. Now, based on [the example of] King Wen's rule, I would like to gather people by the palace, go out to the gate with the crown prince to encourage and show [our concerns for] them.

The ritual protocol Yŏngjo produced included standing arrangements of participants (those from the court stood inside the palace gate facing the people who, led by the heads of the capital city government, stood outside the gate); a bowing ceremony (the bureaucrats were required to bow but not the people); and a symbolic awarding of rice (the heads of local office received it on behalf of the people). Those people who were considered destitute were given a certain amount of rice after the ceremony. Upon examining the ritual protocol, his officials made inquiries concerning it, but could find no legitimate objections.[102]

In about ten days, Yŏngjo, accompanied by his son, appeared at Honghwa Gate before a large congregation of Seoul residents and duly performed the first "ceremony of displaying sympathy to the people." His pronouncement on the occasion was the following:

> Truly, those who entrust us [with the mandate] are the people and those who give us support [in carrying out] our duty are also the people. But in our daily life, [in which the ruler and the people are separated] between palace mansion and village lanes, [the distance is almost as great as] Heaven and Earth. Today, more than ever, we know that [the relationship between] the ruler and his people is [in fact that between] parents and children. Indeed, the sage tells us the truth. King Wen who displayed love for his people shows us the way. But this [way] could become only a formality. Only with a genuine heart, can it be turned into actual rule. King Wen took counsel of teachers and he took advice from ordinary villagers. During his rule, everyone was united. The ruler did not suspect his people and the people did not dare to deceive their ruler. How great! How admirable! Truly splendid! Truly brilliant! . . . Yet though we are the parents of the people, we see them today for the first time. This certainly is not the way of being parents! We are truly ashamed of ourselves, especially [in not following] the sagacious instruction. The Mandate of Heaven upon us is not for the sake of the ruler but for the sake of the people. Therefore the passing or staying of the mandate, that is, turning the people's hearts for or against [us], lies entirely in whether or not we can save the people. This is why Mencius said that if the prince protects the people, none could conquer him. Ah, the sage would not lie to us. But if the ruler were to turn into a solitary man whom the people could find no way to inform [of their troubles] then there would be dire consequences for him. If he does not love his people, and if he does not save the people,

then their hearts will become resentful and the Mandate of Heaven will pass [from him]. For though he dwells in the position of the ruler, he is only a solitary man. When our thoughts reach this, we tremble with fear. . . . Thus, we came to this special occasion today. And though our virtues are deficient and accomplishments meager, in longing memory of King Wen, we speak every word to let our people, suffering hardship far and near, know our concerns. . . . Hereupon we request officials high and low not to take this as a one-time formality and guide the crown prince with undivided care and cooperation. Help us to save the people! Help us to protect the people! . . . The government starts near and extends far. Thus we command each governor of the eight provinces and each magistrate of the two special cities to let our sympathy be known to the people and to specially instruct the local magistates to take the task of protecting the people as their most urgent duty.[103]

If this ritual seemed innocuous and formalistic, it was still a legal channel for direct contact with the people. And with a slight variation, it could be turned into a forum to solicit popular support, which was obviously what Yŏngjo had in mind. Having taken every step that he could in preparation for the reform, Yŏngjo waited for the right moment.

That moment came in 1750, the twenty-sixth year of his reign. A terrible epidemic swept across the country, taking some 300,000 lives, according to the *Sillok*.[104] Unrest caused by large-scale famine or an epidemic was dreaded at the court, especially after the 1728 rebellion. On June 21, in an atmosphere of panic, the king convened a meeting with top-ranking ministers. Yŏngjo pronounced an emergency, declaring that a new crisis might just ignite accumulated resentment unless the government made a serious gesture to ameliorate the condition by instituting the long-overdue military tax reform. Cho Hyŏnmyŏng, Yŏngjo's supporter, who was at the time serving as Prime Minister, concurred. The meeting turned into a forum for a debate on which reform measure should be adopted. Cho Hyŏnmyŏng suggested the landholding tax, while the king expressed preference for the household tax. A rather technical discussion of the merits and demerits of these two taxation systems ensued. Officials were forced to express their opinions as if the adoption of the military tax reform had been already concluded, though there were faint murmurs of resistance. The meeting ended as Yŏngjo had planned—the principle was agreed upon, leaving undecided only the question of details of execution.[105]

Yŏngjo knew, however, that the concession he had exacted at this meeting, which was attended only by top-ranking ministers, was fragile. Before the official community could strengthen its resistance, he turned to the people. And the ritual he instituted in the previous year came in handy. Two days later, on June 23, he went to Honghwa Gate. About fifty commoners and soldiers had been summoned and were waiting there. He had his royal secretary, Hong Iksam, read his announcement to them:

Of all the pernicious practices abusive of the people, none is worse than the present military tax system. If we don't ease [the people's burden], we will not have a base to draw tax from. For the people are like water and the government is a ship. I have never heard of a case where a country is formed without the people or a ship navigated without water. Our sagacious royal ancestors were deeply distressed over this problem [of military tax] and made repeated attempts. . . . Though we have known their heartfelt wishes, we have been to date unable to carry them out. We are nearing sixty years of age and have been on the throne for more than two decades. If we further delay and avoid [solving the problem] now, it would be a betrayal of our mantle and a betrayal of the people. This would be a terrifying and unforgivable error. We have already consulted ministers and searched for a solution to save [the people] and remedy [the situation]. Yet, the matter needs still more attention. Moreover, it is not proper for parents to embark upon such a task for the children without notifying them. . . . So, though we have been recuperating from illness, we came out here today to ask your opinion.

Those congregated were informed of the choices and the majority enthusiastically supported the household tax.[106] The *Sillok* alleges that Pak Munsu, a strong proponent of the household tax, had rehearsed them in anticipation of the king's move.[107] Whatever spurred their preference for the household tax, their support endowed Yŏngjo with something like a popular mandate.

This act played on a fundamental tenet of Confucian ideology — government for the people — to bypass the officials who previously had acted as the sole link between the ruler and his subjects. Its use to impel an important change in a long-standing policy was symbol and rhetoric turned into action. If officials objected at this point, they would have been objecting to the sacred rhetoric they had spent their lives promoting and they would have had to risk appearing as villians, as "betrayers of the people."

Still apprehensive, Yŏngjo rushed to officially promulgate the reform. After his return from Honghwa Gate, in an audience with his officials, he reiterated his conviction that the future of the country depended on the reform. This meeting produced remarkable progress toward finalization. First a tentative agreement was reached on the amount of tax in coin to be levied per household. While this amount represented a concession from the official and yangban class, Yŏngjo matched it by conceding a certain right of the royal house. The lack of funds was to be supplemented by the nationalization of tax levied on fisheries and salt which previously had gone to the royal house. Then the king announced that the royal house was not exempt from the household taxes; his prince's residence would be the first to pay it.

Then he praised his officials, noting that their cooperation would make them meritorious ministers who brought security to the country. He further honored them by assigning them the task of lecturing the heir apparent on the virtue and the necessity of the reform. The *Records of the Royal Secretariat* notes that on the following day, the ministers extolled the merits of the reform to the

110

heir apparent.[108] It does not, however, describe what they really felt.

But Yŏngjo's strategem had not exhausted official resources. In less than ten days, resistance began. The first signs of dissension, which came from Cho Chaeho, director of the Royal Medical Bureau, and Kim Chaero, minister without portfolio, were cautious, concentrating on the difficulties of managing the household tax. Now that it was out in the open, the opposition gradually gained momentum. On July 25, a memorial came from Yi Chongsŏng, the fifth councilor of the State Council. This was the memorial that argued for the special treatment of the yangban appropriate to their role as custodians of Confucian ritual and scholarship and as models for the rest of the population. It called on the state to protect and honor them and criticized the household tax as shortsighted, discriminatory, and counterproductive.[109]

The battle lines were drawn. In one camp were Yŏngjo and his supporters, Cho Hyŏnmyŏng, Pak Munsu, and Hong Kyehŭi. In the other stood the majority of the officials.[110] Just at this time, an itemized reform plan arrived from the Office of Military Affairs that had been drafted by royal request. But to his dismay, Yŏngjo found that the draft was based not on the household tax but on a compromise plan consisting of a reduction by half of the tax paid by non-yangban taxpayers and a series of miscellaneous measures to supplement the differences by collecting revenues from other sources, including the fisheries and salt tax.[111] The plan still did not include any tax to be paid by the yangban.

The opposition was rapidly mounting. Yŏngjo needed a countermeasure. Hoping to find it in the public opinion, he went back to Honghwa Gate. This time, however, the tactic backfired. The yangban community anticipated this move and many of them were awaiting his arrival. Thus, after Yŏngjo's plea for a truly equal military tax, the scene was dominated by none other than those who were enjoying privileged status. One after another, they condemned the household tax. When Yŏngjo finally succeeded in silencing them so as to give commoners a chance to speak, the commoners endorsed the household tax. As soon as they expressed their approval, however, a yangban angrily charged that ordinary people were extremely deceitful and that they would complain of everything among themselves but would always agree with the king in public. Such people, he declared, deserved execution.[112]

The vehemence with which the yangban class opposed the household tax convinced Yŏngjo that he had better wait. Pak Munsu's impassioned memorial advocating the adoption of the household tax was to no avail. Yŏngjo agreed to begin with the compromise plan.[113] On August 10, 1750, as a first step, Yŏngjo ordered a nationwide reduction in a commoner's tax burden by half. On August 12, he established the Office of the Equal Military Tax (*Kyunyŏkch'ŏng*) to implement the partial reform.[114] This time the officials and yangban won; they did not have to pay any military tax.[115]

Yŏngjo was quite wary of the compromise. He knew that it would not generate sufficient revenues and that other revenues would have to be found. His greatest fear, however, was that officials, taking insufficient revenues as an excuse, might press for cancellation of the reform altogether. He took several preventive steps in anticipation of this danger. He appointed trusted officials such as Pak Munsu as inspectors of the equal military tax and sent them out to the provinces to report on the management of the reform.[116] He also sent secret censors[117] to document popular response. In October, Yŏngjo himself took a trip to Onyang, a hot spring resort, ostensibly for reasons of health. The real motive for setting out in the midst of a ravaging epidemic seems to have been to check on the situation himself. On this trip, a rare event indeed, Yŏngjo, as usual, played the concerned ruler-father, once again resorting to his familiar acts of consideration and concern.[118] And he waited.

Soon enough, objections to the partial reform began. As expected, the new system did not raise sufficient revenue and this was cited as the reason for cancelling the partial reform. The question was whether to return to the previous system or to find alternate sources of revenue to make up the shortage. An imposition of modified landholding tax emerged as the most plausible means to cover the difference.[119] This would seriously affect the bureaucratic and yangban class since they owned far more land than commoners. Again, this class was opposed to this solution and urged total revocation of the reform. This time Kim Chaero, who had become Prime Minister in the interim, led the bureaucratic opposition.[120]

By this time, however, Yŏngjo was armed with reports from his secret censors. On June 29, 1751 Chŏng Hongsun, secret censor to Kyŏnggi Province, returned with reports that the populace was delighted with the reform, which reduced their burden, but was quite worried that it might be rescinded.[121] In about two weeks, another censor returned from Chŏlla Province, a seat of periodic unrest. He reported that the people there were intensely happy with the reduction in the military tax and were singing in praise of the king's virtue.[122] With this in hand, Yŏngjo presented the case to the bureaucracy. He contended that repeal was not a possibility as it would result in extreme disappointment and anger among the populace, which might lead to a truly dangerous situation. Official opposition lost its momentum. It was realized that the reduction of the military tax on commoners was a *fait accompli*. The royal house had given up its right to the fishery and salt tax already. Moreover, the royal house was willing to pay the landholding tax as well. Now it was the turn of yangban to pay. Soon, Yŏngjo was able to silence Kim Chaero's opposition.[123] To make sure, Yŏngjo went, on August 8, the Myŏngjŏng Gate to obtain a mandate from the people. Scholars, officials, and soldiers congregated, but they were persuaded by royal argument that there was no alternative to the landholding tax.[124] On August 10, Yŏngjo at last received the bureaucratic concession in a meeting. On August 12, 1751, exactly a year after the partial reform had been instituted and after much debate and numerous setbacks, the landholding tax was finally promulgated,[125] completing the reform.

Admittedly this reform, though it is referred to as the equal military tax, was not equal in the true sense of the world.[126] The reform finally adopted fell short of Yŏngjo's original aim. But what it accomplished was considerable. First of all, it resulted in a substantial increase in state revenues. The total revenues resulting from this reform soon after the adoption were about 630,000 taels of silver, more than double the 232,000 taels that Sukchong had tried to obtain in 1704.[127] It also considerably reduced the burden on commoners. The establishment of the Office of the Equal Military Tax, which came to oversee all aspects of the military service and the associated taxes, with well-prepared figures and statistics at hand, eliminated much of the previous confusion and many devious practices.[128] But most significantly, the adoption of the reform represented a concession by the royal house and the bureaucratic and yangban community to the population at large.

It was no small feat that Yŏngjo broke bureaucratic resistance where his more autocratic father had failed. His success, modified though it was, was based on his utilization and realization of the concept of government for the people, which had been buried in the miasma of Confucian rhetoric. While his use of this idea in his politics of patriarchy marks him as a skilled negotiator and astute politician, the tactic worked because this rhetoric became the medium of expression for his determination and concern. In the end, no one could doubt that Yŏngjo meant what he said.

Even after the adoption of the military tax reform, Yŏngjo did not relinquish the role of ruler-father. In fact, it appears as though this was the role he came to identify with for the last ten years of his life. He routinely went to the city gates to ask people of their woes. He met Seoul residents, merchants, travelers from the countryside, soldiers, and students.[129] He would also stop on some city street or go to the neighborhood where he lived as a prince to speak with people. Frequently, if they complained of hardship, he would reduce their taxes or provide them with rice.[130] He also ordered that the poor be assisted financially with such costly matters as weddings and funerals.[131]

Surely, royal excursions into the streets and alleys provided the king with a means to check on the powerful as well. In the course of his outings and inquiries, Yŏngjo uncovered numerous cases in which officials had taken unfair advantage of commoners and which he subsequently corrected.[132] Yŏngjo certainly was fully aware of the benefits he so accrued. It clearly helped his cause to be perceived by the people as someone on their side, trying to protect them from the powerful. In this way, they would attribute the deficiencies of government to the officials, and the good policies to him. Nevertheless, the degree of persistence and involvement with which Yŏngjo pursued this leads one to wonder whether it was all ideology and politics or whether there might have been some personal component to this. One might say that his disillusion with court politics led him to seek consolation in the streets. One almost senses that he felt more affinity with the people in the streets than with the officials at his court. Could it be that his mother Lady Ch'oe's reputed low origins had something to do with it?

Indeed, Yŏngjo was not satisfied with only going out to see the people. Why shouldn't he bring them into the palace? Why not invite them to palace festivities to "share joy" with them? He first broached the topic in 1743, the nineteenth year of his reign. For his forthcoming fiftieth birthday, he wanted some revision of the celebration. He wanted to keep the party for ladies as usual because his stepmother would preside over it. But as for the party for men, he wanted to turn it into a party for the aged to which commoners would be invited as well.

The impending sight of commoners in the palace sanctuary was apparently repellent to official sensibilities. "Your Majesty, the royal birthday is a great festive occasion. It demands to be celebrated in due propriety," one cautioned. "The party for the aged would distress Her Majesty, the Queen Dowager," another said, "and Your Majesty would be committing an unfilial act." Unfilial, presumably because Yŏngio would not shield his mother from the unsightly scene. "But Her Majesty concurred with me," the king informed them. "It is not her true intention," they insisted. At any rate, under no circumstance could they allow this to happen. "Even if your servant might die in this seat, your servant would not comply with Your Majesty's wishes," each of them announced.[133] Soundly defeated this time, Yŏngjo, for several decades, had to content himself with sharing joys with the people in separate quarters. He sent them gifts instead.[134] In 1765, for instance, he had a list compiled of elderly people in Seoul and sent gifts of rice and meat to each of all 1,700 of them.[135] This became a regular event in his later years. He especially chose those who were as old as he and older.[136]

The first time Yŏngjo could "share joys" with commoners at the same place was in 1773, but this party for people over sixty was held outside the palace.[137] Later, though, for once, he could have them at his palace as his guests. For the celebration marking the completion of his fifty-first year on the throne, the eighty-three-year-old Yŏngjo could invite all persons of his age regardless of social status. To the accompaniment of music, these octagenarian guests danced, and shouted, "Long live the king!" They indeed had reason to be pleased. They went home with armloads of presents.[138]

Right until his death, Yŏngjo was seen roaming city streets asking people about their problems.[139] Evidence suggests that they got his message and were moved by his concern. When they cheered him on the roadside and cried out "Long live the king" in his waning years,[140] their response seems to have been spontaneous and heartfelt. True appreciation came in February of 1776, a month before his death. At a city gate he asked merchants of their woes. The sight of the ailing and enfeebled king touched them deeply. They denied that they had problems.[141] Unlike his officials who bowed fearfully to him, their restraint rose from respect. This was the final tribute to a king who fervently wished that his rule would bring them some comfort. One might say that it is ironic that the group from which Yŏngjo elicited respect and support were his people—the most important group in theory but the most remote and powerless in the practical workings of the monarchy. But this perhaps was also the ultimate vindication of his quest for sagehood.

CHAPTER 4

Yŏngjo's Court: Magnificent Harmony

And they will submit to us gladly and cheerfully. The most painful secrets of their conscience, all, all they will bring to us, and we shall have an answer for all. And they will be glad to believe our answer, for it will save them from the great anxiety and terrible agony they endure at present in making a free decision for themselves. And all will be happy, all the millions of creatures except the hundred thousand who rule over them. For only we, we who guard the mystery, shall be unhappy.

—Dostoyevsky, *The Brothers Karamazov*

WHY *T'ANGP'YŎNG?*

Yŏngjo could not spend all his time in the streets. To rule, he had to constantly deal with the bureaucracy. After all, the makeup of the bureaucracy and the king's relationship with it largely determined the character of the government. The bureaucratic community that Yŏngjo inherited was bitterly torn by factional animosities. In fact, for a good part of his reign, factional issues dominated his court to such a degree that one wonders whether other matters could receive sufficient attention. Yŏngjo obviously felt that, in order to bring stability to his court, it was imperative that factional politics be brought under control. Yŏngjo turned, as he had done in other aspects of his rule, to impeccable rhetoric—*t'angp'yŏng* (magnificent harmony), as he called it—with which he proposed to deal with the problem. Alluding to the Kingly Way

117

(Wangdo) in the *Book of Documents*,[1] *t'angp'yŏng* literally meant the grand harmony achieved through a rule of impartiality.

Adopted from Confucian utopian rhetoric, the *t'angp'yŏng* policy became perhaps the most celebrated theme of Yŏngjo's reign, almost a synonym for his policies. But exactly what was his *t'angp'yŏng* policy? Viewing it purely as an attempt to equalize or nullify factions, modern historians have rated it a noble failure: Yŏngjo succeeded in avoiding the most vicious aspects of factional strife but could not eradicate it. This assessment reflects an assumption, especially prevalent among modern Korean scholars, about the role and the effect of factionalism in Yi politics—an assumption that it was central to court politics and that it was a debilitating force, responsible for the inertia and chaos that eventually led to the demise of the dynasty.[2] The *t'angp'yŏng* policy, applied against the perpetual evil of factionalism, becomes a very natural endeavor for a conscientious monarch. Thus, Yŏngjo is commended for simply pursuing the *t'angp'yŏng* policy. But since he could not eradicate factions, the verdict on the policy's result is far less favorable. More recently a few articles have appeared that have reexamined Yŏngjo's *t'angp'yŏng* policy from a more political and ideological point of view, but they nonetheless fall short of placing it in perspective.[3]

In adopting the *t'angp'yŏng* policy to deal with factional conflict in the bureaucracy, Yŏngjo was acknowledging the impact of factionalism. The immediate question is why the factional aspects of the bureaucracy suddenly became an issue. Factionalism had been a part of Yi politics for many decades. Could it be, as common wisdom would have it, that in all these years of factionalism no king did anything to arrest it while it poisoned the court and crippled the country until Yŏngjo belatedly tried to battle against this all-time evil?

Most unlikely. It is more logical to conjecture that kings did nothing because they saw little harm in it. Otherwise they, or at least some of them, would have somehow tried to curtail it. Sukchong, a master politician, for instance, encouraged factions when they were useful to him and discouraged them when they were not. In fact, it was Sukchong who first invoked the *"t'angp'yŏng* policy" in 1698 when he more or less outgrew his need for factions.[4] Likewise, Yŏngjo, an astute policitian himself, must have perceived that factionalism ran counter to his purposes.

Then, what was Yŏngjo's objective in proposing the *t'angp'yŏng* policy? Can we attribute it to the ideal of restoration which he constantly invoked? It is true that Yŏngjo used the rhetoric of restoration to support the *t'angp'yŏng* policy. It was very useful to do so. True, also, is that he must have wanted some sort of harmony at his court. Indeed who would not? Yet, if harmony was all that he wanted, the *t'angp'yŏng* policy was hardly the way to get it. Denounced by the bureaucratic community from the beginning, the *t'angp'yŏng* policy was resisted to the end, causing dissension and bitterness. In fact, a semblance of harmony would have been achieved more quickly and with less pain if Yŏngjo had favored one faction, as was usual.

Nor can one say that the equalization of factions was really what Yŏngjo had in mind. Though he insisted on a coalition bureaucracy for many years, the balance was always precarious. Moreover, it was a coalition of the Noron and the Soron; other factions that had been out of power, such as the Namin, were excluded. Thus, it is not likely that Yŏngjo wanted equalization among factions in the literal sense. Moreover, while Yŏngjo seems to have abjured factional politics, the end result was not significantly different from the usual pattern. At the time of his accession, the Soron were in power. At the conclusion of his reign, the bureaucracy was dominated by the Noron. Unless this happened totally against his will, a dubious proposition given his record, one cannot say that he wanted to destroy factions altogether.

Instead of seeking a rigid and concise definition of the *t'angp'yŏng* policy, it would be more useful to see it as Yŏngjo's search for an alternative to factional politics. Then what in the factionalism of his day led him to choose this problem-ridden and, in the view of many, not particularly fruitful or rewarding course of action?

Factions, like all political groups, were associations in quest of power. Yet, Confucian ideology rendered it difficult for its practitioners to accept this notion with equanimity. First of all, a longing for harmony made differences of opinion undesirable. This is not to say that Confucians did not see the value of debate. Debate was, in fact, part of the intellectual and political life of Yi Korea. Still, disagreement was an expression of the imperfect state of the world in which inhabitants had not yet attained truth. If they had, then perfect harmony would ensue as it had during the sage kings' era. Trained not to discard this vision as unrealizable, Confucians were unwilling to settle comfortably into an imperfect reality. For what was the worth of man if he did not constantly strive for improvement and perfection? And what was the use of a scholar-official if he did not work toward the realization of a better society, a society harmonized and peaceful? Thus, viewing factions as something other than acutely shameful and at best temporary was not acceptable. This probably was one of the reasons why factions did not achieve the legitimate status that political parties gained in the West.

More important still, the quest for power was held in deep suspicion by the Confucian scholar community. They were indoctrinated to evaluate a person according to whether his activities were governed by concern for the public welfare *(kong)* or the desire for selfish gain *(sa)*. The former was a gentleman, the latter a petty man. The same distinction extended to holding office. One should use the power of the office to promote the public good, not to advance self-interest. Moreover, a truly conscientious scholar, before taking office, first should evaluate whether the government, both morally and functionally, was worthy of his service. If it were not, then he should not serve since he would not be able to discharge his duty as he should.[5] In the Yi scholar community, especially in the later part of the dynasty, there seems to have been a widespread belief that the government was quite corrupt and that abuse of power was prevalent among officeholders. Aside from the fact that power remained concentrated in a small number of powerful families, some scholars, especially those living in Kyŏngsang Province, seem to have deliberately chosen a private life devoted to scholarship.[6] Of course there was no lack of candidates for office and there is no reason to doubt that those who held it did so, to some extent, out of devotion to the Confucian ideal of public duty. Nevertheless, one detects a vague aura of discomfort and ambivalence in a great number of officials with regard to their official careers.[7] The special admiration reserved for those scholars who shied away from public office attests to this trend. For instance, Yun Chŭng, whose activities resulted in the formation of the Soron, never took office despite a continuous bestowal of high positions.[8] When he died in 1714, Sukchong, in grief, wrote a poem:

> *A Confucian recluse respected virtue and the Way*
> *I have always admired him.*
> *When he was alive, I never saw his face.*
> *Now he is dead; my regret is even harder*
> to bear.[9]

Song Siyŏl, the leader of the Noron faction and a representative scholar of the Chu Hsi school, also admired Yun Hyu, his scholarly and political rival, for his refusal to serve.[10]

If the individual quest for power was suspect, collective pursuit of it was all the more so. Despite a distaste for disagreement and a low esteem for power, Confucian scholar-officials, like ever so many politicians, often found themselves in groups contending with other groups for ascendancy. They could not, however, view this as the natural course of events. It is hardly surprising, under the circumstances, that factions distinguished between the faction of gentlemen (ours) and that of petty men (theirs), as did Ou-yang Hsiu of the Sung dynasty,[11] who was often alluded to by Koreans. That is, the practitioners of factionalism justified themselves by the proposition that they were forced into it by their sense of duty to guard the state against a group of unscrupulous self-seekers. In their view, the ruler should see to it that this faction of self-seekers be eliminated so that harmony would return. Thus, the existence of factions was not taken in stride. It signified that someone, though certainly not oneself, was at fault. It was a lapse from the ideal that should be corrected. Consequently, factions were seldom discussed in neutral terms. Rather, discussions about factions tended to be secretive, defiant, and denunciatory, and these qualities hardened into a fixed historiographical tradition.

Ideological ambivalence toward factions, however, does not explain the vicissitudes of factionalism which were rooted in social and political reality. Factionalism was a medium of reverberation for movements originating from at least two principal sources. On the one hand, there were established groupings—familial, regional, scholastic, etc.—which tended to act in unison. On the other hand, political and social issues resulted in shifting tactical alliances. How these elements became related and which were emphasized determined the character of the factionalism of each period.

In the latter half of the seventeenth century, factional debate appears to have been mainly concentrated on the role of the Yi monarchy in the changed world hierarchy. The searing contention between the Sŏin and the Namin in the mourning controversy *(yesong)* was based on their differing views of the definition of the orthodox Confucian tradition, the role of the Yi royal house, and its relationship to the bureaucratic community.[12] During Sukchong's reign, however, the factions became a means through which the throne checked bureaucratic power. This resulted in the purges and deaths of numerous scholar-officials, the loss of power for the Namin, and the division of the Sŏin into the Noron and the Soron.[13]

The consequent schism in the scholar-bureaucrat community was exacerbated during Kyŏngjong's reign. This time the issues centered around Yŏngjo. In 1721, within a year of Kyŏngjong's accession, the Noron pressed for an immediate appointment of Yŏngjo as heir apparent. When this was accomplished, they proposed that he be made a regent.[14] The Noron might have been acting on behalf of Sukchong, who presumably had charged them to protect Yŏngjo to insure his eventual accession.[15] In fact, it was strongly suspected that it was this question that Sukchong had broached in his celebrated and much-criticized secret audience with Yi Imyŏng, one of the "four Noron ministers."[16] But this Noron initiative, coming so soon after the new king's accession, hardly concealed their lack of respect for or confidence in him. Surprisingly however, at first Kyŏngjong, citing his frail health and his wish to see government in his brother's competent hands, concurred. But his resentment at what he perceived as the arrogance of the Noron and, through them, his deceased father's unflattering judgment of him, got the better of him. He changed his mind and gave in to Soron demands. The "four Noron" ministers, Kim Ch'angjip, Yi Imyŏng, Yi Kŏnmyŏng,[17] and Cho T'aech'ae, were executed for charges ranging from treason to signing the memorial accepting Yŏngjo's regency. Other Noron either shared their fate or were banished in dishonor.[18]

By Yŏngjo's reign, the residual animosities left by Sukchong's ruthless exploitation of factions and Yŏngjo's own succession struggle had deprived factional structures of adaptability. When factionalism was concerned with contemporary questions and issues, a certain shift in factional affiliations and alliances was possible. One might choose or change affiliations depending on one's beliefs and inclinations. But by now factional issues were rooted in past events. Thus partisanship was fostered and alliances became rigid and were perpetuated. The familial and social structure of the Yi ruling elite probably exacerbated this trend. The power elite was small and family honor and loyalty were exceedingly important. Such questions as familial and social relations between people of different factions remain to be examined. Nevertheless, one distinctly notes that marriages, friendships, scholarly exchanges, and other social contacts across factional lines became rather uncommon by the eighteenth century.[19] Thus, where factionalism had once been an avenue of expression for issues and ideas, now factionalism itself was an issue.

Driven by differing perceptions and divergent viewpoints, the king and the bureaucracy found themselves in conflicting positions. Polarized by the recent past, the bureaucracy sought vindication. For each faction, honor, prestige, moral credentials, and, ultimately, power and security depended on definitively settling past scores. Both factions, the Noron and the Soron, pressed for this.

Yŏngjo, for his part, could find no advantage in it. His experience as heir apparent had left him with a deep-rooted aversion to powerful factions. Even after the elimination of the Noron, seeing Yŏngjo as the symbol of potential Noron power, some extremist members of the Soron plotted for his life.[20] Kyŏngjong's four-year reign had been indeed a perilous time for Yŏngjo. During this period, his stepmother, Queen Inwŏn, protected him. Kyŏngjong seems to have felt rather ambivalent toward his brother for a while. When he became disillusioned with Soron dominance and with his own ineffectual rule, however, Kyŏngjong also came to his brother's assistance. It appears that, in his last years, he came to view Yŏngjo as his true heir in whom he could invest his failed hopes.[21] If the memory of this period instilled in Yŏngjo a feeling of bitterness toward the extremist Soron, it also implanted in him a strong desire to avoid bloodshed. Moreover, his experience convinced him of the danger of dominance by one faction.

As he saw it, his alliance with one faction or another would neither enhance monarchical power nor serve his tactical needs. In fact, Yŏngjo came to see factionalism as anathema to monarchical power.[22] One of his most pressing problems was to affirm his legitimacy. But factional alliance would only complicate this issue. For he did not want to take a course of action that would imply that he owed his accession or his power to any single group. To ally with the Noron would suggest just that, and was not a very appealing option for Yŏngjo, who wished to establish an absolute legitimacy. On the other hand, he had to face repeated accusations that he had killed his brother. Since he believed that this charge originated with the extremist Soron, exculpation lay in discrediting the Soron and—by the laws of factional politics— honoring the Noron. But the conundrum is not yet complete. Dishonoring the Soron would have traduced his brother's judgment. Ineffectual indeed, if he wished to confirm his loyalty to Kyŏngjong. Most crucially, factional politics would endanger the very foundation of the state. This was brought home to him, vividly and materially, in the outbreak of the 1728 rebellion.

Thus, a confrontation over factionalism itself was inevitable. The form it assumed was determined by the demands of Confucian rhetoric. When bureaucrats demanded justice, Yŏngjo reminded them of their duty to adhere to a transcendent norm of loyalty. When Yŏngjo sought cooperation, bureaucrats responded with demands for adherence to principle. Impatient with the acrimony of debate and taunted by charges of regicide, Yŏngjo enforced his ban on factional defense.

To this bureaucrats could only respond with accusations that he suppressed the official channel for speech *(ŏllo)*. In contrast to China where, with rising monarchical autocracy,[23] the censorial voice increasingly lost its independence,[24] in the Yi monarchy the right to speak given to the censors, referred to as the speaking officials *(ŏn'gwan)*, came to be considered almost sacrosanct. In fact, respect for this channel of speech was considered one of the cardinal duties of the throne, a yardstick by which royal virtue was measured. But censors, divided in their factional allegiances, often acted as spokesmen for their factions. For Yŏngjo, to respect their right of speech meant to let factional issues fester. This he felt he could not afford. Hence, his suppression of speech. True, with the *t'angp'yŏng* policy, Yŏngjo avoided the bloodshed that had frequented his father's and brother's courts. And he succeeded in keeping both the Noron and the Soron in his government, though there was a gradual trend toward Noron dominance. He even silenced the factional debate in his court. But this silence was ominous; it signified his violation of one of the most sacred traditions of his Confucian monarchy. And for Yŏngjo, a ruler who believed his power to be founded upon his moral authority, this was his greatest cross.

DISILLUSION WITH FACTIONAL POLITICS

Despite Yŏngjo's obsession with the *t'angp'yŏng* policy, it was not until several years after his accession that he pursued it in earnest. At first, he tried to make do with factional politics. But both the Soron bureaucracy, which he inherited from Kyŏngjong, and the Noron bureaucracy, with which he replaced it, proved to be, for different reasons, unsatisfying and unmanageable.

With the Soron, distrust of the new king was the main factor. In view of their past relationship to him, their apprehension was justified. Still, when Yŏngjo, as if oblivious, appointed a Soron cabinet headed by three Soron ministers in the State Council, the king and the bureaucrats took tentative steps toward a working relationship.

In dealing with the new king, the bureaucracy took a time-honored approach—intimidation by the Censorate and conciliation by the State Council. Thus, the Censorate soon demanded further punishment of the Noron,[25] while Prime Minister Yi Kwangjwa and the Board of Rites recommended that Yŏngjo honor his own ancestors. The king responded in kind. He deferred to his ministers in matters of form, while conceding very little in matters of substance, especially to censorial demands.

The past, however, could not be laid to rest. In December, 1724, two months after Yŏngjo's accession, a memorial demanding "justice for the Noron" arrived from a country scholar named Yi Ŭiyŏn. In its vindictive tone and moralistic style, it foretold much of what was to come. Using polemical arguments, it defended the Noron while accusing the Soron, "the petty and vicious men" of blind ambition and shameless trickery, and it cited Kim Ilgyŏng, the principal instigator of the 1722 purge, as an example of Soron power seeking.[26]

The subsequent rift seems to have arisen from distrust. What Yŏngjo wanted was to punish Kim Ilgyŏng and his accomplice Mok Horyong, who had repeatedly persecuted him, vilifying him and plotting for his life. The Soron, however, simply could not believe that the matter would end with Kim and Mok. While most Soron cared little for Kim, they defended him, fearing that his punishment would be the beginning of a deluge.

The Soron bureaucracy, fearing the effects of Yi Ŭiyŏn's memorial, pressed for his punishment. Yŏngjo, on the other hand, waited for a Soron concession concerning Kim Ilgyŏng as a sign of loyalty. Yŏngjo's reluctance to grant the Soron's request made them increasingly insecure while Soron insensitivity to Yŏngjo's wish left him humiliated.[27] In the end, ironically, both got their wishes. Both Yi Ŭiyŏn and Kim Ilgyŏng were put on trial.

Yi Ŭiyŏn refused to recant and was tortured to death by Soron interrogators.[28] It was Kim Ilgyŏng's trial, however, that signaled the end of the Soron bureaucracy. His defiance surprised even those accustomed to his audacity. He was ostensibly tried for a passage in the edict that he composed for the throne at the conclusion of the 1722 purge.[29] It was taken as an insinuation of Yŏngjo's involvement in a plot to assassinate Kyŏngjong. At first Kim defended himself, claiming that the passage was a misquotation. But when he sensed that his case was hopeless, he acted the part of a defiant martyr persecuted for his loyalty to his master, Kyŏngjong, by an illegitimate usurper. He refused to behave as Yŏngjo's subject. He addressed Yŏngjo, who presided over the trial as *chinsa*, a term for an ordinary scholar, and declared that his only wish was to die in the footsteps of his master. His wish was soon granted. Mok Horyong also died after a similar trial.[30]

Shaken by Kim's behavior, the Soron attempted a belated apology, but the rupture was too deep. And now that Kim and Mok had died, their embittered followers were flinging accusations of regicide at Yŏngjo, saying that he had poisoned his brother.[31] This prompted the king's decision. It was important to reverse the verdict of the 1722 purge and to clear his name. A Noron bureaucracy offered fulfillment of these objectives. The change of power was completed by June 1725. Soron fears had become a self-fulfilling prophecy.

The weight of the past also guided the Noron bureaucracy. Where fear of retaliation had driven the Soron, the Noron were impelled by a burning desire for revenge, for which their expectations were high. After all, was not the man they believed in, and for whom they had suffered a crushing defeat, now on the throne? Bent on vindication, the Noron were eager to adjudge the Soron as rebels and to inflict on them a loss equivalent to what they had suffered.

Though what the Noron demanded was well precedented and justified by the rules of factional politics in the recent past, it did not suit Yŏngjo. He was determined to avoid a bloody purge. Thus, Yŏngjo again faced a contradiction—to use factional politics in turning to the Noron, while refusing to abide by its rules. The result was several years of bitter contention.

This unhappy situation resulted at least in part from miscalculation. True, Yŏngjo anticipated Noron demands. But he hoped to persuade them of the futility of purges. This ill-placed hope was, ironically, based on his past relationship with the Noron. They had both been humiliated by the Soron. Since he was willing to forego revenge,[32] he expected the same of his officials. As for the trappings of victory, he granted these easily enough. Martyrs and patriarchs were restored to honor,[33] charges were reversed,[34] banishment was lifted, and the Soron were censured.

From the Noron perspective, it was all form and no substance. The measures Yŏngjo took were, as they viewed it, those beneficial to the king. When it came to measures really important to them, he was not sympathetic. Where Yŏngjo had hoped that his past relationship with the Noron would facilitate understanding, it only made the Noron feel more betrayed. They felt that they had paid for his rise in blood. Securely on the throne, Yŏngjo deliberately chose to ignore them, speaking of a greater justice. This of course infuriated them. Steeped in Confucian tradition, the implication that they were pursuing private interests which, by extension, made them morally inferior to the king, was more than they could take. To obtain a royal verdict terming the Soron rebels thus gained an added significance. It was not only a matter of settling scores. They had to show that they were right to demand a Soron purge and that this was in the public interest.

A sure way to undercut the Soron position was to report their crimes to the royal ancestral temple. The Noron thus made two suggestions. The first was to mention Kyŏngjong's illness in a ritual report.[35] Publicly establishing Kyŏngjong's illness would have supported the Noron claim—that it was their concern for dynastic security that had led them to designate Yŏngjo as heir apparent and regent at the earliest possible date and that the Soron's greed for power had obstructed this. It would also exempt Kyŏngjong of responsibility for the purge and place the entire blame on the Soron, who had manipulated an ailing king. This proposal presented problems of propriety. It exonerated Kyŏngjong but by making him an incompetent. Though Yŏngjo was strongly tempted, when reminded of this implication of unfiliality by moderate officials[36] he decided against it.[37] The second suggestion was that the expulsion of the Soron be described as the "subjugation of rebels." Yŏngjo's refusal was even more prompt.[38]

Having failed at a direct onslaught, the Noron attempted a piecemeal approach. They chose five Soron ministers to be dealt with as rebels,[39] but Yŏngjo was heedless. They employed every form of pressure available—joint and individual memorials, personal admonitions and pleas—but to no avail. Finally, on July 29, the bureaucracy vacated office and staged a strike. Yŏngjo remained firm. After two weeks, the king formally requested that they end the strike. The terms he offered were little more than a face-saving formula.[40] After two days of vacillation, on August 14, the bureaucracy ended the strike.

THE BIRTH OF THE *T'ANGP'YŎNG* POLICY

Though Yŏngjo had successfully resisted Noron demands,[41] the resulting strain was enormous. The issue dominated the court, crippling the efficiency of administration. The Noron officials now spoke of withdrawal from service. In the Confucian tradition of "retreat and advancement," this threat implied that the ruler was not worth serving.

At about this time, a different voice was heard. Cho Munmyŏng, who had just returned from China as a member of an ambassadorial mission, denounced factionalism. In a memorial, he expressed his sadness over the fall of the Ming, which he attributed to factionalism, warned of its danger to the present Korean court, and suggested that factions be abolished. Yŏngjo welcomed this timely proposal.[42] The *t'angp'yŏng* policy was declared. Now the alarmed Noron confronted the king over this new policy. In November 1725, Min Chinwŏn, Queen Inhyŏn's brother and a ranking Noron minister, held a conversation with Yŏngjo on the topic. Min, as the king's uncle, was frank, while the king took a conciliatory tone. The conversation is quite revealing:

MIN: "To abolish factions," as the royal secretary Cho Munmyŏng proposed in his memorial, might sound good but there is an important reason why it is not good. . . . When the distinction between right and wrong, correct and devious is made, factions will naturally disappear. But if one does not make these distinctions and concentrates on getting rid of factions, then the state will head for destruction. Munmyŏng is a man of learning. How could he have failed to understand these points? He espoused abolishing factions but was silent on the principles involving abolishing factions. There are reasons why [Munmyŏng's idea] looks good, yet in reality it is not. Your Majesty, however, casually glanced it over and pronounced it good. Surely this was a mistake. The purges of yesteryear can be described as a calamity. It began with [their] rejecting those who were of a different opinion from them, then massacring good people and finally it reached such extremes as to attempt to harm the father of the country. Now, if the request to chastise the evil and punish the criminals is confused with factionalism, then perversion would reign over righteous principle. On the other hand, when the principal criminals receive capital punishment and the rest are punished by lighter degrees, it will be the way of the *t'angp'yŏng*. When this happens, some in the cunning faction will repent. Our correct principle will thus be manifest and evil influence will not be able to infiltrate. If, however, one confuses right and wrong, correct and devious, and indiscriminately regards everything as factionalism, not only will righteous principle come to an end but the country will face destruction.

YŎNGJO: When I read Cho Munmyŏng's memorial, I chuckled over it myself. As far as I was concerned, I did not see anything wrong with it, though from someone else's point of view, it might seem rather impractical. As for making distinctions between right and wrong, correct and devious, I agree that it should be done. Yet, right contains wrong and wrong contains right. A man is not a Yao or a Shun and he cannot be completely good all the time. We cannot say that it is a bad policy to take a man's strong points while discarding his shortcomings, espe-

130

cially in dealing with people with no ulterior motives. Speaking of the disasters of yesteryear, I also feel aggrieved. Yet I realize that it was all ill effects of factionalism. Again, I do admit that I have a feeling of rancor about it. This rancor, however, is what is known as anger, one of the seven emotions. There is an old saying that though anger is most difficult to control, if one does not restrain it, it will invariably lead to excessive behavior. I have already spoken about this during the recent request for punishment. The Censorate's request, that various criminals such as the cosigners of that [Kim Il-gyŏng] memorial should get the severest punishment, might not have been totally outrageous. At the same time, the Censorate's argument was all based on terrible rancor. If the ruler takes this kind of temporary official consensus too seriously and does not attempt to restrain it, the outcome will be far too excessive. I have noticed an instructive anecdote in the *Chronicles of the Successive Rules*. At the end of the Koryŏ dynasty, the powerful ministers permitted someone not of the royal line to rule[43] and for this they deserved execution. Yet, our founder T'aejo did not see the need for any more unnecessary killing. This was an act of supreme virtue and utmost benevolence. And this custom of benevolence and generosity is precisely why our dynasty enjoys longevity equal to that of Han or T'ang. An old saying has it that if you want to emulate Yao and Shun, emulate your royal ancestors. I, too, should emulate our royal ancestors. If I want to do that, I cannot possibly endorse excessive or ungenerous arguments. . . .

MIN: It was not only T'aejo who displayed such virtue. For example, all the criminals of 1623 who participated in the deposal of the Queen Dowager deserved to receive capital punishment.[44] But King Injo only executed six or seven principal figures and banished the rest. He even appointed many of their descendants to office. The present official request only extends to the execution of Yu

Ponghwi and the five cosigners of the memorial and does not demand many unnecessary killings. Its only objective lies in making distinctions and manifesting crimes. The righteous principle of this is clear and indisputable. If Your Majesty reduces this righteous principle to factionalism, the consequence will be grave. When that happens, your servants will be tainted with factionalism and we simply will not have face to stand in this court. If Your Majesty favors only abolishing factions and does not exercise discriminating judgment, heads of the former crowd will sneak in with a hundred intrigues. Once a hundred intrigues sneak in, petty man's schemes will win, bringing untold disaster. The inclination to favor life and to dislike death is a universal human emotion which your servant also shares. Your servant and the Minister of the Right often remark to each other that, due to the positions we occupy, it is not right for us to avoid the issue of law. If, perchance, the tradition of debate were to be changed, your servant cannot hope to preside over the Censorate.

YŎNGJO: The word "suspicion" precisely refers to this situation. If the situation develops in this manner, there will be no place for affection and trust [between the ruler and the officials] and we simply cannot work on state affairs together. The idea of *t'angp'yŏng* and abolishing factions is good. The argument my lord just set forth might seem correct and honest. But as long as it endorses the taking of many human lives, it is not correct and honest.[45]

The above exchange gives the impression that Min Chinwŏn was rabidly moralistic, overbearingly self-righteous, and hell-bent on revenge, while Yŏngjo was a model of moderation and reason. Why was Min so unbendingly harsh on this subject, failing to yield to perfectly rational pleas from Yŏngjo? At the outset, Min was not an unreasonable man. He was a seasoned politician who knew and practiced his share of compromise, a respected scholar, the scion of an illustrious family who had represented his country in China on several occasions, and the veteran of a long and glorious, though troubled, official career.[46] His vehemence of tone, which would be echoed again and again by his fellow Noron who, on other matters, were capable of discretion and reason, requires some explanation.

True, past events and relationships exerted a strong hold on the Noron. Yet, it was not just the past but a certain way of interpreting the past that led to their stance. Certainly this hunger for revenge was not merely a quest for power. It was ultimately linked to power, like almost everything in politics. But, as a strategy for maintaining and enhancing their power, it was not particularly wise and they knew it. Yŏngjo had proven that he was a king with a will of his own, willing and able to make a change of power if it suited him. With such a king, to challenge and defy him was risking a great deal. True, Noron power was not as secure as it would have been had the Soron been definitively eliminated, but it certainly was not so insignificant that it could be traded for "righteous principle" *(ŭiri)* as they were soon to do, unless, of course, this principle was very important to them, more important than power.

The "righteous principle" to which they referred was that Yŏngjo should pass judgment that their opponents had been traitorous rebels. Executions and penalties were not really central to this principle. What was central was that the king, by some formal act, should establish Noron innocence and vindicate them once and for all. If this necessitated bloody reprisals then so be it. Nothing less would justify their identities as public men.

At this point, one is forced to examine the relationship between the concept of a public man and the concept of justice as it was manifested in factional politics. The authority of a Confucian government was based on the assumption that it would induce in society the moral order immanent in the universe. The raison d'être of a public man was to assist in fulfilling this goal. All of his actions, including revenge, thus had to be justified in this framework.

Not that there was a choice. The Confucian belief in the universality of the moral order implied that, in a perfect state, personal and public justice would coincide. In other words, the judgment of a beneficent government should confirm this indivisibility. And conversely, a moral man should not violate this indivisibility. Hence, to be a public man one had first to be a moral man. But this required a recognition that one's motives and actions conformed to public morality. This recognition had to come from the ruler who, in so doing, would make the union between personal justice and public justice complete. This probably was why there was not even a single instance of a secret or personal assassination attempt on members of the opposing faction even during periods of the most bitter factional struggle. For revenge so achieved would have vitiated its purpose.

From this point of view, the *t'angp'yŏng* policy threatened the Noron's self-images as moral beings. For it was based on the indistinguishability between right and wrong. To accept this would deprive them of their long-sought recognition as moral men. Clearly this was out of the question for most Noron. The alternative was to blame the king for failing in his duty. This they did. A few refused to serve the "unworthy" ruler. The majority who remained in office constantly reminded him of his failing.

But if the Noron pressed for vindication, their arguments soon introduced another issue. For in making these demands, they repeatedly pointed out that Yŏngjo was indebted to them. Recalling their support when Yŏngjo was under attack, they perhaps implied to the ever-alert sovereign that he owed his accession to them. One memorial even explicitly said that the king owed his life and throne to the Noron.[47] Now Yŏngjo could not, by ritual observance, place his imprimatur on this viewpoint. For to do so would have attenuated his authority and undercut his claim to legitimacy.

Clearly, the *t'angp'yŏng* policy did not provide an easy answer to the problems of factional politics. Conflict between Yŏngjo and the Noron continued under a new rhetoric. The king insisted that the policy was the public cause to which private desire for revenge, his own included, should submit. The bureaucrats maintained that the punishment of the Soron was essential to achieving justice. After this, harmony and order would naturally prevail.

By early 1727, the situation became so tense and acrimonious that some change was necessary. Yŏngjo replaced Min Chinwŏn and Yi Kwanmyŏng, the hard-liners, with moderates. But as the king's hand-picked successors to Min and Yi, Hong Ch'ijung and Cho Tobin were held in suspicion by their fellow Noron. Any concession on the Soron issue was regarded as a betrayal of the Noron cause. Bombarded with denunciatory memorials, they resigned.

In fact, nothing short of conceding to Noron demands would work. The State Council had for some time been immobilized.[48] When Yŏngjo saw no hope of getting the Noron to cooperate with him, he decided, in August 1727, to change the ministry a second time. Within days, the Soron were back, headed by Yi Kwangjwa and Cho T'aeŏk. Noron officials who had participated in the palace strike one year previously, 101 in all, were dismissed.[49] Thus Yŏngjo relied once again on factional politics in order to avoid its problems. When Cho Hyŏnmyŏng questioned the wisdom of this course, Yŏngjo was apologetic. It was admittedly regrettable, he conceded, but he had to do it to pursue the "great ideal."[50]

Not all was in vain, however. Determined not to repeat past errors, Yŏngjo greeted incoming Soron with an official ban on the defense of factions.[51] Having returned to power under the *t'angp'yŏng* policy, the Soron did not dare to object to it, at least on a rhetorical level. But enforcement of the *t'angp'yŏng* policy was anything but perfect. Yŏngjo's attempt to retain some moderate Noron in the new bureaucracy did not work out. Hong Ch'ijung, for instance, plainly expressed extreme discomfort at being asked to stay while his fellow Noron were dismissed, and he refused to serve.[52] Other Noron more or less followed suit. Yŏngjo was hurt and angered by this[53] but nothing could be done about it. What he could not do with the moderate Noron, he did by finding and promoting supporters of the *t'angp'yŏng* policy. Song Inmyŏng, Pak Munsu, Cho Munmyŏng, and Cho Hyŏnmyŏng, all strong opponents of factional politics, soon found themselves acting as key advisors to the king. Yŏngjo even chose Cho Munmyŏng's daughter as his son's wife.[54] Through their mediation, the Soron were forced to satisfy themselves with the mildest symbolic dishonor to the Noron.[55] For the first time since Yŏngjo's accession, the court showed some semblance of order as factional issues assumed a role secondary to the administrative functions of government.

THE REBELLION OF 1728

Yŏngjo had reason to be anxious to attend to practical matters. The central government, distracted by political turmoil, had failed to respond to social problems. In each sector of the society discontents grew and unrest was manifest. At first, Yŏngjo attributed it to a famine which had started in mid-1727. Though famine was in no way unusual, a large-scale one could easily lead to disorder, and the ruling group was acutely aware of this. Coming as it did on the heels of a problem-ridden succession, accompanied by rumors of cannibalism[56] and social dislocation, the famine galvanized the court. Yŏngjo responded swiftly with such traditional measures as reductions of taxes and the distribution of relief grain. But the fall harvest was meager and by November the south was destitute. Though Yŏngjo did the best he could, it was not enough.

By December, portents appeared. On December 4, Yi Kwangjwa reported that homeless and starving crowds had occupied two mountains in Chŏlla Province, turning unruly and dangerous, and that their growing numbers already made arrest impossible.[57] Soon, it was evident that these events signified more than famine. Seditious posters appeared, first in Chŏlla Province, and spread rapidly to Seoul by January 1728.[58]

The exact content of these posters is unrecorded. They were all burned as *lèse majesté*. Described as "unmentionable," one can glean sufficient information from hints and suggestions in certain official documents and private sources to surmise that they were incitements to revolt against Yŏngjo, citing his "illegitimacy" as a reason.[59]

Posters and unruly mobs suggested an imminent uprising. Discussions of the problem dominated the court. Yŏngjo surprised his officials by urging caution. At first, he was incredulous. There had been no major uprising since Yi Kwal's rebellion in 1642. Why should he now face one despite his concern for the sufferings of the populace? Of course, a rebellion was the ultimate rejection of monarchical authority. To face a rebellion specifically directed against him was the greatest indignity. For Yŏngjo to acknowledge it was to admit failure.

By April 22, evidence of an impending outbreak was overwhelming. Song Chinmyŏng, Magistrate of Suwŏn in Kyŏnggi Province, had reported to the court evidence of a planned uprising in his district. On the night of April 21, Ch'oe Kyusŏ, a former Soron Prime Minister, galloped all night to Seoul with the same information. Still, at an emergency meeting, Yŏngjo stunned and exasperated the officials by overriding their almost unanimous call for speedy mobilization of troops. He insisted that, if the rumors were false, the appearance of troops would needlessly cause consternation among the populace.[60] It took two more days of horrifying reports to persuade Yŏngjo that they were not dealing with mere speculation but with a real rebellion. The king appointed an interrogation committee and personally interrogated the suspects already arrested. The picture was far worse than he had imagined. The most comprehensive information came from one Kim Chungman, who claimed to have participated in the plotting against his will. The gist of his story was the following.

The rebel forces were spread over the southern half of the peninsula and the leadership was drawn from influential local yangban. The plan had long been at work through a combination of local meetings and coordination between leaders. The rebels had decided to join forces at a town called Kumalli in Kyŏnggi Province on April 20 and to attack Ch'ŏngju, the provincial capital of Ch'ungch'ŏng Province, immediately afterwards. This was temporarily postponed when an army from Kyŏngsang Province led by Yi Injwa failed to appear on the appointed date. According to Kim, at his departure, the rebel army had been hiding at Kach'ŏn and Kumalli. Kim then revealed that they planned to attack the capital quite soon. Many, disguised in mourning, had already infiltrated the city so that, upon the army's attack, they could rise and join forces.

Other suspects confessed to having witnessed recruitment and preparations for the uprising or to having seen or heard of the insurgent army. More disturbing still was the discovery that some high military officers such as the commander of the P'yŏngan Army had joined the seditious plot. In fact, it turned out that the royal army in the northern provinces was under heavy rebel influence.[61]

Shaken, Yŏngjo swiftly took countervailing measures. He ordered a mobilization of troops, appointing Kim Chunggi and Pak Ch'ansin as commander in chief and deputy commander in chief, respectively, for the subjugation campaign. He arrested Yi Sasŏng, the commander of the P'yŏngan Army and Nam T'aejing, the commander of the Palace Army, among others, eliminating the most dangerous forces just in time. Mok Siryong, Mok Hyoryong's brother, and Kim Yŏnghae, Kim Ilgyŏng's son, who were suspected of having participated in the scheme, were arrested and executed. In addition to measures of appeasement, news of rewards and punishments was promulgated nationwide. Assistance rendered to rebels would be deemed sedition, and thus the entire family of one involved in such an act would be dealt with by capital punishment. The capture of a rebel, dead or alive, or information leading to such capture, would be rewarded materially and with appointment to office.[62]

Nevertheless, it seemed, at least for a short while, that the royal court was in actual danger. For one thing, the departure of the expeditionary army was delayed. This was caused by reluctance to fight the rebels on the part of the commander in chief, Kim Chunggi, who was apparently in sympathy with, though not a party to, the rebellion. Only on the 25th, when O Myŏnghang, the Minister of Military Affairs, replaced Kim as the commander, did the army get underway. Then, on the following day, the 26th, news that Ch'ongju, the provincial capital of Ch'ungch'ŏng Province, had fallen to the rebel forces on the 23rd reached the court.

Official historiography says that the insurgents took the city by hoodwinking the local authorities by holding a mourning procession in which the rebels participated as mourners, and also by buying the residents' cooperation through bribery and promises. It also mentions the Magistrate Yi Pongsang's failure to take necessary action despite repeated warnings. Yi's post at Ch'ŏngju was the consequence of a recent demotion and in his case his incompatibility with the central government resulted in his own misfortune and death.[63]

What the official historiography does not mention except in the most oblique fashion was something that must have caused Yŏngjo the greatest concern of all—the significance of the mourning. For this, we must turn to contemporary private records. The mourning seems to have been for Kyŏngjong who, according to the rebels, had been poisoned by Yŏngjo and Queen Dowager Inwŏn, Yŏngjo's stepmother. The rebels reputedly carried portable shrines for Kyŏngjong and performed ritualistic wailing morning and night. They maintained that Yŏngjo's unconscionable usurpation of the throne made it imperative that someone with a rightful claim be installed. The person chosen was Prince Milp'ung, a direct descendant of Prince Sohyŏn, King Hyojong's older brother, who had died before accession.[64]

Taking this together with the posters, a consistent theme of the uprising emerges—Yŏngjo's illegitimacy and the restoration of a legitimate heir. This of course was a terrible blow for Yŏngjo. He must have known this from the posters. Still, the dissemination of such posters was one thing and a material threat under cover of mourning for his predecessor was something else again. The most devastating fact lay not in the slogan but in its success. He could rationalize the posters as an unfortunate consequence of recent political events. But the wide support accorded them meant that his mandate was indeed being questioned. In the face of this astonishing reality, Yŏngjo fell into despair. Only constant ministerial consolation and pledges of loyalty sustained him through the worst days.[65]

The worst was soon over. The royal army began to reap victories. Commander in chief O Myŏnghang vanquished the rebel forces in Kyŏnggi Province by May 1, and this news led to a rebel debacle in Chŏlla Province. Local residents' cooperation, encouraged by handsome rewards, led to the arrests of the rebel leaders, Yi Injwa, Pak P'irhyŏn, and Pak P'ilmong, and others, some of whom had been cosigners of Kim Ilgyŏng's notorious memorial. The last stronghold, Kyŏngsang Province, where the rebels had elicited the greatest support among residents, came under the royal army by May 10.[66]

The interrogation of the rebels lasted another two months. Yŏngjo often presided. About one hundred people were executed and most of them were put into the slave register to make their surviving family members slaves. The trials were recorded and the transcripts are the main source of information concerning the identities and motives of those involved.[67] Certainly, this rebellion was an explosion of social and political tension meriting considerable analysis. To understand Yŏngjo's perception of the event, however, the trial transcript seems to be our best guide.

What emerges from the transcript is that the rebellion's principal organizers were extremist Soron who felt that their careers, or all the Soron's for that matter, had come to an end with Yŏngjo's accession.[68] Plans for rebellion were hence initiated soon afterwards. Court politics only strengthened the rebels' convictions. First, Kim Ilgyŏng and Mok Horyong were executed, while Kim's cosigners were banished. This was followed by a Noron bureaucracy of several years' duration characterized by unceasing demands for punishment of the Soron.

The rebels sought each other out, attempting to enlist other groups whom they saw as potential allies. They mainly recruited through familial contacts such as distant cousins, wives' families, etc.[69] The Na family of Chŏlla Province is a good example. They had been out of office for several generations and had no hopes of attaining it in the near future. As they had acquired substantial wealth, the inaccessibility of office was a source of great bitterness. Several members of the Na family were somehow related to Yi Injwa through marriage. They were inducted into the rebellion and were important members of the uprising in the Chŏlla Province.[70] As for manpower, the rebels first counted on their own slaves and dependents. These came to a fair number. They also hired men.

The rebels needed an anti-Yŏngjo slogan, something justifiable and persuasive to the masses. Kyŏngjong's reign and Yŏngjo's succession provided them with a perfect answer—to mark Yŏngjo as Kyŏngjong's murderer and present themselves as restorers of dynastic legitimacy.[71] This was a master stroke, and it put Yŏngjo on the spot. To discuss Kyŏngjong's illness was antithetical to custom, and for Yŏngjo to formally deny that he had murdered his brother would recognize the allegations. The uncontested rumor circulated widely, as the rebels had hoped, and preparations went as planned.

The reappointment of a Soron bureaucracy in August 1727 caught the rebels by surprise. They saw this as gravely damaging to their plans. As one rebel later put it, "though those who reentered the court were moderate Soron, the extremist Soron could also entertain hopes. And as long as one has a hope, his evil mind disappears."[72] Emergency meetings were held to discuss this turn of events. A surprising number of the original planners were inclined toward a temporary halt or even an abandonment of the uprising. But the decision was no longer up to them. Their several years of planning and recruitment had produced a formidable network. Some latecomers had invested substantial resources, energy, and dreams in the plan. More on the fringes than the original planners, they had nothing to gain from Soron power and thus wanted to carry out this plan.[73]

Disruptive though this change of power was, it also brought some real advantages to the rebels in that some sympathizers came to occupy strategic posts. Nam T'aejing and Yi Sasŏng, who were later labeled as among the ten principal rebels, received key military posts. There were people like Kim Chunggi whose reluctance to fight the rebels caused considerable damage to the court. Natural events also seemed favorable. For the rebels, the famine, which drove a large segment of the population to desperation, hopelessness, and anger—an essential ingredient of an uprising—was certainly an encouraging development.

As it turned out, the rebels' apprehensions were accurate. Their downfall, however, had less to do with people's changing their minds once they found themselves in power—in fact, Yi Sasŏng

141

and Nam T'aejing did not change their minds—than with the feverish activities of the moderate Soron. Though the 1728 rebellion was a crucial point which definitively severed the moderate Soron from the extremists, their relationship had long been one of mutual distrust. And yet, there obviously existed between them a network of communications and associations: the extremist elements in the Soron bureaucracy were precisely those who provided the moderates with the knowledge and the impetus to obstruct the plot. With a renewed sense of loyalty and a need to prove it, the moderates quickly informed Yŏngjo of the plot and fought and vanquished the rebels.

There is even a belief that Yŏngjo's recall of the Soron was a calculated move.[74] This theory seems too much benefited by hindsight. If indeed Yŏngjo's strategy had been intended to muffle the explosion, he failed. But the Soron presence undermined overall planning and communications among the rebels. With their plans leaked prematurely and many participants arrested, the rebels could no longer plan for joint action. What could very well have been a serious challenge to the royal house became a minor fracas among outcasts.

This is not to say that, if they had not been recalled, the moderate Soron would have turned their backs on the monarch. Nonetheless their sense of alienation might have resulted in slower action. It is also probable that the Noron response to Soron information might have been mistrustful, delaying the counterattack. In this sense, Yŏngjo's commitment to the *t'angp'yŏng* policy certainly paid off handsomely, though perhaps in a way different from what he had anticipated.

THE POLITICS OF THE *T'ANGP'YŎNG* POLICY

The 1728 rebellion, so traumatic for Yŏngjo, had an enduring impact on him. He was brought face to face with the threat that "his" mandate might just be taken away from him. This determined the course of his politics. His lifelong campaign to win popular trust was one consequence; his extreme zeal for the *t'angp'yŏng*

142

policy was another. He attributed the rebellion to the "evils of factionalism" which produced so many "families embittered by destruction."[75] He now equated factionalism with the challenge to his legitimacy and, thus, came to view it as subversive. This theme, which would emerge as the central defense for the *t'angp'yŏng* policy, was revealed soon after the rebellion. When the Noron, hoping for punishment of the Soron, in the summer of 1728, pressed for royal discrimination between right and wrong, Yŏngjo replied:

> What you ask requires a change of power. Which is more important to you—faction or ruler? Even if you cannot completely forget your faction, some kind of cooperation should be possible. Only after the nation survives can you even indulge in factionalism. If there is no nation, you cannot think of faction.[76]

So thoroughly convinced was he of the danger of a large alienated group that he kept the punishment of the rebels to a minimum[77] and installed a coalition Noron and Soron bureaucracy. The *t'angp'yŏng* policy was to be pursued in earnest.

But the coalition bureaucracy could be maintained only if members of both factions could be persuaded to tolerate each other's presence, to set aside past animosities and work together. In fact, Yŏngjo was asking them for a truce. Fully aware of the delicacy of this proposition, he turned to the arts of persuasion. Collectively, he appealed to their sense of duty, and he cultivated them individually. To Noron officials he emphasized the tactical necessity of having a Soron presence, even suggesting that he viewed the Soron as a necessary and unpleasant evil.[78] To Soron bureaucrats, he stressed his appreciation for their loyalty in time of crisis and their individual merit.[79]

But his persuasion could affect only those who wished to be affected. While the moderates of both factions might occasionally bend to Yŏngjo's ministrations, this was not the case generally. Both factions, in different ways, eluded the king's attempts on the whole.

The Soron, tinged by past associations, could at best offer penance. They certainly could not offer conciliation or forgiveness. Thus, while the Soron leadership lay with the moderates, they were in no position to effectively mediate between the factions. The Noron, untempered since the depredations of Kyŏngjong's reign, were led by less moderate elements. While Yŏngjo carefully chose moderates for his ministers, these men were not factional leaders and were easily depicted as opportunists by the polemicists who guided the faction. Thus vulnerable to pressure, they too were ineffective in bringing about a settlement.

Yŏngjo, on his part, continued his efforts. There was nothing he would not try. He begged and cajoled, raged and wept, persuaded and patronized all to no effect. On several occasions, he attempted to bring the opposing factional leaders together. In 1730, for instance, he brought Min Chinwŏn and Yi Kwangjwa, the leaders of the Noron and the Soron respectively, into the same room. Holding Yi's hand in his left hand and Min's in his right, he entreated them to take each other's hands as a gesture of truce. They both politely, but firmly, refused.[80] A similar scene recurred three years later with no better result.[81]

In the end these efforts were doomed to failure. The factional leaders lacked the ideology, the rhetoric, and the moral outlook to accommodate the *t'angp'yŏng* policy. Their political perceptions, rooted in precedent and sanctioned by tradition, just could not conform to Yŏngjo's desires. The only thing that could be bent to contain the conflict was Yŏngjo's moral image—they could view him as suppressing the censorial voice.

For Yŏngjo, who believed in the moral authority of the throne, it was an unappealing prospect to appear to be blocking the channel of speech, the time-honored privilege of the Censorate regarded as the conscience of the monarchy. But the censorial conscience had a factional heart. Since he could not reach its heart, he sought, at least, silence. Otherwise the court would be consumed by factional issues, a situation he felt he simply could not afford. To justify this course of action Yŏngjo adopted a formula that distinguished between destructive and constructive censorial criticism, and declared factional defense to be destructive. But of course this formula could not work. It was neither flexible enough to handle complex realities nor so unassailable as to disable the bureaucrats, also master practitioners of Confucian rhetoric.

After all, where does constructive criticism end and destructive criticism begin? First of all, the Censorate was an integral part of the bureaucracy, with its members acting and responding to a variety of issues arising from day to day. How an issue would develop and which member would respond to it and in what manner were all very hard to predict. One memorial or a remark, seemingly innocuous and minor at first, could evolve into an all-consuming affair. And this happened again and again, invariably attaining a factional coloration, leaving Yŏngjo distressed and infuriated. For example, a scholar's memorial of June 1737, pleading for the restoration of his teacher's honor, in two months snowballed into factional recriminations involving virtually the entire bureaucracy.[82] Yŏngjo was at his wit's end to stop this factional free-for-all. In desperation, he resorted to self-flagellation and withdrawal, the ultimate weapon. On September 2, he announced that he would abstain from food. To the royal secretaries imploring that he retract the announcement, he said:

> Just as rearing children without decorum is the father's fault, letting officials behave without propriety is the ruler's mistake. I am driven to abstinence by powerful officials. Later generations will surely laugh at my cowardice and weakness but they will also see my agony. Rather than remain so helplessly in the palms of powerful officials, I would prefer to be put to the grindstone by their hands.

He refused the daily visit of the Medical Bureau, ordered no document be sent in except those directly pertaining to the problems of the populace, and locked himself in.

When he granted an audience to ministers several days later, Yŏngjo greeted them derisively: "My lords truly have thick skin. How can you bring yourselves to face me today?" They apologized abjectly. Yŏngjo continued: now that he was driven to the brink of death by starvation, did they consider themselves to be rebels or loyal ministers? Nothing if not politic, the ministers wept. Yŏngjo archly expressed curiosity over their weeping. He declared that his appetite would be restored by one or two heads of the most vehemently factional officials. The court was filled with traitors whose only concern was their faction; beheading them all might be the only way to break this vicious circle, except that the ruler could not govern alone. As he raged he wept, and weeping he raged further. After considerably more raving, weeping, pleading, and cajoling, Yŏngjo emerged the victor. On September 7, 1737, he dismissed every censor and every official who had not ritually awaited punishment.[83]

Where reason and rhetoric failed, Yŏngjo substituted tantrums and abstinence. Though temporarily effective, the flaw in this method was that Yŏngjo was unable to carry out his threats. He needed his bureaucrats not only to govern but also to maintain his throne. It was simply impossible for him to challenge this group whose power bases had long since been firmly established. For instance, most of the officials dismissed in September 1737 soon found their way back into the bureaucracy. And the bureaucrats, knowing this, were not about to succumb to the king so easily.

What censors and other bureaucrats did was a direct attack on Yŏngjo for his repression of the bureaucratic voice in general. To punish those who could be accused of factional defense might be justified. But unless the king was willing to forego even the appearance of respect for the bureaucratic voice and to unabashedly accept an autocratic role, he had to respond to this general criticism. Not to do so would fly in the face of censorial traditions. And Yŏngjo also had to live by the rules.

Verbal criticisms would have been rather meaningless if the censors had not translated their criticisms into action by refusing to serve the king. It was exactly in this that the bureaucrats held an advantage. While Yŏngjo could threaten liberally in anger but had only limited options for action, the bureaucrats, especially the Noron, dissatisfied with the coalition bureaucracy, had no compunctions about actually withdrawing from service if it worked to their advantage. Yŏngjo tried to fight bureaucratic withdrawal by treating it as contempt for the throne. He frequently inflicted symbolic punishment on those who failed to take up posts or to respond to his summons.[84] But here Yŏngjo was treading on very dangerous ground. The right of a Confucian scholar-official to withdraw was long since established. Moreover, short of resorting to physical coercion which Yŏngjo certainly could not do, there was very little the king could do to make one serve. Unable to placate the bureaucrats, Yŏngjo's frustration expressed itself in more tantrums and punishments. This, of course, brought criticism and withdrawal, perpetuating a vicious circle.

SHADOWS OF REBELLION

Had he achieved the stability he sought in cultivating a coalition bureaucracy, Yŏngjo might have felt vindicated. This is not to say that he gained nothing from the *t'angp'yŏng* policy. If the grandiose ideal of its rhetoric remained as elusive as ever, Yŏngjo did at least avert purges. Stability, however, did not end at the palace gates. There were also the rebels, and to control and keep tabs on them Yŏngjo had invested his hopes in a Soron presence.[85] For stability, as well, Yŏngjo tolerated Noron slings and arrows, stubbornly protected the Soron despite his haunting memories of their rejection and persecution of him during Kyŏngjong's reign, and chose to forego the convenience of a unified bureaucracy.

But events did not turn out as Yŏngjo wished. Though no actual rebellion occurred after 1728, specters of it periodically appeared. Not all were connected with the rebellion, but they all touched upon his legitimacy.

In consequence, Yŏngjo found himself feeling increasingly ambivalent toward the Soron. On the one hand, he needed them to check the rebels. To clear his name and assert his legitimacy, however, he had to contend with the Soron position in Kyŏngjong's reign. In the volatile political climate of Yŏngjo's court in which the still-flickering past could cause present conflagration, Yŏngjo had to tread delicately. This then was his dilemma: to negate what the Soron had once stood for without discarding the *t'angp'yŏng* policy.

The best he could do was to limit any reappraisal of the Soron to issues directly involving his legitimacy. The Noron, sensing an opportunity, made their own demands. If Yŏngjo's objective tended to vitiate the *t'angp'yŏng* policy, Noron aims would have required discarding it altogether. He would lose his credibility as the "master of the *t'angp'yŏng* policy" (*t'angp'yŏngju*)[86] which he claimed to be; he would lose those officials who supported him because of his commitment to it, and he would lose the fragile equilibrium at court for which he had struggled so earnestly. But while his legitimacy was in question, he could not leave pertinent issues unresolved.

The year 1728 had visited a more personal misfortune on Yŏngjo. His only son, Crown Prince Hyojang, had died, leaving him without an heir at thirty-five. In March 1729, a private scholar, Hwang So, sent a memorial urging the king to select a capable prince from the royal clan and appoint him heir apparent. This was implied *lèse majesté*, and a furor erupted. In a society where the legitimacy of the royal line was sacred, this verged on rebellion. An intrigue was suspected, but a trial of Hwang revealed nothing.[87] Still, Yŏngjo reluctantly agreed to the execution of Prince Milp'ung, the 1728 rebels' candidate for the throne as the "legitimate" prince.[88]

In the following year, the rebellious phantasm took the form of a palace intrigue. Black magic was reported. It had supposedly been practiced for a few years already, with the explicit aim of bringing death to royal children. Some officials even insinuated that Prince Hyojang might have fallen under the curse. Suspected ladies-in-waiting, under torture, confessed that extremist Soron, the cosigners of Kim Ilgyŏng's memorial, were the principal culprits. One wonders how these extremist Soron engineered the palace intrigue from their remote places of banishment. Presumably it was done through connections and influence, but Yi Chinyu and Yun Sŏngsi died under torture, carrying their secrets with them.[89] While this bizarre incident gave Yŏngjo no pleasure, he at least could use it to justify ridding himself of Kim Ilgyŏng's cosigners, without having to allude to the past with its attendant factional implications.

A more frightening apparition of the 1728 rebellion visited Yŏngjo in the following decade. The early 1730s saw an unusual sequence of natural disasters, even considering the generally grim facts of preindustrial life. An epidemic broke out in the summer of 1731 in the south, and after a year rampaged through the capital with no respite. On its heels came a serious crop failure. Formulaic descriptions of famine—women of scholar families were driven to robbery disguised as men, while the poor were reduced to cannibalism—appeared by the end of 1732. Temporary food stalls were installed for the hungry, and other relief measures were taken, but the government seemed powerless in the face of a famine of this magnitude. By March 1733, even palace guards were dying of starvation.[90] Though a much-anguished Yŏngjo did all he could to display his sympathy for the afflicted, antigovernment sentiment resurfaced in the south. By April, anti-Yŏngjo posters, supposedly similar to those of 1728, complete with warnings of an impending uprising, reemerged in Chŏlla Province and elsewhere. Interrogation, however, revealed no organized plans.[91] By mid-1734, the worst of the famine and epidemic had passed.

Though the government had weathered this crisis, the impact of the posters on Yŏngjo cannot be underestimated. That he felt that he had made a real commitment to win popular confidence probably made them harder to bear. Though his commitment was not weakened, his impatience with challenges to his legitimacy grew noticeably. Hence his rage over the circulation of the anti-Yŏngjo songs that came to his attention in 1739. Traditionally, songs were regarded as sure indicators of popular sentiment, and rebellious songs were often viewed as serious portents of the end of a dynasty. Doggedly attending the trial of the suspects—in fact, these were mostly people from Chŏlla Province who had allegedly circulated posters in 1728—and presiding over grueling interrogations for five and a half months, he meted out the harshest punishment to those adjudged to have been guilty.[92]

The discovery of anti-Yŏngjo songs marks a turning point in Yŏngjo's attitude toward the Soron. He felt that he somehow had to make a royal pronouncement clarifying the course of events leading to his succession. To do so of course required confronting the Soron position. Now the Soron were really terrified. It is reported that Prime Minister Yi Kwangjwa was so petrified that he did not dare to enter the palace to offer consolation after the trial was over.[93] What Yŏngjo did first was to posthumously restore honor to Kim Ch'angjip and Yi Imyŏng, the two of the four Noron ministers still on the criminal register. He had resisted Noron demands to do so partly because of the implication that he was indebted to them for his throne. On occasion, for instance, he had accused the Noron of arguing "as if the ministers chose the king."[94] But now it suited him to restore the honor of two ministers who had died for their support of him. As a next step, he contemplated reassessing the record of the 1722 purge, which attributed to the Noron a plan for the assassination of Kyŏngjong in which he was also implicated.

The Noron waxed enthusiastic. But, characteristically, they went too far. They unleashed demands for wholesale Soron punishment. One Pak Tongjun even accused Yi Kwangjwa of treasonous intent, claiming that he coveted the throne himself. Subsequently, Yi died, allegedly of grief and self-imposed starvation.[95] Alarmed, Yŏngjo declared a renewed commitment to the *t'angp'yŏng* policy.

In November 1741, the seventeenth year of his reign, Yŏngjo emerged with an ingenious resolution. He burned the records of the 1722 purge and promulgated the *Great Instruction (Taehun)*, which he composed. It begins by pointing out that there had been no other heir to the throne than Yŏngjo and that he had been appointed heir apparent on Kyŏngjong's and Queen Dowager Inwŏn's orders. It notes that there had been acts of grave treason during his brother's reign. But it was Kim Ilgyŏng and his cohorts who were responsible for this as well as for the 1728 uprising. The moderate Soron had not been involved, and in the name of justice, they should not be punished. It concludes with the warning that henceforth all discussions of these issues will be forbidden and violators will be accorded heavy punishment.[96] Subsequently, Yŏngjo ritually reported the *Great Instruction* at the ancestral temple, thus rendering it inviolable. On this occasion, he revealed that the punishment for violation would be death.[97] This threat of capital punishment, like most of his other blandishments, was just a threat. No official was actually killed for bringing up factional issues. Nevertheless, it revealed the seriousness of royal intent.

With this pronouncement, Yŏngjo accomplished much indeed— he asserted his legitimacy and reaffirmed his commitment to the *t'angp'yŏng* policy. He also lent form and substance to the *t'angp'yŏng* policy; however, he needed powers of enforcement. For this he required an enhanced monarchical power.

"L'ÉTAT, C'EST MOI"

Yŏngjo now suppressed his bureaucrats with a certain confidence that he was the government. Surely, he had not previously avoided arbitrary measures in his dealings with his officials. But it appears that sometime around 1740 he decided that conciliation was unlikely and that, rather than waste time seeking bureaucratic approval, he should seek bureaucratic acquiescence by force if necessary.

Of course, even in assuming this autocratic role, Yŏngjo turned to Confucian rhetoric. He emphasized his role as a carrier of civilization and his responsibility to the people who, he declared, were the raison d'être of the state and upon whom his mandate depended. No Confucian could find fault with the logic of this stance—except that he used it to deprive his officials of their independence. Their duty was to help the ruler in his mission; were they to deviate from it, either by refusing to serve or by thwarting the monarch's good intentions, they would lose all the rights and privileges accruing to them as dutiful officials. In short, Yŏngjo pitted official criticism against dynastic mission, civilization, and popular welfare. At one point, he even attempted, though unsuccessfully, to establish as orthodoxy the idea that the spirit of Confucian tradition was embodied in respect for the monarch.[98]

Yŏngjo's message was clear—he, as the occupant of the throne uniquely burdened with the sacred mission, knew the right course; at least he knew it better than his officials. Thus he could demand unequivocal and wholehearted official support for any course he might take. Here, the autocratic reasoning that equated his person to the state, and bureaucratic loyalty to submission, was complete.

Within this framework, Yŏngjo tightened his grip on the official community. He changed the procedure for appointing officials so as to lessen the perpetuation of one family or group in office;[99] he imposed sanctions on officials who resigned or refused appointments in protest;[100] he regulated the writing styles of civil officials,[101] and he established lecture sessions for civil and military officials.[102]

In addition, Yŏngjo tried to curtail the power base of the official-bureaucrat community. His sporadic attempts to disseminate power more widely did not work. But he succeeded in reducing the number of private academies. By the eighteenth century, with their financial independence, their claim as guardians of Confucian scholarship, and their distinctive identification with certain schools of thought and factions, private academies posed an implicit challenge to the state. In 1741, Yŏngjo abolished about 170 academies and shrines, built after 1714 without governmental approval, dedicated to or associated with well-known scholars. He also announced punitive measures against their future construction.[103] He withstood uproars, protests, and pressures and succeeded in slowing their growth.[104]

But Yŏngjo had yet to confront his most onerous task—the total suppression of the censorial voice. Previously, he had repressed censorial criticisms pertaining to factional defense. He had not blocked the Censorate's remonstrative role—addressing royal lack of virtue. Even as late as February 1743, he accepted with equanimity censorial criticism that he was obstructing the bureaucratic right to speak and not delighting in official admonition. But progressively tighter controls on the bureaucracy brought correspondingly louder outcries. A censorial memorial from Cho Chunghoe, which arrived in January 1744, the twentieth year of Yŏngjo's reign, illustrates the degree of vehemence. A long list of charges of royal misbehavior began with the following criticism:

The obstruction of the channel of speech has not seen worse days than now. Memorials and admonitions all have met the same intractable [royal] response. Your Majesty invariably suspects factional defense [in them], banishes [officials] in dishonor to detain [them] within hedges of brambles, one after another. It has reached such an extreme that even wooden cangues, fetters and handcuffs are used in interrogation [of officials]. That is why the Censorate has adopted hesitancy and indecisiveness as a common practice and at court, morale and integrity have sunk and become extinguished. Thus, customs are subverted and trampled and the way of the world has suffered ruinous decline. Isn't this cause for worry? How much more [must one worry] over the portents of Heaven and the disasters of Earth? Eclipses, grain, trees, lightning and thunder all signal misfortune frightening our hearts. [They are] benevolent and loving warnings [of Heaven] which are becoming more piercing and urgent. Yet, these have produced neither [royal] admissions of guilt nor a search for advice. The advice offered by the Royal Secretariat and the Office of Special Counselors have long since been met with silence and casual dismissal. With this, how could [the king] hope to move and turn the heart of Heaven around to rid us of disasters?[105]

For charging that Yŏngjo had elicited the wrath of Heaven, Cho elicited the wrath of the king, displayed in his unprecedented severity with Cho. He dismissed him and had his name expunged from the official register.[106] He also dismissed a majority of the Censorate for failing to demand Cho's punishment. Several officials whom Yŏngjo suspected of having collaborated on the memorial received the same penalties as Cho.[107] This was the first time that Yŏngjo had ever punished a censor for admonishing the monarch for his general conduct; it was a bridge of no return. Afterwards Yŏngjo would find it necessary to take progressively harsher measures to justify his position until, at length, his authority would be questioned only in silence.

THE SEARCH FOR ESCAPE

Yŏngjo could so punish Cho Chunghoe only because he had found a monarchical equivalent to bureaucratic retreat—the threat of abdication. If bureaucratic retreat expressed a negation of the hope that communal efforts could bring progress toward the utopian goals of the Confucian state, monarchical abdication expressed despair not only of these efforts, but of the very structures in which they were expended. Of course, abdication to a successor fully prepared for the burden of rule was regarded as a virtuous act intended to ease the transition of power. But when Yŏngjo attempted abdication, his only son and heir, Prince Sado, was clearly too young and inexperienced to function as a ruler. While Yŏngjo's act may have superficially conformed to accepted notions, under the circumstances it was an expression of despair and, in so far as it would have left the government dysfunctional, it was clearly a threat.

While this threat became, in Yŏngjo's hands, a powerful monarchical tool, it also expressed a yearning to escape his role, a role he increasingly felt to be at odds with his idea of a truly virtuous king. This discomfort grew from his attempts to control and stifle the bureaucratic voice. He felt that such measures were unavoidable, but nonetheless his anguish over his imperfect kingship intensified. Disillusioned by his court and restless with his limitations, Yŏngjo sought an escape, a release from the burden of rule. But his longing for escape, expressed in threats to abdicate, was the very instrument that gave him power over his officials and solidified his rule.

There is a strong correlation between the birth of Prince Sado and Yŏngjo's increasing tendency toward repression. The seven years from 1728, the year of the rebellion and the death of Yŏngjo's first son, Prince Hyojang, to 1735, when Sado was born, were the most precarious for the throne. If the instability resulting from the rebellion was not enough, the king had no heir. Anxiety was pervasive. In 1732, for instance, Min Chinwŏn urged Yŏngjo to take virtuous and healthy young women as secondary consorts.[108]

During this period, Yŏngjo's behavior toward his officials was

154

nearly that of a model king. He resorted to harsh measures only to deal with sedition and opposition to the *t'angp'yŏng* policy. On other occasions, he approached his officials with genuine respect. After Sado's birth, however, his actions were more arbitrary. His temper worsened, and he became impatient and authoritarian.[109] More to the point, after 1735 Yŏngjo's tantrums were increasingly overbearing. Beyond refusing audiences, he refused to take medicine, fasted, and confined himself to his private quarters. This was a rather effective method of getting his way, and whatever his motives were, he staged this sort of scene over and over again.

This behavior culminated in his attempts to abdicate to his son. This was the ultimate weapon available to a monarch. Perhaps because of its extreme implications, it was not very often employed by other Yi monarchs. The first time Yŏngjo promulgated an edict of abdication was in February 1739. At the time, Prince Sado was only five years old. Abject ministerial pleas led to a royal rescission on the same day.[110] The next decree of abdication appeared after the discovery of anti-Yŏngjo songs in 1740. This was Yŏngjo's response to Noron demands for severe action against the Soron.[111] In both instances, it was an act of protest against an attack on the *t'angp'yŏng* policy.

In these threats of abdication, Sado had never been mentioned. He was still very young and though his existence made Yŏngjo's abdication possible, it was only a theoretical possibility. As Sado got older, he seems to have become, in Yŏngjo's mind, a solution to his problems, an agent offering an avenue of escape. This emerges quite clearly in an incident of 1742 when Sado was eight years old, ready to begin his formal study.

In March 1742, Yŏngjo received a memorial. It was sent by Min Ch'angsu in compliance with the wish of his brother, Hyŏngsu, who had recently died. The two brothers had collaborated on its composition. They were the sons of Min Chinwŏn, who had headed the Noron until his death in 1736. The memorial was bitterly factional. It defended Noron activities during Kyŏngjong's reign, leveled charges against the Soron and some neutral officials like Cho Hyŏnmyŏng, and lamented the injustices that the Noron, both dead and alive, had borne.[112]

This subjected Yŏngjo to a sharp conflict of loyalty. The year before, he had promulgated the *Great Instruction*. Min Ch'angsu was the first to violate it, and was thus subject to the death penalty. Now, Yŏngjo was the captive of his own law. To maintain credibility, he had to kill the first violater. But he did not want to kill Min, whose aunt was Queen Inhyŏn, his late stepmother, for whom he had great affection.

In seeking a way out of this predicament, Yŏngjo turned to Sado for the first time. He announced that he would exonerate Min out of indebtedness to Queen Inhyŏn, but out of shame for this private act, he would relinquish his position. Pressed for an explanation, Yŏngjo answered that his son could take the throne. Using this threat Yŏngjo was able to spare Min from death, but official pressures forced him to interrogate him and banish him to a remote place.[113]

On this occasion, Yŏngjo's opponents were the supporters of the *t'angp'yŏng* policy whose principles did not allow exceptions to the *Great Instruction*. Cho Hyŏnmyŏng, who was regarded as the spokesman for this policy, was particularly uncompromising. He refused to come to court, sending memorials of protest, seven in all, and requesting to be relieved of his post.[114] In response Yŏngjo retreated to his private quarters. After seven weeks of this, on April 18, Yŏngjo sent out an edict of abdication. In it he cites his wretched state of mind as a reason for the decision. This wretchedness is attributable, it notes, to factional officials who resent him for the *t'angp'yŏng* policy, on the one hand, and to those who criticize him for neglecting it, on the other. When Cho Hyŏnmyŏng still failed to appear, a disappointed Yŏngjo announced Sado's regency. Cho finally came to await punishment, sending a customary memorial of apology. Yŏngjo revoked Sado's regency and sent Cho a reply. It was not the time for resignation. They had to save the country together, and Cho should immediately return to his duties. But Yŏngjo only revealed the depth of his feelings later when he told a sympathetic Song Inmyŏng, "that edict was the most ardent wish of my troubled heart."[115]

Sado's revoked regency was prophetic. Yŏngjo's doubt and disillusion increased as the reality he faced degenerated, at least from

156

his point of view. Correspondingly, Sado loomed ever larger in his mind as an escape and a solution. In fact, Sado became almost an obsession. Whenever Yŏngjo found himself in a predicament, Sado was mentioned. He used the threat of abdication to Sado in two ways. First, he used it to suppress the censorial voice when the *t'angp'yŏng* policy required that he silence factional demands. Then he used it in his attempt to clear himself of the charge of regicide. In this attempt he came into conflict with the *t'angp'yŏng* policy and had to override the objections of its supporters, a difficult task indeed for Yŏngjo, whose policy it was to begin with.

Troubled though he was in repressing the bureaucratic voice, Yŏngjo's torment remained more theoretical than real when the repressed voice was that of the censors. While the repression of the censorial voice was, symbolically, his most directly autocratic policy, its practical effect was not that great. The exclusive and limited function of the censors, and their relative youth and inexperience, made repression rather simple. The same cannot be said of the king's close ministers, whom he trusted and respected and whose cooperation was essential to his ability to carry on state affairs. Three of them, Cho Hyŏnmyŏng, Pak Munsu, and Song Inmyŏng, emerge conspicuously, at least during the first half of his reign.

These three ministers enjoyed a uniquely close relationship to Yŏngjo, a relationship based on a shared commitment to the *t'angp'yŏng* policy and a common concern for popular welfare. In fact, they were the mainstays of the official support, which made it possible for Yŏngjo to enforce the *t'angp'yŏng* policy and to enact reforms like the equal military tax despite overwhelming opposition. They stood behind Yŏngjo unshaken by repeated denunciations by fellow officials[116] and they saw their monarch through difficult times. Yŏngjo rewarded them with nearly complete trust and appreciation. Their open disapproval of his repression of the censorial voice did not hinder them in supporting his pursuit of policies they believed in.

But in one area they would differ from the king. When the all too familiar charges of regicide and allegations of illegitimacy would reappear to taunt Yŏngjo, they would not deviate from the

Great Instruction. When the troubled sovereign would feel that his only hope for vindication lay in reevaluating the events of Kyŏngjong's reign, they would not sympathize.

THE THREE STALWARTS

Though the three ministers, Cho Hyŏnmyŏng, Song Inmyŏng, and Pak Munsu, were close in age and shared certain political ideals and a commitment to public service, they were quite different in temperament, personality, and intellectual outlook. Though they worked closely together and had great respect for one another, each had a separate and distinct relationship to Yŏngjo. Pak Munsu, perhaps the most colorful of the three, seems to have enjoyed Yŏngjo's closest affections. Guileless and unpretentious, he was the only official who could make Yŏngjo laugh. Not unfamiliar with the Confucian classics, he held book learning in contempt, "a way to lose one's true nature," as he put it.[117] Instead, he exemplified the activist tradition in Confucianism. After playing a significant role in the military campaign against the rebels in 1728, he repeatedly worked on famine relief. He was a strong advocate of the equal military tax and worked for it tirelessly. His report on the ill effects of the old tax system (the outcome of a traveling investigation) and his success in generating popular support were essential to the adoption of the reform in 1751.

Frequently sent to the provinces as a secret censor, Pak was the emissary of Yŏngjo's good will to the people. His celebrated hatred for corruption and his impatience with official exploitation of the powerless seem to have completely won the confidence of the people, in whose imagination he gained a stature similar to that of the incorruptible Judge Pao in China. This fearlessness and straightforwardness had a counterpart in his manner, which was described as indecorous. On one occasion, for instance, he was censured for looking straight at the king's face while speaking to him. He loudly protested that the relationship between the ruler and a minister was like that of father and son and that he saw nothing wrong with looking at the king's face.[118] There are numerous records of his shouting at Yŏngjo, and on several occasions he brought Yŏngjo to rage and tears by his blunt insistence on a point of principle. Though these incidents occasionally elicited real anger from the king,[119] Yŏngjo's affection for him was unabated and he once publicly announced that Pak was like his own brother.[120]

Song Inmyŏng, on the other hand, was the consummate statesman. Flawless in manner, refined in speech, reasonable yet flexible, he was the negotiator in troubled situations. He was deeply concerned with the exclusivity of the bureaucracy and with discriminatory practices based on faction, region, school, and family, and he repeatedly urged the king to open doors to as many different groups as possible. He was totally opposed to bloodshed and always counseled Yŏngjo to choose the lightest punishment possible. Serving on the State Council until his death in 1746, he was a mediating and enlightening influence. Always ready with thoughtful and kind words, even in his disagreements or admonitions, it was he to whom Yŏngjo turned for consolation and understanding.

But it was Cho Hyŏnmyŏng whom Yŏngjo respected and feared the most. The most intellectual of the three, yet deeply committed to activist ideals, he embodied the principled, dedicated, rational, and uncompromising Confucian official. Militarily active in the 1728 subjugation campaign, Cho served the central government in various capacities, becoming the Minister of the Right in 1740 and Prime Minister in 1750. While Pak Munsu was the king's emissary to the people, Cho was the Confucian conscience of the court. While Pak translated his impatience with injustice into action, Cho articulated the principles of justice. While Pak garnered popular support for the military tax reform, Cho worked out the details of the reform as the director of the Office of the Equal Military Tax.[121] Unlike Pak, who had a natural and instinctive affinity for the underdog, Cho's concern with the people arose from his strict sense of duty. In voicing their differences to the king, they were equally fearless but, where Pak was impetuous, Cho was rational. Unlike Song, whose compassion always led him to plead for minimal punishment, Cho insisted on the impartial and faithful application of the law. Yŏngjo regarded Cho's opinion as the barometer of Confucian principle. His esteem for Cho was such that nothing distressed him more than Cho's disapproval. In Yŏngjo's drive to clear his name his efforts were mainly expended in coming to terms with these three ministers.

In 1741, when Yŏngjo, spurred by the rebellious songs of 1739, had sought to clear his name, these three ministers had stood guard over the *t'angp'yŏng* policy. The court had roundly agreed to burn the transcripts of the 1722 purge, but there was some debate on how, in what would become the *Great Instruction*, to treat those Noron who had been implicated in the alleged plots to assassinate Kyŏngjong. Pak Munsu, Song Inmyŏng, and Cho Hyŏnmyŏng had all insisted that they be termed as rebels, while the Noron, led by the Prime Minister Kim Chaero, pressed for exoneration.[122] Yŏngjo's three ministers won, and the *Great Instruction* followed a general outline prepared by Cho Hyŏnmyŏng.

The destruction of the transcript of the 1722 purge and the promulgation of the *Great Instruction* succeeded in making Yŏngjo officially innocent, but it did not allay darker suspicions that he might have poisoned Kyŏngjong. Though this topic could only rarely be broached at court, and then only in so far as it had been a rallying cry for the rebels of 1728, it must have been a sore spot for Yŏngjo. To establish his innocence, however, Yŏngjo had to officially announce the cause of Kyŏngjong's death. But Kyŏngjong was said to have suffered an "unseemly" illness. This would have sullied the memory of a royal ancestor. This was why Yŏngjo had balked in the past. Worse still, this issue lay at the center of factional conflict. For if Kyŏngjong's illness were to be announced publicly, this would have implied a judgment on the Soron—that they had been cunning plotters manipulating a frail and ailing monarch. Indeed, it would have justified Yŏngjo's regency, which had precipitated the purge of 1722. It was this implication that had made such discussions impolitic in the years following the rebellion when the *t'angp'yŏng* policy was paramount. And it was one more reason why Yŏngjo hoped that the *Great Instruction* would lay questions of his innocence to rest.

These hopes, however, were misplaced. In 1745 rebellious posters appeared again. They were found in late October and the inquest lasted from November 1745 to April 1746. The culprits were, in the main, related to the rebels of 1728 and were, in fact, their next generation. Some suspects attributed their rebellious intentions to disappointment with the current political climate which, despite the *t'angp'yŏng* policy, did not allow them to transcend the past to attain official positions.[123]

The limitations of the *t'angp'yŏng* policy were clearly revealed in this complaint. It appeared that the exclusion of the extremist Soron from the bureaucracy was directly responsible for the continuing charges of regicide. But could they be accommodated? Yŏngjo apparently did not think so. What would the Noron reaction be? Just keeping the moderate Soron at court had required suppressing the bureaucratic voice. More than that, there were his own feelings of resentment and bitterness. He would rather confront Kyŏngjong's illness which would, hopefully, discredit the rebel charges of regicide.

But to do so required support from some quarter; and this would certainly not come from his three ministers. In fact, he was deeply concerned with parting from their position. No mean politicians themselves, the posters had alerted them to flaws in the *t'angp'yŏng* policy as it was practiced. Their response was to reaffirm and strengthen the policy so that it would be able to function as it should. Song Inmyŏng was quick to point out that, despite the *t'angp'yŏng* policy, power was perpetuated within a small group of favored individuals. The king might not be able to change the system but he might at least employ the next generation of extremist Soron, all from respectable families. Otherwise, Song warned, the *t'angp'yŏng* policy would be just a euphemism for closing doors to outsiders.[124] Gently but indefatigably, Song petitioned Yŏngjo to drop the distinction between extremist and moderate which had such polarizing effects.

While Song urged conciliatory measures, Cho Hyŏnmyŏng had requested that he, Cho, be relieved of office for his failure to help the king to maintain harmony and order. At first his memorials of resignation were pleading and guilty, but they grew critical and accusatory.[125] Yŏngjo could thus not turn to him for assistance.

161

Pak Munsu could never be counted upon to support measures that might weaken the Soron, and to turn to the fractiously partisan Noron would be catastrophic. Yŏngjo needed some new source of support, and he needed it badly. It should be someone respectable, neutral of factions and preferably an outsider. Precisely at this time, Pak P'ilchu appeared on the scene. Seventy-two years of age in 1746, a scholar of high repute and factionally neutral, he had served periodically in previous reigns. He was known for his predilection for a quiet and meditative life and his distaste for factional politics. He had briefly visited the court at Yŏngjo's behest to tutor his son in 1743. A relative of one of Hyojong's sons-in-law, he could claim high birth and a connection to the royal house.[126] His credentials made him a perfect candidate to suit Yŏngjo's needs.

While royal motives in summoning Pak are clear, it is harder to gauge just how Yŏngjo communicated his purpose or, for that matter, how Pak intuited the king's intentions. In any case, in an unusually cordial exchange of letters, Yŏngjo appointed Pak P'ilchu Minister of Personnel in April 1746. The letters reveal nothing.[127] But when Pak arrived at the court on July 12, he at once broached the question of Kyŏngjong's illness. He urged that a description of Kyŏngjong's illness be included in the *Great Instruction*. Yŏngjo was visibly excited and responded with an appreciative remark: "But for you, who would have dared to bring this up?"[128]

But this suggestion resulted in a predictable reaction in the bureaucracy—Noron demands for Soron punishment and Cho Hyŏnmyŏng and Pak Munsu's firm opposition. Pak P'ilchu subsequently left the court.[129] And, in respect for his three ministers' insistence that under no circumstance should a solemn decree such as the *Great Instruction* be tampered with, Yŏngjo settled for a separate pronouncement, which attributed Kyŏngjong's death to poor health.[130]

Suddenly in September, Song Inmyŏng died. He had until the last minute argued for an open door policy to the extremist Soron. Yŏngjo was grief-stricken. Still, he turned the situation to his advantage. He enacted the mild form of symbolic punishment for

Kyŏngjong's Soron ministers.[131] Out of respect for Cho Hyŏnmyŏng's sentiment, Yŏngjo accepted his resignation. His remark to Cho was, "though the measures I took this time were intended to allay the troubles of the world, I feel sad and ashamed when I see you."[132] Several weeks later, Yŏngjo awarded Cho Hyŏnmyŏng a citation for his "service of integrity."[133]

A period of loneliness and self-doubt awaited Yŏngjo. Though he had been cautious in clearing his name, he was troubled by the compromise he had made with his ideals. After all, in publicly discussing Kyŏngjong's health and dishonoring his ministers, Yŏngjo had done more than diminish the *t'angp'yŏng* policy; he had approached the limits imposed by the demands of filial piety for his predecessor. Song Inmyŏng was dead and Cho Hyŏnmyŏng, who rejected service on the State Council but remained at court as a minister without portfolio, was a constant reminder of failure. Perhaps to compensate for this, Yŏngjo frantically engaged in self-improvement—he read late into the night, wrote on his daily toils, and was obsessed with frugality. Simultaneously he became progressively more autocratic to protect the *t'angp'yŏng* policy from total collapse. Opponents of the policy, taking advantage of the departure of its supporters, openly discussed its uselessness. To Yŏngjo's dismay, they quoted Song Inmyŏng out of context, citing his remark that the policy only benefited a small group.[134]

This was not a happy time for the officials either. None of the groups, neither the Noron nor the Soron nor the supporters of the *t'angp'yŏng* policy, was untroubled. Yŏngjo's increasingly overbearing manner made them reluctant to appear at court. Censors, especially, who took the brunt of royal repression, were frequently absent.[135]

By the summer of 1747, after twenty-three years on the throne, Yŏngjo seems to have felt genuinely weary of his role. On July 29, in an audience with his ministers, Yŏngjo confessed to a longing for a rest from the burden of administration. Pleading feeble health and mental inertia, he begged them to accept a proposal to appoint his son a regent. While offering sympathy, they insisted that he continue.[136] Two days later, Yŏngjo brought the same proposal to Cho Hyŏnmyŏng in private. Cho offered scant satisfaction.[137] Failing to obtain official approval, Yŏngjo retreated to his private quarters for a while, pleading illness. Finally, in September, Cho Hyŏnmyŏng chided him for not appearing at the State Hall and for not being properly attired when he received officials. Yŏngjo admonished Cho for failing to understand his distress and for speaking of his impropriety. But later he remarked that "Since I know that he spoke out of affection for the ruler, I forgive him."[138]

Through this exchange, however, Yŏngjo and Cho Hyŏnmyŏng came to an understanding that they both had to get back to work in earnest. There were important tasks awaiting them. By October, Cho Hyŏnmyŏng was back on the State Council. Soon, Cho spoke of the necessity of reforming the military tax. Pak Munsu was recalled and, by May 1748, was appointed Minister of Taxation. The preparation of the equal military tax occupied these three until it was finalized several years later.

Still, 1748 was not a happy year for Yŏngjo. In April, rebellious posters reappeared at the palace gates. Their origin remained a mystery.[139] The appearance of these posters shattered Yŏngjo's hopes that his mention of Kyŏngjong's poor health in the 1746 pronouncement would effectively put a stop to this type of challenge. Then Yŏngjo suffered a personal tragedy. In July, his beloved daughter Princess Hwap'yŏng died. Grieved over his daughter's death, he ceased attending state affairs and moved back to Ch'angdŏk Palace.[140] It was closer to his daughter's house, and he could easily oversee funeral arrangements there. By early 1749, his desire to escape his duty seems to have overwhelmed him.

On March 9, 1949, Yŏngjo promulgated an edict of abdication:

Unable to disobey the instructions of three royal ancestors, we have occupied the throne. Yet, we have not enjoyed it even one day of the last twenty-five years. Each day, we waited for the prince to grow. Now fortunately, he has reached fifteen *se*. This decision is based on three considerations. First, we want to have the face to greet the royal brother on our return to the nether world. Second, we want to follow our desire to leave the throne. Third, our health has been poor

164

since the *kapcha* year (1744). It is difficult to improve one's health overnight and therefore, we wish to look after our health relieved of our duties.[141]

This edict of course caused a furor. Prince Sado and the officials all wept, begging for retraction. Eventually, Yŏngjo conceded to a regency for his son.[142] Now, Sado was the regent. And he became an official agent of his father's hopes and despairs and the vessel of his apprehension over Kyŏngjong.

CHAPTER 5

Yŏngjo's Tragedy:
The Prince of Mournful Thoughts

> . . . let us sit upon the ground
> And tell sad stories of the death of kings!
> How some have been deposed, some
>   slain in war,
> Some haunted by the ghosts they have
>   deposed,
> Some poisoned by their wives, some
>   sleeping killed—
> All murdered; for within the hollow
>   crown
> That rounds the mortal temples of a
>   king
> Keeps Death his court; and there the
>   antic sits,
> Scoffing his state and grinning at his
>   pomp; . . .
>
> —Shakespeare, *Richard II*

THE GREAT KING OF THE RICE CHEST

Sado's regency ended in a sealed rice chest thirteen years after it began. This then was where Yŏngjo's hopes were laid to rest. For on July 4, 1762, Yŏngjo confined his son to a chest to suffocate and die. Sado was at the time twenty-eight years of age, and Yŏngjo was sixty-nine with no other son. This was the only public execution of an heir apparent by a reigning father in Yi history.

Sado's tragedy encapsulates the contradictions of Yŏngjo and his reign: Yŏngjo, one of the greatest kings, resorted to filicide, of

166

which no other Yi king was guilty; he was obsessed with rule by virtue, yet violated the basic tenets of Confucian humanism; he insisted on being a father to his people, yet killed his own son; he struggled to silence suspicions of fraternal regicide, yet turned irrevocably to filicide; and, though valiantly dedicated to a policy to end bloody purges, he snuffed out the life of his own son Sado, groomed from birth to fulfill a dynastic mission, but who died to safegu ird that selfsame mission.

If this incident is easily recognized as the dramatic climax of Yŏngjo's reign, the driving furies behind the tragedy cannot be apprehended so simply. Indeed, what did lead Yŏngjo to kill his only son? To answer this requires extreme caution. For one thing, Sado is a legend. The sadness of the event and the gruesomeness of the execution captured the Korean imagination, which sees Sado as a victim of the ruthlessly self-serving power seekers surrounding his father.[1] As the "Great King of the Rice Chest" (*Twiju taewang*), even today Sado reigns supreme over the tragic domain in the popular imagination. Thus, one truly does have to distinguish fact from legend.

Then there are modern scholarly views. These are split roughly into two groups. In what can be called the historical view, the whole incident is viewed from the perspective of factional and political strife. A typical proponent argues that differences in political and factional sympathies created the incident.[2] Viewing it as ancillary to factional conflict, this school has produced no study of the incident. The other group sees the event as the culmination of a personality conflict. This is a more literary approach. Its adherents use as their source *A Journal Written in Leisure* (*Hanjungnok*), a memoir written by Sado's wife, Lady Hong of Hyegyŏng Palace (Hyegyŏnggung Hong Ssi). One article, for instance, attempts a Freudian analysis based on Lady Hong's journal. It goes so far as to suggest that "the rumor from the inner palace," which was decisive in Yŏngjo's final decision, might have been that Sado was guilty of incest with his sister, Princess Hwawŏn, Yŏngjo's most favored daughter.[3]

None of the these views is entirely without merit, but each focuses on only one aspect of the incident. It may be quite satisfying to explain the incident entirely in terms of psychological conflict or political strife, but where in Yŏngjo's reign was the line between political force and psychological compulsion so clearly drawn? We need a more comprehensive picture, if only to do justice to the actors in this drama who, struggling valiantly in all their fallibility, played out this tragedy which scarred them to the least player.

Bafflement mounts when we find that the official historiography, departing from its usual comprehensiveness, is laconic and circumspect in approaching the incident. For one thing, portions of the *Records of the Royal Secretariat* (*Sŭngjŏngwŏn ilgi*) dealing with Sado were destroyed. This would otherwise be the most complete record of the king's and the regent's public activities. The destruction was done at Chŏngjo's (r. 1776–1800) request in 1776, a month before Yŏngjo's death.[4] Chŏngjo was Sado's son. At the age of eleven, he witnessed his father's death and he eventually was to devote a great deal of attention to clearing his father's name. This was his duty as a Confucian monarch and Yŏngjo would have understood it. Given Yŏngjo's[5] and Chŏngjo's[6] extreme zeal in preserving historical documents, one is tempted to speculate that the deleted portion contained material quite damaging to Sado. Lady Hong suggests as much in her journal. In any case, the destruction virtually barred details of Sado's behavior from inclusion in the *Sillok*, since the *Records of the Royal Secretariat* was a major source in compiling it. Certain restraints under which the compilers labored, like the taboo on unseemly behavior of members of the royal family, further affected the *Sillok*. At any rate, though it is somewhat more informative than the *Royal Secretariat*, the *Sillok* is generally oblique where Sado is concerned. For example, it does not explicitly say that Yŏngjo had his son killed.

One need not despair, however. Yi historians were nothing, if not historically minded. In the *Sillok*, they did leave suggestions and allusions for those willing to disentangle them. Of course they must be used in conjunction with other sources. In the official historiographical tradition, there are the countless memorials sent to Yŏngjo and Sado, the *Records of the Crown Prince Office* (*Seja*

168

tonggung ilgi), and records of various kinds. There are also private writings by Sado's contemporaries, including Lady Hong. If Lady Hong, writing under conflicting allegiances thirty years after the incident, is frequently less than candid, she does offer valuable insights. Then there are the "wild histories" (*yasa*). While extreme caution is required in using them, they are at times rather revealing, if only of contemporary views and later myths. Lastly, an obscure journal kept by Yi Kwanghyŏn, a royal secretary, who witnessed the execution, survives. With a historian's meticulousness, Yi records the details of Sado's last days.

Of course, even with the help of this formidable array of sources, a definitive explanation of the incident remains elusive. In history, as in life, truth escapes entrapment. Yi Kwanghyŏn acknowledges this in the concluding sentence of his journal. Nonetheless, it is possible to formulate a working hypothesis by piecing together information from available accounts.

The picture that emerges is indeed complex and terrifying. If the tensions of eighteenth-century Korea were crystallized in Yŏngjo, Yŏngjo's conflicts found their most virulent expression in his attitude toward Sado. Sado was the vessel for Yŏngjo's yearning for sage kingship and his desires for vindication. These conflicting needs had led Yŏngjo to seek escape through Sado, but for Sado there was only death. For few sons could have satisfied either of these demands and none could have fulfilled both. Sado too sought escape, first in insanity, then through travels in disguise, and eventually through attempting annihilation of the very object from which he wished to escape—the image of his father. In the end, the only escape for him was extinction in a sealed chest of forty *ch'ŏk*.

HOPE ETERNAL, HOPE INCHOATE

My ancestor's line was about to be extinguished but now it will continue. Fortunately, I now have the face to meet my ancestors. My happiness is indeed great![7]

169

Thus exuberantly did Yŏngjo greet Sado's birth on February 13, 1735. Lady Yi (Yi Yŏngbin) of Sŏnhŭi Palace, who had long since enjoyed royal affection and had already given him several daughters, finally gave birth to a son. Euphoria enveloped the court. The next few days were spent in exchanging congratulations, promulgating amnesties, and performing sacrifices to celebrate the occasion. At the age of forty-two, Yŏngjo at last had an heir. And it was as an undisputed heir that Sado's life progressed. In September 1735, Yi Chae, a celebrated Noron scholar, Chŏng Chedu, a renowned Wang Yang-ming scholar, and Yi Chinmyŏng, who had been Yŏngjo's own tutor, were appointed as head tutors in the Guidance Office of the Primary Prince (*Wŏnja poyangch'ŏng*).[8] This was the first step in establishing Sado as an heir apparent. His formal designation followed in April of the next year. Fourteen months old at the time, Sado was the youngest heir apparent in Yi history.[9] Sado was housed in the crown prince's residence, which was located within the same palace precinct as, but was separate from, his father's and mother's quarters. It consisted of several buildings, one for daytime use, a sleeping quarter, one for holding lecture sessions, and others intended for his family such as his wife and children, when the time came. The Crown Prince Tutorial Office (*Seja sigangwŏn*) and the Crown Prince Protection Office (*Seja igwisa*) were situated in proximity. Nine ladies-in-waiting and several tens of eunuchs who held varying palace rank served him. About seventy to ninety slaves, most of them male, belonged to his establishment. There were fourteen military guards in the Crown Prince Protection Office, who escorted him by turns. When Sado was eight years old, thirteen full-time tutors were appointed as his instructional staff at the Crown Prince Tutorial Office, and he began his formal studies with them.[10]

After Sado's capping ceremony, Yŏngjo, in September of 1743, initiated a search for a wife for his son. After three months of screening, he chose a daughter of Hong Ponghan of the illustrious P'ungsan Hong clan. Ministers were dispatched to Lady Hong to announce the formal decision. In his own writing, Yŏngjo welcomed her and cautioned her. As the wife of the heir apparent and the foundation of the nation's future, she should be a source of myriad blessings. Hence, it was of the utmost importance that she should always support her husband with her virtue.[11] On February 23, 1744, the wedding took place at Ŭidong Palace. A week later, Yŏngjo, accompanied by the newlywed couple, both ten years old, ceremonially announced the marriage to the ancestral temple, completing the five-month royal wedding.[12]

From early 1745, Sado's studies expanded. In addition to reading with his tutors, he now participated in lecture and discussion sessions provided by the Crown Prince Tutorial Office. By the time Sado was appointed a regent in 1749, none of the details of his preparation as a future monarch had been neglected. The regency seemed, at least superficially, a continuation of his smooth progression toward the throne. At the age of fifteen, he was perhaps a trifle young but nonetheless he was an adult by the standards of that society. He consummated his nuptials with Lady Hong this year, for instance.[13] In every way, Sado was exceptionally well qualified for the role he was about to assume.

Perhaps so, but appearance and reality are too often distinct. As the future monarch, Sado was future hope incarnate. If the common hope conjoined wishes for a virtuous and able king, individual hopes depended on political and ideological standing and determined distinct and different expectations. The supporters of the *t'angp'yŏng* policy looked to him to inherit and perfect the policy.[14] Factional officials hoped for his eventual sympathies. Indeed, on his day of birth, Pak Munsu had counseled Yŏngjo to enforce the *t'angp'yŏng* policy to assure dynastic integrity for the newborn prince.[15] In any case, the young prince was soon an object of lavish attentions. When Sado was about four months old, Yŏngjo brought him to an audience with his ministers. Two tufts of hair sprang out from a black cap. In a robe of blue silk, and a girdle of red, Sado lay in the arms of a palace attendant. When the infant prince made a valiant attempt to stand grasping a table, the ministers all joined in praising him as the child of Heaven. Everyone present from Min Chinwŏn down took turns in asking Yŏngjo for permission to hold the child. Permission, of course, was granted by the proud father.[16]

Very soon, Sado was praised for scholarly precocity and moral virtue. At three, Sado was asked by Yŏngjo to display his reading and writing ability. Sado chose the *Classic of Filial Piety* (*Hsiao-ching*) and recognized the characters for King Wen. Then, upon his father's urging, he wrote. With a brush rather large in his hand, he wrote what were taken to be characters for Heaven, Earth, king, and spring. The ministers present all exclaimed over the prince's intelligence and asked for the paper on which he wrote.[17] At about this time, he is said to have refused a cookie decorated with engravings of hexagrams. This was taken to mean that, at this tender age, he was respectful of venerable symbols.[18] This type of episode continued to occur throughout his childhood. His performance thus began in the public eye and was watched with bated breath by a hovering and anxious court.

The most intensely hopeful observer was, of course, his father. But with these hopes came equally intense anxieties. And as is often the case with an anxious and hopeful parent, Yŏngjo's expectations were, to say the least, unrealistic and even contradictory. We know that Yŏngjo sought in Sado, unbeknownst to the young prince, the miracle of vindication for the charge of regicide without jeopardizing the *t'angp'yŏng* policy. While this in some way required dealing with factional issues, Yŏngjo was passionately opposed to letting his son know about them.[19] When Sado asked what factionalism was on one occasion, Yŏngjo thundered that there was no need for him to know about it.[20]

One cannot say that Yŏngjo did not harbor secret hopes that his son would someday dishonor the Soron for the humiliations his father had suffered.[21] Effected by Sado, punishment of the Soron would be filial piety. Done with the proper concern for political repercussions, it could accomplish what Yŏngjo could not. But even to obliquely suggest this to his son was unimaginable to Yŏngjo. Moral perfectionist that he was, his son should be nothing less than a latter-day sage king. His son was to vindicate him by sheer force of moral authority, not through devious revenge.

With characteristic thoroughness, Yŏngjo set about making his son into a sage king. With regularity, the official historiography mentions Yŏngjo's blandishments. He chose books and tutors with meticulous care. He lectured the tutors on the necessity of teaching the principles of propriety and morality in addition to the classics. And he also frequently intervened personally in his son's education. He quizzed the prince on passages from the classics, composed numerous instructions on virtuous rule, and lectured on the brilliant accomplishments of the sage kings.[22]

At first Sado seems to have responded quite well to his father's attentions, according to the somewhat formulaic rhetorical praise of royal precocity in the official historiography. He was always ready with the right answers and always serious in manner. In fact, throughout his childhood, his brilliance and industriousness were never in doubt.[23] The only voice of apprehension was that of Yŏngjo who, in 1743, expressed concern that the prince was too earnest and unbending and asked the tutor Yi Chongsŏng to mitigate this quality.[24]

This uniform praise for Sado continued until early 1746. In February, he was said to have worked hard despite illness.[25] In April, he was answering questions well enough to please his father.[26] But sometime around late 1746, the entries on Sado change their tone subtly but unmistakably. One day in October, Sado could not clarify the meaning of a passage from a book. Yŏngjo scolded him, saying that he should not be ashamed of consulting his attendant.[27] After this, Sado answered fewer and fewer questions. This elicited successively harsher admonitions from Yŏngjo. Eventually, in December 1748, the king was so angry at this son's sloth that he put his tutors under censure.[28] Yŏngjo also summoned Sado at one point to tell him that thunder on the previous night was a warning that he should develop moral virtue.[29] At about this time, Pak P'ilchu, whom Yŏngjo had invited as a tutor, resigned because of the futility of teaching the prince.[30] In January 1749, Cho Hyŏnmyŏng, then serving as the Minister of the Left, spoke to the king about the importance of guiding the heir apparent.[31] As this implied that something had gone awry in Yŏngjo's dealings with Sado, we can be quite certain that serious problems had appeared.

Sado's difficulties had begun much earlier, according to Lady Hong, Sado's wife. In *A Journal Written in Leisure*, Lady Hong attributes it to the physical separation between father and son which had been effected very early in Sado's life. In his eagerness to set his son up in the crown prince's establishment, Yŏngjo had moved Sado to a separate residence complete with lecture halls when he was about three months old, even before his appointment as heir apparent. This new residence, located as it was rather far from those of Yŏngjo and Lady Yi, Sado's mother, made it difficult for them to spend as much time with the prince as they might have otherwise.

Moreover, this residence had been occupied by Queen Sŏnŭi, Kyŏngjong's widow, until her death in 1730. The ladies-in-waiting who would serve the prince had served Kyŏngjong and his queen. According to Lady Hong, this arrangement was quite damaging. The primary loyalties of these servants of Kyŏngjong and his queen were with their former master and mistress. They were rather arrogant with the new king and outright contemptuous of Lady Yi who, as was usual with secondary royal consorts, was of rather humble origins. Lady Hong surmises that this haughty attitude caused Sado's parents to visit their son less frequently than they might have. She blames Yŏngjo for short-sightedness in retaining these ladies.

In any case, Sado was left almost entirely to the care of these ladies-in-waiting who, in Lady Hong's view, preferred indulgence to discipline. One in particular, Lady Han, taught Sado military games with toy weapons. Naturally this caught the child's fancy. Pampered by his attendants and neglected by his parents, the prince turned more to games than to his studies. Knowing that he was not doing what was expected of him, Sado began to fear his father. The result was a barrier between Yŏngjo and Sado.[32]

Though these events took place before she entered Sado's life and she recounts them with some uncertainty, Lady Hong is nonetheless revealing. Certainly, Yŏngjo's haste in providing Sado with the formal grandeur appropriate to his status is conspicuous. This must, at least in part, be attributed to a desire to spare Sado of all too familiar questions of legitimacy. Though Yŏngjo successfully resisted ministerial suggestions that Sado be formally adopted by his legal consort, Queen Chŏngsŏng, from whom he had long been estranged, Lady Yi's rather humble origins must have contributed to his obsessive concern with the details of his son's upbringing.

But still Yŏngjo was delivering Sado over to his brother's cohorts. Given his considerable desire to neutralize suspicions that he had murdered his brother, one cannot but wonder if, in this, he was attempting to demonstrate his loyalty to Kyŏngjong. Otherwise, why choose Queen Sŏnŭi's residence, and why retain her and her husband's ladies-in-waiting for Sado, despite their attitudes? In this sense, Yŏngjo seems, quite unwittingly, to have relinquished his son to Kyŏngjong. Perhaps with benefit of hindsight, contemporary sources often refer to a striking resemblance between Kyŏngjong and Sado. Several sources recount that Yi Kwangjwa dreamt that Sado was in fact a reincarnation of Kyŏngjong.[33] If this sounds apocryphal, it is not farfetched to imagine that these ladies-in-waiting probably represented Kyŏngjong to Sado in a sympathetic light.

Be that as it may, the prince's arrangements did cause some concern. In an entry of 1740, for instance, the *Sillok* contains a memorial by a tutor on the unwholesome and dangerous effects of indulgent and careless attendants.[34] Lady Hong says that Yŏngjo did dismiss Lady Han in 1741, but that the situation remained fundamentally unchanged. After all, ladies-in-waiting had no authority over the price, and they probably gave into his whims.

Lady Hong furnishes an account of the deteriorating relationship between father and son. Once he began to fear his father, Sado became tongue-tied and hesitant in his presence. This worried Yŏngjo, and rather than responding gently, he became harsh and disparaging. Predictably, Sado's difficulties merely intensified. Soon after her marriage, Lady Hong noticed that the prince delayed dressing in the morning as much as possible to put off confronting his father. Attributing a part of the conflict to personality differences—Yŏngjo was quick and observant, Sado was slow and reticent—she gives Yŏngjo's severity as the underlying cause for Sado's behavior. She was also somewhat put off by the strict code of behavior at the court which required a young prince of ten to bow prostrate to his father and to call himself "your servant" (*sin*) in conversation with him. In any case, as early as 1745, she noted rather sinister developments in Sado's personality.[35]

These observations seem to ring true. With his exacting standards, Yŏngjo must have been an extremely demanding father. As a king whose preparation for the throne came late and with great difficulty, he might have been displaying something of the harshness of the self-made man. It is not unreasonable to imagine that he was hard put to sympathize with a son who seemed to be making so little of the very opportunities that had been denied to him. His belief in discipline and moral rigor, in this case, was no help.

The *Sillok*, indeed, documents the continuing deterioration. On December 12, 1747, while Yŏngjo was routinely quizzing Sado, the young prince appears to be making an oblique criticism of his father:

YŏNGJO: Of all Han emperors, who was the most eminent?
SADO: I think it was Wen-ti.
YŏNGJO: Why don't you praise Kao-ti?
SADO: It is because Wen-ti's and Ching-ti's reigns were most splendid.
YŏNGJO: I would have thought, considering your personality, that you would like Wu-ti and yet you prefer Wen-ti. Why?
SADO: Though Wu-ti was quick and keen, he was in many respects too hasty and coarse.

Yŏngjo requested a clarification of this remark. Sado responded evasively, and his father chose to see this as ineptness. Yŏngjo responded with a long lecture evaluating merits of various Han emperors and he ended by admonishing Sado to work harder.[36]

The exchange is shot through with an inexplicable undercurrent of tension and conflict. Inexplicable, that is, unless each sensed a certain parallel between Yŏngjo and Wu-ti. In any case, what should have been a simple study session seems more like a suppressed quarrel. And it was in just such an atmosphere of oblique acrimony that Sado became regent in 1749.

176

THE TWO COURTS OF CH'ANGDŎK PALACE

Procedurally, Sado's regency was based on that of Kyŏngjong, who had been appointed regent in 1717, three years before Sukchong's death.[37] The regent could administer and make decisions except for appointments, punishments, and the use of troops. In these matters, the king retained direct control. The regent was also to confer with the king and to obtain his approval in matters of special importance. The king reserved the right to veto any of the regent's decisions. The regent would be treated as a ruler, however. Officials would refer to themselves as "your servant" (*sin*) in addressing him.[38]

On the day of enactment, both the king and the new regent were appropriately solemn. Yŏngjo composed an admonitory piece, the *Instructions on Rule* (*Chŏnghun*),[39] for the occasion. He exhorted the regent to cultivate his moral nature, to honor the worthy, to be affectionate to kin, to be respectful of ministers, to be considerate of officials, to care for the people as if they were his children, to encourage artisans, to be kind to strangers, to be wary of dissension and debauchery, to be strict with palace attendants, and so on. After this was read, Sado, prostrate, pledged devotion. He would heed the sacred instruction and would strive for peace and happiness. Pleased, Yŏngjo requested the cooperation of his officials and warned them against factional dispute and extortion of the powerless, which could reduce the country to barbarism.[40]

The ministers were more apprehensive. To begin with, a regency contained an implicit tension. Unlike a clear-cut abdication, power was not completely transferred. Thus officials would only reluctantly agree to a regency when, like Kyŏngjong's, it was an apprenticeship for the heir apparent in the last years of an enfeebled king. Sado's regency was enacted under this rhetoric, but Yŏngjo, at fifty-six, was neither feeble nor eager to relinquish power. He did not see Sado's regency as a transition. Rather it was a tool of governance to complement, expand and, ultimately, to perfect his rule. And this is why Cho Hyŏnmyŏng, fearing conflict, cautioned the prince to always consult the king before making decisions.[41]

But even this advice would prove inadequate. Recently, the burden of rule had weighed heavily on Yŏngjo. He was under pressure to clear his name, but could not imperil the *t'angp'yŏng* policy. Thus, more bureaucratic confrontation and moral compromise seemed to lie ahead. Indeed, in discussing these problems with a minister in 1749, he had complained that "the way of the world" was nearly driving him mad.[42] More immediately, there was the equal military tax, a lifelong project. He was determined to complete the reform, and correctly perceived that it would require his undivided attention and energy. Thus he had turned to Sado in genuine need, seeking solutions to his thorniest problems.

Within a year of the regency, Yŏngjo, in rapid succession, transferred to Sado most of the functions he had originally intended to fill himself. In July, he commanded Sado to preside over the biannual evaluation of officials. In September, he announced that he would no longer participate in audiences. Originally, the regent was to hold four of six monthly audiences (*ch'adae*), and the king and the regent would jointly hold the remaining two. In November, Yŏngjo ordered that military affairs be taken care of by the regent.[43]

Officials protested vigorously, maintaining that the gulf between Yŏngjo and his officials, which had been caused by suppression of the bureaucratic voice, would widen further. Moreover, thrusting too great a burden on the young prince so soon might overwhelm him. Yŏngjo was adamant. He insisted that the regency had been enacted for this very purpose—to share the labors of rule.[44] In delegating so much responsibility to Sado, Yŏngjo really was seeking a way out of his predicament. He must have hoped that, in spite of his poor performance in recent years, actual responsibility would call forth some untapped reserves in Sado's character.

Unrealistic as Yŏngjo's expectations may have been, it was not so much the expectations as his failure to adequately communicate them that would have such dire consequences. True, Sado faced difficult issues in a difficult situation. But still, with a careful division of labor, father and son might have devised a more fruitful approach to rule. One can imagine Sado expeditiously dealing with charges of Yŏngjo's regicide and Yŏngjo blithely enforcing the *t'angp'yŏng* policy all the while. This certainly would have loosed official clamor and protest directed at them jointly and separately. But even this could have been weathered with a prior agreement and firm trust and understanding between king and regent.

In essence, in order to use Sado effectively, Yŏngjo had to transcend his role, perhaps at the expense of his idea of kingship. True, he had brought up Sado hoping that he would be a latter-day sage king. But now, he had appointed his son as regent and entrusted him with power. Was he now to compromise his ideal even temporarily, by asking his son to vindicate him? No. This was impossible for Yŏngjo. For to do so would have been to appropriate the heir apparent as his private son. No matter how much he secretly hoped that his son would do this of his own accord, he could not succumb to his desires as a private father by instructing him thus. This would have negated the raison d'être of the very throne to which Sado was heir. Sado, the heir apparent, was the king's public son, and public son he would remain.

Nor could Sado hope to play the private son on his own initiative. The moral considerations that made it impossible for Yŏngjo to communicate his private desires to Sado also made it impossible for Sado to attempt to satisfy his father's desire. The Confucian emphasis on paradigm and harmony demanded that the regent-son emulate the king's policies in each detail. Nothing less than Yŏngjo's explicit instructions would have justified the regent's taking a course that might contradict the king's public stance. Thus Sado could not contravene the *t'angp'yŏng* policy without Yŏngjo's expressed wish. And since Yŏngjo constantly expounded upon the dangers of factionalism, Sado had no choice but to pursue a course clearly consistent with the *t'angp'yŏng* policy. Thus, the moral restraints under which Yŏngjo and Sado labored as public men effectively eliminated the possibility of their communicating as private father and son.

Yŏngjo and Sado presided over separate courts, each constrained by morality and custom, each uneasy with his power and uncertain of his role. These courts now unfolded into the turbulence of politics. The first years of the 1750s were among the stormiest of Yŏngjo's reign. The equal military tax reform had been concluded in 1751. It had brought its share of passionate protest. But Yŏngjo had anticipated this, and his commitment to the reform was such that he could weather it with ease. But in this period, he further encountered political and factional tensions in their more extreme manifestations. In 1755, Yŏngjo resorted to more ruthless measures than he had before. The accompanying trials were, needless to say, of a new nature and magnitude. Against this background, conflict between Yŏngjo and Sado intensified.

The patterns of political confrontation were all too familiar. In early 1750, Yŏngjo posthumously removed several Noron from the criminal register. They were persons purged in 1722 under the accusation that they had participated in the Kyŏngjong assassination plot.[45] This was followed by inevitable censorial demands for further sanctions against the Soron. In March 1751, the Censor-General Yi Chonjung championed this cause. In August, he was seconded by Min Paeksang, Min Chinwŏn's grandson. Yŏngjo banished them for violating the *Great Instruction*.[46] This triggered a cycle of official protest, followed by royal punishment which lasted for nearly two years. Indeed, during this period, Yŏngjo seems to have been dismissing and banishing officials either en masse or individually almost daily. Officials were less content in service than ever. Chŏng Hwiryang, Minister of the Right, for instance, wrote 103 times to obtain permission to resign.[47] Before they left, either for their homes or their places of banishment, these officials criticized Yŏngjo for repressing the bureaucratic voice, while the king charged them with factional misconduct. When Yi Ch'ŏnbo, Minister of the Right, criticized the king in August 1752 for burning censorial memorials, the king retorted that they were not memorials of admonition but memorials of factional defense. By December, realizing that some gesture of support for the *t'angp'yŏng* policy was necessary, Yŏngjo posthumously rehabilitated one Soron minister who had been dishonored.[48]

The battle may have seemed familiar, but there was something new in it. There was the regent. He had been an embodiment of hope; now that he held real power, the entire court turned to him for mediation. Official demands were explicit. After Yŏngjo banished Yi Chonjung in March 1751, for instance, the Censorate memorialized Sado. Royal obstruction of the censorial voice had a discouraging effect on morale. Sado should press the king to rescind Yi's punishment. Sado refused.[49] Yŏngjo's expectations, on the other hand, went uncommunicated. Even if the officials had urged Sado to vindicate his father, their advice, coming as it would have from obviously interested parties, would have been suspect. This left Sado at a loss. He knew that his behavior was unsatisfactory to his father—Yŏngjo's disapproval said as much. But Sado was unable to devise a solution. As acrimony at court grew, so did his discomfort. In December 1752, he could no longer contain himself. He remarked that, in the four years of his regency, he had been unable to ease his father's burden. To show his desolation, he refused medical attention. He did manage to punish several officials who had defended several victims of Yŏngjo's wrath,[50] but this had no visible effect. Soon, there was a general agreement that the regency was not a source of mediation but rather a one of further division. Yi Ch'ŏnbo, for instance, in mid-1752, spoke of the inconvenience and superfluity of maintaining two courts.[51]

FILIAL PIETY, THE HOPE THAT FAILED

Yŏngjo was openly disappointed in Sado, and his displeasure must have been noticed by others. The Prime Minister, Kim Chaero, as early as August 1752, counseled the king to be a little more gentle with his son; the regent was always looking up to his father, trying his best to please him.[52] Worse, the king was suspicious that the regent might become an agent of official protest, which of course further hindered Sado from taking any action. This might have prompted Yŏngjo to end the regency; instead it deepened his commitment to transferring power to his son. He thought that, freed of restrictions, his son might be able to vindicate him. Now Yŏngjo looked to his son with an equal measure of high expectation and bitter disappointment.

If this lay beneath nearly all their encounters it became quite

181

explicit in early 1753. Toward the end of 1752, Yŏngjo learned, to his immense chagrin, that the rumor that he had poisoned his brother was being whispered through the court. When and why this rumor was revived or how it reached Yŏngjo are unclear but it upset him enough to unleash one of his extraordinary outbursts. For several weeks Yŏngjo expressed his distress through his refusal to take medicine, his unwillingness to return to the palace from visits to his daughter's house,[53] and his flat refusal to allow his officials to plan for his fifty-ninth birthday. To accept such celebration when he was faced with this evil rumor would be, he declared, extremely "unfilial" to his deceased brother Kyŏngjong.[54]

On January 11, 1753, he finally spoke of his decision to abdicate. It was a cold and snowy day and the king went to a courtyard, and sat there. Ministers came running. Pak Munsu, pointing out that the royal order was not something officials could comply with, asked for his reason for it. His answer was: "Only when I take off this robe [of the king], will my heart be revealed." He continued, "If I had remained Prince Yŏning, then I would not have had this pain. If I don't take this robe off, with what face could I greet my royal brother upon my death?" Prince Sado came and, prostrate, pleaded for revocation of the order. Yŏngjo replied: "You simply don't understand my mind. T'aejo abdicated to Chŏngjong. . . . Now I want to do this in accordance with precedents set by our ancestors. If you want to set your father's mind at ease, then you had better let me change this robe to that of an ordinary person." All present objected and finally Kim Sangno, Minister of the Right, said: "Even if your servants might not be worthy of consideration, please at least take pity on the heir apparent." Yŏngjo said: "I'd rather choose to be an unloving father. It's simply unbearable to remain unfilial to my predecessor." When everything failed, Queen Dowager Inwŏn interceded. Her dozen or more handwritten messages appealing to his sense of filial piety not to cause her immense anxiety finally induced him to relent.[55]

These scenes might be by now familiar—Yŏngjo's threats of abdication, the prince's and ministers' entreaties and the queen dowager's parental pleas to which he had to succumb. What is new in this episode and what continued for another fortnight or so was his persistent return to the theme of filial piety. On the 12th, regretting that he had succumbed to Queen Dowager Inwŏn's entreaties against abdication, Yŏngjo said: "Yesterday, I missed a good chance. Long ago, Han Seryang observed that there were neither two suns in the sky nor two kings in one country. Isn't the regent a king? After the abdication, one palace cannot accommodate two masters. Therefore, I should leave and find another place outside." Two days later, Yŏngjo made a seemingly strange request. He wanted to hear a poem from the *Book of Odes*. The poem, "Thick grows that tarragon" (*Lu wo*) was reputedly written by a filial son in contemplation of his parents.[56] He read the poem. Then he reiterated his view that in his present predicament, there was no way to prove that he had not been covetous of the throne other than to relinquish it. The frustrated Pak Munsu, in his usual outspoken manner, accused the king of using this threat because he knew that ministers could not, as his subjects, comply with it. No matter, the next day the same scene was repeated. He read the same poem on filial piety. Around 11 o'clock at night, Prince Sado came in. The king waved him away. Then, on second thought, he said to the prince: "I'll read a poem to you. If you cry, that proves your filial piety. For that I'll retract my order." Faced with this prospect, Sado indeed wept. While Yŏngjo was reading the poem, tears streamed down Sado's face. But this proved insufficient to cause Yŏngjo to revoke his decree of abdication. When his ministers insisted that he should, his fury was such that he ordered the banishment of all present, from the Prime Minister down to the royal secretaries.

On the 18th, it seemed as though Yŏngjo really would abdicate. He had already retracted many of the punitive measures he had taken in the last two years. All of the officials he had banished were released. Now he went to a city gate and apologized to crowds congregated there for the small benefits his thirty-year rule had brought. Then he went to the shrine of his mother, Lady Ch'oe, to perform a ritual. Afterwards, he handed to a royal secretary an edict that said he intended to obtain the queen dowager's permission to abdicate and that he would enact it according to precedent. The royal secretary declared that he would die before complying with the royal order. Other ministers began to wail. The king turned to his soldiers and bid them farewell. Everyone cried. The king, shedding tears, left for Ch'angŭi Palace, and locked himself in.

It was now a time of memorials. Sado walked a part of the way to Ch'angŭi Palace and sent in the first memorial:

> From the time your ten thousand times, a hundred thousand times unfilial servant received appointment as a regent, morning and night, he has lived in mortal fear of error. Receiving now this order, beyond dreams or wildest imaginings, heart and gall plunge into the lower depths of abysses and chasms, and [your servant is driven to] a state of complete loss and dazzlement. Your servant is indeed unfilial and contemptible. Your servant faces yet another day unable to move and change the sagacious heart. This is truly your servant's crime, truly your servant's crime. Even though your servant wants [out of shame] to bore a hole in the ground and disappear into it he could not attain it. At the moment, sagacious rule is at its most bountiful, its influence having penetrated throughout the eight directions. Receiving this untenable order, this heart dissolves in fright and shatters in agitation. How can your servant, even for a minute, retreat [into his own residence]? Risking ten thousand deaths, your servant awaits punishment on a straw mat outside the gate, daring to cloud the sagacious heart. Your servant deserves death, deserves death. Humbly begging and wishing, out of sagacious consideration for the ancestral altar, the retraction of the order now at the Royal Secretariat.

Prostrate on the cold snowy ground, Prince Sado sent in countless memorials for three consecutive days, only to be rebuffed. To one of his pleas, the king's answer was:

> Even if Her Loving Majesty would come in person, it would be difficult to comply. How much less should I [be moved]

184

by you? The warmth of the *ondol*[57] is there but you let it go cold. Is this the way of a son? When you receive this message, you had better return immediately.

Another answer was:

I'd rather be an unloving father. It is unbearable to remain an unfilial descendant. Now cold air rises. You had better return immediately.

By this time, however, the pressure for retraction was mounting. Virtually everyone in office or, for that matter, out of office, including students, physicians, merchants, and Seoul residents, sent in joint memorials by groups. And of course, Queen Dowager Inwŏn announced her immanent departure to Ch'angŭi Palace, pleading her inability to sleep or to take food in the king's absence. Thus, this episode ended.

On January 22, Yŏngjo was seen outside of a palace gate asking the people about their problems. On the same day, he also heard from ministers about Sado's grief over the days past. The prince walked instead of using the palanquin; he awaited punishment prostrate in the snow-covered ground in the open air when he could have used a tent; he did not eat or drink, he cried continuously and whenever he saw an official, he asked for the best way to change his father's mind. Yŏngjo was moved by this tale of filial piety. He shed tears and said, "Did the prince really behave like that?"[58]

What, then, was the meaning of Yŏngjo's concern with filial piety? This was not the murmuring of an aging monarch. Filial piety was a many-faceted thing. On one level, it clearly referred to his relationship to Kyŏngjong, which was held in the worst suspicion. Considering the importance of filial piety and loyalty to one's predecessor in a Confucian monarchy, it is not at all surprising that Yŏngjo reacted so vehemently to the charge of fraternal regicide. Faced with this charge, which had been discussed openly in his own court, he may even have been justified in feeling that he could not rule without an effective rebuttal. And yet, he was in his usual predicament. There was the factional implication that he had to contend with. But most of all, whatever he chose to do, he could not challenge his brother and predecessor.

And precisely in this, Sado could be of service. For Sado's primary loyalty was to his father and so he could, under the rhetoric of filial piety, posthumously punish Kyŏngjong's ministers and find a way to announce Yŏngjo's innocence. While this was a course riddled with unfilial implications for Yŏngjo, it would have been a filial one for Sado. Thus, filial piety in Sado would establish filial piety in Yŏngjo.

But now, while Yŏngjo could not press for vindication, he could press for virtue. Or so he hoped. Yŏngjo, the Confucian monarch, who wished to rule by virtue, could surely instruct his heir in virtue. And the public son could publicly gratify the private man. For by now, in Yŏngjo's mind, an act of vindication initiated by Sado had become the sure test of Sado's virtue as a public man, and a perfect solution to Yŏngjo's perennial dilemma.

Perfect, of course, only if Sado grasped his intention. But Sado did not. Ever hopeful, Yŏngjo returned again and again to filial piety in his instructions. If he quizzed Sado, he quizzed him on filial piety. And whenever he referred to historical anecdotes, to his own writings, or to the sage king Shun, the paragon of filial piety, Yŏngjo was talking about Sado's filial piety.[59] For vindication born of filial piety was the major thing, perhaps the only thing he wanted of his son.

But still Sado showed no indication that he grasped what his father had in mind. He appears to have been puzzled by his father's incessant references to filial piety, and increasingly frustrated at his inability to satisfy him.[60] Even if he suspected what his father had in mind, he had neither the means to verify it nor the courage to test it. More insecure and fearful than ever, Sado seems to have retreated into a state of near-complete passivity, verging on paralysis. He meekly tried to comply with the guidelines his father set forth in his *t'angp'yŏng* policy. He certainly could not conceive of reversing a decision made by his father. After all, no filial son could do so. Nor could he take any initiative. For instance, the followers of Song Siyŏl and Song Chun'gil, the patriarchs of the Noron, had long been pressing to have their mentors canonized at the Confucian temple. Approval of this request might have brought some satisfaction to Yŏngjo,[61] but Sado was too terrified to make a decision on such a weighty and sensitive matter. Not only did Sado lose the opportunity to prove himself, he lost all interest in his public function. He barely attended to routine matters, giving succinct and noncommittal answers to ministerial suggestions and advice.[62] His performance at study sessions rapidly declined.[63]

Yŏngjo attributed this silence and withdrawal to Sado's lack of virtue and filial piety. Never doubting that his demands could be understood by any filial son, Yŏngjo saw Sado's non-compliance as willful neglect. Disappointed, he rejected his son privately and denounced him publicly. Thus, Yŏngjo's emphasis on filial piety, so conspicuous since 1752, accompanied a growing harshness toward Sado. On Sado's nineteenth birthday in 1753, for example, citing the insolence of the regent's court, he dismissed several of Sado's tutors.[64] Soon he publicly admonished Sado for his unkempt clothing.[65] He also attributed official criticism to Sado's faults. In December 1754, for instance, Yŏngjo banished two censors who had made *ad hominem* attacks on the Prime Minister, Yi Ch'ŏnbo.[66] The Censor-General Sin Wi memorialized to Sado, protesting that this punishment was "unfair." When Yŏngjo read this he was incensed. Sin had insulted the king to the regent. He banished Sin. Still furious, the king declared that the true reason for this insolence lay in Sado's careless use of language. An attempt at appeasement only elicited what is described as an "unbearable" admonition. Helpless and terrified, Sado then sent a memorial begging to be relieved of the regency, citing his incompetence as the reason. The king's answer to Sado, who waited for it prostrate on the stone pavement, again contained "unbearable" phrases. Crying continuously, Sado lay prostrate till dawn.[67]

Yŏngjo's harshness toward Sado now became a matter of concern to the officials. Pak Munsu, for instance, broached the topic to the king. In March 1753, he gently advised Yŏngjo. It was correct to maintain a strict regimen in the royal house, but it was not the best thing to keep exchanges between father and son excessively severe. Yŏngjo replied that he merely intended to aid the regent in attaining moral virtue through exhortation. The custom of the royal house had always been rigorous.[68]

"I DID NOT DO IT"

Yŏngjo's extremities, which blinded him to his son's predicament, were paralleled by anguish at having to punish the Soron and, by extension, Kyŏngjong. Sado's unresponsiveness in the matter left him no choice but to do it himself. This drove him to despair. How else could one interpret this dream, which he had on October 4, 1754: He was walking on a street when he saw a member of one faction nearly killing a member of the other. A woman from a Soron family approached, weeping, and asked why things had reached such an extreme. He answered that it was a pregnant lesson on the dangers of current factional practice. Since the nation belonged neither to the Noron nor the Soron, but to him, he would punish both. Feeling happy, he woke up. In reflecting on the dream, Yŏngjo remembered three persons whom he had killed and whose deaths he had come to regret.[69] Soon afterwards, Yŏngjo began to drink heavily, behavior quite out of character for him. Official critcism of royal indulgence in drinking and women appeared in December of the same year.[70]

Yŏngjo's distress reached its highest point in 1755 when, forced by events, he finally carried out the long-feared act. In March, the governor of Chŏlla Province reported that rebellious posters had appeared at Naju City. Officers of the State Tribunal were speedily dispatched. They succeeded in arresting the suspects. When the trial began on April 1, it was evident that it was another extremist Soron plot.[71] On April 12, Yŏngjo decreed that Kim Ilgyŏng's cosigners and several Soron ministers including Cho T'aegu and Yu Ponghwi were to be posthumously adjudged rebels. In addition, Yi Kwangjwa and Ch'oe Sŏkhang were to be posthumously stripped of their posts. On April 15, the definitive judgment on the Soron came. Yŏngjo ceremonially announced the vanquishing of the rebels at the ancestral temple. To avert further repercussions for the *t'angp'yŏng* policy, Yŏngjo commanded that memorials requesting further punishment of the Soron be returned to their senders.[72] The trial lasted until May 10, implicating many extremist Soron. During the trial, Yŏngjo's anguish was evident. He drank constantly, "to calm my troubled mind," as he later explained to Pak Munsu.[73]

His ordeal was not yet over. Just when he felt that the trouble was behind him, his legitimacy was challenged anew. On June 11, Yŏngjo presided over a special *munkwa* examination held in celebration of the recent "subjugation of rebels." The examination papers included one by a certain Sim Chŏngyŏn, which alluded to Yŏngjo's regicide. Another, anonymous, contained a still more virulent denunciation of the king.[74] The trial of Sim Chŏngyŏn soon involved other extremist Soron, including a number of Kim Ilgyŏng's relatives. To Yŏngjo's chagrin, the defendants were defiant. They admitted their rancor toward the royal house but denied that they were wrong.[75]

The incident enraged him to no end. To be challenged again, so soon after taking, against his better intentions, what he had hoped would be definitive steps, was a colossal blow. He had hesitated so long and endured such humiliation before taking this action. But he had not doubted its efficacy. When all else had failed, he had stifled his misgivings and moved, but all was in vain. Now he had to find another way. What could he do? Would anything work?

Yŏngjo's conduct during the trial reached unprobed extremes. On June 15, in interrogating one Yun Hye, he discovered that Yun possessed writings blasphemous to his royal ancestors. Dismayed, he went to the ancestral altar. He cast himself down at the foot of its steps and wept, crying that now his deficient virtue had brought disgrace even to his ancestors, he could no longer live. He proceeded to a bridge and announced to congregated onlookers that he was ashamed of his thirty-year reign. Then he went to a pavilion atop one of the city gates. In helmet and armor, he ordered the military band to play. He resumed the interrogation. Yun Hye insisted that he had written the papers himself. Yŏngjo ordered his officials to stand. He turned to Kim Sŏngŭng, the

189

commander of the Military Training Army, and directed him to behead Yun and bring his severed ears. Yi Chongsŏng objected, citing regulations. Criminals were to be executed by the appropriate board and under no circumstances would it be done in the royal presence. Yŏngjo, in fury, dismissed him. He also had Kim Sŏngŭng beaten and banished for intransigence. Yŏngjo was on this occasion roaring drunk. He repeated his order, this time demanding that Yun's severed head be pierced on a flagpole. This produced no response. Several dozen times he screamed, challenging any official of the same mind as Kim Ilgyŏng to step forth and face him. Then he went into a small tent and collapsed in a drunken torpor. The band blared on and the water in a water clock dwindled almost to nothing. At dawn, he came out of the tent and stopped the music. In armor and helmet, he returned to the palace.[76]

The trial concluded. It resulted in a number of executions and a display of severed heads. Yŏngjo now came to a resolution. He simply had to publicly deny the charge of regicide. He appointed several ministers to a committee formed to write a book on this. The book, the *Illuminating Mirror of Righteousness* (*Ch'ŏnŭi sogam*), completed in December 1755, explicitly denies the charge that had been rumored—that Yŏngjo had sent preserved crab to Kyŏngjong through Queen Dowager Inwŏn, and that Kyŏngjong had died eating it. The *Illuminating Mirror* begins with Yŏngjo's preface. It states that the crabs did not come from the queen dowager's kitchen but from Kyŏngjong's own. The rest of the book, written by the committee members, is devoted to proofs of Yŏngjo's legitimacy and his filial affection for Kyŏngjong.[77] For a wider dissemination of the book for the masses, who were not versed in classical Chinese, a Korean version was also prepared and published.[78] In any case, after the publication of the *Illuminating Mirror* the charges of regicide seem to have ended. Very few incidents of a rebellious nature occurred afterwards. Of course this may just as well have resulted from the virtual elimination of the extremist Soron in 1755.

The two "subjugations of rebels" in a row and the publication of the *Illuminating Mirror* seriously threatened the *t'angp'yŏng* policy. There was a real possibility that the Noron, taking advantage of recent events, might demand a Soron purge. If that were to happen, resistance would have been rather difficult. The Soron, frightened by this prospect, were already leaving the court en masse. Yŏngjo realized that a certain degree of Noron dominance was inevitable. He even anticipated having to honor Noron patriarchs. Under no circumstances, however, would he tolerate a purge.[79] He had had enough of death and he certainly had no desire to sacrifice innocent Soron. Moreover, he was determined to keep the bureaucracy open to qualified Soron, if fewer in number.

Aware of the urgency of the situation, Yŏngjo struck a blow before the Noron could act. Immediately after the trial, he launched a full campaign against factionalism. Almost daily, he passionately denounced factionalism, attributing to it all the evils of his reign—rebellions, charges of regicide, etc. He repeatedly referred to his dream of a crying Soron wife, he cited historical examples, he mentioned his writings, he evoked the memory of his brother, and he mortified himself.[80]

This was all intended to exact official promises to denounce factionalism. Such promises he repeatedly received. But nothing less than written pledges would satisfy him. On October 26, about seventy Noron officials from the Prime Minister down sent to the throne written notes pledging that they would abstain from factionalism. Relieved, Yŏngjo nonetheless expressed displeasure at seeing so many Noron pledges and none from the Soron[81]—a tactic clearly intended to leave an opening for the Soron. Official pledges in hand, Yŏngjo carried out his side of the bargain. In December, he ordered sacrifices to Min Chinwŏn and Min Chinhu. In March 1756, he announced that Song Siyŏl and Song Chun'gil would be canonized at the Confucian temple, a great honor for Noron patriarchs. Several weeks later, Song Siyŏl was further honored by a posthumous promotion to Prime Minister. But Yŏngjo did not forget to display his commitment to the *t'angp'yŏng* policy. In late December 1755, he performed a sacrifice to its supporters, including Song Inmyŏng and Cho Hyŏnmyŏng. Yŏngjo and the Noron achieved a reasonable compromise. The Noron had prestige and formidable, though not total, power. Yŏngjo avoided a purge, and kept the *t'angp'yŏng* policy, if only in rhetoric.

If Yŏngjo's political problems were held somewhat in check, he paid a price in his relationship to his son. Their relationship deteriorated beyond the point of repair, particularly in 1755 and 1756. For in confronting the problem of his own legitimacy Yŏngjo had given up his most cherished expectation of Sado. In failing to fulfill his hope, Sado elicited ever greater rejection. For instance, in 1755, Sado had a son born of a concubine. Yŏngjo took no note of the child. As far as he was concerned, Sado's son by Lady Hong, born in 1752, sufficed. As a future heir apparent, he would inherit the dynastic line. The king had no desire to acknowledge any more of Sado's children. There were several months of pleading. Only after Pak Munsu forcefully reminded him of the custom in the royal family of not neglecting children by secondary consorts did he reluctantly agree to hiring a wet nurse.[82]

Yŏngjo's anger at his son was exacerbated by Sado's ineffective public performance. Uncomfortable with his recent acts, and especially concerned that he might be expressing unfiliality to Kyŏngjong,[83] Yŏngjo probably hoped that his son would furnish some support. Paralyzed with fear and insecurity, Sado could initiate nothing. A month after Yŏngjo ordered the composition of the *Illuminating Mirror,* students memorialized Sado, suggesting that he publish a book enumerating the crimes of Kyŏngjong's Soron ministers. Sado refused.[84] He also refused Noron requests for the two Songs' canonization, so that Yŏngjo had to do it himself. Exasperated at Sado's uselessness, Yŏngjo, in March 1756, told secretaries that Sado's answers to certain memorials should not even be sent out.[85] It is difficult to imagine that Yŏngjo's estimate of his son could fall any lower.

WITHDRAWAL

At this point, one must ask why Yŏngjo maintained his son's regency after 1756. Having cleared his name and come to a decision that his son was politically useless, Yŏngjo had no apparent reason for keeping the regency. But he did, and it is a mystery that cannot be easily fathomed. Probably, coming hard upon Sado's ineffectiveness and his own negative evaluation of the regency, the retraction of the regency would have appeared tantamount to deposing Sado as heir. But then, perhaps Yŏngjo's disenchantment with Sado was so deep that he did not care. Perhaps the memory of his own abortive regency deterred him. Perhaps he was concerned with the symbolic significance of ending a regency enacted under the rhetoric of emulating his brother Kyŏngjong. But then, perhaps he still hoped, even against his better judgment, that his son would eventually come around and turn into the latter-day sage king he so desired him to be. Whatever Yŏngjo's motives may have been, he had no other son and Sado remained the regent.

Sado was perforce regent in body, but he could escape in spirit. He began to conspicuously withdraw from public function. In addition to his passivity in administration, he turned derelict in his studies. His formal lecture sessions with the Crown Prince Tutorial Office had begun in 1742. Until 1749, he held them regularly. In 1750, he missed a few sessions. In 1751, for reasons of health, he cancelled them for a week or ten days at a time. From 1752, however, he was truant for several months at a time, using as a pretext every imaginable illness—headache, stomachache, toothache, eye disease, dizziness, etc. By 1756, he was even using cold weather as an excuse. He held very few sessions in 1757. This of course provoked deep concern. His officials constantly admonished him to be careful of his health, diligent in his studies, and judicious in administration.[86]

Now, Sado's terror of his father left him unable to behave properly in his presence. Lady Hong reports that when Queen Chŏngsŏng died in 1757, Sado cried pitifully, as a filial stepson should. As soon as Yŏngjo entered the room, however, he could no longer cry but merely remained prostrate.[87] Yŏngjo, of course, disapproved of this dry-eyed unfiliality and communicated this by pointedly praising his grandson's virtuously ample tears.[88]

This terror led Sado to greater default—he began to omit his regular greetings to his father. This irritated Yŏngjo tremendously. One day in December of 1757, he told Kim Sangno and Sin Man, the Ministers of the Right and the Left, that Sado had not visited him for three months. Pressed for a reason, Sado burst into tears, admitting unfilial behavior. Informed of the prince's remorse, Yŏngjo requested a written apology. Sado wrote one. Somehow, the apology did not satisfy Yŏngjo, and so it elicited an all too familiar scene.

Several days later, in the evening, a number of senior officials were summoned to the palace. They found the king, in hempen clothes, prostrate upon the ground, wailing aloud. The regent, also in hempen clothes,[89] lay prostrate behind the king. Startled, they immediately prostrated themselves and, in tears, asked the king for the reason. The king replied that he had found the prince's apology wanting in effort. He had summoned him hoping for a verbal admission of his misdeeds. But the prince had refused to say anything. The ministers explained that the prince was usually too much in awe of the king to speak as he intended. They counseled the king to let them advise the prince quietly. Instead, Yŏngjo threatened abdication, accusing Sado of insincerity.

Seeing Sado dissolve into tears, the minsiters took courage and protested Yŏngjo's severity. Yu Ch'ŏkki, the Magistrate of Seoul, was the first to speak.

> In teaching and instructing sons and brothers, there is no difference between the noble and the base. Speaking from observation of ordinary practices, if fathers or elder brothers are too severe, the young become fearful and frightened. Their relationship will be distant at the very least, and it might even turn into something sick and dreadful. If elders guide mainly with love and harmony to awaken the way and reason, then [children's] gratitude and righteousness will both be complete, and thereby affection and aspiration would have been successfully communicated. In Your Majesty's case, severity and authority take precedence. This leaves His Highness always in fear and dread. When he has to answer his father, he cannot but be hesitant. Your servant humbly begs Your Majesty to turn to harmony and peace. Even if His Highness were to err, speak to him quietly, solicit him gently

and patiently guide him along the right path one day and another day. This will naturally bring the desired effect.

The Minister of the Right, Sin Man, was next:

The way of teaching and instructing is like taking medicine. One cannot hope it will take effect after one dose. Only after taking it for a long time without stopping, can one see its natural effect.

Councilor Hong Ponghan, Sado's father-in-law, followed:

Whenever His Highness finds himself in Your Majesty's presence, he becomes so frightened and terrified that, even if the answers expected of him were something he knew well, he gets tongue-tied. This is because he has been treated with excessive severity.

The Minister of the Left, Kim Sangno, spoke last:

On each occasion when Your Majesty is displeased with His Highness, Your Majesty has summoned and scolded him. This has deprived His Highness of peace and comfort and that is why the situation has developed to the present impasse.

This onslaught of ministerial criticism left Yŏngjo quite dumbfounded. Sado was permitted to leave. But he was beside himself with mortification. On his way out, Sado fell down the steps and lost his consciousness. Only after receiving medication did he come to his senses.[90]

Thus the relationship worsened day by day amidst ministerial concern and royal grief. The gap between father and son widened, especially now that most of the effective mediators had died. Yŏngjo's three closest ministers had all died. Song Inmyŏng was the first, in 1746, followed by Cho Hyŏnmyŏng in 1752.[91] Pak Munsu, who had persuasively pleaded for Sado, followed them in 1756, dying in the care of Yŏngjo's own royal physicians. Yŏngjo, with most of his contemporaries dead, was surrounded by younger officials. Having no one to confide in, and no one who could speak to him intimately, Yŏngjo became more arbitrary in his isolation. Then Queen Dowager Inwŏn and Queen Chŏngsŏng, both Sado's protectors, died in succession early in 1757. Sado seemed genuinely grieved at his stepmother's death. Queen Chŏngsŏng, childless and estranged from her husband, had been especially sympathetic to her stepson, probably feeling that they shared the same fate. Sado wrote a conspicuously large number of commemorative writings such as tomb inscriptions and eulogies for her.[92] He also frequently performed sacrifices at her shrine. Yŏngjo, in accordance with custom, remarried in 1759 but the new queen, Queen Chŏngsun, was only fifteen years of age at the time, ten years Sado's junior. Her youth probably made it difficult for her to fully grasp the complex relationship between Yŏngjo and his son. We know very little of what role Sado's mother, Lady Yi, played except in the last moment of Sado's life. Though she enjoyed a long and stable relationship with Yŏngjo, bearing him many children, she seems to have stayed in the background as her status as a secondary consort dictated.

There were, of course, new ministers and officials, many of whom did their best to improve Yŏngjo's relationship with Sado. Often risking royal wrath, they would plead with the king for generosity and with Sado for patient filial devotion. Yi Ch'ŏnbo, for instance, who served as Prime Minister during this period, emerges as a conspicuous mediator. He would emphasize the preservation of civilization, long since lost everywhere else, which now depended on Sado's virtue.[93] For the most part, official efforts were wasted.

There were, however, occasional attempts at reconciliation. From time to time, Yŏngjo would respond to ministerial suggestions to show tenderness for his son. Sado would respond in remorse, making desperate efforts to please his father. In October 1758, for example, Yŏngjo agreed to hold joint study sessions with Sado if Sado were to attend three sessions within the next ten days. When Sado was informed of this, he was deeply moved. He asked Yi Chongsŏng whether awaiting punishment would express his sincerity. Yi thought that it would. Pleased at the opportunity to show his feelings of regret, he immediately went outside to lay prostrate on the ground.[94] Afterwards, Sado indeed attended his study sessions. Though there were gaps, his performance was rather good until July of the following year, when he again began to cancel sessions.[95]

As desirous as they were of a better relationship, Yŏngjo and his son just could not achieve it. Isolated by a total failure of communication and constrained by rigid patterns of behavior, they simply could not resolve their differences. In August 1760, Yŏngjo moved to Kyŏnghŭi Palace, leaving Sado in the Ch'angdŏk Palace compound. Their relationship had become so unbearable that they could no longer live in one palace compound.

But then, according to Lady Hong, it was even worse than appearances suggested. Her journal depicts a life of sheer terror. Perhaps speaking with bitterness as the wife of an estranged son, she criticizes Yŏngjo for his irrational severity, enumerating his greatest lapses into harshness. Yŏngjo had clear favorites among his children and treated them with a peculiarly intense discrimination. Among other things, in visiting his favored children, he wore different clothes and used different roads and gates than in visiting the children he disliked. Princess Hwap'yŏng, who died in 1748, and Princess Hwawŏn, born in 1738, were his favorites, while Sado and Princess Hwahyŏp, who was two years Sado's elder and who died in 1752, were among his less-favored offspring.[96] His distaste for Sado, however, was particularly intense. He would not invite him to festive occasions or bring him to visit tombs—the only outings from the palace—and requested his presence only at unpleasant activities such as criminal trials.

Nor would Yŏngjo show any restraint in expressing disapproval of Sado's performance. If Sado consulted him on administrative matters, he would angrily complain that the regency was no help, but if his son failed to consult him, he would be infuriated because his opinion had not been sought. He would publicly disparage Sado when he could not answer questions, and he soon found fault with his son's deportment and appearance, especially his clothing.

By 1750, Sado's terror of his father was already quite pitiable. When Lady Hong bore a son (he would die a few years later), Sado seemed to seriously doubt that his father would accept the child.

But soon, his terror provoked alarm. In 1752, Sado read a Taoist text, openly hoping to become a master of the supernatural. Soon he began to hallucinate and he developed an acute fear of thunder. When it thundered, he would lie prostrate, covering his ears, until it stopped.

The birth of a child by Sado's concubine in 1755 provoked reproaches unusual even for Yŏngjo. The king himself had fathered two daughters by a newly acquired concubine, Lady Mun, in 1753 and 1754.[97] Moreover, the practice of concubinage, especially for a prince in his sexual prime, had long been taken for granted in the royal house. But Yŏngjo's disapproval of his son knew no bounds. By this time, the prince was so disabled by disease that he could no longer regularly perform administrative duties or attend study sessions. Questioned by his father on the new child, he would only shrink in fear. He groaned continuously for several days and openly expressed a desire to die. In July 1756, unjustly upbraided for drinking, Sado attempted to jump into a well. This decline in performance and health was paralleled by a renewed interest in military games. Whenever Yŏngjo left the palace, Sado would ride horses and practice archery in the palace grounds. He equipped eunuchs with weapons and flags and led military marches to the accompaniment of a band.

But Lady Hong also notes Sado's responsiveness to his father's attentions. Yŏngjo attempted reconciliation in the summer of 1756. He invited Sado to Queen Dowager Inwŏn's seventieth birthday celebration—her last, it turned out—and took him to Sukchong's tomb. In consequence, Sado's behavior improved markedly.

This was but a brief interlude, however. In the several months between the deaths of Queen Chŏngsŏng and Queen Dowager Inwŏn and their funerals, the father and the son frequently met at the wakes. Yŏngjo was impressive in his mourning for his stepmother, but he found his son wanting in grief. His criticism of Sado's conduct and his clothing grew severer than ever.

Now Sado turned violent. He began to beat eunuchs, and, shortly afterward, to kill them. The first death occurred in July, 1757. To his wife's utter horror, Sado entered the room carrying a severed head dripping blood. This was when he was stricken with what

Lady Hong calls clothing disease. This was an extreme difficulty, perhaps even a terror, in putting on his clothes. Before he could successfully get one suit of clothing on, many would be destroyed.

In October of that year, Sado became enamored of a certain Pingae and installed her in a separate apartment. She had been a lady-in-waiting to the deceased queen dowager. Such a liaison was rigidly proscribed by custom. When Yŏngjo found out about it several months later, he demanded that Sado send her back. Now, for the first time, Sado defied his father. As an emergency measure, Lady Hong chose a woman resembling Pingae and sent her back, hiding the real Pingae at Princess Hwawŏn's residence outside the palace. Yŏngjo rebuked the prince sharply for having taken Pingae in the first place. On his way back to his residence, Sado again jumped into a well to die. He was saved only because the well was frozen.

Yŏngjo made another attempt at reconciliation in 1758. He was deeply disturbed by the killings committed by his son. Yŏngjo went to see him and asked why he had killed. This is Lady Hong's description of the encounter:

> In his replies that day the prince said, "When anger grips me, I cannot contain myself. Only after I kill something—a person or maybe an animal, even a chicken—can I calm down."
> "Why is that so?" His Majesty asked.
> "Because I am deeply hurt."
> "Why are you so hurt?"
> "I am sad that you don't love me, and terrified when you criticize me. All this turns to anger."
> Then he reported the people he had killed in detail, giving their number and hiding nothing. At this moment, His Majesty, perhaps, for a time, responding to his natural instincts as a father, or perhaps allowing his sagacious heart to be overcome with pity, said,
> "From now on I will not be that way."

But Sado remained pessimistic. To the jubilant Lady Hong, he predicted his death. He declined steadily. His clothing disease worsened. In dressing, not only did he destroy many suits of clothing, but he also killed the attendants who assisted him. His murders became commonplace and he hallucinated, seeing people and objects. He grew conspicuously disrespectful of his mother and frighteningly harsh to his children.

There was a drought in the summer of 1760. Yŏngjo upbraided his son, attributing the disaster to Sado's abandonment of virtue. "Military games" were his only solace. This was when Sado decided that he could not live in the same palace compound as his father. He turned to his sister, Princess Hwawŏn, Yŏngjo's favorite daughter, to persuade their father to move to another palace. This is what had prompted Yŏngjo's move. At this time, Sado may have felt a premonition of what was to come, for he threatened to harm Hwawŏn with his sword if anything befell him.[98]

ESCAPE

Though Yŏngjo had moved to another palace, it was not far enough for Sado. For the palace itself had become, to his crazed mind, a prison, a symbol of his father's reproval and his own failure. Soon he sought escape, and his travels began. Now death loomed ever larger. In fact, the last two years of his life were one long dance with death. Now he courted it, now he flew from it, but death remained at the center of his consciousness. Faced with Sado's macabre and destructive behavior, the court was plunged into turmoil. Torn between the present and the future monarchs, fearful of their fates and concerned for the dynasty, officials responded variously. There was a movement to end Sado's life, and there were a number of suicides. In the end, Yŏngjo felt that he had no choice but to kill his mad and dangerous son, if only to safeguard dynastic continuity. Though this ended Sado's unhappy life and terminated Yŏngjo's unrealizable dreams, its personal and political repercussions continued through Chŏngjo's reign.

On Sado's first trip, in 1760, he went to Onyang. Lady Hong says that he obtained Yŏngjo's permission through Princess Hwawŏn. Another source attributes the king's permission to ministerial counsel.[99] However it came about, this Onyang trip was a normal royal excursion. The king allowed it for his son's health. Sado's entourage contained his tutors, 120 persons carrying luggage, an escort of 795 soldiers, and a military band, all totaling close to 1,000 people.[100] A royal trip of this sort often imposed great expense on local households, damaged farms, and caused numerous disruptions. Sado is said to have been extremely careful to ease the burden on the local populace and to minimize the damage inflicted. He was scrupulous in reimbursing local residents for any expenses attributable to his travels. He won admiration and praise for his concern.[101] Released from his confinement, was he so elated that reason prevailed?

Perhaps. But the trip could not last forever. After three weeks, Sado returned to the palace. He was greeted by officials who congratulated him for his conduct and urged him to maintain it in the future.[102] But Sado, back in the palace, reverted. The killings, the clothing disease, and the military games became totally unrestrained. By early 1761, his fits of violence were utterly uncontrollable. Pingae had by now borne him two children. Nonetheless, he beat her to death while she helped him to dress.[103]

Now Yŏngjo gave up all hope in Sado, for he had begun to transfer his hopes to Sado's son, later Chŏngjo, who had been appointed grand heir (*Seson*) in 1759.[104] Now Yŏngjo openly declared that the survival of the three-hundred-year dynasty lay with the grand heir.[105] Lady Hong responded in fear. She did all she could to hide Yŏngjo's praise of her son from her husband lest he, in a moment of violence, harm the child.[106]

In this atmosphere of terror, Sado began excursions in disguise. For several months, he is believed to have roamed the environs of the city. Then, three ministers of the State Council died mysteriously in an interval of two months. Prime Minister Yi Ch'ŏnbo, who had emerged as Sado's protector, was the first to die on February 9, 1761. He left a deathbed memorial to Yŏngjo pleading against rash actions. The Minister of the Right, Min Paeksang, was next, on March 21, followed by the Minister of the Left, Yi Hu, on April 8. These deaths are believed to have been self-inflicted and the causes are attributed to Sado.[107] Presumably, as the highest-ranking officials in the state, they died feeling responsible for Sado's misdeeds. Still, what did this imply? Where, in fact, was Sado going and what did he do? We find, in *Imo ilgi*, a collection of writings concerning the Sado incident, a memorial sent by an official to Sado criticizing him for his unruly behavior. It mentions such activities as traveling with gangs and terrorizing the people.[108] Though we may deduce from hints that Sado was engaged in quite destructive activities, we remain ignorant of what he, in his distorted frame of mind, attempted.

Then on May 6, Sado left for P'yŏngyang still in disguise and of course without royal permission. Again, Sado's activities on this trip are unknown. But it caused a panic. Lady Hong describes the frantic activities of Sado's court to hide his absence. A eunuch lay in an inner chamber giving orders in imitation of the prince, while another tended him as if he were Sado.[109]

Sado returned in three weeks, this time to a chorus of official criticism. Censors and officials admonished him for the trip. Some asked that those who had allowed it be executed.[110] Sado, however, successfully withstood demands that he visit his father until the night of June 17. Lady Hong's father, Hong Ponghan, to whom Sado felt rather close, managed to persuade him. Two days later Sado went to Kyŏnghŭi Palace to visit Yŏngjo. Sado also held quite a few study sessions in the course of a month.[111] He may have done this by way of expiation; illness, however, forced him to stop the sessions.

Several months later, when Sado had recovered, Yŏngjo discovered his P'yŏngyang trip. On October 17, in the course of reading the *Records of the Royal Secretariat*, Yŏngjo came across the memorials sent to Sado rebuking him for his trip. Enraged that a matter of such gravity had been kept a secret from him, Yŏngjo dismissed Hong Ponghan, who was serving as the Minister of the Right, several royal secretaries, and many of Sado's tutors, and banished his attendants. On this occasion, Sado anticipated his death. When Lady Hong tried to ease his fears, in sudden lucidity he predicted his impending death and Yŏngjo's decision to make Chŏngjo an adopted son of Prince Hyojang, his older brother who had died in 1728.[112] He told Hong Ponghan that this fear left him unable to sleep or to get out of bed.[113] But Yŏngjo was not yet ready to fulfill his predictions. In a week, Hong Ponghan was back on the State Council, this time as Prime Minister. On November 2, Yŏngjo finally relented to ministerial pleas that he take pity on Sado, who had been awaiting punishment in the courtyard without food or medical care. He should forgive him, if only to ease the tension of the court. On the 5th, Yŏngjo received Sado, ending the episode.

From this point on, the *Sillok* is conspicuously reticent about Sado except in recording his presence at regular audiences and at Chŏngjo's wedding ceremony. According to Lady Hong, his son's marriage brought Sado both grief and joy. The joy was just his delight at his new daughter-in-law, but his grief came when his father ordered him, because of his slovenly carriage, to leave the ceremony.

Unmentioned in the official historiography, Sado was reaching the final stages of insanity. He rebelled against anything that was, in his mind, connected with his father. He drank, he held parties with entertainers and nuns that he had picked up on his travels, and he ordered his attendants and ladies-in-waiting to loudly shout things disparaging to his father. Now he killed not merely servants who helped him to dress but also court physicians, fortune-tellers, messengers, and palace servants belonging to other establishments including one of his mother's.

And now he courted death. He decorated his room like a funeral chamber complete with commemorative banner. He held parties there occasionally attended, under threat, by Princess Hwawŏn. He slept in this room in a box resembling a coffin. Then in May 1762, he dug an underground chamber resembling a crypt. He covered it with planks and then with earth, leaving only a small opening. In this crypt, lit by a jade lamp and surrounded by his weapons, he spent increasing amounts of time.

In June, Lady Yi visited her son, Sado, in his residence. As if he knew that this would be his farewell, he had a feast prepared and composed a poem wishing her a long life. To his mother's horror and dismay, he insisted on holding a military parade, with her in a palanquin escorted by armed soldiers and accompanied by a military band. This deranged display of filial affection convinced her that he was beyond all hope. Tearful, she took leave of him after a few days.[114]

Astonishingly, from mid-May to mid-June, he held lecture sessions. This rekindled Yŏngjo's paternal hopes.[115] But these too took a morbid turn. In the past, Sado's most frequent question had been why this or that virtuous person had not received his just reward.[116] Now his question turned to death. "If Fu-su had not been killed, the Ch'in dynasty would not have gone to ruin. Can one say that Fu-su was filial in accepting death?"[117] "The Emperor An-ti always bore remonstrance very well. Why suddenly did he kill Yang Chen for just one word?"[118] Wide awake with insomnia, he would summon his tutors in the middle of the night and ask these questions.[119] Could it be that he was identifying with these victims?

But these activities ended on June 14. On this day, Na Kyŏngŏn's report, which enumerated ten heinous crimes committed by Sado, came into Yŏngjo's hand. Na was a brother of Na Sangŏn, a palace guard. Though the contents of the report are suggested only obliquely in the *Sillok*, we know that the charges must have been quite grave. The following is a rough summation of the *Sillok* account. Yŏngjo read a few lines of the report and then, clapping his hands together, screamed: "Disaster is around the corner! I should conduct a personal interrogation [of Na]." The governor of Kyŏnggi Province, Hong Kyehŭi, who happened to be present at the court, advised the king to keep military guards around him. Yŏngjo then ordered that the city gates be closed and the palace gates lowered. He ordered eight people, including Hong Ponghan, to serve on the interrogation committee. Yŏngjo started to read Na's report again and before finishing it, he shouted again: "I was worried that this disaster might happen." He then gave it to Hong Ponghan to read. Hong, upon finishing it, said: "Your servant requests to die first." The king said to the present officials: "Those who wear a cap and carry insignia [on the official robe] at this court are all criminals. Na Kyŏngŏn managed to send me this report to let me know the heir apparent's misdeeds. There was not one among you who informed me of the same. Aren't you all ashamed to look at Na?" Hong Ponghan let the storm subside, and told Yŏngjo that Sado was in such a state that if he were to learn of the report from anyone else, he would become quite uncontrollable. Thus, he, Hong Ponghan, should be permitted to inform the prince. The king agreed.

When Sado was informed, he went to a palace gate and lay prostrate awaiting punishment. Soon Yŏngjo summoned him. The *Sillok* contains a description of the confrontation:

> Upon seeing the prince, the king shouted,
> "You beat the mother of royal grandchildren to death, brought nuns and monks into the palace and sneaked off to P'yŏngyang and roamed the northern suburbs; how can this be called the conduct of an heir apparent? All those who wear caps have been deceiving me; if it were not for Na's report, how could I have known about the mother of royal grandchildren? You were so infatuated with her at first that you even jumped into a well for her. How could you beat her dead in the end? Only because Na is honest and criticized your behavior to me did I come to know this. Furthermore, sons of nuns will call themselves royal grandchildren in the future and will come and visit me. With a situation like this, how can the country avoid ruin?"
> Overwhelmed with anger, the prince asked for a face-to-face confrontation with Na. The king again shouted:
> "Are those not words to cause the ruin of the nation? How can a prince-regent want a confrontation with a criminal?"
> "It is because of the symptoms of your servant's disease which is caused by frustration," the prince said, weeping.
> "Is it right to go into a fit? Don't you have to try to fight it back?"
> Asking this, the king ordered the prince to leave.[120]

Did Na Kyŏngŏn's report contain something more than Sado's misdeeds? Did it charge Sado with having engaged in something more sinister, more directly threatening to the king? Yŏngjo certainly was behaving as though he were in danger. The closing of the city gates and tight surveillance of the palace gates indicate that much. But at the same time, the interrogation of Na does not seem to have revealed any serious plots. Yŏngjo thundered at him demanding truth: now that he had alarmed the ruler by talking about impending disaster, he had better furnish evidence. Na named a few names but they were inconclusive and incoherent. Evidently, at least judging by the *Sillok* account, he had no first-hand knowledge of what could be called a serious plot. Official attitudes support this. They all demanded that Na be punished as a traitor—his disloyalty to the regent was disloyalty to the throne. And Na was executed on the same day.[121] Had he revealed some real evidence of Sado's plotting, perhaps they would not have been so insistent. Or at least, there would have been more interrogation. But at the same time, no one seriously pleaded for royal exoneration of the regent. This suggests that Sado had been charged with something truly grave.

In this charged atmosphere, the last act of the tragedy unfolded. Father and son, separately, until their fateful last meeting several weeks later, played out their painful roles. Sado awaited his father's summons by Kŭmch'ŏn Bridge all night, returning to his residence in Ch'angdŏk Palace only at dawn. But upon royal order, Ch'angdŏk Palace was sealed and there from June 16, Sado began his long wait for punishment in the courtyard of Simin Hall. And the prince's daily waiting is the only reference the *Sillok* makes to Sado until July 4. Sado, intermittently, sent messages of greeting to Yŏngjo but Yŏngjo did not answer.

Yŏngjo was in fact busy mending the damage that Sado had done. He went to Hŭnghwa Gate and asked the merchants there to tell him if any of their goods had been appropriated by the prince or his cronies, and ordered the concerned board to compensate them for their losses.[122] He also executed several people who had allegedly intimidated the populace and kidnapped and raped women by pretending to be the prince.[123]

The king also raged at his officials for their silence and uncooperativeness concerning Sado. Their slightest attempt to defend Sado was attributed to ulterior motives in wishing to insure their future. When officials requested that Na Kyŏngŏn be post-

humously enslaved, he fell into a tantrum. He raged that the officials were splitting the court into a father faction and a son faction. They were all traitors.[124]

Officials were indeed caught between the father and the son,
and between the present and the future. Though gravely charged,
Sado was still their regent and the heir apparent. Moreover, even
if Sado were to be eliminated, they still had to worry about Chŏngjo,
Sado's son, who would almost certainly succeed his grandfather,
and who might eventually seek to settle old scores. They must
have felt as if they were walking on thin ice. One wrong word,
one wrong move could be fatal. Each day, they were terrified of
going into the court lest they be asked to do something that might
prove to be dangerous, but they could not stay away lest this be
viewed as something worse. Then, of course, beyond these concerns, they each had their own relationships to the king and to
the prince. They were torn, fearful, and sad.

And Yŏngjo was desolate. He refused medicine.[125] Feeling guilty
and angry, he kept on wondering what he had done to turn his
son into a madman. On June 22, he even asked Hong Ponghan
how Sado could have reached such a state. His son had shown
innate intelligence and so, in the beginning, he had dearly loved
him. He then regretted not having followed the advice of a eunuch
who told him long ago that he should not be too indulgent with
the young prince.[126] On July 1, upon reading a biography that described a son's effort to avenge his father, the king exclaimed that
this was a filial son indeed.[127]

Whatever was on Yŏngjo's mind, Sado's wait ended on July 4.
On that day, Yŏngjo went to Ch'angdŏk Palace and demoted Sado
into a commoner and had Sado locked in a rice chest. After twenty
days of vacillation, why this act? The following is the *Sillok* account of what led up to it:

> After Prince Hyojang's death, the king had been without an
> heir for a long time until the birth of the crown prince [Sado].
> [The prince] was talented and superior, and the king loved
> him dearly. From about ten years of age, [the prince] began

to show increasingly less interest in his studies. After the regency, [he] became quite ill and began to lose his senses. At
first it was not so serious and so people hoped that he would
be cured. But in the *chŏngch'uk* year (1757), his illness took
a turn for the worse and when it acted up, he would kill palace servants and eunuchs. Afterwards, the prince would regret the killings. The king admonished him severely each time
it happened and consequently the prince became exceedingly fearful, which worsened his illness. After the king's move
to Kyŏnghŭi Palace, deep suspicion and an insurmountable
barrier developed between them. Moreover, [the prince] carried on with nuns and entertainers with no regard for propriety. And [he] completely abandoned the ritual duties to
the three courts. The king was displeased, but he had no other
heir. Hence, he was exceedingly worried for the future of the
dynasty. After the incident of Na Kyŏngŏn, the king wanted
to depose the heir apparent, but had no heart to issue the
proclamation. Suddenly there was a rumor from the inner
court. The king was truly astounded and went to Ch'angdŏk
Palace.[128]

What was this "rumor from the inner court" which had such a
decisive impact on Yŏngjo? It is nowhere explicitly recorded. But
we know that the informant was Sado's mother, Lady Yi. Lady
Hong reports that Lady Yi, after conveying the rumor to Yŏngjo,
said:

> The horrible disease gradually worsens; there is no hope. As
> a mother this humble person can hardly bear to say this, but
> it is only right that Your Majesty secure the dynasty by pro-
> tecting [your] sagacious person and the grand heir. Please
> make this decision.[129]

Were Yŏngjo and the grand heir in real danger?

The peril to the grand heir was obvious. He was after all a young
child of eleven, living in the same palace quarters as Sado. Even
under the best of circumstances, his continuing development would

have made Sado no longer indispensable. Given Sado's deteriorating condition and Yŏngjo's confidence in his grandson, Sado's
replacement as heir apparent must have emerged as an increasingly real, if unspoken, possibility. It did occur to Sado, who reputedly once said that he did not see why his father should save
him as long as there was a grand heir.[130] A general fear that Sado
might, in consequence, act against the grand heir set in. It was
just this that had led Lady Hong and those close to the young
child to conceal Yŏngjo's praise of his grandson from Sado. During this last period, both grandmother and mother displayed acute
concern for the child's safety.

Yŏngjo had been acting as if he too were in danger. Later Chŏngjo
would charge that "that traitor, Hong Kyehŭi" had tried to make
Sado's trip to P'yŏngyang into a treasonous plot.[131] It was Hong
who urged Yŏngjo to keep bodyguards around him and to close
the city gates. But evidence was inconclusive and the king was
left in discomforting suspicion. Despite the peril he sensed and
the threat to his grandson, Yŏngjo vacillated for three weeks. Yet,
the mysterious rumor provoked him to decide immediately and
irrevocably for death.

The rumor must have been that Sado planned patricide. Lady
Hong, on several occasions, ruefully refers to his weapons and the
underground chamber as the instruments of his downfall.[132] Then
she reports that Sado announced, "I am going to go to the upper
palace[133] through a water passage (*sugu*)." On two nights, the nights
of July 2 and 3, preceding the fateful day, he had actually attempted this but failed. On the second night, he injured his back
in the attempt. According to her, these acts had caused the rumor.
She explains it as madness,[134] but the court must have seen it as
attempted murder. It is also very likely that, judging by the extra
caution Yŏngjo was taking in guarding the gates as soon as he
heard the rumor, he suspected that his son was expecting some
outside help in his attempt. Still, to what extent Yŏngjo felt any
real peril in this attempt is a moot question, for he now had other
very real concerns. If Sado could, in his desperation, attempt regicide, what else might he do? Even setting aside the problem of

personal safety there was the grand heir's life to be considered. In this sense, the dynasty itself was at stake. At any rate Yŏngjo must have seen it this way when he said to his son:

If I die, our three-hundred-year dynastic line would end. If you die, the dynasty can be preserved. It would be better if you died.

This then was how Yŏngjo's hopes would be interred. This was where his endless toil to escape shadowy suspicions of regicide ended. He had given Sado over to his brother's attendants to be raised. He had delivered Sado into a regency just like his brother's that he might learn rule. And now, Sado had come full cycle, incarnating that very essence in his brother's rule that Yŏngjo had fled in his night of peril to Queen Dowager Inwŏn's palace,[135] in his *t'angp'yŏng* policy, in his endless quest for vindication, and in his long lonely striving on his troubled throne. After Sado's death, in interrogating one of his associates, a former minister named Cho Chaeho,[136] he would discover a connection to Kim Ilgyŏng's group, the extremist Soron.[137]

And so Yŏngjo decided to act. But even in this most painful and private act, the public constraints of the monarchy impinged with great force. That action is described in three different sources— in the *Sillok*, in a journal kept by Yi Kwanghyŏn, a minor royal secretary, and in Lady Hong's memoir. For purposes of comparison and for some hope of historical accuracy, these three accounts are presented here in full.

THE *SILLOK*[138]

Then [the king] went to Ch'angdŏk Palace, and performed the ceremony of obeisance to Sŏnwŏnjŏn.[139] Then [he] released the crown prince from waiting and ordered that he accompany him to Hwinyŏngjŏn[140] to perform a ceremony.[141]

The prince, pleading illness, did not go. The king dispatched the first royal secretary Cho Yŏngjin to urge the prince to perform the ceremony. The king then headed toward Hwinyŏngjŏn. [He] passed through the crown prince's residence, but saw no sign of preparation.

But the prince was waiting outside Chibyŏng Gate and followed the king's carriage to Hwinyŏngjŏn. After the king finished with his ceremony the crown prince, in the courtyard, bowed four times.

The king abruptly clapped his hands and said, "You officials also heard these words from the spirits? Queen Chŏngsŏng has just said to me, 'Disaster hangs on your very breath.' "

The [the king] commanded that the palace gates be shut and watched by four or five rows of palace guards, that the officers patrol the palace with bare swords and that city gates be closed and guarded by military troops blowing horns. None, not even officials, were to be allowed to pass through the gates except the Prime Minister, Sin Man.

The king ordered the crown prince to prostrate himself, to remove his coronet and shoes, and to place his head on the ground. The king issued an order unbearable to hear, and urged [the prince] to take his own life. The prince knocked his head against the ground repeatedly until it bled.

The Prime Minister, Sin Man, the Minister of the Left, Hong Ponghan, the minister without portfolio, Chŏng Hwiryang, the first royal secretary, Yi Ijang, the royal secretary, Han Kwangjo and others rushed in. Before they could say a word, the king dismissed the three ministers and Han Kwangjo. The four of them left.

The grand heir came in, removed his cap and outer robe, and prostrated himself behind the crown prince. The king sent [the grand heir] to the Tutorial Office, and ordered Kim Sŏngŭng and his son to guard [the young prince] lest [he] enter again.

The king, sharply rapping his sword, repeatedly issued orders unbearable to hear, urging the crown prince to commit suicide. The crown prince tried to throttle himself, but was loosened by his tutors from the Crown Prince Tutorial Office.

The king then stripped [the prince] of his rank and made [him] a commoner. At this time, Sin Man, Hong Ponghan and Chŏng Hwiryang entered again but they dared not admonish or contend with [the king].

The king then ordered that the prince's tutors from the Crown Prince Tutorial Office be ejected by the palace guards. Im Tŏkche, a diarist, alone remained immovably prostrate on the ground. The king sternly reprimanded, "The crown prince has been demoted. There should be no diarist." [He] then had [Im] dragged out by the arms.

Holding fast to Im's clothes, the prince followed him out, crying and saying, "Now even you are going. Upon whom can I rely?" Then [the prince] went toward a gate and consulted with his tutors about what he should do. The fourth tutor, Im Sŏng, suggested that he return to await a royal decision.

The prince, crying, went back and prostrated himself on the ground. [He] pleaded and begged, promising that he would correct his errors and be good.

The king became more stern and told [the prince] what [Lady Yi] Yŏngbin had reported. Yŏngbin was the crown prince's mother, and it was she who had informed the king in secret.

The first royal secretary Yi Ijang asked, "How can Your Majesty, based on the words of a woman deep within the inner court, shake the very foundation of the nation?" The king, trembling with rage, ordered the execution [of Yi], but then rescinded the order.

Subsequently, [the king] ordered that [the prince] be locked up. The grand heir hurried in. The king ordered that the crown prince's consort, the grand heir, and her other children be sent to the house of the Minister of the Left Hong Ponghan.

By this time, half the night had passed. The king dictated a royal edict to be promulgated to the nation, but the historian was so afraid that he could not write it.[142]

Yŏngjo's Tragedy: Mournful Thoughts

LADY HONG, *A JOURNAL WRITTEN IN LEISURE*[143]

That day, intending to hold an audience, His Majesty remained in the throne room, Kyŏnghyŏn Hall in the Kwan'gwang Pavilion. There, Lady [Yi of] Sŏnhŭi [Palace] came to see him. In tears, she said, "The horrible disease gradually worsens; there is no hope. As a mother this humble person can hardly bear to say this, but it is only right that Your Majesty secure the dynasty by protecting [your] sagacious person and the grand heir. Please make this decision." She continued, "With the affection of a father, Your Majesty might hesitate to do this. But all is caused by disease; he is not a criminal. Though he cannot be saved, he cannot be blamed. Though you must settle this, please extend your grace to the grand heir and his mother."

As the wife [of the prince], I dare not say that what she did was right. The situation, however, had reached an irreparable point. The right thing for me would have been to follow him to death and then I would have been spared of knowing what proceeded. But I did not. I could not; the thought of the grand heir prevented me. I can only grieve the painfulness of life, the misery of fate.

When His Majesty heard it, he did not hesitate or ponder, but at once ordered the departure for Ch'angdŏk Palace.

Sundering her maternal love and crushing her parental attachment, Lady Sŏnhŭi, for the sake of great principle, had brought herself to inform [the king]. Once this was done, she was seized by pain and could hardly breathe. She trod back to her residence Yangdŏk Hall and took to bed, abjuring all food. Has there ever been such a painful predicament?

There were two paths of royal procession to Sŏnwŏnjŏn. One was through Manan Gate, which carried no suggestion of misfortune. The other, through Kyŏnghwa Gate, signified misfortune. That day the procession was ordered to proceed through Kyŏnghwa Gate.

His Highness the prince had hurt his back entering the water passage on the night of the [lunar] eleventh. On the twelfth,

213

he was at T'ongmyŏng Hall. That day, the main beam of the hall made a loud crack as if the wood was breaking. Frightened, the prince groaned, "What could this mean? It must foretell my death."

A little before this, early in the fifth month, my late father had elicited royal wrath. Dismissed, he had to stay in the eastern suburb for about a month. His Highness the prince must have felt the danger and he had directed Cho Yujin of the Crown Prince Protection Office to send word to Cho Chaeho, a former minister, who was in Ch'unch'ŏn, to come up. In matters of this sort, he scarely seemed inflicted by disease. Strange, the ways of Heaven!

The news of the royal departure on that day terribly alarmed him. Quietly he ordered that military weapons and horses be hidden. And he set out for Tŏksŏng Hall through the back of Kyŏngch'un Hall. Before entering the palanquin, he sent word that I come to see him.

In recent days, if anyone was caught in his sight, it resulted in tragedy. So, when he rode the palanquin, he had it enclosed on top and all four sides covered with banners. To his tutors and to anyone outside, it was claimed that he was suffering from a disabling fever.

It was about noon when I received his summons to Tŏksŏng Hall. Suddenly, as I watched, an innumerable flock of magpies surrounded Kyŏngch'un Hall and in unison began to cry out. I was seized by an ominous foreboding. The grand heir was staying at Hwan'gyŏng Hall. I had been in a state of terrible agitation, but now gripped by anxiety over my son, I ran to his residence and said to him, "No matter what happens, don't be alarmed. Bear everything in stride." I really did not know what to do.

Somehow, the royal arrival was delayed. News reached us that His Majesty might not reach Hwinyŏngjŏn until three in the afternoon.

His Highness again sent word that I should come to Tŏksŏng Hall. When I arrived, I found him drained, without his usual energy but with no sign of derangement in his face or in his voice. He was sitting with his back resting on the wall, his head lowered in a deep, meditative manner, his face drained of color.

I was expecting that my appearance would lead to rage. This premonition, that my life would end that day, had caused me to plead with the grand heir and to warn him. Contrary to my anticipation, he calmly said, "It looks very bad, but they will let you live. Oh, how fearful I am of their intentions." In deep consternation, I sat there silently, just rubbing my hands, while tears rolled down my face.

The royal procession had reached Hwinyŏngjŏn and a messenger came to summon the prince. How strange! The prince did not say, "Let's escape," or "Let's run away." Nor did he beat anyone nearby. With not a trace of rage, he asked for the dragon robe [of the crown prince]. While he was putting it on, he said "I am going to say that I am suffering from a disabling fever. Bring the grand heir's winter cap."

As the grand heir's cap was small, I thought it would be better for him to wear his own, so I asked a lady-in-waiting to fetch it. This brought from the prince a completely unexpected response: "You are truly frightening and malevolent. You want to live long with the grand heir at your side. Since I will die today, when I get out there, you don't want me to wear his cap lest it bring misfortune [to your son]. How very well I can fathom your treacherous heart."

I did not know that he would meet that disaster on that day. I just could not see how it would all end. It was the sort of thing that could end in death for all. What would become of my son, of me? And so his words, coming as a thunderbolt, tormented me. I fetched the grand heir's cap and gave it to him, saying, "What you said was indeed out of my reckoning. Please wear this." "No, why should I wear what you wish to keep from me?" he refused. Could one have thought these the words of a diseased person? Oh! Why did he go so obediently? It was, I guess, all Heaven's will. Only pain and misery remain.

It grew late, and, much urged, the prince went out. His

Majesty, seated before Hwinyŏngjŏn, rapping his sword, carried that order out. It was too cruel; I cannot bear to record the scene. Oh, grief!

When the prince left, one could hear the fury of His Majesty's voice. Hwinyŏngjŏn was not far from Tŏksŏng Hall; I had someone go to the wall. He returned to say that the prince had already taken off the dragon robe and was prostrate upon the ground. I realized that it was the final decision; Heaven and Earth seemed to sink around me; my heart and innards felt as though they were being torn to pieces.

Too restless to stay at Tŏksŏng Hall, I went to the grand heir's residence. We hugged each other desperately, not knowing what to do.

At about four o'clock, I was informed that a eunuch had come asking for a rice chest from the kitchen. I could not understand what it meant but I was too agitated to let him have it.

Realizing that a decision of an extreme nature had been taken, the grand heir went inside the gate and begged, "Please spare my father." His Majesty ordered sternly, "You leave here." The grand heir left and went to the waiting room at the prince's residence. My state at the time was simply beyond comparison to any ever known. After sending out the grand heir, the sky and the earth seemed to come together; the sun seemed to be losing light, and everything went dark. I had no desire to linger in this world for even one more second. I took a knife and was about to end my life, but someone took it and I could not get my wish. I desperately wanted to kill myself; I looked for something sharp but found nothing.

I went out, passed Sungmun Hall and reached Kŏnbok Gate which leads to Hwinyŏngjŏn. I could see nothing. I only heard the sound of the sword that His Majesty was rapping, and His Highness' pleas: "Father, father. I have done wrong. Herewith, I will do everything as you say, I will study, I will obey you in everything, I promise. Please do not do this to me." My liver and gall were breaking into bits; everything was black around me. I just beat my breast. But what was to be done? What would be of use?

With your strength and with your energy, couldn't you have avoided getting into that chest even if it was a royal command? Why did you get in? Oh, why! At the beginning he tried to come out but in the end he was pressured into facing that dreadful fate. How could Heaven be so cruel? There is only unparalleled grief. I wailed and wailed beneath the wall, but there was no response.

Since His Highness had been already stripped [of his position], his wife and children ought not to have remained in the palace. Moreover, I was too fearful to let the grand heir stay out. I sat beneath the gate and wrote a letter to His Majesty: "Now under Your Majesty's decision, it is most discomforting for the criminal's wife and son to stay at the palace. It is all the more fearful to let the grand heir stay out for long, and so this person humbly begs permission to leave for her [father's] home." I added, "By Your Majesty's heavenly grace, this humble person begs for the protection of the grand heir." I managed to find a eunuch and asked him to deliver it.

Not long afterwards, my brother came in and said, "There was a royal decree commanding that, in accordance with the changed status [of the crown prince], his family should leave for [his wife's] family home. We are bringing a palanquin for Her Highness and a sedan chair for the grand heir. So please come in them." Brother and sister embraced, crying bitterly.

I was carried on someone's back to the inner gate of Chŏsŭng Hall passing through Ch'ŏnghwi Gate. A palanquin was waiting there. A lady-in-waiting, named Yun, rode with me and eunuchs carried the palanquin. All the ladies-in-waiting followed wailing. Can there have been such a pitiful scene, ever?

When I entered the palanquin, I fainted. The lady-in-waiting Yun desperately massaged me, and I came back but my misery was too much to bear.

When we reached my father's house, I was laid in a room

in the inner quarter. The grand heir came accompanied by my uncle and my brother. The grand heir's consort, together with Ch'ŏngyŏn,[144] was brought in a palanquin sent by her family. What a pathetic sight.

I was just too miserable to live. I again attempted to kill myself, and again failed. On second thought, I simply could not bear to inflict added grief upon the grand heir. Without me, who would see to his safety, his growing up? I restrained myself, and preserved this cruel life of mine. I just cried out to Heaven. What a cruel fate!

At home, I met the grand heir. One could see his shock and grief. He had just witnessed, at his tender age, a scene of such terror and fright. Who could imagine the depth of his sorrow. Lest it make him ill, I hid my own sorrow and said, "This is truly unbearable. But there is no way to deny that it is all Heaven's will. Only if you stay in good health, and are good, only then will the country be at peace, so that we can repay the sagacious grace. Though we are in deep sorrow, you should not bring harm to yourself."

. . . As the days passed, it was just too horrid to imagine His Highness' state. Unable to think of anything else, I spent days in near collapse. On the fifteenth, His Majesty had [the chest] bound very tightly [with rope], covered deeply [with grass], and moved to the upper palace. All hope was lost. . . .

On the twentieth, at about four o'clock in the afternoon, there was a torrential rain with much thunder. The thought that [the prince] was terrified of thunder made me so restless. I just could not bear to imagine it. All through this period, I constantly thought of dying: I wished to die of starvation; I imagined jumping into deep water; I handled towels; and I frequently grabbed knives. But because of my weakness, I could not bring myself to complete the final act. But I could not eat at all, I could not drink water or eat wet gruel.

The prince was reported to have responded until [the storm], so it must be that he died during that rain.[145]

218

YI KWANGHYŎN'S DIARY[146]

The eleventh of the intercalary fifth month, *imo* year [July 2, 1762]: Yi Kwanghyŏn was appointed as a temporary replacement for Kim Hwajung, the recorder [in the Royal Secretariat].[147]

The twelfth [July 3]: On duty at Ch'angdŏk Palace. Pak Sanap, a royal secretary, Im Tŏkche, a diarist, and the officials of the Medical Bureau asked the prince how he was.

"Right now, I am shivering with fear, waiting for punishment. Though I am seriously ill, I can't allow myself to be examined," the prince answered.

The palace physician retired.

The thirteenth [July 4]: On duty at Ch'angdŏk Palace. The royal secretary Cho Chunghoe, the diarist Im Tŏkche, the second tutor Yi Manhoe, the fourth tutor Im Sŏng, and the officials of the Medical Bureau asked after the prince.

"I am a little better today," he replied. They left. Han Kwangjo, a division chief of the Medical Bureau, had just returned from a visit home and so he requested an audience.

The prince said, "Can't you see I am waiting for punishment? How can I give you an audience?"

At seven in the morning, the king announced that he was leaving for Ch'angdŏk Palace. When his tutors asked for an audience the prince answered, "I've come down with a horrible illness. I just simply can't perform the ceremony."

Next the royal secretary begged for an audience.

The prince answered, "I just told the tutors I can't because of my condition. Why is the royal secretary bothering me again?"

The king directly entered Chinjŏn.[148] Before going toward Hwinyŏngjŏn, he ordered, "Even though it is hot, the crown prince has to perform the ceremony."

The royal secretary Cho Chunghoe, diarist Im Tŏkche, recorder Yi Kwanghyŏn, the medical division chief Han Kwangjo, the second tutor Yi Manhoe, the third tutor Pyŏn

Tŭngnyang, the fourth tutors Im Sŏng and Kwŏn Chŏngch'im, all went to the central gate and prostrated themselves begging for an audience. By now, the king's retinue had arrived at the road in front of the Crown Prince Tutorial Office and they repeated His Majesty's order that the prince perform the ceremony.

The crown prince soon appeared from Chinhyŏn Gate and walked to Hwinyŏngjŏn. Then, the king entered the shrine. In the courtyard a platform had been erected for the ceremony. On the platform, the prince performed the ceremony and prostrated himself. The tutors, the royal secretaries and the historians all prostrated themselves in attendance.

The king summoned the military guards. They came at once. He ordered them to draw their swords. They hesitated. The king drew his own sword and shouted angrily, "Why do you not draw them?" They drew them all at once.

The king summoned a herald and whispered something to him. It was an order for the palace guards. Presumably, it was about procedures for guarding the palace and the city.

It was almost nine and the morning sun bore down like fire. The prince, still on the platform, seemed extremely uncomfortable. He was panting and seemed near collapse. The tutors requested that the royal secretaries suggest to the king that the prince's health might give out. The king said something, but most of the officials could not hear it.

The prince removed his coronet, came down from the platform and prostrated himself on the ground.

Alarmed, the tutors asked him, "Did His Majesty order Your Highness to take off your coronet like that?"

He answered, "After his order, how can I wear my coronet?"

The tutors asked again what the order was.

"I can't repeat it," he said.

Just then they heard the king. Brandishing his sword, he screamed, "If you kill yourself, you will die as crown prince of Chosŏn. You had better die fast!"

All in the court wailed.

220

The prince answered, "The relationship between father and son is woven in Heaven and bound on Earth. [Your servant] can't bear to do such a horrible thing before my lord and father."

He asked permission to commit suicide outside. Then he went to the southern end of the courtyard, removed his outer robe and threw himself to the ground with his head to the north. The tutors, the royal secretaries and the historians all took off their caps and lay prostrate in attendance.

The king came down from the shrine, walked to the moon viewing platform and said, "If I die, our three-hundred-year dynastic line would end. If you die, the dynasty can be preserved. It would be better if you died."

He went on, "By just saving your head, should I let the dynasty end?"

The prince wailed pounding his head on the ground.

All the officials, from the Minister of the Military Affairs down, took off their caps. Wailing, they asked, "Your Majesty, what is the meaning of this?"

The king grew still angrier and thrust his sword at [the prince]. Terrified, the officials stood up not daring to utter a sound.

"Kill yourself fast," the king kept repeating.

"Your Majesty, when you struck your servant with your sword, you struck not using the edge, only to frighten me. Now your servant begs for death," the prince answered.

The king thrust out his chest and cried out, "Just look at what he is saying! How horrid!"

"Your servant has this unbearable misery in his heart," the prince went on.

Rather than answer, the king said, "Why don't you just kill yourself?"

"Your servant requests to kill himself," the prince said.

He then untied his girdle and with the string succeeded in strangling himself till he passed out and slumped to the ground.

Whispering among themselves, the tutors rushed [to him]

221

and undid the cord. They surrounded [the prince], crying, and hastily ordered the recorder to go to the division chief of the Medical Bureau to arrange for an examination by the palace physician. Then the tutors dissolved some heart-clearing pills in warm water and, with a spoon, forced it into the prince's mouth.

The prince, in his misery, refused to swallow it. Weeping, they kept on urging him until he took three or four spoonfuls and sat up. He had not yet finished half of it when he burst out wailing. He gave the rest to his tutors, saying, "You have some too."

The king, who had been watching intently, said, "That's the way they are: the wretch counted on them and became even more wicked."

The division chief of the Medical Bureau, Han Kwangjo, rushed in with medicine. The king stripped him of his post and turned him away.

At just this moment, the king saw the physicians entering through the side gate. Brandishing his sword, he shrieked, "Pang, Pak, you scum! Just you dare!" He ordered that their heads be chopped off.

At this point, the prince was lying on the ground. The first royal secretary, Yi Ijang, came from the shrine, asked about the prince and left.

Then Kim Yangt'aek, the Minister of the Military Affairs, came to wait upon the prince.

The prince gazed searchingly at Yangt'aek and said, "If they were all like you, I would have died long ago. Out, now!"

The prince sat up and started banging his head on the stone pavement. The fourth tutor Im Sŏng put his hand on the ground where the prince's head was hitting. Soon the skin on the back of his hand was peeled and torn.

The king's anger grew more intense as he continued to urge the prince to kill himself.

At about this time, stern orders were given but Yi Kwanghyŏn had been in and out of the side gate on errands and so he missed much of what went on.

Then the fourth tutor Im Sŏng went to the foot of the steps and threw himself prostrate. With his head to the ground, he wailed to the king. "Though His Highness the prince failed in virtue, couldn't Your Majesty, in benevolence and love, open a new road for him so that he could have a fresh start?"

The king stared at him silently for a while. Then he shook his head saying, "That's Im Sŏng."

Now, the side gate was shut tight and guards surrounded the gates so that ministers could not get in. The tutors discussed it and decided that the ministers should be informed of the situation immediately. They ordered the recorder to go and tell them. Because he bore a brush and inkstone [of a historian], Yi Kwanghyŏn could pass through the gate.

Outside, on the steps, the Prime Minister, Sin Man, said, "If we could only get in through the side gate!"

Hong Ponghan, the Minister of the Left, beating his breast, said, "We are not even allowed in. How could we save him?"

Chŏng Hwiryang was silent.

Then Yi Kwanghyŏn told them. "If the ministers were to request an audience, the palace guards would not dare to stop you. When you reach the gate, there will be some way to get through."

When they got to the gate, they were obstructed as expected. Yi Kwanghyŏn went in first addressing the guards. "The ministers are requesting an audience and you are blocking them. You know that it might cost your lives?"

The gatekeepers whined, "This is the king's command. What can we do?"

Seizing the opportunity, Yi Kwanghyŏn pushed them aside and told the ministers to run in and they did.

By the time Yi Kwanghyŏn reported their entry to the tutors and turned around, the Prime Minister was already leaving. Yi Kwanghyŏn went after him, saying, "Why is your lordship leaving so soon?"

"I was met with a very severe command," he answered.

Next, Minister Hong started to leave. Yi Kwanghyŏn asked, "How could your lordship leave now?"

"The royal order was extremely stern. What else can I do?" Hong answered. Then he turned and addressed the tutors, "Under His Majesty's command, I cannot but leave."

Watching the three ministers leave, the tutors conferred again and decided that the only way left to move the celestial heart was to let the grand heir [appeal].

The fourth tutor Im Sŏng went out to watch and the second tutor Hong Surhae came in leading the grand heir.

While he was approaching the gate, the grand heir took off his coronet and clasped his hands together pleading.

The king caught a glimpse of him. "Does he think he can get out of this by using the grand heir?" he quivered in rage.

The prince tugged at Yi Kwanghyŏn's hand and asked that the grand heir come close to him. By now the grand heir had crossed the gate and, though he lay prostrate, he was edging up to his father.

Seeing this, the king at once ordered the military guards to carry him out. When a guard was about to pick up the grand heir, he fended him off.

The prince drew Yi Kwanghyŏn's hand close and demanded, "What is that rascal's name?"

"Your servant does not know his name. He serves in a special military unit which receives direct royal orders," he replied.

The prince turned to the guard and said, "Don't you know the difference between the highness of Heaven and the lowness of Earth? The grand heir should be left to leave on his own. How dare you force him? What is your name?"

That guard, terrified and embarrassed, answered, "Humbly, sir, this person is Kim Sujŏng. This humble person is under royal orders and cannot but obey." Then he carried out the grand heir.

The prince again drew Yi Kwanghyŏn's hand close and said, "He is repulsive. He could easily harm me."

It was already about four, and the king once again urged, "Aren't you ever going to kill yourself?"

The prince picked up his robe, tore off the hem and strangled himself. Again the tutors saved him. Han Kwangjo, who had been dismissed as division chief of the Medical Bureau, was standing just outside the side gate. Yi Kwanghyŏn went for medicine and got some heart-clearing pills and offered them to the prince.

This all happened about three times.

Suddenly, a huge chest was brought in and placed in the middle of the courtyard. It was about three and a half *ch'ŏk* high and the same in width.[149]

The king ordered harshly, "Get in, fast."

The prince walked to the chest, and was about to get in. The tutors grabbed him and pulled him back. With much shouting and sobbing, they threw themselves to the foot of the chest.

Raving mad and pointing at the tutors, His Majesty shouted, "Traitors, traitors! All of you! You all lose your post! Out! Right at this minute!"

The tutors still would not leave.

The king shouted, "You are all banished to the Six Extremities![150] Get out! This instant!"

The tutors had to leave. Only the tutor, Kwŏn Chŏngch'im, because he was responsible for the prince's wardrobe, and the historians remained.

The king raved at the prince, "Formerly, in a case like this, even a reigning sovereign had to go to Kyodong in Kanghwa Island.[151] How dare you not get in?"

Then he said, "You royal secretaries and historians, you lose your posts too. Out!"

One royal secretary, Cho Chunghoe left.

By this time, each of the prince's officials, having been dismissed from his post, had departed. Only the diarist and the recorder remained. The prince held the diarist Im Tŏkche's hand and Tŏkche held Kwanghyŏn's hand and thus they supported each other.

Kwanghyŏn turned to Tŏkche, "The secretaries and historians have been dismissed from their posts. The secretaries have already left. The historians ought to leave too. What are you going to do?"

"You do what you think best. I just cannot leave," Tŏkche answered.

Kwanghyŏn remained with them. Prostrate, they looked up at the king from time to time.

Sword in hand, the king rushed over to the eastern steps. From the way the palace guards were acting, it seemed that the king was giving them orders. Since it was quite far, the historians could not hear. The guards and soldiers all dropped their muskets to the ground and let out loud screams.

Thrashing at the tent posts with his sword the king roared, "These ruffians are afraid of that wretch. They don't think I am the ruler."

Just then the king ordered the herald to haul out a palace custodian, behead him and hang the severed head outside the gate. The herald dragged out a palace custodian.

Then the king gave orders to two palace guards, "First drag these two out and execute them as severely as the law will allow."

"These two" meant Im Tŏkche and Yi Kwanghyŏn. The guards dragged Kwanghyŏn off first and left him just beyond the side gate. He sat on the steps and peered in. Soon Im Tŏkche was dragged out. The prince followed him and came out through the gate.

By now the sun had set and it was dark. Torches began to appear. The palace guard filed in forming ranks on the left and right. They shouted to the tutors telling them to make the prince go back at once. If they failed, they would be executed in the severest way.

The tutors had been waiting just outside the side gate. When they saw the prince come out, they rushed to him and asked, "Your Highness, why did you come out?"

The prince did not answer. He just let out a long mournful groan.

He walked several dozen steps to the wall, leaned on it and

urinated. Then he sat on the ground. Feeling extremely thirsty, he asked for something to drink. A eunuch, weeping, brought a porcelain bowl with some warm water and heart-clearing pills in it and offered it to him.

The crown prince drank it up. Then between sobbing, he asked, "What should I do?"

The tutors said, "Today, Your Highness has no way but to reverentially obey His Majesty's decision. Wait until he changes his celestial heart, even if it takes all day and all night. Only then will Your Highness be able to come out."

The prince said, "That's true."

He got up and went back. When he disappeared into the gate, his attendants, including Im Tŏkche and Yi Kwanghyŏn, tried to follow him in. But at the gate the guards stopped them all and so they could not enter.

It was about eight. They were peering through the gate trying to figure out what was going on, but they could not hear well because of the distance.

Then they saw the prince pull up his garment, place his hands on both sides of the chest and look up at the king. Crying piteously, he implored, "Father, let me live." Then he jumped into the chest.

Through all this the tutors could do nothing but stay outside the gate crying.

Suddenly a herald named Kim secretly told them that there was a hole in the chest through which one might pass food and drink.

At some point, the side gate was left open a crack so that it was possible to sneak in but none of them had caps. Yi Kwanghyŏn stole in through the gate and fetched two scholar's caps. He gave one to Im Sŏng and put one on himself.

As they crept in, they saw that on the south side of the chest there was a hole, some sort of break. There was a eunuch standing there, one whose name they did not know.

Im Sŏng offered some medicine and something to drink to the prince through the hole.

After he had taken it, the prince took off his jacket of lined

227

silk inside the chest. He handed it to Im Sŏng and asked for
a thinner one with no lining. Im Sŏng took it and went to
the eunuchs. He got an unlined silk jacket from one of them
and gave it to the prince.

"This is silk. Could you go back and get a hempen one?"
he asked.

Im Sŏng took it, found a short hempen jacket and brought
it to the prince.

While this was going on, Yi Kwanghyŏn prostrated himself
before the chest right by the hole. Though it was pitch dark,
the prince recognized him at once and greeted, "Oh, you
came." He asked what His Majesty was doing.

All Yi Kwanghyŏn could say was that His Majesty's anger
still seemed to be at full blaze and showed no sign of abate-
ment and that, since he could not get close to him at all, he
had no way of knowing what was going on.

Then Yi Kwanghyŏn managed to get a bowl of wet gruel
from a eunuch and offered it to the prince.

The prince finished. Then Kwanghyŏn prostrated himself
again and said, "Your humble servent is under grave royal
injunction to await execution. Your servant must take leave."

Im Sŏng likewise prostrated himself before the chest.

Suddenly, Im Sŏng tugged at Kwanghyŏn's coat, got up
hastily and left. Kwanghyŏn got up quickly and followed him
out.

On the way out, Kwanghyŏn turned around and looked up
at the Audience Hall. He saw a lighted lamp coming down
the steps toward the chest. Apparently word had reached the
Audience Hall that a board in the chest had a hole in it. Now
the king had personally come to seal it up tightly.

Just then there was an official at the side [of the chest].
Later Kwanghyŏn heard that it was Kim Igon, one of the
prince's attendants from the Crown Prince Protection Office.[152]

At about midnight, a royal edict was issued deposing the
prince and making him a commoner. Just then, a royal sec-

retary, Chŏng Sun'gŏm came out. The tutors at the gate asked him what was happening.

"The king commanded me to take down the edict," Chŏng explained. "But I just could not comply with the order, so I was dismissed."

Just before that, the first secretary, Yi Ijang, had received the same command. He responded by reprimanding the king, "Your Majesty, how could you do this unprecedented thing just on the words of one woman. Your servant does not dare to accept the royal decree." The king ordered his execution and sent him out. Then he commanded Chŏng Sun'gŏm. When Chŏng too refused to obey, the king had to write it himself.

Shortly afterwards, the king decreed that none of the orders that he issued that day be carried out. This meant that all his injunctions, the dismissal and banishment of eunuchs, the executions of historians and royal secretaries, were rescinded.

Then the king ordered that the chest be moved to the front of the Office of Diplomatic Correspondence.

On that day, though it is not clear just when, Yun Suk, a diarist from the Royal Secretariat, came upon the ministers sitting outside the gate. Rather agitated, he shouted at them, "You lords, don't you understand anything but high posts and fat salaries? What are you going to do with them?"

The next day [July 5], the Minister of the Left Hong Pong-han informed the king that Yun Suk had berated the ministers. Consequently, Yun was banished to a remote place. On the same day, Im Tŏkche also was banished.[153] His crime was that he had wailed too loudly when they read the edict making the prince a commoner.

Later at about two in the morning, the crown prince's consort and the grand heir, now commoners because of the edict, left the palace through Tanbong Gate.

Yi Kwanghyŏn, Im Tŏkche and many other officials lay prostrate by the road as they saw them off.

On the twenty-first day [July 12], when they dressed the

body, a fan was discovered in the chest. It is not known who gave it to the prince.[154]

THE PRINCE OF MOURNFUL THOUGHTS

Sado died on July 12, 1762, in a rice chest of four-feet cubed after eight days of confinement. This truly gruesome method of execution requires some explanation. One can only say that if the causes for his downfall had to be sought in the difficulties of his role, the way he died also was a result of his position. Yi royal custom prohibited bloodletting or disfigurement of the body in executing members of the royal family. Thus, giving a cup of poison was the standard method of execution. But a standard execution implied criminality, perhaps even treason. In this case, Sado's family was bound to share the guilt and possibly the punishment. Certainly the legitimacy of his issue would be in question. A criminal's son simply could not ascend the throne. Since Yŏngjo had no other sons or reasonably close male relatives, this alternative would drastically weaken the line of dynastic succession. Hence Sado had to die in a way that carried no definitive judgment of criminal status. Hence Lady Yi's statement: "But all is caused by disease; he is not a criminal. Though he cannot be saved, he cannot be blamed. Though you must settle this, please extend your grace to the grand heir and his mother." And Lady Hong was clearly extremely disturbed by these implications. Hence such statements as: "I simply could not see how it would all end. It was the sort of thing that could end in death for all. What would become of my son, of me?" Or later: "Now under Your Majesty's decision, it is most discomforting for the criminal's wife and son to stay at the palace. It is all the more fearful to let the grand heir stay out for long, and so this person humbly begs permission to leave for her [father's] home."

This implication further explains the prudence of making Chŏngjo a posthumously adopted son of Prince Hyojang.[155] For then even if Sado's activities were called into question by later scholars, Chŏngjo's line would remain untainted.

For these reasons, Sado had to die, in some sense, by his own hand. Self-strangulation was one alternative. Sado tried this several times, but each time he was revived by his tutors. They could not interfere while he was in the act but it was their duty as tutors, with their primary loyalties to him, to save him. If self-strangulation was impossible, all that remained was the rice chest. Sado entered on his own, if under royal orders. Tutors and historians were also neutralized either by direct order where applicable or by being forced to await an execution that would never come. And there in the confines of the chest Sado could have succeeded in fulfilling the "unbearable" order. Possibly Yŏngjo was hoping for that. Sado did not so choose. Nonetheless, dying as he did, it did not have to be recorded that he was killed. The *Sillok* simply states that Sado was locked in and that his death followed eight days later.

On July 12, when Yŏngjo heard of the death, he composed an edict:

> When we hear these tidings, we cannot help but think about this father-son relationship which lasted three decades. In consideration of the grand heir's sentiments and in deference to my minister's wishes, we restore his title and post. And hereafter may he be known as the Prince of Mournful Thoughts (Sado).[156]

LEGACY

In dying, Sado joined his ancestors to cast long shadows. The court now lived in the umber of the incident. Lady Yi died in August 1764, after two years of grief and self-doubt. In commemoration of her "courage, rare among women" in informing him on that fateful day, Yŏngjo composed a eulogy, the *P'yoŭirok* (Record of Manifest Righteousness). In it, Yŏngjo pays tribute to her "loyalty transcending private love, which saved the dynasty from the brink of ruin."[157] He then conferred a title on her, "Shining Righteousness" (*Ŭiyŏl*). These posthumous honors were scant reward.

Lady Hong lived another fifty-three years to see her family cast

231

aside in the tumult of court politics. She survived her only son, Chŏngjo, by fifteen years. From 1795 to 1805, she composed her celebrated memoir, *A Journal Written in Leisure.*

The event also clung stubbornly to many officials who had participated in it. Some were later punished by Chŏngjo[158] for their supposed roles in Sado's downfall. Some of Sado's tutors and royal secretaries who had made last-minute efforts to save him, men like Im Sŏng[159] and Kwŏn Chŏngch'im,[160] spent the remainder of their lives mourning the prince, refusing public service. Yi Kwanghyŏn, who served in the Royal Secretariat for those few fateful days and left a description of the incident, disappeared into oblivion.

Yŏngjo, who resumed full administrative duties upon Sado's deposal with an announcement that he would receive no congratulations for the occasion, reigned another fourteen years. His shattered hopes, however, seem to have turned him, in some ways, from a man of vision into a man of delusion. His obsession with the *t'angp'yong* policy continued. For a time he forbade marriages between families of the same faction;[161] on another occasion he composed a *New Great Instruction.*[162] But his preoccupation with asserting his legitimacy and authority kept him in continuing conflict with the predominantly Noron bureaucracy. As his suppression of the bureaucratic voice grew sharper, the *t'angp'yŏng* policy, which had begun in a vision of a government in harmony, became mainly a medium of repression.

Undeterred by his personal tragedy, he continued in his quest for sage kingship until his death. The discrepancy between the ideal of his vision and the reality of his rule was at its sharpest in the most intimate of his relationships—the killing of his son. The discrepancy was less sharp, though considerable, in his dealings with the bureaucracy. He became an indisputable autocrat to his officials. Yet, it can be argued that his autocracy was necessitated, at least in part, to avoid bloodshed. The gap almost disappeared in his role as ruler-father to the people—the most remote, if most important, group in the monarchy. Yŏngjo, who killed his own son, could become father to his people, the fulfillment of a public paternal role at the expense of a private one.

These disparate paternal roles that reached varying degrees of fulfillment in inverse proportion to their distance from Yŏngjo found more harmonious coexistence in his successor. Chŏngjo nearly realized the ideals of moral rule of the Confucian kingship. Chŏngjo's reign was a glorious chapter in the Yi Confucian monarchy, deserving of the epithet "restoration" that later historians confer on his and Yŏngjo's reigns. The factionalism that had plagued the court for about a century came under control while the bureaucratic voice was freed. The agrarian economy developed and intellectual life flourished.

Chŏngjo, however, had his own sadness. He could not be a full-fledged son to his father. Since Yŏngjo had made him an adopted son of Prince Hyojang in 1764 as Sado had predicted, this proscribed him from conferring honors on Sado as the father of the reigning monarch. This remained a source of profound unhappiness for him. Chŏngjo's pronouncement on the day of his accession clearly reveals this:

> Alas, I am really Prince Sado's son. The Late Majesty made me an adopted son of Prince Hyojang since he thought the main line of the family should be given precedence. Isn't it sad! . . . Though propriety must be strict, human emotion cannot but be expressed.[163]

Throughout his twenty-four-year reign, Chŏngjo devoted immense care and attention to his father's memory, but he was never free of the restriction imposed by his adoption.[164]

He too contemplated abdication so that his son, under the rhetoric of filial piety to his father, could extend honor to Sado, his grandfather.[165] He died in 1800, his wish unfulfilled. All through his life, in the awesome train of his grandfather, in pursuing his ideal of moral rule, he would be haunted by pale images of his father, especially his image of him on that day when he, Chŏngjo, was eleven, when he begged for the life of him who lay prostrate in front of him quaking in madness and terror, that day which, for him, would chafe the luster off his brilliant rule.

APPENDIX 1

Genealogical Table of the Yi Royal House

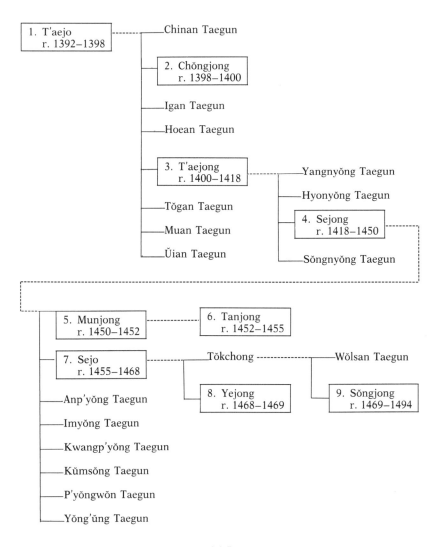

Appendix 1

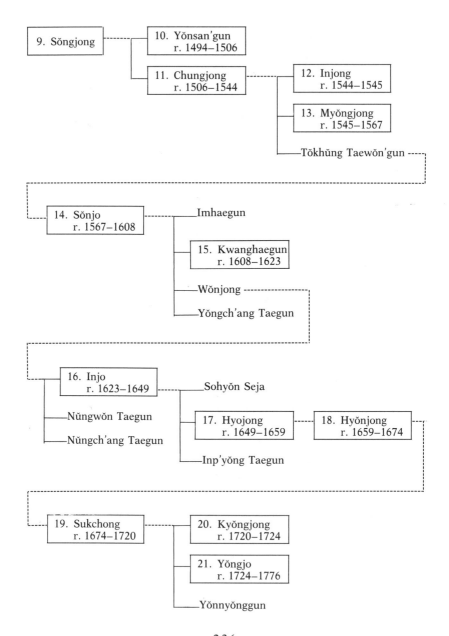

Genealogy of Yi Royal House

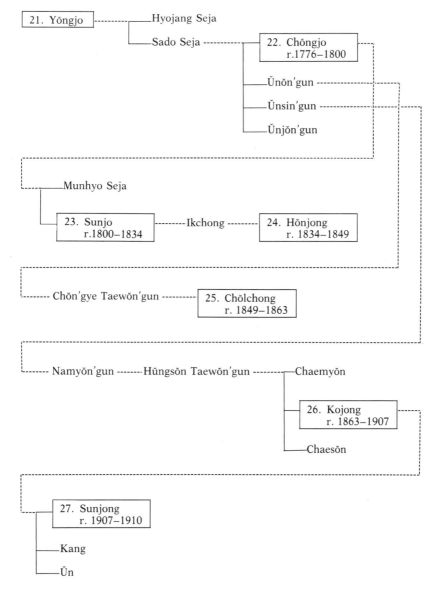

APPENDIX 2

Historical Chart of Factional Development

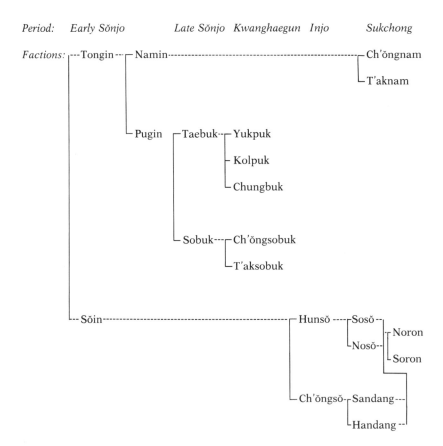

Period: *Early Sŏnjo*   *Late Sŏnjo* *Kwanghaegun* *Injo*   *Sukchong*

SOURCE: This chart is based on that of Yi Kibaek, *Hanguksa sillon*, p. 252.

APPENDIX 3

Yŏngjo's and Sukchong's Curricula in the Royal Lecture

Kyŏngyŏn

Title	Yŏngjo	Sukchong
The Analects (Lun-yü)	1/5/1725–5/18/1725 (4 months)	12/20/1674–3/5/1676 (16 months)
	2/29/1763–6/5/1763 (4 months)	
Mencius (Meng Tzu)	7/8/1725–4/17/1727 (21 months)	3/20/1676–9/5/1677 (18 months)
	9/22/1763–9/1/1764 (12 months)	
The Doctrine of the Mean (Chung-yung)	4/25/1727–1/26/1728 (9 months)	9/24/1677–4/8/1678 (7 months)
	5/6/1756–3/29/1758 (22 months)	
	4/6/1758–7/11/1758 (3 months)	
	7/21/1758–9/3/1758 (2 months)	
	9/4/1758–9/22/1758 (1 month)	
	5/11/1760–5/6/1761 (12 months)	
	9/1/1761–2/23/1762 (6 months)	
	Intercalary 5/1/1762– 9/16/1762 (4 months)	

The curricula are based on *Yŏlsŏngjo kye kang ch'aekcha ch'aje*. The dates are given in the lunar calendar.

239

Appendix 3

Kyŏngyŏn

Title	Yŏngjo	Sukchong
The Book of Documents (Shu-ching)	2/8/1728–6/3/1731 (42 months) Intercalary 2/4/1762– 9/16/1762 (7 months)	5/1/1678–10/11/1678 (5 months)
The Book of Rites (Li-chi)	8/3/1731–5/17/1734 (33 months)	4/2/1709 (one day)
The Book of Odes (Shih-ching)	6/22/1734–5/28/1736 (23 months) 9/10/1764–2/10/1765 (5 months)	10/16/1680–4/11/1683 (30 months)
The Book of Changes (I-ching)	6/3/1736–10/7/1737 (16 months)	6/9/1685–9/11/1690 (52 months)
The Spring and Autumn Annals and Collected Commentaries (Ch'un-ch'iu chi-chuan)	10/16/1737–6/21/1741 (44 months)	1/29/1702–3/21/1709 (86 months)
The Classic of the Mind (Hsin-ching)	7/15/1741–11/4/1744 (40 months) 2/21/1765–intercalary 2/2/1765 (10 days)	1/11/1681–6/5/1685 (53 months)
The Rites of Chou (Chou-li)	11/7/1744–4/18/1749 (53 months)	
The Great Learning (Ta-hsüeh)	10/2/1758–11/8/1759 (1 month) 6/12/1759–7/19/1759 (1 month) 2/5/1760–4/19/1760 (2 months) 9/2/1760–11/8/1760 (2 months) 5/11/1761–7/26/1761 (2 months) 3/1/1762–5/7/1762 (2 months) 9/8/1762–11/8/1762 (2 months) 6/9/1763–7/13/1763 (1 month)	

240

Yŏngjo's and Sukchong's Curricula

Kyŏngyŏn

Title	Yŏngjo	Sukchong
Reflections on Things at Hand (Chin-ssu lu)	4/22/1765–11/26/1765 (6 months)	
The Elementary Learning (Hsiao-hsüeh)	5/8/1766 (one day) 5/12/1769 (one day) 1/12/1772 (one day) 2/3/1776 (one day)	
The Extended Meaning of the Great Learning (Ta-hsüeh yen-i)	1/4/1770 (one day) 3/1/1772 (one day)	
An Essential Guide for the Learning of the Sage (Sŏnghak chibyo)[1]	3/1/1762–5/9/1762 (2 months)	6/1/1697–6/1/1701 (48 months)

Sodae

Title	Yŏngjo	Sukchong
An Outline and Digest of the General Mirror (T'ung-chien kang-mu)	10/7/1721–6/1/1726 (56 months) 2/8/1735–7/3/1736 (17 months) 5/6/1763–7/21/1763 (2 months)	1/3/1675–3/15/1698 (278 months)
The Mirror of the Sung (Sung-chien)[2]	6/5/1726–1/9/1727 (7 months) 8/10/1763 (one day)	4/9/1698–12/14/1699 (20 months)
The General History of the Imperial Ming Dynasty (Hwang Myŏng t'onggi)[3]	1/16/1728–2/23/1728 (one month)	12/21/1699–Intercalary 6/21/1702 (31 months)
A Chronological History of the Ming (Ming-chi p'ien-nien)[4]	2/24/1728–3/7/1728 (one month)	6/21/1702–6/27/1702 (last four chüan)
The Classic of the Mind (Hsin-ching)	10/2/1724–3/6/1728 (41 months) 12/15/1744–4/15/1746 (16 months) 7/8/1758–3/4/1759 (8 months)	

Appendix 3

Sodae

Title	Yŏngjo	Sukchong
	1/17/1761–12/3/1761 (11 months)	
	2/18/1762–5/17/1763 (15 months)	
The Letters of Master Chu (Chu Tzu feng-shih)	3/12/1728–6/8/1728 (3 months)	
The Extended Meaning of the Great Learning	6/2/1728–Intercalary 7/4/1729 (14 months)	
	11/2/1769 (one day)	
A General Mirror of the Eastern Kingdom (Tongguk t'onggam)[5]	Intercalary 7/5/1729– 5/26/1731 (22 months)	12/11/1702–1/26/1708 (61 months)
An Essential Guide for the Learning of the Sage	6/1/1731–1/8/1732 (7 months)	
	5/25/1749–4/23/1750 (10 months)	
	10/6/1759–1/16/1761 (15 months)	
The General Mirror of the T'ang (T'ang-chien)[6]	1/11/1732–2/19/1732 (one month)	2/4/1708–2/30/1708 (one month)
The Selected Letters and Essays of Chu Hsi (Chŏlchak t'ongp'yŏn)[7]	2/20/1732–10/16/1733 (20 months)	3/10/1708–7/6/1711 (40 months)
The Memorials and Discussions of Lu Chih (Lu-Hsüankung tsou-i)[8]	12/9/1733–1/27/1734 (one month)	
Reflections on Things at Hand (Chin-ssu lu)	1/29/1734–4/3/1734 (2 months)	
	3/17/1735–11/2/1735 (8 months)	
The Memorials and Discussions of Li Kang (Li Chung-tingkung tsou-i)[9]	4/15/1734–6/5/1734 (2 months)	

242

Yŏngjo's and Sukchong's Curricula

Sodae

Title	Yŏngjo	Sukchong
The Tso Commentary (Tso-chuan)	6/9/1734–9/7/1734 (3 months)	
Discussions and Memorials of the Famous Ministers of History (Li-tai-ming-ch'en tsou-i)[10]	9/8/1734–12/18/1734 (3 months)	8/24/1711 (one day)
Essentials of the Governance of the Chen-kuan Era (Chen-kuan cheng-yao)[11]	12/20/1734–2/5/1735 (2 months)	
Record of the Words and Deeds of the Famous Ministers of the Sung (Sung ming-ch'en yen-hsing lu)[12]	7/5/1736–10/14/1737 (15 months)	
A Continuation of the Outline and Digest of the General Mirror (Hsu Tzu-chih t'ung-chien kang-mu or Sung Yüan kang-mu)[13]	10/12/1736–10/14/1737 (12 months)	
A Supplement to the Extended Meaning of the Great Learning (Ta-Hsüeh yen-i pu)[14]	10/15/1737–10/5/1740 (36 months)	
Selections from the Classified Conversations of Master Chu (Chu Tzu yü-lei ch'ao)	10/2/1740–3/4/1741 (5 months) 5/5/1750–8/4/1750 (3 months, not finished)	
A General Mirror for Aid in Government (Tzu-chih t'ung-chien)	3/21/1741–4/3/1749 (97 months)	
An Outline of Koryŏ History (Yŏsa chegang)[15]	4/19/1749–5/4/1749 (one month, from 7 kwŏn)	
A Mirror for Historical Rulers (Li-tai chün-chien)[16]	7/22/1763–8/9/1763 (one month)	

243

Appendix 3

Sodae

Title	Yŏngjo	Sukchong
The Precious Mirror of the Yi Dynasty (Kukcho pogam)[17]	11/7/1730–12/8/1733 (37 months)	
A Royal Self-Reflection (Ŏje chasŏng p'yŏn)	12/7/1755 (one day) 12/13/1755 (one day) 1/17/1756 (one day)	
An Admonition on Rising Early and Retiring Late (Sukhŭng yamae cham)[18]	1/28/1760 (one day) 2/3/1770 (one day) 2/6/1770 (one day) 2/27/1770 (one day)	

244

APPENDIX 4

A Historiographical Discussion and Evaluation of Several Sources

SILLOK

One of the main sources for this work is the *Sillok,* an official account of each king's reign. The *Chosŏn wangjo sillok* covers the reigns of twenty-five Yi kings, from that of T'aejo (r. 1392–1398) to that of Ch'ŏlchong (r. 1849–1863), in 1,893 *kwŏn.* Though the actual compilation of the *Sillok* of each reign did not begin until the death of the king under discussion, the process began from the moment of his accession. At the inception of the Yi dynasty, the Bureau of State Records (*Ch'unch'ugwan*) was established. The total number of officials in the bureau was seventy-eight; they concurrently served in other offices. The bureau was headed by the Prime Minister and the Ministers of the Left and the Right, but the most important members were eight diarists from the Office of Royal Decrees (*Yemun'gwan*). Commonly referred to as the historians (*sagwan* or *hallim*), the diarists by turns attended all the public functions of the court, especially those presided over by the king, and they recorded everything that went on. All other documents pertaining to state affairs were made available to them. Based on each diarist's report and other documents, they then wrote the *Sijŏnggi* (Records of Administration). No one including the king was allowed to see either the diarists' report or the *Records of Administration,* which served as the main sources for the *Sillok.*

Another important source for the *Sillok* was the *Sŭngjŏngwŏn ilgi* (Records of the Royal Secretariat). The Royal Secretariat was the agency that took care of the king's daily schedule including all the interactions between him and the bureaucracy. The two recorders of the secretariat also attended all the public activities of the king, and were responsible for recording them. This included discussions in royal audiences, both formal and informal, Royal Lecture sessions, memorials to the throne, royal answers to them, and other royal decrees and pronouncements. Unlike the records prepared by the diarists, the *Records of the Royal Secretariat* was open to view by the king and other officials.

The portion of the *Records of the Royal Secretariat* that dealt with the earlier period of the Yi dynasty was destroyed by fire, and only the records from 1623 to 1894 are extant. Entered on a daily basis, each month produced usually one *kwŏn*, sometimes two. It is a voluminous record and the parts covering Yŏngjo's reign alone are much longer than the entire *Sillok* of the Yi dynasty.

At any rate, upon a king's death, the new monarch set up a Committee on Compilation of *Sillok* (*Sillokch'ŏng*). The committee consisted of anywhere from thirty to over a hundred people.[1] The three highest-ranking officials of the state, the Prime Minister, and the Ministers of the Left and the Right, as well as a few scholars specially invited to serve on the committee were appointed as directors. Under them was the office of general compilation. Anywhere from six to twenty compilers headed this office, each responsible for a certain period of the reign. At times, a few directors also doubled as compilers. The compilers often included outside scholars. Under them were division offices which worked on the first draft of the period for which each office was responsible. There were clerks and copyists assigned to each of these offices. In the case on the Committee of the Compilation of the *Yŏngjo sillok,* there were five directors, seventeen compilers, twenty-seven heads of division offices, and another one hundred and forty-five people working in various capacities.[2]

All of the pertinent documents were made available to those on the committee. In addition to the diarists' reports, the *Records of Administration,* the *Records of the Royal Secretariat,* and other records kept by each public office, any sources deemed relevant, including private writings by scholars, were consulted. Once the first draft was prepared by division offices, they were sent to the office of general compilation, where the second draft was prepared. Then the directors and compilers, after further editing, completed the final version. Subsequently, the diarists' reports, the *Records of Administration*, and the first and second drafts were destroyed. The whole process of compilation usually took several years.

Once the *Sillok* was completed, no one including the king was allowed to read it. This was to insure the autonomy of the historians and compilers as well as the objectivity of the historical records. King Sejong (r. 1418–1450) set the precedent by following official advice not to ask to read the *Sillok* of his father's reign.[3] His successors followed this rule. Only four copies of the *Sillok* were made and each was deposited in a separate historical archive. This was to ensure its preservation in case of fire or other unforeseen disasters at one or the other of the archives. Only when a certain important decision required consulting precedents were historians permitted to view the relevant section of the *Sillok* and to report their findings.

While every precaution was taken to ensure the accuracy and objectivity of the *Sillok*, no historical work is, so to speak, completely value free. As a joint venture of the establishment, sponsored by the court and summing up a reign, the *Sillok* certainly is official historiography par excellence with all of the attendant merits and demerits of works of this kind. The *Sillok* historians and compilers not only labored under such pervasive cultural influences as the concept and purpose of historical work and the moral and other criteria with which one's actions were evaluated; they were also constrained by social customs and taboos regarding their freedom to discuss the royal family.

Moreover, the role of the specific editors, especially the final editors, cannot be underestimated. This is why, during the period of intense factionalism, the phenomemon of compiling revised *Sillok* occurred. Two versions of the *Sŏnjo sillok* set the precedent. First there was the *Sŏnjo sillok*,[4] completed in 1616, supposedly representing Pugin (Northerners') views. Once the Pugin lost power with the dethronement of King Kwanghae (r. 1608–1623), the Sŏin wanted to put forth their positions in a revised version. Thus, the compilation of the *Sŏnjo sujŏng sillok* began in 1641 and was completed in 1657.[5] Similarly, Hyŏnjong's reign (r. 1659–1674) was represented by the Namin-biased *Hyŏnjong sillok*,[6] completed in 1677, and the *Hyŏnjong kaesu sillok*,[7] completed in 1683 by the Sŏin.

The compilers of the *Sukchong sillok*[8] sought a different solution. Sukchong's reign (r. 1674–1720) was not only arguably the most violent period of Yi factionalism, it was also followed by an almost equally volatile period. The *Sukchong sillok* took seven years to finish, from 1720 to 1727, during which period Noron power alternated with Soron power. Most of the *Sukchong sillok's* compilation was done by the Noron, but before it went into print, the Soron came to power in 1727. The result was Soron preparation of the *Pogwŏl chŏngo* (Additions and Corrections) which were distributed at the end of each *kwŏn*.

The *Kyŏngjong sillok*,[9] dealing with a hardly less problematic period, was completed in 1732. Though it is presumably Soron biased, Yŏngjo, with his commitment to the *t'angp'yŏng* policy from which he was reluctant to deviate since 1728, did not allow the Noron a revision. It was only in 1778, after Chŏngjo acceded, that the Noron was permitted to compile a revision, *Kyŏngjong sujong sillok*,[10] which was completed in 1781. The *Yŏngjo sillok*,[11] was compiled during the same period, and it is safe to assume that it represents Noron views. That no revised version of the *Yŏngjo sillok* appeared, or for that matter that of any reign after his, indicates that the more virulent forms of factionalism disappeared mainly because of continued Noron dominance.

Then, how do these versions differ from each other? A comparison of a key factional issue as it is presented in two versions might indicate certain differences. There was hardly a more contentious issue than that of Kyŏngjong's appointment of Yŏngjo as the regent and the subsequent retraction of it. But the descriptions of the day of the retraction in the *Kyŏngjong sillok* and the *Kyŏngjong sujŏng sillok* are surprisingly similar. In fact, when it comes to recounting how the event unfolded on that day, who said and did what and when and where, the *Kyŏngjong sujong sillok* follows the *Kyŏngjong sillok* almost verbatim.[12]

Where they differ from each other is in the historians' comments that come afterwards. In the *Kyŏngjong sillok,* consistent with the Soron view, the four Noron ministers' action is adjudged to have been motivated by their self-interest and their desire to establish their claim as the prime force behind Yŏngjo's rise to power. It does not refute the merit of Yŏngjo's regency which would have relieved Kyŏngjong of the burden of administration to tend to his frail health. But the way the Noron went about it is termed devious and their motives impure.[13] The historians' comments in the *Kyŏngjong sujŏng sillok,* on the other hand, attribute the same action of the Noron ministers to their loyalty and commitment to preserve the well-being of the state. Kyŏngjong was deeply ill, which had been admitted by the Soron themselves, and this led to the Noron ministers' reluctant acquiescence to Yŏngjo's regency.[14] Thus, in this case, it is in the interpretation of motives, not in the description of what happened, that the two versions differ from each other.

There are other ways in which the two versions disagree— through the inclusion of certain material and the omission of other material. The entry on Yun Chŭng's death is a good example. Yun Chŭng was the founder of the Soron, who parted from his teacher Song Siyŏl, the Noron patriarch, after a protracted quarrel. The *Sukchong sillok,* after entering Yun's death, his post, and age, says that the king was deeply grieved over the news and conferred upon him the honorary title Munsŏng. Then it goes on to enumerate Yun's "crimes." His "betrayal" of two teachers is mentioned and is termed the greatest and most truly unforgivable crime against the entire scholarly establishment.[15] The *Additions and Corrections* takes a different approach. After giving biographical data, it records Sukchong's eulogy, which is full of praise for Yun—his noble character, his erudition and commitment to scholarship, his filial piety, and his integrity in refusing to serve in the government, though this was regrettable to the throne.[16]

Since the *Yŏngjo sillok* is presumed to have been compiled under Noron influence, it might be useful to investigate how it treats the Soron. Under the entry of the death of Yi Kwangjwa, the representative Soron minister, it records Yŏngjo's grief, and his praise of Yi at length. The historians' comments that follow, however, are quite derogatory of Yi's political judgment and career.[17]

All in all, when it comes to factional issues, the historians and compilers of the *Sillok* made conscious efforts to distinguish between what they considered to have been facts and their own views, between objectivity and personal judgments.

Our more direct concern here is how the *Sillok* portrays the activities of the king and his family. In this, the historians were guided by certain conventions such as those specifying certain formulaic praise, or taboos which led to frequent use of euphemism. But once this barrier of rhetorical convention is overcome, one sees that the historians applied to the king basically the same moral criteria as they did to others. For instance, throughout the *Yŏngjo sillok*, the historians' comments praise what they considered royal virtue, such as Yŏngjo's exercise of frugality, and condemn what they saw as vice, such as the suppression of the bureaucratic voice.

Still, certain taboos leave one frustrated. For instance, the *Sillok* does not mention what the precise nature or specific symptoms of Kyŏngjong's or Sado's illnesses had been; it vaguely suggests some kind of mental disorder. But if the *Sillok* at times does not reveal detailed information, it does not distort the picture. It leaves enough clues and circumstantial evidence. One can piece the puzzle together and arrive at an educated guess. This of course needs to be verified by comparisons with other sources. Though laconic, the *Sillok* mentions Sado's travel in disguise, his bringing of entertainers and nuns into the palace, his terrorizing of people, his killing of his servants, his extortion of merchants, etc. In fact, one is surprised to find as much as one does. If the historians considered a certain event to be of importance, they might have resorted to euphemism, but they somehow found a way to say it.

Where one should be cautious in using the *Sillok* is not in the deliberate choices the historians made. One can penetrate and evaluate them if one is familiar with the issues and the rhetorical conventions of the period. It is rather the moral view of the period, certain beliefs and assumptions that they embraced unconsciously, that might mislead us. This is something all historians have to face and is a most difficult barrier to overcome. Except

A Historiographical Discussion

by trying to develop a fine-tuned sensitivity to the mentality of the time, there does not seem to be an easy way to deal with it.

SŬNGJŎNGWŎN ILGI
(THE RECORDS OF THE ROYAL SECRETARIAT)

The *Sŭngjŏngwŏn ilgi* is another source that I consulted quite often. As I have already mentioned, this is a record of the king's public life and his interactions with the bureaucracy. Entered on a daily basis, it records the king's daily schedule, his ritual functions, his Royal Lecture sessions, his dealings with diplomatic matters, and the memorials and other written communications he received, as well as his answers to them and his audiences and discussions with officials. Unlike the *Sillok*, this is an unedited source, and as such offers a closer view of the workings of the royal court. During Prince Sado's regency, the *Records of the Royal Secretariat* records his daily schedules as well. But since the portions that deal with his specific activities were deleted in 1776, the entries are perfunctory.

CHANGHŎN SEJA TONGGUNG ILGI
(THE RECORD OF PRINCE SADO'S TUTORIAL OFFICE)

This is a record kept by the Crown Prince Tutorial Office. Entered on a daily basis, it records the time of the prince's lecture sessions, the names of the tutors who held each session, the books read and discussed, the names of the tutors on night duty, etc. It does not, as a rule, record the contents of the discussion. Nevertheless, one can get a fairly accurate picture of the prince's scholarly schedule.

YI KWANGHYŎN'S DIARY (YI KWANGHYŎN ILGI)

I used Yi Kwanghyŏn's diary to describe Sado's execution. I found it in the Changsŏgak, the Yi royal family private collection, formerly housed in Ch'angdŏk Palace, now moved to the Academy of Korean Studies. It is in the form of a copied manuscript. The diary is extremely revealing, but perhaps one should evaluate its authenticity.

From the time of his appointment as regent, Sado had been assigned a royal secretary and a recorder. They belonged to the Royal Secretariat of the king, but by turns they were sent to serve the regent. At the beginning of the diary, Yi Kwanghyŏn claims that, on the eleventh of the intercalary fifth month (July 2), 1762, he was appointed a recorder as a temporary replacement for Kim Hwajung. According to the secretariat roster, Kim Hwajung had been ill and absent since the fifth.[18] Consistent with his word, Yi Kwanghyŏn appears on the secretariat roster as a recorder assigned to Sado on the twelfth and thirteenth. Also, the royal secretaries on duty at the crown prince's court on the twelfth and the thirteenth were Pak Sanap and Cho Chunghoe, as Yi says.[19] The thirteenth was the day when Sado was put into the rice chest. From the fourteenth, no separate court was listed in the *Records of the Royal Secretariat.*

As a recorder, Yi was allowed to record everything that went on that day. His report would have been included in the *Records of the Royal Secretariat* except for the fact that in 1776, Chŏngjo requested and received Yŏngjo's permission to delete those portions in the *Records of the Royal Secretariat* that concerned Sado. Hence, the entries on Sado in the *Records of the Royal Secretariat* are very bland indeed.

Nevertheless, the question remains of whether the version of Yi Kwanghyŏn's diary that I found at Changsŏgak is indeed the one written by Yi Kwanghyŏn. The diary is included in a book called *Imo ilgi* (Records Concerning the Year 1762). The book is a collection of documents related to the incident of Prince Sado. Except for Yi Kwanghyŏn's diary, which is the first document in the book, all the documents in the book are public in nature. The book includes such documents as Yŏngjo's tomb inscription for Lady Yi, Sado's mother, Chŏngjo's declaration that Sado was his father and numerous memorials to Yŏngjo, Sado and Chŏngjo bearing directly on the incident. The Changsŏgak catalogue (*Changsŏgak tosŏ Han'gukp'an ch'ongmongnok*) gives the editors as Yi Kwanghyŏn et al., but this probably just reflects the fact that the first document in the book is his. There is no evidence that he participated in collecting the materials in the book. The public documents in the book can be firmly dated and on this basis one can deduce that they could not have been collected before the last decade of the eighteenth century. It was most likely assembled much later, perhaps in the nineteenth or the twentieth century.

There are two editions of *Imo ilgi* in Changsŏgak. Both bear the seal of the Yi royal family library. One is a manuscript edition in one volume of 79 pages. It bears a statement that copying was completed in 1924. The other edition is a printed edition in one volume of 98 pages. It does not bear a precise date but it indicates that the initial copying was done between 1911 and 1940.

It is highly unlikely that only one document in the collection would be inauthentic but still one should evaluate the document on the basis of internal evidence. I would venture to say that the document is authentic. First of all, details match with descriptions in other sources. For a work of imagination, it is too accurate. In fact, it is difficult to imagine that it is written by someone who was not on the scene. Not many were there, and only a few historians were allowed to record what was going on. Further, a detailed minute-by-minute account suggests that it was not recorded from memory but from the scene; Yi Kwanghyon was one of a few people who could have done it.

The *Sillok* does not mention Yi Kwanghyŏn but this does not contradict his presence. The *Sillok* does not mention everyone who was on the scene. Yi was quite insignificant, a new, temporary recorder. He disappears from sight after that day. Probably not many people would have known his name in the first place and even those who did probably forgot him promptly afterwards. That it was a time of terrible confusion makes it all the more likely that Yi came and went with no trace.

Except, of course, for his diary. It is possible or even likely that Yi exaggerates his role. In his description, one detects a certain zeal, that of someone new to the job witnessing a truly unusual event. But his account on the whole rings true.

Appendix 4

LADY HONG, *A JOURNAL WRITTEN IN LEISURE* (*HANJUNGNOK*)

In 1795, thirty-three years after Sado's execution, his widow, Lady Hong of Hyegyŏng Palace, began a series of memoirs. The original manuscript is lost, and there are various copies, somewhat different from each other in some passages and arrangements. Professor Kim Tonguk compared the three major versions and prepared a modern text. Since this is widely available, I referred to the Kim Tonguk edition for the sake of convenience.

The journal consists of four memoirs (six chapters in the Kim edition) each written for a specific audience. The portion I use is from the last memoir, which was written in 1805 for King Sunjo (r. 1800–1834), her grandson. In the preface to this memoir, Lady Hong says that Sunjo should be informed of events involving his forebears and that she was the only one who could provide such information.

In some sense, Lady Hong's memoir is self-serving, especially in her defense of her family, the Hongs. At the time of Sado's execution, her father, Hong Ponghan, served as Minister of the Left. Perhaps because of his relationship to Sado, lest he be suspected of an overly protective attitude toward his son-in-law, Hong might have taken a deliberately cool attitude toward Sado's execution. At any rate, in the volatile political climate after Sado's execution, Hong suffered royal disfavor.

Lady Hong's obvious bias toward her family notwithstanding, *A Journal Written in Leisure* is a very valuable and moving account of the conflict that developed between Yŏngjo and Sado. Though she is rather critical of Yŏngjo for his harshness toward his son, which she sees as the original cause for Sado's insanity, she gives a remarkably balanced picture. As for the final decision to execute Sado, she seems to even agree with its inevitability. She extends sympathy to all involved for the painful role each had to play and the duty each had to perform.

Writing so many years after the incident, for separate audiences and for special purposes, Lady Hong might not be as accurate or

254

as candid as one might wish, especially when it comes to certain details. But her psychologically insightful account of the growing tensions between father and son, and the details of Sado's gradual deterioration, not found anywhere else, provide us with an invaluable understanding of the complexities of the situation.

A COMPARISON OF THE DESCRIPTIONS OF SADO'S EXECUTION

I have presented the portions of the *Sillok* and Lady Hong's journal that deal with Sado's execution and Yi Kwanghyŏn's diary. Perhaps it might be useful to briefly compare these three accounts.

There is no glaring discrepancy between the *Sillok* account and Yi's diary. Since the *Sillok* is a much shorter summary of that day, the sequence of events, such as who came in at what point, is not always very clear. This might give an impression that it differs from what Yi Kwanghyŏn says, but in most instances, this is because Yi's account is more detailed. There is one point on which the accounts do differ, however. The *Sillok* says that the three ministers came in twice, but Yi Kwanghyŏn mentions that they came in only once, and on his insistence, at that. But Yi says that he had been in and out of the scene on errands, and he might have missed their second entry. Moreover, as is common with a young person new to a big organization, Yi seems to have been predisposed to think that high-ranking older ministers were only concerned with their own safety.

The above two sources and Lady Hong's journal are different in nature. Lady Hong starts with what Sado said to her before he went to see his father. The other accounts are certainly not privy to that. But once Sado encounters his father, Lady Hong, who was not present at the scene, reports from outside on what she found out by sending someone to the scene and what she overheard by eavesdropping from behind the wall.

Since she writes in Korean, while the other two accounts are written in classical Chinese, what Sado was supposed to have said to his father comes across differently. Her version seems to be more like what one imagines a son would say to his father.

There is, however, one obvious discrepancy between her description and Yi's—time reference. According to Yi, Yŏngjo left for Ch'angdŏk Palace around seven in the morning and Sado was already prostrate in front of Yŏngjo by nine. Lady Hong says that Yŏngjo's arrival was delayed and that Sado did not leave for Hwinyŏngjŏn until sometime in the afternoon. Since the *Sillok* does not mention time until the very end, it does not help to solve this mystery. True, it was not the period of quartz watches, but rather of mostly guessing by looking at the sun. Still, the gap is rather disconcerting. One might allow for Lady Hong's flustered frame of mind. Also, it was in early July, when the day was longest. In addition, it was reported to have been a very hot day.[20] Thus, with the sun already quite high and the temperature very hot, and having already done several psychologically taxing things, she may have overestimated the lateness of the hour. And when she was writing her memoir forty-five years after the event, it is likely that it was not the actual time of the day that she remembered but rather a certain atmosphere. Whatever the reason, there is a time gap, and if one believes Yi Kwanghyŏn's diary to be authentic, his time reference, as an official historian, should be more credible. When it comes to when the day ended, however, all three accounts seem to be in agreement—very late at night.

NOTES

1. Confucian Kingship and Royal Authority in the Yi Monarchy

1. *Shu-ching*, V:1:1:3; Legge, *Chinese Classics*, III:II:285.

2. See *Yao-tien, Shun-tien, Ta Yü-mo,* and *Kao-t'ao-mo* in *Shu-ching*, in Juan Yuan, ed., *Shih-san-ching chu-su*, 1:117–59.

3. *Mencius*, I:1:3:3; Legge, *Classics*, II:128.

4. *Mencius*, IV:1:6:3; Legge, *Classics*, II:294.

5. *Shu-ching*, V:1:2:7; Legge, *Classics*, III:II:292.

6. The kind of popular sovereignty expressed in the Confucian kingship was not linked to public participation in government as it was in the West. It may be said that the concept of a popular mandate both in Christian Europe and Confucian East Asia had at its base the belief in the commonality of men. But the emphasis on the commonality of men in the West diminished the authority of both the church and the monarchy. The notion of the "brotherhood of all believers" that emerged with the Reformation, by establishing individuals' relationships to God, further circumvented the unique role of the Church as the mediator of divine love. Moreover, in western European states individual rights and interests gained ascendancy after the French Revolution through wider public participation in government. See Bendix, *Kings or People*, pp. 8–9. But in a Confucian monarchy, the idea of the commonality of men did not necessarily undermine hierarchy.

7. Liu, "How Did a Neo-Confucian School Become the State Orthodoxy?" p. 503.

8. Fan Tsu-yü, *Fan t'ai-shih chi*, 14:11a. Translation adopted from de Bary, *Neo-Confucian Orthodoxy and the Learning of the Mind-and-Heart*, p. 30.

9. de Bary, *Neo-Confucian Orthodoxy*, pp. 27–38.

10. Chu Hsi, *Hui-an hsien-sheng Chu Wen-kung wen-chi*, 11:35b–36a. Translation adopted from de Bary, *Neo-Confucian Orthodoxy*, p. 34.

11. On the origins of imperial autocracy in the Ming dynasty, see Dardess, *Confucianism and Autocracy*.

12. Institutional apparati including such elements as the palace (secret) me-

1. Confucian Kingship in Yi Monarchy

morial system clearly reflected as well as contributed to such power. Wu, *Communication and Imperial Control in China.*

13. On Ch'ien-lung's image building, see Harold L. Kahn, *Monarchy in the Emperor's Eyes.*

14. *T'aejo sillok,* 1:43a–45a.

15. This was made possible, at least in part, because of the changing and unstable situations in neighboring countries. In the 1350s, the last years of the Mongol rule of China, many anti-Mongol secret societies had sprung up. One of them, the Red Turbans, had become powerful and for a while contended with the Chu Yüan-chang forces. The Red Turbans even entered Korea, ransacking P'yŏngyang and plundering Kaesŏng, the Koryŏ capital. At the same time, the Korean coastal regions were being frequently raided by Japanese pirates. With no strong central authority to contain them after decades of civil war, the Japanese pirates were marauding the Korean coasts with impunity. There were not just one or two ships but often fleets of two hundred to three hundred ships with as many as several thousand pirates organized into infantry and cavalry. From 1375 to 1388, there was an average of twenty-seven raids per year. In this situation, generals who fought successfully, driving out the Red Turbans and defending the coastal regions against the pirates, gained fame and power. Yi Sŏnggye was one of the generals who achieved prominence through this endeavor. By 1388, Yi vanquished his rivals and became a virtual ruler except in name. Yi formed an alliance with a group of Neo-Confucian scholars. With Yi Sŏnggye's blessing, these scholars carried out a land reform, nationalizing most of the land. The confiscation of the large estates held by the pro-Yüan Koryŏ elite effectively stripped that group of its financial bases. Having already gained political, military, and economic control, Yi Sŏnggye took the throne in 1392. Han Yŏngu, *Chosŏn chŏn'gi sahoe kyŏngje yŏn'gu,* pp. 20–21, 32–43.

16. Dardess argues that they heavily leaned toward strong central leadership. Dardess, *Confucianism and Autocracy,* pp. 131–81.

17. Han Yŏngu, *Chosŏn chŏn'gi,* pp. 11–50.

18. Chŏng Tojŏn, *Chosŏn kyŏnggukchŏn,* pp. 204–10. See also Chung Chai-sik, "Chŏng Tojŏn: 'Architect' of Yi Dynasty Government and Ideology," pp. 63–73.

19. Chŏng Tojŏn, *Kyŏngje mun'gam,* pp. 167–77.

20. Yi Sŏngmu, "The Influence of Neo-Confucianism on Education and the Civil Service Examination System in Fourteenth- and Fifteenth-Century Korea," pp. 135–60.

21. Concerning this process, see Deuchler, "Neo-Confucianism: The Impulse for Social Action in Early Yi Korea."

22. Deuchler, "The Tradition: Women During the Yi Dynasty," pp. 1–13.

23. Ch'oe Honggi, *Han'guk hojŏk chedosa yŏn'gu,* pp. 73–103.

24. For examples, see Yi Sugŏn, *Yŏngnam sarimp'a ŭi hyŏngsŏng.*

25. Yi Kwanggyu, "Chosŏn wangjo sidae ŭi chaesan sangsok."

26. Peterson, "Women without Sons," pp. 39–43; Ch'oe Chaesŏk, *Han'guk kajok chedosa yŏn'gu,* pp. 588–635.

27. Song Chunho, "Han'guk e issŏsŏ ŭi kagye kirok ŭi yŏksa wa kŭ ihae," pp. 116–26.

28. Kawashima, "The Local Gentry Association in Mid-Yi Dynasty Korea," pp. 113–24.

1. Confucian Kingship in Yi Monarchy

29. For the contents of several community compacts in the sixteenth century, see Sakai Tadao, "Yi Yulgok and the Community Compact."

30. Sohn, *Social History of the Early Yi Dynasty 1392–1592*, pp. 124–45.

31. On the financial remunerations and social prestige granted to them, see Wagner, *The Literati Purges*, pp. 5–10.

32. From 1452 to 1492, for instance, only three out of twenty men who served as high ministers in the State Council were not merit subjects. *Ibid.*, p. 13.

33. There were four purges (*sahwa*), in 1498, 1504, 1519, and 1545, respectively. For the first three purges, see *ibid.*, pp. 23–120.

34. Haboush, "The Education of the Yi Crown Prince," pp. 210–11.

35. Yi Yulgok, *Tongho mundap.*

36. Yi Yulgok, *Sŏnghak chibyo.*

37. On the Yi social class structure, see Wagner, *The Literati Purges*, pp. 11–12.

38. The social origins of yangban of the early Yi are much disputed. Han Yŏngu, for instance, paints a picture of rather fluid social mobility in the early Yi. Han Yŏngu, *Chosŏn chŏn'gi*, pp. 393–413. Yi Sŏngmu, on the other hand, believes that a more rigid structure took root very early in the dynasty. Yi Sŏngmu, *Chosŏn ch'ogi yangban yŏn'gu.*

39. The social origins of the new elite of the sixteenth century are disputed. A large proportion of them seem to have come from the same social strata as the old elite, though there was some new blood. For their social origins, see Yi Pyŏnghyu, *Chosŏn chŏn'gi Kiho sarimp'a yŏn'gu;* Yi Sugŏn, *Yŏngnam sarimp'a ŭi hyŏngsŏng.*

40. Wagner. "The Ladder of Success in Yi Dynasty Korea," p. 4.

41. *Ibid.*, pp. 4–8.

42. E.g., *Kukcho inmulchi;* Min Iksu, *Yŏhŭng Min Ssi kasŭng kiryak.* For a sampling of eighteenth-century officials, see Haboush, "A Heritage of Kings," pp. 117–18.

43. This resulted from the change in marriage custom. During the Yi dynasty, a man was allowed to have only one legal wife and so concubines were generally taken from lower social classes. Discrimination against concubines' children revealed class bias but it also reflected the importance of the maternal line in Korean society. From the Silla period (58 B.C.–935 A.D.), a mother's social status had been an important factor in determining her children's status. For about fifty years in the mid-sixteenth century, children by concubines of commoner status were allowed to take higher government examinations, but this was later reversed. Yi T'aejin, "Sŏŏl ch'adae ko."

44. Wagner, *The Literati Purges*, p. 2.

45. Hi-woong Kang, *The Development of the Korean Ruling Class from Late Silla to Early Koryŏ.*

46. Yi Sŏngmu, "Education and Civil Service Examination System," pp. 135–60.

47. Palais, *Politics and Policy in Traditional Korea*, p. 114.

48. According to Taga, there were about three hundred *shu-yüan* in Ch'ing China. Taga Akigorō, *Chūgoku kyōikushi*, p. 99.

49. Yi Pŏmjik, "Chosŏn chŏn'gi ŭi kyosaeng sinbun," pp. 323–41.

50. Yu Hongnyŏl, "Chōsen ni okeru shoin no seiritsu (2)."

51. There were 741 posts in the central civil bureaucracy, but of these, 95 were unsalaried while 105 were supernumerary posts. Yi Sŏngmu, *Yangban*, pp. 125–

1. Confucian Kingship in Yi Monarchy

27. These figures are based on the *Kyŏngguk taejon*, a late fifteenth-century book of statutes of the Yi government. By the eighteenth century, the bureaucracy had expanded a bit, but not significantly.

52. The military bureaucracy consisted of 319 posts in the central government, 502 provincial posts, and 3,005 supernumerary posts. Yi Sŏngmu, *Yangban*, pp. 125–27.

53. E.g., eunuchs. Crawford, "Eunuch Power in the Ming dynasty," pp. 115–16.

54. E.g., the Manchu bannermen, the palace memorial system, and bond servants. Wu, *Communication*.

55. A similar, if slightly less strict, policy concerning the imperial clan was in force during the Ming dynasty. Nunome Chōfū, "Minchō no shoōseisaku to sono eikyō."

56. In fact, the Chŏnju Yi constituted the largest number of *munkwa* passers from one clan during the Yi dynasty. Wagner, "The Ladder of Success," p. 7.

57. Wagner, *The Literati Purges*, pp. 14, 23–50.

58. Ch'oe Sŭnghŭi, *Chosŏn ch'ogi ŏn'gwan ŏllon yŏn'gu*, pp. 99–153.

59. Wagner, *The Literati Purges*, pp. 22–123.

60. *Hyojong sillok*, 21:15b.

61. Song Siyŏl reports what went on. Song Siyŏl, *Toktae sŏrhwa*.

62. *SS*, 60:5a–b.

63. *SS*, 60:8a–9a; 60:15b–17a.

64. Haboush, "A Heritage of Kings," pp. 61–68.

65. A group of social critics, known as the school of practical learning (*sirhak*), expressed somewhat different views. But these outside intellectuals still emphasized the importance of the king's performance. *See* Haboush, "The *Sirhak* Movement of the Late Yi Dynasty."

66. Yi Yulgok, *Tongho mundap*, 15:6b.

67. Yang Lien-sheng, "Historical Notes on the Chinese World Order."

68. E.g., Cantos 18, 25, 44, 66, 79, 82, 104, 106. Lee, *Songs of Flying Dragons*, pp. 173, 178, 198, 217, 229–30, 232, 251, 253.

69. Han Young-woo, "Kija Worship in the Koryŏ and Early Yi Dynasties: A Cultural Symbol in the Relationship Between Korea and China," in de Bary and Haboush, eds., *The Rise of Neo-Confucianism*, pp. 359–60.

70. Deuchler, "Neo-Confucianism," pp. 81–84.

71. As an example of this attitude, see Meskill, *Ch'oe Pu's Diary*.

72. Deuchler, "Reject the False and Uphold the Straight," pp. 400–01.

73. The *Sŏnjo sillok* gives 50,000 as the number of Ming soldiers in Korea at the conclusion of the war. *Sŏnjo sillok*, 105:15a–b.

74. When Kwanghae sent troops to assist the Ming army in 1618, he was alleged to have instructed Kang Hongnip, the commander, to surrender to the Manchus if the situation became hopeless and to inform them that Korean participation was exacted under duress. Kang did exactly that. This was used as a reason for Kwanghae's deposal (*Kwanghaegun ilgi*, 187:8b). Ibana Iwakichi suspects that this was a fabrication. See his *Kōkaikun jidai no Man Sen kankei*, pp. 186–96. According to a diary kept by one of Kang's officers in the battle, however, Kwanghae's instructions seem to have been well known. See Yi Minhwan, *Ch'aekchung ilgi*.

75. *Injo sillok*, 1:5a–6a. But of course, there were other factors in his dethronement. For details, see Haboush, "A Heritage of Kings," pp. 34–36.

1. Confucian Kingship in Yi Monarchy

76. Haboush, "A Heritage of Kings," pp. 36–37.
77. *Ibid.*, pp. 61–86.
78. On the Ming Restoration movement, see Struve, *The Southern Ming*. On the Ch'ing subjugation of resistance movements, see Wills, "Maritime China from Wang Chih to Shih Lang."
79. Yun Hyu, "Tok Sangsŏ," in *Paekho chŏnsŏ*, p. 1647; "Toksŏgi, Chungyong," in *ibid.*, p. 1447.
80. Song Siyŏl, "Ŏrok," in *Purok*, 5:30a, in *Songja taejŏn*.
81. Miura Kunio, "Orthodoxy and Heterodoxy in Seventeenth-Century Korea."
82. This was at the bottom of the celebrated rites controversy (*yesong*) between the Sŏin and the Namin. For a fuller discussion of these issues, see Haboush, "A Heritage of Kings," pp. 40–61.
83. *Ibid.*, pp. 61–86.
84. For details, see, *T'ongmun'gwanji*, 9:1–12:12.
85. For their travel diaries, see, *Yŏnhaengnok sŏnjip*. See also Ledyard, "Korean Travellers in China."
86. The scholars of the practical learning school grappled with this question. Hong Taeyong and Pak Chiwŏn used the notion of "the civilized and the barbarous" (*hwai/hua-i*). Hong challenged the traditional classification which made China and the Chinese "civilized" and the rest of the world "barbarous." See Hong Taeyong, "Ŭisan mundap," in Hong Taeyong, *Tamhŏnsŏ*, 1:4:36b–37b. Pak Chiwŏn accepted the traditional distinction, arguing instead for a separation between political and cultural entities. The Manchu domination had not annihilated Chinese culture which was intact and functioning in China. See Pak Chiwŏn, *Yŏrha ilgi*, in Pak Chiwŏn, *Yŏnamjip*, 12:2a–4a. See also Min Tugi, "*Yŏrha ilgi* ŭi iryŏn'gu." Yi Ik and Chŏng Yagyong, on the other hand, sought to define the Korean identity independent of the traditional division between the "civilized" and the "barbarous," leaving the Manchu problem as a special case. Yi Ik believed that Korea, as an equal of China, should have her own source and tradition of legitimacy independent of, but parallel to, that of China. See Yi Ik, "Punya," in Yi Ik, *Sŏngho sasol*, 1:31:33. See also Yi Usŏng, "Yijo hugi kŭn'gi hakp'a e issŏsŏ ŭi chŏngt'ongnon ŭi chŏn'gae." Chŏng Yagyong accepted the Chinese designation of Korea as not "civilized" but he downgraded the importance of this notion. Korea was an autonomous entity with her own customs and culture, civilized or not, and this should be a considerable source of pride. See Chŏng Yagyong, "Ch'ŏlpal wiron" and "Tonghoron," in Chŏng Yagyong, *Chŏng Tasan chŏnsŏ*, 1:12:7a–b and 1:12:7b–8a. See also Haboush, "The *Sirhak* Movement of the Late Yi Dynasty."
87. For a discussion of this, see Haboush, "The Education of the Yi Crown Prince," pp. 168–171.
88. The scholars of practical learning reexamined this moral view of history. They did not categorically reject the idea that history manifested a certain moral principle, but they argued that historical events were the result of composite temporal factors. To formulate conclusions on the basis of the morality of an age or its principal figures would obscure rather than illuminate historical principles. This belief in the autonomy of history and the inevitability of historical forces led them to emphasize that an understanding of history required the examination of the complex external factors governing an event, unhindered by simple moralistic cause-and-effect formulas. See Yi Ik, "Kangmok," in Yi Ik, *Sŏngho sasŏl*, 2:6. See

261

1. Confucian Kingship in Yi Monarchy

also Hwang Wŏn'gu, "Sirhakp'a ŭi sahak iron." It is interesting to compare this to a similar phenomenon in China and Japan at the time. See Demiéville, "Chang Hsüeh-ch'eng and His Historiography," pp. 167–85; see also Maruyama Masao, *Studies in the Intellectual History of Tokugawa Japan*, pp. 97–101.

89. See Han Young-woo, "Kija Worship," pp. 349–74.

90. For example, Wang An-shih of the Sung dynasty and Huang Tsung-hsi of the early Ch'ing dynasty all referred to the ideal of the sage kings' era in an exhortation for reform. See de Bary, "A Reappraisal of Neo-Confucianism," pp. 100–06. See also his article, "Chinese Despotism and the Confucian Ideal." Yu Hyŏngwŏn, a seventeenth-century Korean scholar of the practical learning school, took the law of the sage kings' era as a reference point in his call for change. See Yu Hyŏngwŏn, *Pan'gye surok*, 2:17a–18a; 17:17b; 25:71-b. See also Chŏng Kubok, "Pan'gye Yu Hyŏngwŏn ŭi sahoe kaehyŏk sasang." The *Rites of Chou (Chou-li)* was one of the main sources of inspiration for Chŏng Tojŏn's *Chosŏn kyŏnggukchŏn.* Chung Chai-sik, "Chŏng Tojŏn," pp. 63–64.

2. Yŏngjo's Reign: Images of Sagehood

1. *YS*, 1:1a–2a

2. *KS*, 5:36a–b.

3. For details, see Haboush, "A Heritage of Kings," pp. 86–105.

4. Sukchong had three sons who survived to adulthood, Kyŏngjong, Yŏngjo, and Prince Yŏnnyŏng. Sukchong seems to have been partial to Yŏnnyŏng, his youngest son. But Yŏnnyŏng died in 1718 at the age of twenty.

5. Yi Chae, *Samgwan'gi*, 2:22b, in *P'aerim*, 9:331–401.

6. Min Chinwŏn, *Tanam mallok*, 2:8b–9a.

7. See Wright, *The Last Stand of Chinese Conservatism*, pp. 43–48.

8. *YS*, 3:30a–b.

9. The founder of the Ming dynasty began his reign on this note. See his imperial proclamation in Wang Ch'ung-wu, *Ming-pen-chi chiao-chu*, p. 107.

10. Chinese emperors like Han Wu-ti and T'ang T'ai-tsung offered the *feng* and *shan* sacrifices but this symbolized their status as Sons of Heaven. Shryock, *The Origin and Development of the State Cult of Confucius*, pp. 36, 153. After the Yi dynasty was declared to be completely independent of China in the late nineteenth century, the Yi monarch performed sacrifices to Heaven and Earth for the first time in 1897. *Chŭngbo munhŏn pigo*, 54:1b–2a.

11. For details, see *Kukcho oryeŭi* and *Kukcho sok oryeŭi.*

12. *Kyŏngguk taejŏn*, 1:259–60.

13. *Chosŏn wangjo ŭi chesa*, pp. 33–36.

14. *Sok taejŏn*, p. 148.

15. For discussions of ritual, see Wechsler, *Offerings of Jade and Silk.* See also Wright, "Sui Legitimation," pp. 36–37.

16. E.g., *YS*, 7:19b; 42:1a; 63:32a; 79: 25b.

17. E.g., *YS*, 29:30b–39a; 31:29b; 79:25b; 87:6b.

18. *YS*, 7:14b; 29:33a–b; 31:32b; 122:11b.

19. *YS*, 79:25b–28b.

20. *YS*, 42:22b–23a; 96:15b–16a; 126:1a.

21. *YS*, 32:27a; 45:27a–b; 46:2b; 107:6b.

22. *YS*, 97:23b.
23. *SS*, 39:2a–5b.
24. *SS*, 39:24a–b.
25. *SS*, 40:50b–51a.
26. *YS*, 11:5a.
27. *YS*, 69:22a.
28. *YS*, 69–25a.
29. *YS*, 69:25a–26b. Incense and paper money were burned in ancestral sacrifices. If the Ming had been able to continue such sacrifices, then the Korean practice would have been a sacrilege.
30. *YS*, 69:26b–27a.
31. *YS*, 69:27b–32b.
32. The puns were the characters for sun and moon which combine to form the character for Ming, which means "brightness."
33. *YS*, 103:11a–15a.
34. *YS*, 8:13b.
35. *YS*, 9:28a–29b; 9:33b.
36. E.g., Empress Kao's *Nai-hsün* in 1723; Chiao Hung's *Yang-cheng t'u-chieh* in 1749; a revised version of *Hwang Myŏng t'onggi*; and *Hwanghwa chip* in 1773.
37. *YS*, 120:26a.
38. A Korean ship was driven to the China coast by a storm. Chinese officials inquiring into the matter discovered the Ming reign year on the mariners' identification plaques. *YS*, 26:16a.
39. *YS*, 26:17b.
40. *SI*, 45:92–158.
41. *SI*, 45:275–83; 45:558–61.
42. *SI*, 45:704.
43. E.g., *YS*, 41:8b.
44. *YS*, 28:16a.
45. They suggested that the Yi kings' tablets should bear the Ming rather than Ch'ing reign year. *YS*, 63:14a; 66:3a–b.
46. Yŏngjo's decision to have the Ming reign title inscribed on the plaques for successful candidates in the special examination of 1764 is a good example. *YS*, 103:5b.
47. *SI*, 56:572b.
48. *Chŭngbo munhŏn pigo*, 64:7b–17a.
49. *SI*, 50:339–40.
50. *YS*, 63:19a; 29:40b; 49:23b; *Chŭngbo munhŏn pigo*, 64:11a.
51. *YS*, 31:3b.
52. *YS*, 67:6b–7a.
53. *YS*, 90:6b.
54. *YS*, 9:40b.
55. *YS*, 13:38b–39a; 29a:1a; 60:12b; 67:26a.
56. *YS*, 52:19a–20b.
57. *YS*, 99:16b.
58. *YS*, 11:17a–b; 31:3b.
59. *YS*, 31:3b; 32:9a–b.
60. Yŏngjo read this book in 1749. See Appendix 3.

263

61. *SI*, 57:430.

62. *Chŭngbo munhŏn pigo*, 64:4b–7b.

63. E.g., *YS*, 11:6b; 49:24a; 49:26a; 64:7a–b; 94:11b.

64. For details, see *Sajik ŭigwe*.

65. *Chongmyo ŭigwe*.

66. E.g., *YS*, 61:25a–26b.

67. *Chŭngbo munhŏn pigo*, 59:1a–61:8b.

68. *YS*, 61:25b–26a.

69. *YS*, 37:25b; 57:37b.

70. *YS*, 58:7b.

71. *YS*, 57:37b; 67:6b.

72. *YS*, 45:21a.

73. *Hyojong kasang ikho togam ŭigwe*.

74. *SI*, 71:368. For Yongjo's gift to Hyojong's son-in-law, see *YS*, 63:1a.

75. *Kyŏngjong taewang kukhyul tŭngnok*.

76. *Sŏnwŏn segye*, 31b, 32b.

77. The Yi kings who were honored in this way are the following: Sejong, Sejo, Sŏngjong, Chungjong, Sŏnjo, Injo, Hyojong, Hyŏnjong, Sukchong, Yŏngjo, Chŏngjo, Sunjo, and Hŏnjong. It appears that the practice became more common in the later period of the dynasty. *Sŏnwŏn segye*, 11b, 15a, 18a, 21a, 25a, 28a, 30a, 31a–b, 32b, 41a, 42b, 45b.

78. Sŏ Myŏngŭng, "Haengjang," in *Wŏnnŭngji*.

79. *SI*, 66:490.

80. *Sŏnŭi Wanghu kukhyul tŭngnok*.

81. *Inwŏn Wanghu ch'ilchonho chonsung togam ŭigwe; Inwŏn Wanghu ch'usang chonho okch'aengmun; Inwŏn Wanghu ojonho chonsung togam ŭigwe;* and *Inwŏn Wanghu yukchonho chonsung togam ŭigwe.*

82. *Yŏlsŏng ŏje*, pp. 137–38.

83. Sŏ Myŏngŭng, "Haengjang."

84. *KS*, 5:36a–b.

85. *Inwŏn Wanghu kukhyul ch'o tŭngnok.*

86. *SI*, 63:742–78.

87. E.g., Yŏngjo, *Yŏngse ch'umorok* and Yŏngjo, *Yŏngse sok ch'umorok*.

88. *Sŏnwŏn segye*, for instance, does not record secondary consorts.

89. *YS*, 1:10b–11a.

90. *YS*, 8:30b–31a.

91. Lady Ch'oe's father was posthumously given the post of the Prime Minister. *YS*, 37:29a–b.

92. *YS*, 50:3b.

93. *YS*, 50:4a.

94. *YS*, 50:4b–5a.

95. *YS*, 50:4b–5a.

96. *YS*, 50:5b–6a.

97. Kahn, *Monarchy in the Emperor's Eyes*, pp. 87–97. On rites controversies in China, see Fisher, "The Great Ritual Controversy."

98. *YS*, 50:8b–9a.

99. *SS*, 39:9b.

2. Yŏngjo's Reign: Images of Sagehood

100. Kim Yongsuk, "Yijo kungjung p'ungsok ŭi yŏn'gu," in Kim Yongsuk, *Yijo yŏryu munhak mit kungjung p'ungsok ŭi yŏn'gu*, p. 307.

101. Yi Munjŏng, *Sumunnok*, 1:39a in *P'aerim*, 9:224.

102. *YS*, 50:9a.

103. *SS*, 25:12b.

104. *Sukpin Suyang Ch'oessi myoji*.

105. *Sukchong sillok* offers two explanations. One confirms Lady Ch'oe's role. The other is that Min Chinwŏn and Min Chinhu had informed Sukchong of Lady Chang's "evil" activities in compliance with Inhyŏn's request that they do so after her death. *SS*, 35B:11b–12a.

106. Min Chinwŏn maintains, however, that it was Lady Ch'oe who had informed the king. Min Chinwŏn, *Tanam mallok*, 1:46a.

107. *Sukpin Suyang Ch'oessi myoji*.

108. Min Chinwŏn, *Tanam mallok*, 2:15a.

109. *YS*, 59:3a.

110. *YS*, 59:15a–16a.

111. *YS*, 79:31b–32a.

112. *Yuksanggung sangch'aengin ŭi*.

113. *YS*, 80:6b–7a.

114. *YS*, 80:18b–19a.

115. *SI*, 61:126–28.

116. *YS*, 63:32a. The temple name, conferred upon the King on his death, was decided upon by a committee appointed by his successor. The *Sillok* makes no reference to the fact that the committee that chose Yŏngjong (in Chinese, Ying-tsung) was aware of the King's pronouncement on the matter made in 1746 (*Chŏngjo sillok*, 1:3a). Yŏngjong was changed to Yŏngjo, a more exalted name, in 1889.

117. *YS*, 109:28a–b.

118. *YS*, 105:12a–b.

119. Ssu-ma Ch'ien, *Shih-chi*, 8:2459–69.

120. *SI*, 74:970–72. The *Sillok* or *Sŭngjŏngwŏn ilgi* does not mention the content of the phrase. Ch'ae Chegong, a minister of a board at the time, refers to it. Ch'ae Chegong, "Tok No Chungnyŏnjŏn," in Ch'ae Chegong, *Pŏnam sŏnsaengjip*, kwŏn 59.

121. *YS*, 125:7a–8a.

122. *SI*, 76:881–82.

123. *Hwihoch'ŏp*.

124. Later Ikchong, posthumously, and Kojong, while on the throne, received similar titles. *Munjo Ikhwangje ch'usang chonho okch'aengmun; Kojong kasang chonho okch'aengmun*.

125. *SI*, 76:948.

126. *SI*, 76:954–55.

127. *SI*, 77:2.

128. This section, in a shorter form, was previously published. See Haboush, "Confucian Rhetoric and Ritual as Techniques of Political Dominance."

129. Haboush, "The Education of the Yi Crown Prince," pp. 161–64.

130. Kwon, "The Royal Lecture of Early Yi Korea (1)."

131. Haboush, "Education," pp. 164, 211.

265

132. Some Ch'ing emperors took the role as arbiter with impunity. They lectured to officials rather than being lectured to. Sakai Tadao, *Chūgoku zensho no kenkyū*, pp. 7–8. See also Nivison, "Ho-shen and His Accusers," pp. 222–23.

133. I am grateful to Professor Pei-yi Wu for providing me with this information.

134. For details, see Kwon, "The Royal Lecture," pp. 90–104.

135. *SI*, 32:1295.

136. *SI*, 32:3.

137. E.g., *SI*, 32:65–80.

138. *YS*, 17:32b.

139. In the early Yi, the distinction between the curriculum of the *kyŏngyŏn* and that of the *sodae* was less marked. Haboush, "Education," pp. 191–92.

140. See Appendix 3.

141. For records of the Royal Lecture from Hyojong (r. 1649–1659) to Kojong (r. 1863–1907), see *Yŏlsŏngjo kye kang ch'aekcha ch'aje*. For Sejong and Sŏngjong (r. 1469–1494), see Kwon, "The Royal Lecture," pp. 106–07.

142. The only text Sejong reread was the *Extended Meaning of the Great Learning* (*Ta-hsüeh yen-i*). He read it twice. Kwon, "The Royal Lecture," p. 106.

143. Chŏng Chedu, "Yonju," in Chŏng Chedu, *Hagokchip*, pp. 50–62. Chŏng was a Wang Yang-ming scholar.

144. *Ibid.*, p. 54.

145. *YS*, 41:36a.

146. *YS*, 42:1a.

147. *SI*, 51:730.

148. *YS*, 56:15b–16a.

149. *YS*, 47:43b.

150. *YS*, 56:16a.

151. *SI*, 54:796–869.

152. *SI*, 54:875–901.

153. *SI*, 55:594–96; 693–95; 700–02.

154. *SI*, 57:197.

155. *SI*, 57:404.

156. Yŏngjo, *Ŏje chasŏng p'yŏn*.

157. *SI*, 58:392–93.

158. *SI*, 63:74–75.

159. See chapter 5.

160. *SI*, 70:217–18. After this, Yŏngjo held *kyŏngyŏn* once in a great while, and his last one was on April 1, 1776 (*SI*, 77:36–37). He died on April 22 of that year.

161. These works are in the Changsŏgak Library, now housed in the Academy of Korean Studies in Korea.

162. There are roughly five thousand entries in the *Catalogue of Holdings in the Changsŏgak* (usually ten to fifteen titles per page and 392 pages in total) devoted to Yŏngjo's writings in the last ten years of his life. Many of them are copies of the same work, appearing two or three times as separate entries. See *Changsŏgak tosŏ Han'gukp'an ch'ongmongnok*, pp. 676–1072.

163. *YS*, 125:1b.

164. On the sovereign's role as a model, see Munro, *The Concept of Man in Early China*, pp. 96–112.

2. Yŏngjo's Reign: Images of Sagehood

165. Sŏ Myŏngŭng, "Haengjang."

166. One *p'yŏng* was 35.586 square feet.

167. *Kyŏngguk taejŏn,* 1:179–80.

168. One *kan* was 1.818 meters or 5.965 feet. 60 square *kan* is about 2,100 square feet.

169. *Sejong sillok,* 90:18a–b.

170. Yun Changsŏp, *Han'guk kŏnch'uksa,* p. 273.

171. The Yi bureaucrats' public attire corresponded to that of the Ming officials two degrees below them in rank. In other words, Yi officials of the first rank wore the same costume as Ming officials of the third tank. Kim Tonguk. *Yijo chŏn'gi poksik yŏn'gu,* pp. 81–121.

172. This can be seen in a conversation Yŏngjo had with his officials, full of self-congratulation on the subject, soon after his accession. *YS,* 5:27a.

173. The Yi king's costume was modeled after that of Ming princes. *T'aejong sillok,* 3:11b–12a.

174. *YS,* 70:17a; 102:28a.

175. *YS,* 10:19a–b; 109:4b–5a.

176. *YS,* 10:20b–21a; 37:24b–25a; 64:24a–25a; 65:3a–b.

177. *YS,* 68:27a–b; 98:20a; 102:28b.

178. *YS,* 31:33a. This style of coiffure first appeared in late Koryŏ, and by the late fifiteenth century had gained popularity in the cities. By Yŏngjo's time, the fashion is said to have spread to the countryside and to women of lower social classes as well. Kim Tonguk, "Yijo chung-hugi ŭi yŏbok kujo," pp. 27–28.

179. *YS,* 70:16a–b; 90:36–b; 102:28a.

180. *YS,* 56:13a–b; 6:2a.

181. *YS,* 10:20a–21a; 23:26b; 29:39a; 30:27b; 33:3a; 99:5a; 100:28a; 124:9b.

182. *YS,* 88:21b; 90:24a.

183. *YS,* 90:24b–25a.

184. *YS,* 90:30b.

185. *YS,* 29:39a; 31:31b–32a.

186. *YS,* 90:30b; 102:3b.

187. *YS,* 108:6a.

188. *YS,* 114:39b.

189. *YS,* 3:3a; *Sok taejŏn,* pp. 78–79.

190. *YS,* 21:2a.

191. *YS,* 5:34a–b; 11:29b.

192. The exact social class from which ladies-in-waiting were selected is not very well understood. Toward the end of the Yi dynasty, those who were selected for service in the king's residence came from the *chungin* class, the technical functionaries who occupied a social position between the yangban and commoners. It is also believed that ladies-in-waiting tended to come from families that had already supplied them in the past. Kim Yongsuk, "Yijo kungjung p'ungsok," pp. 287–91. Yŏngjo's orders suggest that life at court in this capacity was not considered very desirable.

193. *YS,* 63:16b.

194. Pak Munsu, ed., *T'akchi chŏngnye.*

195. *YS,* 65:8a.

196. *Wangseson karye tŭngnok.*

197. *Wangja karye tŭngnok; SS,* 39:15b.
198. *YS,* 60:23b.
199. *YS,* 70:17a–b.
200. *YS,* 66:31a.
201. *YS,* 71:7b–8a.
202. *YS,* 59:28b.
203. *YS,* 82:24b.
204. *YS,* 84:12b–13a.
205. *SI,* 51:730.
206. *YS,* 45:4a–b.
207. *YS,* 102:35b. His nine dragon marks were duly recorded in the biographies of Yŏngjo. Sŏ Myŏngŭng, "Haengjang"; Kim Yangt'aek, "Chimun," in *Wŏnnŭngji.*

3. Yŏngjo's Rule: Politics of Patriarchy

1. *SI,* 58:151–54.
2. *Mencius,* I:1:3:3; Legge, *Classics,* II:128.
3. There is little documentary evidence on the class division in early Yi society. But a general impression is that the majority of the population consisted of commoners who had small plots of land or tenant farmers and slaves. The slave population seems to have been rather large. One scholar estimates the slave population in the early Yi at 1,500,000 out of a total population of four to five million. Shin, "Some Aspects of Landlord-Tenant Relations in Yi Dynasty Korea," pp. 49–52.
4. Shikata, "Richō jinkō ni kansuru mibun kaikyu betsuteki kansatsu."
5. Shin, "The Social Structure of Kŭmhwa County in the Late Seventeenth Century."
6. Wagner, "Social Stratification in Seventeenth-Century Korea."
7. Shikata, "Richō jinkō."
8. A study on the Ulsan district shows that yangban, commoners, and slaves composed 19.9 percent, 49.57 percent, and 31.04 percent of the population, respectively, in 1729, but by 1765 the ratios changed to 32.11 percent, 50.83 percent, and 17.06 percent. But the slave population remained more consistent through the nineteenth century, at 22.99 percent in 1804 and 14.66 percent in 1867. Chŏng Sŏkchong, *Chosŏn hugi sahoe pyŏndong yŏn'gu,* pp. 248–51.
9. The social makeup of the population in the Sangju district changed from 19.4 percent yangban, 59.8 percent commoners, and 20.8 percent slaves in 1720, to 30.1 percent yangban, 49.3 percent commoners, and 20.6 percent slaves in 1738. Kim Yongsŏp, "Chosŏn hugi e issŏsŏ ŭi sinbunje ŭi tongyo wa nongji soyu," in *Chosŏn hugi nongŏpsa yŏn'gu,* p. 427.
10. A study on the Tansŏng district shows that in 1717 the population breaks down into 19.9 percent yangban, 52.5 percent commoners, and 27.6 percent slaves, while in 1786, the ratio changed to 32.2 percent yangban, 59 percent commoners, and 8.8 percent slaves. Kim Sŏkhŭi and Pak Yongsuk, "18 segi nongch'on ŭi sahoe kujo," 3 pp. 31–37.
11. Kim Yongsŏp, "Sinbunje ŭi tongyo," pp. 420–25.
12. The scholars of the Yŏngnam school, mostly out of power by the eighteenth

3. Yŏngjo's Rule: Politics of Patriarchy

century, continued the study of *i/li* (principle) as successors to Yi T'oegye (Yi Hwang), while the scholars of the Kiho school developed Yi Yulgok's (Yi I) study of *ki/ch'i* (material force). Takahashi, "Richō jugakushi ni okeru shuriha shukiha no hattasu," pp. 225–67.

13. Yi Ch'unhŭi, *Yijo sŏwŏn mun'gogo*, p. 17 and Appendix, pp. 1–35.

14. Kawashima, "Local Gentry Association," pp. 129–33.

15. Chŏng Sŏkchong, *Sahoe pyŏndong*, pp. 243–78.

16. Kim Yongsŏp, "Sinbunje ŭi tongyo," p. 434; Kim Yongsŏp, "Yangan ŭi yŏn'gu," pp. 133–56; Shin, "Land Tenure and the Agrarian Economy in Yi Dynasty Korea," pp. 44–72.

17. Kim Yongsŏp. "Sinbunje ŭi tongyo," pp. 420–22.

18. Shin, "Land Tenure," pp. 98–109.

19. When this practice first appeared in 1593, it was actually a sale of official posts and commoners were excluded from buying them. The next year, military rations were depleted and the government responded by selling empty ranks which could be bought by anyone in exchange for a certain amount of grain. *Sŏnjo sillok*, 35:25b–16a; 50:8b–9a.

20. This purchase did not entitle the buyer to full privileges, but it was the beginning of a process. After buying the status, people gradually moved up in social status through gray areas which functioned as buffer zones between classes. Kim Yongsŏp, "Sinbunje ŭi tongyo," p. 410–14, 420–22, 432–33.

21. Chŏng Sŏkchong, *Sahoe pyŏndong*, pp. 243–78.

22. For a fuller discussion of the Yi civil examination system, see Yi Sŏngmu, "Education and the Civil Service Examination System," pp. 149–52.

23. In the course of the Yi dynasty, there were 229 preliminary examinations and 47,749 people passed. Of these 162 were regular examination and 67 were irregular. Moreover, 34,159 people passed the regular preliminary examinations and 13,589 passed the irregular examinations. There were 744 *munkwa* examinations, of which 163 were regular. A total of 14,620 passed the *munkwa* examination of which 6,063 passed the regular *munkwa*. Song Chunho, *Yijo saengwŏn chinsa-si ŭi yŏn'gu*, p. 19.

24. At first, passing one of the two preliminary examinations and a stay of 300 days at Sŏnggyun'gwan, the Royal College, were prerequisites to taking the *munkwa* examination. These requirements were first relaxed for the irregular *munkwa*. Gradually, relaxation of these requirements spread to the regular *munkwa* examination. *Ibid.*, pp. 16–24.

25. *Ibid.*, pp. 36–38, 57.

26. Wagner, "The Ladder of Success in Yi Dynasty Korea," p. 4.

27. *Ibid.*

28. *Ibid.*, pp. 7–8.

29. A study of the Ch'angnyŏng district in Kyŏngsang Province shows that membership in the local gentry association grew, but it was accounted for almost entirely by the increase in population within the yangban class. This suggests that the new yangban were not accepted in this association. Kawashima, "Local Gentry Association," pp. 130–34.

30. *YS*, 65:9b–10a.

31. Wagner, "The Ladder of Success," pp. 6–7.

3. Yŏngjo's Rule: Politics of Patriarchy

32. YS, 2:53b–54b.
33. YS, 52:6a–b.
34. YS, 56:23b–24a.
35. YS, 62:3b–4a.
36. YS, 119:18a–b. "Pure officials," strictly speaking, refers to those holding posts in the Office of the Special Counselors (Hongmun'gwan), one of the three offices constituting the Censorate. But officials in the other two offices in the Censorate were also loosely called "pure officials." On this occasion, three of them were appointed to the Censorate but not to the Office of the Special Counselors.
37. E.g., YS, 29:39a; 31:31b–32a.
38. YS, 3:30b.
39. YS, 3:42b–43a.
40. YS, 31:33a.
41. YS, 35:25b.
42. YS, 51:21b.
43. YS, 59:38b.
44. YS, 105:2a–b.
45. Hyojong sillok, 14:21b; 18:4b–5a; 21:6b–9b; 21:12a–b.
46. When a parent was over seventy, one male child was exempt from service. When a parent was over ninety, all children were exempt. Kyŏngguk taejŏn, 2:123.
47. Ibid., 2:123–24.
48. Yi Sangbaek et al., Han'guksa, 3:218–19.
49. The unit called the kapsa (first-class division) consisted of the descendants of officials who were talented in military arts. Ibid., 3:221.
50. Kyŏngguk taejŏn, 2:125.
51. One p'il of cloth means a bolt. That is, it was the length of cloth that could be woven unbroken by a loom. As might be imagined, the actual quantities of cloth vary tremendously with the time period, the region, and the kind of fabric. At any rate, here one p'il of cloth refers to cotton, roughly two by forty feet. The actual tax collected was not cloth, but its equivalent value in coin.
52. Ch'a Munsŏp, "Imnan ihu ŭi yangyŏk kwa kyunyŏkpŏp ŭi sŏngnip (1)," pp. 117–19.
53. Sŏngjong sillok, 197:18a–b; 275:19a–20a. See also Ch'a Munsŏp, "Yangyŏk (1)," p. 122.
54. Chungjong sillok, 62:43b–45b. See also Ch'a Munsŏp, "Yangyŏk (1)," p. 123.
55. Ch'a Munsŏp, "Yangyŏk (1)," pp. 125–29.
56. Yi Sangbaek et al., Han'guksa, 4:144.
57. Sŏnjo sillok, 61:14a–15a.
58. Sok taejŏn, p. 258.
59. Yi Sangbaek et al., Han'guksa, 4:146–48.
60. Ch'a Munsŏp, "Yangyok (2)," pp. 85–89.
61. Shin, "Land Tenure," pp. 99–105.
62. One pu of land is approximately one-fiftieth of an acre.
63. Shin, "Land Tenure," pp. 44–80.
64. The recorded Korean population was two million in ca. 1450, 5,018,644 in 1666, 6,828,881 in 1717, 7,238,522 in 1777, and 7,561,403 in 1807. The total arable land was 1,619,257 kyŏl in ca. 1450, 1,246,310 kyŏl (excluding P'yŏngan Province) in 1666, 1,395,333 kyŏl in 1720, 1,437,975 kyŏl in 1780, and 1,456,592 kyŏl in 1801.

3. Yŏngjo's Rule: Politics of Patriarchy

Shin, "Land Tenure," p. 75. One *kyŏl* was about two and one fourth acres of the most fertile category of land in the early Yi dynasty.

65. In 1769, the taxable land was only 56.7 percent of the total. Ch'ŏn Kwanu, *Han'guk t'oji chedosa*, 2:1507.

66. Kim Yongsŏp, "Sagungjangt'o ŭi sehugyŏngje wa kŭ sŏngjang."

67. Shin, "Land Tenure," p. 118.

68. Ch'a Munsŏp, "Yangyŏk (2)," pp. 107–11. Also *SS*, 7:1b.

69. *SS*, 33:49a.

70. *Hyŏnjong sillok*, 16:14b–15a.

71. *Hyŏnjong sillok*, 20:51b.

72. *SS*, 5:26b–27b; 6:28a.

73. *SS*, 6:63b–64a; 7:1a.

74. *SS*, 11:31a–32b.

75. *SS*, 12:56a; 12:60a–62b; 12:65a.

76. *SS*, 13A:18a–b.

77. This was when the government discovered 10,358 people who were illegally receiving protection from central government agencies. The project was initiated by the Prime Minister, Yu Sangun. *SS*, 33:33a; 33:49a.

78. *SS*, 33:49a; 56:29a–30b.

79. One *p'il* of cloth came to mean a piece of roughly two by forty feet. *SS*, 38A:2a–3b; 38A:8a–10a; 40:54a–59b.

80. *SS*, 50:12b–14a.

81. *Pibyŏnsa tŭngnok*, 26:320–25; 26:554–57.

82. *SS*, 55:31a–32a.

83. *KS*, 4:20a.

84. *KS*, 11:3a–b.

85. *YS*, 10:10a–b; 14:3a–b.

86. For a discussion of this rebellion, see chapter 4, pp. 000–000.

87. *YS*, 37:11a–b.

88. *YS*, 56:28b.

89. The ostensible reason Yŏngjo gave for sending secret censors was to investigate the administration of lawsuits in the provinces. A more immediate purpose was to find out what kind of a reform of the military tax the people preferred. *YS*, 61:3b–4b.

90. Cho Hyŏnmyŏng, ed., *Yangyŏk silch'ong*.

91. *Shu-ching*, II:1:8; Legge, *Classics*, 3:1:35–37.

92. Spence, *Emperor of China*, p. 148.

93. Harold L. Kahn, "Politics of Filiality: Justification for Imperial Action in Eighteenth-Century China."

94. *SS*, 51:10a; *KS*, 4:28a–b.

95. E.g., *YS*, 50:4a–b.

96. *YS*, 63:6a.

97. *YS*, 99:19a–b.

98. *YS*, 111:6a–b.

99. *YS*, 7:37a.

100. *YS*, 52:20a.

101. Chiao Hung wrote this book in 1594 when he was a lecturer to the eldest son of Emperor Wan-li. It was an illustrated collection of moral sayings and com-

mendable acts selected from history. Though he wrote it to present it to the prince, he was unable to do so. Ch'ien, "Chiao Hung and the Revolt Against Ch'eng-Chu Orthodoxy," p. 278.

102. *YS*, 70:5a–b.
103. *SI*, 57:646–47.
104. *YS*, 71:18b.
105. *SI*, 58:86–91.
106. *SI*, 58:94–95.
107. *YS*, 71:20a–b.
108. *SI*, 58:95–99.
109. *SI*, 58:151–54.
110. *YS*, 71:18a.
111. *SI*, 58:162–66.
112. *SI*, 58:168–74.
113. *SI*, 58:190–94.
114. *YS*, 71:32b–33b.
115. *SI*, 58:190–94.
116. *SI*, 58:253–55.
117. The throne periodically sent secret censors to the provinces to check on local government. Though they were sent rather discreetly, their comings and goings and their reports to and audiences with the king are duly recorded in the *Records of the Royal Secretariat.* They were not personal agents of the king. Chŏn Pongdŏk, *Han'guk pŏpchesa yŏn'gu*, pp. 21–186.
118. *Onhaeng ilgi.*
119. Hong Kyehŭi was the strongest proponent of this alternative. *SI*, 58:942.
120. *SI*, 58:826–27.
121. *SI*, 58:933–95.
122. *SI*, 59:25–26.
123. *SI*, 59:31–32.
124. *SI*, 59:43–45.
125. *SI*, 59:56–59.
126. The inadequacies of this reform, which grew progressively more visible through the nineteenth century, are discussed in Palais, *Politics and Policy in Traditional Korea*, pp. 86–109.
127. Yi Sangbaek et al., *Han'guksa*, 4:218–39; Ch'a Munsŏp, "Yangyŏk (2)," pp. 139–43.
128. *YS*, 74:11b–12a.
129. E.g., *YS*, 110:32a; 112:4a; 113:10b–11a; 118:32b; 118:33a; 120:13a–b; 120:21a–b; 125:5b–6b.
130. E.g., *YS*, 112:4a; 113:10b–11a; 116:1a–1b; 124:18b.
131. E.g., *YS*, 61:3b; 110:6b.
132. E.g., *YS*, 102:15a; 113:11a.
133. *SI*, 52:603–06.
134. On Queen Dowager Inwŏn's seventieth birthday, he sent gifts to persons over seventy throughout the country. *SI*, 63:459.
135. *YS*, 106:20b.
136. *YS*, 120:16a; 123:1b; 124:18b.
137. *YS*, 120:13a–b.

4. Yǒngjo's Court: Magnificent Harmony

138. For the celebration marking the beginning of his fifty-second year, Yǒngjo demanded and received official concurrence for a reduction of taxes on farmers, totalling 10,000 sǒk of rice, and a similar curtailment of taxes on merchants. *SI*, 76:881–83.
139. *SI*, 76:187; *YS*, 125:15b.
140. *YS*, 122:1a.
141. *SI*, 76:909–10.

4. Yǒngjo's Court: Magnificent Harmony

1. It is one of the precepts that Kija (Chi Tzu) was supposed to have presented to a Chou king. *Shu-ching* in *Shih-san-ching chu-shu*, 190b.
2. This is the standard view. E.g., Yi Sangbaek et al., *Han'guksa*, 3:567–83; Yi Kibaek, *Han'guksa sillon*, pp. 252–56; Sǒng Nakhun, *Han'guk tangjaengsa*, pp. 282–88.
3. Chǒng Manjo, "Yǒngjodae ch'oban ǔi t'angp'yǒngch'eak kwa t'angpy'ǒngp'a ǔi hwaltong"; Ch'oe Wan'gi, "Yǒngjojo t'angp'yǒngch'aek ǔi ch'anbannon kǒmt'o."
4. *SS*, 32:5a.
5. Chu Hsi, the model for Korean scholars, for instance, expressed deep reservations toward public service in a corrupt government. Schirokauer, "Chu Hsi's Political Career."
6. Many families who produced high officials in the early Yi, for instance, settled into a life in the countryside toward the mid-Yi dynasty with little connection to government. Some of these choices seem to be deliberate. See *Kwangsan Kim Ssi Och'ǒn komunsǒ; Puan Kim Ssi Uban komunsǒ;* and Yi Sugǒn, ed., *Kyǒngbuk chibang komunsǒ chipsǒng.* Peterson discusses the "new outlook" among scholars in seventeenth-century China according to which the pursuit of scholarship was superior to government service. Peterson, *Bitter Gourd.* Though the Korean situation seems to bear a certain similarity to this, it remains to be investigated.
7. Scholar-officials' collected works as a rule contain numerous memorials requesting that they be relieved of office. Even if one discounts them as purely *pro forma* acts, still one senses a general longing for a life in retirement.
8. The highest post offered to him was that of Minister of the Right in the State Council. Yun wrote eighteen memorials in fourteen months requesting to be relieved of it before Sukchong accepted his resignation. Yun Chǔng, *Myǒngjae sǒnsaeng yugo*, 7:6a–22b.
9. Quoted from Hyǒn Sangyun, *Chosǒn yuhaksa*, p. 259.
10. Song Siyǒl, "Ǒrok," *Purok*, 15:22a, in Song Siyǒl, *Songja taejǒn;* Haboush, "A Heritage of Kings," pp. 41–42.
11. Ou-yang Hsiu, *Ou-yang Yung-shu chi*, 3:22–23. For a discussion of Ou-yang's stand on factionalism, see Liu, *Ou-yang Hsiu*, pp. 52–64.
12. Haboush, "A Heritage of Kings," pp. 40–61.
13. *Ibid.*, pp. 61–87.
14. *Ibid.*, pp. 90–91.
15. *Ibid.*, pp. 83–87.
16. What went on in the audience is not clear. Min Chinwǒn, a Noron minister, gives this account: Sukchong expressed serious doubts concerning Kyǒngjong's ability to rule and alluded to problems with the heir apparent in the Ch'ing court.

4. Yŏngjo's Court: Magnificent Harmony

Sukchong was referring to problems concerning Yin-jeng, the Emperor K'ang-hsi's initial heir apparent. But Yi Imyŏng defended Kyŏngjong and promised that the ministers would guide him. Min Chinwŏn, *Tanam mallok*, 2:9a–10a. Concerning Yin-jeng, see Spence, *Emperor of China*, pp. 125–36. Subsequently, in a public conference with his ministers, Sukchong expressed great anxiety over Kyŏngjong. *SS*, 60:5b–7b.

17. Yi Kŏnmyŏng, rather than being given a cup of poison, the customary method of execution for scholar-officials, was beheaded, a humiliating way to die. His two sons, after burying him, committed suicide. Yu Sukki, *Kyŏmsanjip*, 14:30.

18. Haboush, "A Heritage of Kings," pp. 91–104.

19. E.g., Yŏngjo's lament over the practice of not marrying outside of one's faction. *YS*, 70:16b.

20. *Ibid.*, p. 100. *KS*, 6:18b–19b.

21. Haboush, "A Heritage of Kings," pp. 104–5.

22. See Levenson's discussion of Emperor Yung-cheng's distaste for officials' factional loyalty which might precede their loyalty to the throne. Levenson, *Confucian China and Its Modern Fate*, 2:69–73.

23. For a discussion of this, see Dardess, *Confucianism and Autocracy*.

24. For the evolution and decline of the censorial voice (*yen-lu*) in China, see Hucker, "Confucianism and the Chinese Censorial System."

25. The Censorate demanded that Kim Ch'angjip and Yi Imyŏng, who had died by cups of poison, be posthumously beheaded. *YS*, 1:18a–b.

26. *YS*, 2:5b–6a.

27. Despite the numerous signals Yŏngjo sent out, no one requested Kim's punishment. *YS*, 2:11a–14a.

28. For Yi's trial, see *Ŭiyŏn ch'uan*.

29. The passage in question was "treading upon blood in the palace garden" (*chŏphyŏl kŭmjŏng*).

30. *Ilgyŏng Horyong tŭng ch'uan*.

31. One Yi Ch'ŏnhae shouted this charge at Yŏngjo as he was returning from Kyŏngjong's tomb. An investigation revealed that the accusation of regicide originated with Sim Yuhyŏn, Kyŏngjong's first wife's brother, who had attended Kyŏngjong's deathbed. Sim allegedly said that Kyŏngjong had vomited bile and that later his corpse looked very strange. This was taken to indicate poisoning. This rumor had apparently spread widely. One functionary mentioned it in his memorial, and was executed for spreading a groundless rumor. *YS*, 3:25b–29a; 3:11b–12b; 3:19b–30a.

32. Yŏngjo foreswore revenge, saying that it would be detrimental to accomplishing restoration. *YS*, 3:30a.

33. The four Noron ministers were posthumously restored to honor, and Song Siyŏl's private academies were restored. *YS*, 4:2b–3a; 4:10a–b; 3:26a; 3:33a.

34. Allegations of the Kyŏngjong assassination plots were declared to have been fabricated. *YS*, 4:24a–30b.

35. *YS*, 5:1a–3b.

36. *YS*, 5:9a–b; 5:13a–b.

37. *SI*, 31:195–96.

38. *YS*, 5:1a; 6:2a; 6:7a–b.

39. Two of them were dead, three alive.

4. Yŏngjo's Court: Magnificent Harmony

40. Of the three living Soron ministers, one was banished and two were barred from entering the capital. *YS*, 7:3a–b.

41. The ritual report to the ancestral temple which announced the reversal of the 1722 verdict mentioned only the horrible crimes of Kim Ilgyŏng and his cohorts. *YS*, 7:27a–28a.

42. *YS*, 8:2b.

43. King U (r. 1375–1388) and his son, King Ch'ang (r. 1388–1389). The founders of the Yi dynasty maintained that U had not been fathered by King Kongmin but by a monk.

44. King Kwanghae (r. 1608–1623) had his stepmother, Queen Dowager Inmok, put under house arrest. This unfilial act was one of the reasons cited for his deposal in 1623.

45. *SI*, 32:991.

46. For Min's biography, see Min Pyŏngsŭng, *Tanam sŏnsaeng yŏnbo*.

47. See Yi Mansi's memorial in *YS*, 8:7b–8b.

48. The *Sillok* says that the ministers of the State Council had not attended it for six months. *YS*, 11:20a.

49. *YS*, 11:47b–49a.

50. *YS*, 12:12b.

51. *YS*, 12:4a–5a.

52. *YS*, 12:23b–24a.

53. *YS*, 12:29a.

54. *YS*, 12:37a.

55. *YS*, 13:30a–31b.

56. *YS*, 11:36b.

57. *YS*, 13:39a.

58. Song Inmyŏng, ed., *Kamnannok*, 1:1b.

59. The posters seem to have charged that Yŏngjo had killed Kyŏngjong. *Ibid.*, 2:38b–39b. They also seem to have claimed that Yŏngjo was not Sukchong's son. Ku Suhun, *Isunnok*, 1:22a–b, in *P'aerim*, 9:417.

60. Song Inmyŏng, ed., *Kamnannok*, 1:1b–3a.

61. *YS*, 16:9a–10a.

62. *YS*, 16:9b–12b; 16:14a–b.

63. *YS*, 16:7b–8a.

64. Min Chinwŏn, *Tanam mallok*, 2:66a–b.

65. *YS*, 16:15a.

66. *YS*, 16:19b; 16:22b–27b; 16:34a–40b; 17:1a–3b.

67. *Musin yŏgok ch'uan*.

68. *Ibid.*, the entry of the 20th of the 3d month in *ch'aek* 1.

69. Those declared the "ten principal rebels" were all close to each other through political or familial connections.

70. The entries of 19th of the 3d month, and the 5th, 6th, and 7th of the 4th month. *Musin yŏgok ch'uan*, *ch'aek* 1, 2.

71. Sim Yuhyŏn, Kyŏngjong's brother-in-law, denied that he was responsible for the accusation of regicide. (*Ibid.*, the entry of the 29th of the 3d month, *ch'aek* 2). One Min Ikkwan confessed that he had composed the slogan. He took the cue from someone who said he had heard it from Pak P'irhyŏn who had cosigned Kim Ilgyŏng's memorial. (*Ibid.*, the entry of the 28th of the 3d month, *ch'aek* 2).

72. *Ibid.*, the entry of the 1st of the 5th month, *ch'aek* 3.
73. *Ibid.*
74. Yi, Kŏnch'ang, *Tangŭi t'ongnyak*, p. 139.
75. *YS*, 16:30a–b; 7:28a–31a.
76. *YS*, 18:8a.
77. Song Inmyŏng, usually a proponent of milder punishment, cautioned the king against this. *YS*, 17:14b–15b.
78. E.g., Yŏngjo's conversation with Hong Ch'ijung. *YS*, 24:1a–3a.
79. E.g., Yŏngjo's letters and his audience with Yi Kwangjwa. *YS*, 18:33a; 22:29b; 24:3a–7a.
80. Yi Kwangjwa, *Un'gok silgi*, 2:13a–b.
81. *Ibid.*, 2:18b–19b.
82. *YS*, 44:6b–8b; 44:17b–21a; 45:1b–3b.
83. *YS*, 45:3b–10b.
84. E.g., *YS*, 39:10b; 42:6b–7a; 64:21b–22a.
85. *YS*, 24:1a–3a.
86. This was how he referred to himself. *YS*, 42:28b.
87. *Choein Hwang So ch'uan.*
88. *YS*, 21:43b.
89. *Ch'uan kŭp kugan, ch'aek* 146–51.
90. *YS*, 32:25a–26b; 33:3b; 33:18a.
91. *Ch'uan kŭp kugan, ch'aek* 163–68.
92. *Ch'uan kŭp kugan, ch'aek* 172–73.
93. *YS*, 50:10b.
94. *YS*, 40:10a–b; 40:25a–26a.
95. *YS*, 51:27a.
96. Yŏngjo, *Ŏje taehun.*
97. *YS*, 54:29b–30a.
98. *YS*, 59:1b–2a; 61:7b; 61:10a.
99. *YS*, 52:22b–23a; 53:24a–b.
100. E.g., *YS*, 52:30b; 54:38a–b; 64:11b–12a.
101. *YS*, 53:25b–26a.
102. *YS*, 53:27b–28a.
103. Only eighteen new private academies were founded in the second half of the eighteenth century. Palais, *Politics and Policy*, p. 116.
104. *YS*, 53:23b; 53:21a; 53:29a–b; 53:37a–b; 53:42a; 54:1b–2a.
105. *YS*, 58:32b.
106. But Cho Chunghoe was reinstated before long.
107. *YS*, 58:33b–35a.
108. *YS*, 31:1b.
109. During the first ten years of his reign, I could find only two occasions on which he really lost his temper. The first was just before he instituted the change of power from Noron to Soron (*YS*, 12:1a–b). The second was an outburst at Pak Munsu for insisting that the ministers were superior to the royal clan (*YS*, 36:9b–11a).
110. *YS*, 48:2b–3b.
111. *YS*, 51:26a–27a.
112. *YS*, 55:6b–9a.

5. Yŏngjo's Tragedy: Mournful Thoughts

113. *Ch'uan kŭp kugan, ch'aek* 190.
114. Cho Hyŏnmyŏng, *Kwinokchip*.
115. *YS*, 55:17a–18b.
116. E.g., *YS*, 42:33a–34b; 42:4b.
117. *YS*, 45:27b.
118. *YS*, 33:11a–b.
119. E.g., *YS*, 36:9b–11a; 60:42b.
120. *YS*, 58:10b.
121. See Cho Hyŏnmyŏng, ed., *Yangyŏk silch'ong*.
122. *YS*, 54:20b–27b.
123. *YS*, 62:16a; 62:17a–63:8a.
124. *YS*, 63:2a–b.
125. See the memorials in *YS*, 63:1a; 63:11a–b.
126. For Pak's biography, see Pak Suwŏn, *Yŏho sŏnsaeng yŏnbo*.
127. See the letters in *SI*, 54:456; 54:762–63.
128. *YS*, 63:21b–24a.
129. *YS*, 63:26b–27a; 63:28b; 63:29a–30a.
130. The term used here is *wiye*, or "poor health," a very noncommittal term. Yŏngjo said that this decree was intended only to absolve Kyŏngjong of responsibility for the purge. *YS*, 63:28b–29a.
131. Yi Kwangjwa, however, was excluded. *YS*, 64:6b–7a; 64:8a–10a; 64:11a–12a.
132. *YS*, 64:13a.
133. *YS*, 64:14b.
134. *YS*, 65:16b–17a.
135. *YS*, 64:22b.
136. *YS*, 65:31b–32a.
137. *YS*, 65:32b–33a.
138. *YS*, 66:2a–b.
139. The trials of the suspects revealed very little. *YS*, 67:24a–b.
140. Ch'angdŏk Palace was actually his main palace. He also stayed at Kyŏngdŏk Palace from time to time. *SI*, 56:780–82.
141. *YS*, 69:5b–6a.
142. *YS*, 69:6a–b.

5. Yŏngjo's Tragedy: The Prince of Mournful Thoughts

1. E.g., *Taech'ŏnnok, ch'aek* 1; Pak Chonggyŏm, *Hyŏn'gogi, ch'aek* 1, and *Hyŏn'gu kisa*.
2. Sŏng Nakhun, *Han'guk tangjaengsa*, pp. 378–80.
3. Kim Yongsuk, "Sado seja ŭi pigŭk kwa kŭŭi chŏngsin punsŏkhakchŏk koch'al."
4. *YS*, 127:14b–15a.
5. For instance, Yŏngjo employed historians to reconstruct the *Records of the Royal Secretariat* from 1623 to 1721, which had been destroyed by fire. Though the task only took a year and a half—from July 1746 to February 1748—it involved the use of enormous manpower. Nakamura Hidetaka, "Chōsen Eisō no *Shōseiin nikki* kaishu jigyō." pp. 648–51.
6. Chŏngjo had written a series of reflections on daily events called *Ilsŏngnok*

5. Yŏngjo's Tragedy: Mournful Thoughts

(Daily Reflections) since he had been heir apparent. He continued the practice throughout his reign. The custom was maintained through later reigns and *Ilsŏngnok* became an official historical record. Chŏngjo also established a special library called the Kyujanggak. Initially intended to collect royal writings, it published numerous works and became a repository for a wide variety of documents and writings. After it was abolished in 1894, its collection was maintained as a government archive for a time. It eventually passed to Seoul National University where it remains preserved to the present day.

7. *YS*, 40:4a.

8. See the entries of the 25th and 26th of the 7th month, *ŭlmyo* year in *Kyŏngmogung poyangch'ŏng ilgi*.

9. The more usual practice was to appoint an heir apparent at about eight years of age. Both Kyŏngjong, who was appointed heir apparent in his third year, and Sado were deviations from the norm. Haboush, "The Education of the Yi Crown Prince," pp. 177–88.

10. *Ibid.*, pp. 188, 204.

11. *YS*, 59:2a–b.

12. *Changjo Hŏn'gyŏnghu karye togam ŭigwe.*

13. Hyegyŏnggung Hong Ssi, *Hanjungnok*, p. 121.

14. See, for instance, Cho Hyŏnmyŏng's farewell audience with Sado. *YS*, 75:3b–4a.

15. *YS*, 40:4b.

16. *YS*, 40:29a.

17. *YS*, 43:15a.

18. *YS*, 45:9b.

19. One day in November 1747, Yŏngjo told Kim Chaero that the only way for parents to teach their children to abjure factionalism was to prevent them from getting involved in it in the first place. *YS*, 66:22b.

20. *SI*, 54:43.

21. For instance, Sado was present at Yŏngjo's audience with Pak P'ilchu on July 2, 1746. Pak suggested a revision of the *Great Instruction* to show the extremist Soron's evil doings, and Yŏngjo expressed deep pleasure at Pak's suggestion (*YS*, 63:21b–24a). While official sources do not explicitly attribute to Yŏngjo a desire that Sado vindicate him, several so-called wild histories allege that Yŏngjo had openly expressed this desire to his close ministers. See *Taech'ŏnnok, ch'aek* 1; Pak Chonggyŏm, *Hyŏn'gogi, ch'aek* 1.

22. *YS*, 52:30a; 55:6a–b; 53:19b–20a; 59:14b; 61:34a.

23. E.g., *YS*, 55:6a–b.

24. *YS*, 58:25b.

25. *YS*, 63:4a–b.

26. *YS*, 63:10a.

27. *YS*, 64:7b–8a.

28. *YS*, 68:28a.

29. *YS*, 66:17a.

30. *YS*, 66:9a–b.

31. *YS*, 68:33a–34b.

32. Hyegyŏnggung Hong Ssi, *Hanjungnok*, pp. 97–107.

5. Yongjo's Tragedy: Mournful Thoughts

33. E.g., *Taech'ŏnnok, ch'aek* 1; Pak Chonggyŏm, *Hyŏn'gogi, ch'aek* 1, and *Hyŏn'gu kisa.*

34. *YS*, 52:28a–b.

35. Hyegyŏnggung Hong Ssi, *Hanjungnok*, pp. 107–13.

36. *YS*, 66:30a–31b.

37. For the implications of this regency, see Haboush, "A Heritage of Kings," pp. 83–86.

38. *SI*, 27:194; *YS*, 66:30a–31b.

39. See Yŏngjo, *Ŏje chŏnghun.*

40. *YS*, 69:10a–11a.

41. *YS*, 69:17b.

42. *YS*, 69:40b.

43. *YS*, 69:39b; 70:2b–3a; 70:13a.

44. *YS*, 69:38a; 69:39b; 70:3a; 70:14a; 70:15a–b.

45. They included some eunuchs who had served Yŏngjo when he was heir apparent. *YS*, 73:10a–13a; 74:12a–13b.

46. *YS*, 73:10a–13a; 74:12a–13b.

47. *YS*, 73:14b.

48. *YS*, 78:6a–7a.

49. *YS*, 73:13b.

50. *YS*, 78:5b; 78:7a–b.

51. *YS*, 77:7a–b.

52. *YS*, 74:10b.

53. Princess Hwahyŏp died after an illness and Yŏngjo was visiting her during her illness and after her death. *YS*, 78:9a–10a.

54. *YS*, 78:10a.

55. *YS*, 78:10b–12b.

56. Poem number 202 in the Mao version. It is one of the "Lesser Odes" (*Hsiao-ya*). The Waley translation reads:

> *Thick grows that tarragon.*
> *It is not tarragon; it is only wormwood.*
> *Alas for my father and mother,*
> *Alas for all their trouble in bringing*
>   *me up!*
>
> *Thick grows that tarragon.*
> *It is not tarragon; it is mugwort.*
> *Alas for my father and mother,*
> *Alas for all their toil in bringing me up!*
> *"That the cup should be empty*
> *Is a humiliation to the jar."*
> *Than to live the life of the common people*
> *Better to have died long ago!*
>
> *Without a father, on whom can we rely?*
> *Without a mother, whom can we trust?*
> *At every turn we should encounter trouble,*
> *At every turn meet failure.*

5. Yongjo's Tragedy: Mournful Thoughts

My father begot me,
My mother fed me,
Led me, bred me,
Brought me up, reared me,
Kept her eye on me, tended me,
At every turn aided me.
Their good deeds I would requite.
It is Heaven, not I, that is bad.

The southern hills, they rise so sharp,
The storm-wind blows so wild.
Other people all prosper;
Why am I alone destroyed?

The southern hills, they rise so jagged,
The storm-wind blows so fierce.
Other people all prosper;
I alone can find no rest.

Arthur Waley, tr., *The Book of Songs*, pp.
316–17.

57. This is the traditional method of heating. The floor is heated from below by an intricate set of flues.

58. *YS*, 78:10b–20a.

59. E.g., *SI*, 61:326–28; 61:422; 61:457–58. *YS*, 81:28b. See also Yŏngjo, *Ŏje hoegap monyŏnsŏ si wŏllyang.*

60. Sado expressed such frustrations to his tutors. See the entry of the 21st of the 9th month, the *kyeyu* year in Cho Ch'ŏngse, *Sŏyŏn kangŭi.*

61. Their canonization occurred in 1756.

62. For Sado's answers in this period see Sado Seja, *Nŭnghŏgwan man'go.*

63. See the memorials by Ch'ae Chegong and Pak P'ilkyun in *YS*, 79:21a–b; 81:17a–18a.

64. *YS*, 81:5a.

65. E.g., *YS*, 82:24a–b.

66. The accusation was that Yi had forcefully taken a woman and killed her husband. *YS*, 82:30a–b.

67. *YS*, 82:31b–37b.

68. *YS*, 79:10b–11a.

69. *YS*, 82:14b–15a.

70. *YS*, 82:24b.

71. For the trial, see *Ch'uan kŭp kugan, ch'aek* 191–92.

72. *YS*, 83:18a–21b.

73. *YS*, 84:5a.

74. *YS*, 81:11a.

75. For the trial, see *Ch'uan kŭp kugan, ch'aek* 193–94.

76. *YS*, 84:12b–13a.

77. See *Ch'ŏnŭi sogam.*

78. See *Ch'ŏnŭi sogam ŏnhae.*

79. For Yŏngjo's reputed distaste for killing, see *YS*, 84:10b–11a.

80. E.g., *YS*, 84:25a; 84:26b–27a; 85:18b–20a.

5. Yŏngjo's Tragedy: Mournful Thoughts

81. *YS*, 85:22b–24b.

82. *YS*, 84:5a–b.

83. For his expressed concern, see *YS*, 85:22b–23a.

84. *YS*, 85:7b–8a; 85:9b.

85. *YS*, 87:11a–b.

86. For details of Sado's performance in the study session, see *Changhŏn Seja tonggung ilgi.*

87. Hyegyŏnggung Hong Ssi, *Hanjungnok*, pp. 165–69.

88. *YS*, 90:1b.

89. Both Yŏngjo and Sado were in mourning, hence they were in hempen clothes.

90. *YS*, 90:26b–29a.

91. See Cho's autobiography. Cho Hyŏnmyŏng, *Chajo kiyŏn*, in *Kwinokchip*, 20:1a–35b.

92. Sado Seja, *Nŭnghŏgwan man'go*, 7:1b–9a.

93. Yi Ch'ŏnbo, *Chinamjip*, 5:16b–24b.

94. *YS*, 92:12a–b.

95. *Changhŏn Seja tonggung ilgi, ch'aek* 25–27.

96. Yŏngjo had fourteen children, two sons and twelve daughters, by four women. The sons were Prince Hyojang (died in 1728) and Prince Sado. Seven of the twelve daughters reached adulthood. The princesses Hwap'yŏng, Hwahyŏp, and Hwawŏn and Prince Sado were born of Lady Yi. *Sŏnwŏn segye.*

97. Lady Mun was supposedly anxious to have a son who might replace Sado as heir apparent. At any rate, Lady Hong was suspicious of her ambition. Hyegyŏnggung Hong Ssi, *Hanjungnok*, pp. 177–79. Lady Mun was later put to death by Chŏngjo for allegedly plotting against him. Several others were also put to death for the same charges. Kim Ch'iin, ed., *Myŏngŭirok.*

98. Hyegyŏnggung Hong Ssi, *Hanjungnok*, pp. 121–215.

99. The entry of the 10th of the 7th month, *kyŏngin* year (1760) in *On'gung sasil.*

100. *Ibid., ch'aek* 2.

101. *YS*, 96:5a.

102. *YS*, 96:8b.

103. Hyegyŏnggung Hong Ssi, *Hanjungnok*, p. 223.

104. This was Yi practice—designating the first son of the heir apparent as his eventual successor.

105. *YS*, 97:2b.

106. Hyegyŏnggung Hong Ssi, *Hanjungnok*, pp. 219–21.

107. The *Sillok* just mentions their deaths. Hwang Kyŏngwŏn's tomb inscription for Yi Ch'ŏnbo says little on the cause of the Yi's death. See Hwang Kyŏngwŏn, *Kanghanjip*, 16:1a–25a. But Hwang's preface to Yi's collected writings cryptically refers to his extreme depression preceding his death. See Hwang's preface in Yi Ch'ŏnbo, *Chinamjip*. Yu Ch'ŏkki's biography of Min Paeksang suggests that he willed his death. See Yu Ch'ŏkki, *Chisujaejip*, 14:22a–34b. *Taech'ŏnnok* contains the following statement: "In the garden, there were three pine trees in a row which Hyojong had planted. They were named the pine trees of the three ministers. Some say that the heir apparent chopped them down and therefore the three ministers died at once." *Taech'ŏnnok, ch'aek* 1.

108. Yi Kwanghyŏn et al., eds., *Imo ilgi.*

109. Hyegyŏnggung Hong Ssi, *Hanjungnok*, pp. 225–27.

5. Yongjo's Tragedy: Mournful Thoughts

110. E.g., the memorials by Sŏ Myŏngŭng and Yun Chaegyŏm. *YS*, 97:21b–22a.

111. See the entry of the 14th of the 5th month to the 10th of the 6th month, *sinsa* year in *Changhŏn Seja tonggung ilgi, ch'aek* 28.

112. Hyegyŏnggung Hong Ssi, *Hanjungnok*, p. 231.

113. *YS*, 98:19a.

114. Hyegyŏnggung Hong Ssi, *Hanjungnok*, pp. 233–51.

115. Kwŏn Chŏngch'im, *P'yŏngam sŏnsaeng munjip*, 3:3b–5a.

116. E.g., Sado Seja, *Nŭnghŏgwan man'go*, 6:6a–8a.

117. Fu-su was the elder son of Ch'in Shih-huang-ti, the first emperor of the Ch'in dynasty. While he was in disfavor with his father, his younger brother had him killed. The common belief was that if Fu-su had lived, the Ch'in dynasty would have survived.

118. Yang Chen was a scholar in the Later Han dynasty who remonstrated Emperor An-ti. He was slandered and the emperor consequently gave him poison in 122 A.D.

119. Kwŏn Chŏngch'im, *P'yŏngam*, 3:3b–30a, esp. 14b–16b.

120. *YS*, 99:17b–18b.

121. *YS*, 99:18a–19a.

122. *YS*, 99:19a–b.

123. *YS*, 99:21a.

124. *YS*, 99:21b.

125. *YS*, 99:20a.

126. *YS*, 99:20b.

127. *YS*, 99:22a.

128. *YS*, 99:22a–b.

129. Hyegyŏnggung Hong Ssi, *Hanjungnok*, pp. 255–57.

130. *Ibid.*, p. 231.

131. Chŏngjo, *Hyŏnyungwŏnji*, in Chŏngjo, *Hongjae chŏnsŏ*, 16:1a–26a, esp. 21a–b.

132. Hyegyŏnggung Hong Ssi, *Hanjungnok*, pp. 107, 249.

133. I.e., Yŏngjo's residence in Kyŏnghŭi Palace. The implication here is that Sado was attempting to enter Yŏngjo's quarters in order to kill him.

134. Hyegyŏnngung Hong Ssi, *Hanjungnok*, pp. 253–57.

135. While he was Crown Prince, Yŏngjo, in 1721, had to flee an extremist Soron plot to harm him, and sought protection under Inwŏn. *KS*, 5:36a–b.

136. Cho Chaeho was the son of Cho Munmyŏng, the first proponent of the *t'angp'yŏng* policy. He was interested in practical learning and Catholicism. See Cho Chaeho, *Sonjae sŏnsaeng munjip*, esp. 2:5b–11b; 12:11b–26b.

137. See *Ponggyo ŏmbyŏnnok*.

138. For a historiographical discussion of the *Sillok*, see Appendix 4.

139. The Yi royal ancestral altar. Yŏngjo's ceremony was to announce to his ancestors his decision to kill the heir apparent.

140. It was the shrine of Queen Chŏngsŏng. This was a memorial hall within the Ch'angdŏk Palace compound. *Tongguk yŏji pigo*, p. 32.

141. Sado was required to perform a ceremony of farewell to his deceased stepmother.

142. *YS*, 99:22b–23a.

Appendix 3

143. For a historiographical evaluation of this journal, see Appendix 4.
144. Ch'ŏngyŏn was Sado's and Lady Hong's daughter. They also had another daughter, Ch'ŏngsŏn.
145. Hyegyŏnggung Hong Ssi, *Hanjungnok*, pp. 255–67, 271–73.
146. For a historiographical evaluation of Yi's journal, see Appendix 4.
147. Yi Kwanghyŏn appears on the roster of the Royal Secretariat on only two days, the 12th and 13th of the intercalary 5th month, 1762. *SI*, 67:580–581.
148. Chinjŏn was another name for Sŏnwŏnjŏn, the Yi royal ancestral altar.
149. Three and a half *ch'ŏk* is about four feet one inch.
150. Actually, Six Garrisons. This refers to six fortresses on the Tuman River which were conceived of as the furthest extremities of Korea.
151. Yŏngjo was referring to King Yŏnsan (r. 1494–1506) who was deposed and confined to Kyodong in Kanghwa Island.
152. According to his biography, Kim Igon pushed his way through the palace guards and somehow "clawed" in causing bleeding wounds to all ten fingers. Sim Naksu, "Kin Igon chŏn," in Sim Naksu, *Ŭnp'a san'go*, 8:28b–29b. On his grief of Sado's death, see Hong Naksun, "Kim Hujae jimun," in Kim Igon, *Pongnokchip*.
153. The *Sillok* also records their banishment. *YS*, 99:23a.
154. Yi Kwanghyŏn, *Yi Kwanghyŏn ilgi*, in Yi Kwanghyŏn et al., eds., *Imo ilgi*, 1a–6b.
155. *YS*, 103:8a.
156. *YS*, 99:24b. Since Sado was restored to royal rank, his funeral was that of an heir apparent. *Sado Seja sangjang tŭngnok*.
157. Yŏngjo, *Ŏje p'youirok*.
158. E.g., Kim Sangno was posthumously stripped of his post and his sons were banished. *Chŏngjo sillok*, 1:11a–b. Hong Kyehŭi and his heirs met with the same treatment. *Chŏngjo sillok*, 4:33b.
159. Sim Naksu, *Ŭnp'a san'go*, 8:16a–20a.
160. Kim Sŏnggŭn, *Kwŏn'gong Chŏngch'im ikchang*.
161. *YS*, 109:21a; 109:36a.
162. *YS*, 102:6b.
163. *Chŏngjo sillok*, 1:2b.
164. E.g., ten days after Chŏngjo ascended the throne, he conferred upon Sado a posthumous honorary title, Prince Changhŏn. But, a day earlier, he had already conferred a posthumous title, the Great King Chinjong, on Prince Hyojang. *Chŏngjo sillok*, 1:5a–b. Hyojang's title was one appropriate to the father of a reigning monarch. Chŏngjo could never confer such a title on Sado.
165. Hyegyŏnggung Hong Ssi, *Hanjungnok*, pp. 519–23.

Appendix 3: Yŏngjo's and Sukchong's Curricula in the Royal Lecture

1. Yi Yulgok (Yi I) wrote this in 1575 explicitly for the purpose of aiding royal study and offered it to king Sŏnjo. Yŏngjo published it in 1759 with his own preface.
2. Another title for this book is *Tseng-hsiu fu-chu Tzu-chih t'ung-chien chieh-yao hsu-pien*. It was edited by Liu Yen and revised by Chang Kuang-ch'i of the Ming dynasty.

Appendix 3

3. This book had been in circulation at the Yi court but it was not until 1771 that it was put into final form and published under Yŏngjo's order. It covers the period from 1368 to 1627.

4. This book was written by Chung Hsing of the Ming and revised by Wang Ju-nan of the Ch'ing dynasty.

5. This is a chronological history of Korea from the Tan'gun Chosŏn to the end of the Koryŏ dynasty. It was completed in 1484 by Sŏ Kŏjŏng.

6. It was written by Fan Tsu-yü. His judgments of historical events were supposedly valuable.

7. Song Siyŏl edited this, selecting what he saw as the most important points from the *Chu Tzu ta-ch'üan.*

8. This is a collection of the writings of Lu Chih, a famous minister of the T'ang dynasty in the late eighth century.

9. This is the collected writings of Li Kang, who was a minister under Kao-tsung of the Southern Sung dynasty. He was an ardent proponent of war against the Jürchen (the Chin dyansty).

10. This was compiled by Huang Huai and Yang Shih-ch'i in 1417 under an order of Emperor Yung-lo.

11. This was compiled by Wu Ching under T'ang T'ai-tsung's order. It consists of forty important aspects of Confucian government.

12. This was first compiled by Chu Hsi and continued by Li Yu-wu of the Sung dynasty. Chang Pien of the Ming dynasty added critical comments.

13. This was compiled by Shang Lu of the Ming dynasty under an imperial order.

14. This was edited by Ch'iu Ch'ün of the Ming dynasty.

15. This was written by Yu Kye of the Yi dynasty in 1667.

16. This was edited by the Emperor Ching-ti of the Ming dynasty.

17. This was a chronological history of the Yi dynasty. Compilation began in the fifteenth century and ended in 1909.

18. This was edited by Ch'en Po who is believed to have lived during the Sung dynasty. No Ujin of the Yi dynasty annotated the text. Yŏngjo wrote a preface in 1746.

Appendix 4: A Historiographical Discussion and Evaluation of Several Sources

1. G. M. McCune says it was about thirty people. G. M. McCune, "The Yi Dynasty Annals of Korea," *Transactions of the Korea Branch of the Royal Asiatic society* (1939), 29:66. But usually it involved more than thirty people.

2. *Yŏngjong taewang sillokch'ŏng ŭigwe.*

3. G. M. McCune, "Yi Dynasty Annals," pp. 57-58.

4. *Sŏnjo sillok.*

5. *Sŏnjo sujŏng sillok.*

6. *Hyŏnjong sillok.*

7. *Hyŏnjong kaesu sillok.*

8. *Sukchong sillok.*

9. *Kyŏngjong sillok.*

10. *Kyŏngjon sujŏng sillok.*

11. *Yŏngjo sillok.*
12. *KS,* 5:13a–16a. *Kyŏngjong sujŏng sillok,* 2:25b–28a.
13. *KS,* 5:13a–b.
14. *Kyongjŏng sujŏng sillok,* 2:28a–b.
15. *SS,* 55:1b.
16. *SS,* 55A:1a.
17. *YS,* 51:27a–b.
18. *SI,* 67:572.
19. *SI,* 67:580–81.
20. *SI,* 67:581.

GLOSSARY

An-ti 安帝
Anp'yŏng (Taegun) 安平(大君)
Ansun 安順
Anŭm 安陰
chach'in 慈親
ch'adae 次對
Ch'ae Chegong 蔡濟恭
Chaemyŏn 載冕
Chaesŏn 載先
Chagyŏng 慈敬
chajŏn 慈展
Ch'ang (wang) 昌(王)
Chang Hŭibin 張禧嬪
Chang Kuang-ch'i 張光啓
Chang Pien 張采
Ch'angdŏk (kung) 昌德(宮)
Changhŏn (Seja) 莊獻(世子)
Changsŏgak 藏書閣
Ch'angŭi (gung) 彰義(宮)
Changŭi hongnon 章義弘倫
Ch'ech'ŏn kŏn'gŭk 體天建極
Chen-kuan cheng-yao 貞觀政要
Ch'en Po 陳栢
Chen Te-hsiu 眞德秀
cherye 祭禮
Chia-ching 嘉靖
Chiao Hung 焦竑
Chibyŏng (mun) 集英(門)
Ch'ien-lung 乾隆
Chihaeng sundŏk 至行純德

Ch'in Shih-huang-ti 秦始皇帝
Chin-ssu lu 近思錄
Chinan (Taegun) 鎭安(大君)
Ch'ing 淸
Ch'ing T'ai-tsung 淸太宗
Ching-ti 景帝
Ching-yen 經筵
Chinhyŏn (mun) 進賢(門)
Chinjŏn 眞殿
Chinjong 眞宗
chinsa 進士
chinsa-si 進士試
Ch'iu Ch'ün 邱濬
Cho Chaeho 趙載浩
Cho Chunghoe 趙重晦
Cho Hyŏnmyŏng 趙顯命
Cho Munmyŏng 趙文命
Cho T'aech'ae 趙泰采
Cho T'aegu 趙泰耈
Cho T'aeŏk 趙泰億
Cho Tobin 趙道彬
Cho Yŏngjin 趙榮進
Cho Yujin 趙維進
Ch'oe Kyusŏ 崔奎瑞
Ch'oe Sŏkhang 崔錫恒
Ch'oe Sukpin 崔淑嬪
chogang 朝講
chŏk 適
ch'ŏk 尺
Chŏlchak t'ongp'yŏn 節酌通編

Ch'ŏlchong 哲宗
Chŏlla (do) 全羅(道)
Chŏng Chedu 鄭齊斗
Chŏng Chin'gyo 鄭震僑
Chŏng Hongsun 鄭弘淳
Chŏng Hwiryang 鄭翬良
Chŏng Mongju 鄭夢周
Chŏng Sun'gŏm 鄭純儉
Chŏng Tojŏn 鄭道傳
Chŏng Yagyong 鄭若鏞
Chŏngdŏk 貞德
ch'ŏnggwan 清官
Ch'ŏnggyech'ŏng 撿戒廳
Chŏnghun 政訓
Ch'ŏnghwi (mun) 清輝(門)
Chŏngjo 正祖
Chŏngjong 定宗
Ch'ŏngju 清州
Chongmyo 宗廟
Ch'ŏngnam 清南
Ch'ŏngsŏ 清西
Ch'ŏngsobuk 清小北
Ch'ŏngsŏn 清璿
Chŏngsŏng (Wanghu) 貞聖(王后)
Chŏngsun (Wanghu) 貞純(王后)
Chŏn'gye Taewŏn'gun 全溪大院君
Ch'ŏngyŏn 清衍
chonho 尊號
Ch'ŏnjo 天朝
Chŏnju Yi 全州李
Ch'ŏnmyŏng 天命
Ch'ŏnŭi sogam 闡義昭鑑
Ch'ŏnŭi sogam ŏnhae 闡義昭鑑諺解
chŏphyŏl kŭmjŏng 蹀血禁庭
Chosŏn 朝鮮
Chosŏn wangjo sillok 朝鮮王朝實錄
Chŏsŭng (jŏn) 儲承(殿)
Chou 周
Chou-i 周易
Chou-li 周禮
Chu Hsi 朱熹
Chu-ko Liang 諸葛亮
Chu Tzu chia-li 朱子家禮
Chu Tzu feng-shih 朱子封事
Chu Tzu ta-ch'üan 朱子大全
Chu Tzu yü-lei ch'ao 朱子語類抄
Chu Yüan-chang 朱元璋
chugang 晝講

Ch'un-ch'iu chi-chuan 春秋集傳
Ch'unch'ŏn 春川
Ch'unch'ugwan 春秋館
Ch'ung-chen 崇禎
Chung Hsing 鍾惺
Chung-yung 中庸
Chungbuk 中北
Ch'ungch'ŏng (do) 忠清(道)
chunghŭng 中興
chungin 中人
Chungjong 中宗
chungsa 中祀
erh mu pei yeh 而母婢也
Fan Tsu-yü 范祖禹
feng 封
Fu-su 扶蘇
hallim 翰林
Han 漢
Han (Sanggung) 韓(尚宮)
Han Ingmo 韓翼謨
Han Kao-ti 漢高帝
Han Kwangjo 韓光肇
Han Seryang 韓世良
Han Wen-ti 漢文帝
Han Wu-ti 漢武帝
Handang 漢黨
Hanjungnok 한중록
hoegang 會講
Hoean (Taegun) 懷安(大君)
Hong Ch'ijung 洪致中
Hong Iksam 洪益三
Hong Kyehŭi 洪啓禧
Hong Ponghan 洪鳳漢
Hong Surhae 洪述海
Hong Taeyong 洪大容
Honghwa (mun) 弘化(門)
Hŏnjong 憲宗
Hŏnnyŏl 獻烈
hop'o 戶布
Hsiao-ching 孝經
Hsiao-hsüeh 小學
Hsiao-tsung 孝宗
Hsiao-ya 小雅
Hsin-ching 心經
Hsu Tzu-chih t'ung-chien kang-mu
　　續資治通鑑綱目
Huang Huai 黃淮
Hullyŏn togam 訓鍊都監

288

Glossary

Hǔnghwa (mun) 興化(門)
Hǔngsǒn Taewǒn'gun 興宣大院君
Hung-wu 洪武
Hunsǒ 勳西
Hwagyǒng 和敬
Hwahyǒp (Ongju) 和協(翁主)
hwa-i (hua-i) 華夷
Hwang Kyǒngwǒn 黃景源
Hwang Myǒng t'onggi 皇明通紀
Hwang So 黃爐
Hwan'gyǒng (jǒn) 歡慶(殿)
Hwap'yǒng (Ongju) 和平(翁主)
Hwawǒn (Ongju) 和緩(翁主)
Hwayang 華陽
Hwidǒk 徽德
Hwijǒng 徽靖
Hwinyǒngjǒn 徽寧殿
hyangan 鄉案
hyanggyo 鄉校
hyangyak 鄉約
Hyegyǒnggung Hong Ssi 惠慶宮洪氏
Hyesun 惠順
Hyojang (Seja) 孝章
Hyojong 孝宗
Hyǒnik 顯翼
Hyǒnjong 顯宗
Hyǒnjong kaesu sillok 顯宗改修實錄
Hyǒnjong sillok 顯宗實錄
Hyonyǒng (Taegun) 孝寧(大君)
hyulmin 恤民
hyulmin ǔi 恤民儀
hyungnye 凶禮
i/li 理
I-ching 易經
Igan (Taegun) 益安(大君)
Ikchong 翼宗
Ilsǒngnok 日省錄
Im Sǒng 任珹
Im Tǒkche 林德躋
Imhae (gun) 臨海(君)
Imo ilgi 壬午日記
Imyǒng (Taegun) 臨瀛(大君)
in 仁
In'gyǒng (Wanghu) 仁敬(王后)
Inhyǒn (Wanghu) 仁顯(王后)
Injo 仁祖
Injong 仁宗
Injǒng (mun) 仁政(門)

Inp'yǒng (Taegun) 麟平(大君)
Inwǒn (Wanghu) 仁元(王后)
Kach'ǒn 加川
Kaesǒng 開城
Kaet'ae kiyǒng 開泰基永
kan 間
Kang 堈
Kang Chihwan 姜趾煥
Kang Hongnip 姜弘立
K'ang-hsi 康熙
Kanghwa (do) 江華(島)
Kangwǒn (do) 江原(道)
Kangsǒng 康聖
Kao-tsung 高宗
kapsa 甲士
karye 嘉禮
ki/ch'i 氣
Kiho hakp'a 畿湖學派
Kija (Chi Tzu) 箕子
killye 吉禮
Kim Chaero 金在魯
Kim Ch'angjip 金昌集
Kim Chu 金澍
Kim Chunggi 金重器
Kim Chungman 金重萬
Kim Hwajung 金和中
Kim Igon 金履坤
Kim Ilgyǒng 金一鏡
Kim Sangno 金尙魯
Kim Sangsaeng 金尙生
Kim Sǒngǔng 金聖應
Kim Suhang 金壽恒
Kim Sujǒng 金守貞
Kim Tonguk 金東旭
Kim Yangt'aek 金陽澤
Koguryǒ 高句麗
Kojong 高宗
Kolbuk 骨北
komyǒng 誥命
Kǒnbok (mun) 建福(門)
kong 公
Kǒn'gon konnyǒng 乾健坤寧
kongsin 功臣
Koryǒ 高麗
Koryǒ T'aejo 高麗太祖
Kuan Yü 關羽
Kukcho pogam 國朝寶鑑
kǔkhaeng 極行

289

Glossary

Kŭm 昑
Kumalli 九萬里
Kŭmch'ŏn (gyo) 禁川〔橋〕
Kŭmhwa 金化
Kŭmsŏng (Taegun) 錦城〔大君〕
Kŭmwiyŏng 禁衛營
kunnye 軍禮
Kwanghae (gun) 光海〔君〕
Kwangin tonhŭi 光仁敦禧
Kwangp'yŏng (Taegun) 廣平〔大君〕
Kwangsŏn 光宣
Kwangsuk 光叔
Kwan'gwang (ch'ŏng) 觀光〔廳〕
Kwanjemyo 關帝廟
kwŏn 卷
Kwŏn Chŏngch'im 權正忱
Kyodong 喬桐
Kyŏngch'un (jŏn) 景春〔殿〕
Kyŏngdŏk (kung) 慶德〔宮〕
Kyŏnggi (do) 京畿〔道〕
Kyŏngguk taejŏn 經國大典
Kyŏnghŭi (gung) 慶熙〔宮〕
Kyŏnghwa (mun) 景華〔門〕
Kyŏnghyŏn (dang) 景賢〔堂〕
Kyŏngjong 景宗
Kyŏngjong sillok 景宗實錄
Kyŏngjong sujŏng sillok 景宗修正實錄
Kyŏngsang (do) 慶尙〔道〕
Kyŏngsun (wang) 敬順〔王〕
kyŏngyŏn 經筵
Kyujanggak 奎章閣
kyunyŏk 均役
Kyunyŏkch'ŏng 均役廳
Li-chi 禮記
Li Chung-ting-kung tsou-i 李忠定公奏議
Li Kang 李綱
Li-tai chun-chien 歷代君鑑
Li-tai ming-ch'en tsou-i 歷代名臣奏議
Li Yu-wu 李幼武
Liu Yen 劉剡
Lo Hsiang-chih 駱尙志
Lu Chih 陸贄
Lu Chung-lien 魯仲連
Lu Hsüan-kung tsou-i 陸宣公奏議
Lu wo 蓼莪
Lun-yü 論語
Manan (mun) 萬安〔門〕
Mandongmyo 萬東廟

map'ae 馬牌
Meng Tzu 孟子
Milp'ung (gun) 密豐〔君〕
Min Ch'angsu 閔昌洙
Min Chinhu 閔鎭厚
Min Chinwŏn 閔鎭遠
Min Hyŏngsu 閔亨洙
Min Ikkwan 閔翼觀
Min Paeksang 閔百祥
Ming 明
Ming-chi p'ien-nien 明紀編年
Mok Horyong 睦虎龍
Mok Siryong 睦時龍
Muan (Taegun) 撫安〔大君〕
Mun (Sugŭi) 文〔淑儀〕
Munhyo (Seja) 文孝〔世子〕
Munjong 文宗
munkwa 文科
Munmyo 文廟
Munsŏng 文成
musuri 무수리
Myŏngjong 明宗
Myŏngjŏng (mun) 明政〔門〕
Myŏngŭi chŏngdŏk 明義正德
Na Kyŏngŏn 羅景彥
Na Sangŏn 羅尙彥
Naju 羅州
Nam T'aejing 南泰徵
Namin 南人
Namyŏn (gun) 南延〔君〕
No Ujin 盧宇愼
Noron 老論
Nosŏ 老西
Nŭngch'ang (Taegun) 綾昌〔大君〕
Nŭngwŏn (Taegun) 綾原〔大君〕
O Myŏnghang 吳命恒
obok 五服
Ogunyŏng 五軍營
"Ŏje chamun chadap" 御製自問自答
"Ŏje chaso" 御製自笑
"Ŏje chasŏng" 御製自醒
Ŏje chasŏng p'yŏn 御製自省編
"Ŏje ch'ing che Yo" 御製稱帝堯
Ŏje hoegap munyŏnsŏ si wŏllyang 御製回
　　甲暮年書示元良
"Ŏje ilganggae" 御製日憬慨
"Ŏje ilmin" 御製日悶
"Ŏje kanggae" 御製憬慨

Glossary

Ŏje kogŭm yŏndae kwigam 御製古今年代龜鑑

"Ŏje kosusim" 御製固守心

"Ŏje koyŏsim" 御製固予心

"Ŏje kŭn'gyŏn paekse kusipse su chikchiin ch'umo kihoe" 御製近見百歲九十歲壽職之人追慕記懷

Ŏje kyŏngse mundap 御製警世問答

Ŏje kyŏngse mundap songnok 御製警世問答續錄

Ŏje kyŏngse p'yŏn 御製警世編

"Ŏje minyajang" 御製悶夜長

"Ŏje mo tae Sun" 御製慕大舜

"Ŏje munyŏsim" 御製問予心

Ŏje paekhaengwŏn 御製百行源

"Ŏje simmin" 御製心悶

"Ŏje so ilse" 御製笑一世

"Ŏje so ilse" 御製笑日勢

"Ŏje sungya simyujaemin" 御製夙夜心惟在民

ŏllo 言路

ondol 溫埃

ŏn'gwan 言官

Onjo 溫祚

Onyang 溫陽

oryun 五倫

Ou-yang Hsiu 歐陽修

Owi 五衛

Ŏyŏngch'ŏng 御營廳

Paekche 百濟

Pak Chiwŏn 朴趾源

Pak Ch'ansin 朴纘新

Pak Munsu 朴文秀

Pak P'ilchu 朴弼周

Pak P'ilkyun 朴弼均

Pak p'ilmong 朴弼夢

Pak P'irhyŏn 朴弼顯

Pak Sanap 朴師訥

Pak Tongjun 朴東俊

Pao (kung) 包(公)

p'il 疋

Pingae 빙애

pinnye 賓禮

Pogwŏl chŏngo 補闕正誤

Pogyŏng (dang) 寶慶(堂)

pu 負

Pugin 北人

Pukhak 北學

P'ungsan Hong 豐山洪

Pyŏn Tŭngnyang 邊得讓

p'yŏng 坪

P'yŏngan (do) 平安(道)

P'yŏngwŏn (Taegun) 平原(大君)

P'yŏngyang 平壤

P'youirok 表義錄

sa 私

sach'in 私親

Sado (Seja) 思悼(世子)

saengwŏn 生員

saengwŏn-si 生員試

sagwan 史官

sahak 四學

sahwa 士禍

Sajik 社稷

Samsŏngsa 三聖祠

Sandang 山黨

Sangju 尙州

San-kuo-chih yen-i 三國志演義

se 歲

Seja igwisa 世子翊衛司

Seja sigangwŏn 世子侍講院

Seja tonggung ilgi 世子東宮日記

Seje 世弟

Sejo 世祖

Sejong 世宗

sesil 世室

Seson 世孫

shan 禪

Shang Lu 商輅

Shih-chi 史記

Shih-ching 詩經

Shih-tsung 世宗

Shu-ching 書經

Shun 舜

Sijŏnggi 時政記

Silla 新羅

Sillok 實錄

Sillokch'ŏng 實錄廳

Sim Chŏngyŏn 沈鼎衍

Sim Yuhyŏn 沈維賢

Simin (dang) 時敏(堂)

sin/ch'en 臣

Sin Man 申晚

Sin Wi 申暐

Sinim sahwa 申壬士禍

Sirhak 實學

sŏ 庶
Sŏ Kŏjŏng 徐居正
Sŏ Myŏngŭng 徐命膺
Sobuk 小北
sodae 召對
Sohyŏn (Seja) 昭顯(世子)
Sŏin 西人
sŏk 石
sŏkkang 夕講
sŏng 誠
Song Chinmyŏng 宋眞明
Song Chun'gil 宋浚吉
Song Ikhwi 宋翼輝
Song Inmyŏng 宋寅明
Song Siyŏl 宋時烈
Sŏnggong sinhwa 聖功神化
Sŏnggyun'gwan 成均館
Sŏnghak chibyo 聖學輯要
Sŏngjong 成宗
Sŏngnyŏng (Taegun) 誠寧(大君)
sŏngwang 聖王
Sŏnhŭigung Yi Ssi 宣禧宮李氏
Sŏnjo 宣祖
Sŏnjo sillok 宣祖實錄
Sŏnjo sujŏng sillok 宣祖修正實錄
Sŏnŭi (Wanghu) 宣懿(王后)
Sŏnwŏnjŏn 璿源殿
Soron 少論
sosa 小祀
Sosŏ 少西
sŏwŏn 書院
Such'ang 壽昌
sugu 水口
Sukchong 肅宗
Sukchong sillok 肅宗實錄
Sukhŭng yamae cham 夙興夜寐箴
Sung 宋
Sung-chien 宋鑑
Sung Jen-tsung 宋仁宗
Sung ming-ch'en yen-hsing lu 宋名臣言行錄
Sung Ying-tsung 宋英宗
Sung Yüan kang-mu 宋元綱目
Sungdŏkchŏn 崇德殿
Sunginjŏn 崇仁殿
Sŭngjŏngwŏn 承政院
Sŭngjŏngwŏn ilgi 承政院日記
Sungmun (dang) 崇文(堂)

Sungnyŏlchŏn 崇烈殿
Sungnyŏngjŏn 崇靈殿
Sungŭijŏn 崇義殿
Sunjo 純祖
Sunjong 純宗
Suŏch'ŏng 守禦廳
Suwŏn 水原
Ta-hsüeh 大學
Ta-hsüeh yen-i 大學衍義
Ta-hsüeh yen-i pu 大學衍義補
Taebodan 大報壇
Taebuk 大北
Taegu 大邱
Taehun 大訓
T'aejo 太祖
T'aejong 太宗
taesa 大祀
Taesŏng kwangun 大成廣運
T'ai-tsung 太宗
T'akchi chŏngnye 度支定例
T'aksobuk 濁小北
T'ang T'ai-tsung 唐太宗
T'ang-chien 唐鑑
T'angnam 濁南
t'angp'yŏng 蕩平
t'angp'yŏngju 蕩平主
Tan'gun 檀君
Tanjong 端宗
Tansŏng 丹城
Tanŭi (Wanghu) 端懿(王后)
T'ien Tzu 天子
Tŏgan (Taegun) 德安(大君)
tŏk 德
Tŏkchong 德宗
Tŏkhŭng Taewŏn'gun 德興大院君
Tŏksŏng (hap) 德成(閤)
Tongguk t'onggam 東國通鑑
Tongin 東人
T'ongmyŏng (jŏn) 通明(殿)
Tongmyŏng (wang) 東明(王)
Tso-chuan 左傳
Tu Yen 杜衍
T'ung-chien kang-mu 通鑑綱目
Twiju taewang 뒤주대왕
Tzu-chih t'ung-chien 資治通鑑
U (wang) 禑(王)
Ŭian (Taegun) 宜安(大君)
Ŭidong (gung) 義洞(宮)

Glossary

Ŭijŏngbu 議政府
ŭiri 義理
Ŭiyŏl 義烈
Ulsan 蔚山
ŭm 蔭
ŭn 垠
Ŭnjŏn (gun) 恩全(君)
Ŭnŏn (gun) 恩彦(君)
Ŭnsin (gun) 恩信(君)
Wan-li 萬歷
Wan-shou (shan) 萬壽(山)
Wang Ju-nan 王汝南
Wang Yang-ming 王陽明
wangdo 王道
Wen (wang) 文(王)
Wen-ti 文帝
Wen T'ien-hsiang 文天祥
wiye 違豫
Wŏlsan (Taegun) 月山(大君)
Wŏn Kyŏngha 元景夏
Wŏnja poyangch'ŏng 元子輔養廳
Wŏnjong 元宗
Wu Ching 吳兢
Wu San-kuei 吳三桂
Yang Chen 揚震
Yang-cheng t'u-chieh 養正圖解
Yang Shih-ch'i 楊士奇
yangban 兩班
yangdŏk (tang) 養德(堂)
Yangnyŏng (Taegun) 讓寧(大君)
Yangsŏnghŏn 養性軒
Yangyŏk sajŏngch'ŏng 良役查正廳
Yangyŏk silch'ong 良役實總
Yao 堯
yasa 野史
Yejong 睿宗
Yemun'gwan 藝文館
yen-lu 言路
yesong 禮訟
Yi (jo) 李(朝)
Yi Chae 李縡
Yi Chinyu 李眞有
Yi Ch'ŏnbo 李天輔
Yi Chongsŏng 李宗城
Yi Ch'ŏnhae 李天海
Yi Chonjung 李存中
Yi Chujin 李周鎭
Yi Hu 李珝

Yi Hyŏngman 李衡萬
Yi Ijang 李彝章
Yi Ik 李翼
Yi Imyŏng 李頤命
Yi Injwa 李麟佐
Yi Kŏnmyŏng 李健命
Yi Kwal 李适
Yi Kwanghyŏn 李光鉉
Yi Kwangjwa 李光佐
Yi Kwanmyŏng 李觀命
Yi Manhoe 李萬恢
Yi Mansi 李萬蒔
Yi Pongsang 李鳳祥
Yi Samyŏng 李師命
Yi Sasŏng 李思晟
Yi Sŏnggye 李成桂
Yi T'aejo 李太祖
Yi T'oegye (Yi Hwang) 李退溪(李滉)
Yi Ŭiyŏn 李義淵
Yi Yŏngbin 李暎嬪
Yi Yulgok (Yi I) 李栗谷(李珥)
Yin-jeng 胤礽
Yomyŏng Sunch'ŏl 堯明舜哲
Yongbi ŏch'ŏn'ga 龍飛御天歌
Yŏngbok 永福
Yŏngch'ang (Taegun) 永昌(大君)
Yŏngjo 英祖
Yŏngjong 英宗
Yŏngjo sillok 英祖實錄
Yŏngmo ŭiyŏl 英謨毅烈
Yŏngnam hakp'a 嶺南學派
Yŏngnyŏngjŏn 永寧殿
Yongsŏng (Taegun) 龍城(大君)
Yŏngŭng (Taegun) 永膺(大君)
Yŏning (gun) 延礽(君)
Yŏnnyŏng (gun) 延齡(君)
Yŏnsan (gun) 燕山(君)
Yŏsa chegang 麗史提綱
Yu Ch'ŏkki 俞拓基
Yu Hyŏngwŏn 柳馨遠
Yu Kye 俞棨
Yu Ponghwi 柳鳳輝
Yu Sangun 柳尙運
Yu Segyo 柳世僑
Yu Sŏngnyong 柳成龍
Yüan 元
yuhak 幼學
Yukpuk 肉北

Glossary

Yuksang (gung) 毓祥(宮)
Yun Chaegyŏm 尹在謙
Yun (Sanggung) 尹(尚宮)
Yun Chǔng 尹拯
Yun Hye 尹惠

Yun Hyu 尹鑴
Yun Suk 尹塾
Yung-cheng 雍正
Yung-lo 永樂
Yunghwa 隆化

BIBLIOGRAPHY

Abbreviations used:
KS   *Kyŏngjong sillok* 景宗實錄
SI   *Sŭngjŏngwŏn ilgi* 承政院日記
SS   *Sukchong sillok* 肅宗實錄
YS   *Yŏngjo sillok* 英祖實錄

Manuscripts and Old Publications Housed in Archives

Ch'ae Chegong 蔡濟恭. *Pŏnam sŏnsaengjip* 樊巖先生集 (Collected Writings of Master Ch'ae Chegong). 27 *ch'aek*. 1824. Kyujanggak.

Changhŏn Seja tonggung ilgi 莊獻世子東宮日記 (Records of Prince Sado's Tutorial Office). 30 *ch'aek*. Ms. 1738–1762. Kyujanggak.

Changjo Hŏn'gyŏnghu karye togam ŭigwe 莊祖獻敬后嘉禮都監儀軌 (The Record of the Wedding of Prince Sado and Lady Hong). Ms. 1744. Kyujanggak.

Chiao Hung 焦竑. *Yang-cheng t'u-chieh* 養正圖解 (Diagrams and Explanations on the Cultivation of Correctness). With Yŏngjo's preface. 2 *ch'aek*. 1749. Changsŏgak.

Cho Chaeho 趙載浩. *Sonjae sŏnsaeng munjip* 損齋先生文集 (Collected Literary Writings of Master Cho Chaeho). 2 *ch'aek*. N.d. Kungnip tosŏgwan.

Cho Ch'ŏngse 趙靖世. *Sŏyŏn kangŭi* 書筵講義 (Lectures of the Crown Prince Tutorial Sessions). Ms. 1789. Kyujanggak.

Cho Hyŏnmyŏng 趙顯命. *Kwinokchip* 歸鹿集 (Collected Writings of Cho Hyŏnmyŏng). 20 *ch'aek*. N.d. Kyujanggak.

—— ed. *Yangyŏk silch'ong* 良役實總 (Facts and Statistics of the Military Service). 20 *ch'aek* (*ch'aek* 1, 3 and 10 are missing). 1748. Kyujanggak.

Cho T'aech'ae 趙泰采. *Iudangjip* 二憂堂集 (Collected Writings of Cho T'aech'ae). 3 *ch'aek*. N.d. Kyujanggak.

Cho T'aeŏk 趙泰億. *Kyŏmjaejip* 謙齋集 (Collected Writings of Cho T'aeŏk). 20 *ch'aek*. N.d. Kyujanggak.

Choein Hwang So ch'uan 罪人黃燦推案 (Trial Record of the Criminal Hwang So). In *Ch'uan kŭp kugan, ch'aek*, 144. Ms. Kyujanggak.

Chŏngjo 正祖. *Hyŏnyungwŏnji* 顯隆園誌 (Writings Composed for Prince Sado's Tomb). In Chŏngjo, *Hongjae chŏnsŏ* 弘齋全書 (Complete Works of Chŏngjo). 100 *ch'aek*. 1814. Kyujanggak.

Chongmyo ŭigwe 宗廟儀軌 (Rituals Concerning the Ancestral Temple). Ms. 1706. Changsŏgak.

Ch'ŏnŭi sogam 闡義昭鑑 (Illuminating Mirror of Righteousness). 3 *ch'aek*. 1755. Kyujanggak.

Bibliography

Ch'ŏnŭi sogam ŏnhae 천의소감언해 (Illuminating Mirror of Righteousness, Translated Into Korean). 1755. Kyujanggak.

Ch'uan kŭp kugan 推案及鞫案 (Records of Trials at the State Tribunal). 331 *ch'aek*. Ms. 1601–1892. Kyujanggak.

Hong Kyehŭi 洪啓禧, ed. *Kyunyŏk sasil* 均役事實 (Facts of the Equal Military Tax). 1752. Kyujanggak.

Hwagyŏng hwidŏk ansun Sukpin kasang ikho ch'ingha ch'ŏp 和敬徽德安純淑嬪加上謚號稱賀帖 (Album of Titles Offered to Lady Ch'oe Sukpin). Ms. 1724–1776. Changsŏgak.

Hwang Kyŏngwŏn 黃景源. *Kanghanjip* 江漢集 (Collected Writings of Hwang Kyŏngwŏn). 15 *ch'aek*. 1790. Kyujanggak.

Hwang Myŏng t'onggi 皇明通紀 (A Chronological History of the Imperial Ming Dynasty). 24 *ch'aek*. 1771. Changsŏgak.

Hwanghwa chip 皇華集 (Anthology of Imperial Splendors). 25 *ch'aek*. 1773. Changsŏgak.

Hwihoch'ŏp 徽號帖 (Album of Titles). Ms. 1777–1800. Changsŏgak.

Hyojong kasang ikho togam ŭigwe 孝宗加上謚號都監儀軌 (The Record of the Ceremony of Offering Additional Posthumous Titles to Hyojong). Ms. 1740. Kyujanggak.

Ilgyŏng Horyong tŭng ch'uan 一鏡虎龍等推案 (Trial Record of the Criminals Ilgyŏng and Horyong). In *Ch'uan kŭp kugan, ch'aek*, 133.

Injŏp sŏrhwa 引接說話 (A Report of an Interview). Ms. 1721. Kyujanggak.

Inwŏn Wanghu ch'ilchonho chonsung togam ŭigwe 仁元王后七尊號尊崇都監儀軌 (The Record of the Ceremony of Offering the Seventh Title to Queen Inwŏn). Ms. 1751. Kyujanggak.

Inwŏn Wanghu ch'usang chonho okch'aengmun 仁元王后追上尊號玉冊文 (The Offering of Posthumous Titles to Queen Inwŏn). 1890. Changsŏgak.

Inwŏn Wanghu kukhyul ch'o tŭngnok 仁元王后國恤草謄錄 (The Record of Queen Inwŏn's Funeral). 1757. Changsŏgak.

Inwŏn Wanghu ojonho chonsung togam ŭigwe 仁元王后五尊號尊崇都監儀軌 (The Record of the Ceremony of Offering the Fifth Title to Queen Inwŏn). Ms. 1740. Kyujanggak.

Inwŏn Wanghu yukchonho chonsung togam ŭigwe 仁元王后六尊號尊崇都監儀軌 (The Record of the Ceremony of Offering the Sixth Title to Queen Inwŏn). Ms. 1747. Kyujanggak.

Kim Ch'angjip 金昌集. *Mongwajip* 夢窩集 (Collected Writings of Kim Ch'angjip). 5 *ch'aek*. N.d. Kyujanggak.

Kim Ch'iin 金致仁, ed. *Myŏngŭirok* 明義錄 (The Record of Clarifying Righteousness). 1777. Changsŏgak.

Kim Igon 金履坤. *Pongnokchip* 鳳麓集 (Collected Writings of Kim Igon). 2 *ch'aek*. 1778. Kyujanggak.

Kim Sŏnggŭn 金聲根. *Kwŏn'gong Chŏngch'im ikchang* 權公正忱謚狀 (Eulogistic Biography of Kwŏn Chŏngch'im). 1899–1906. Changsŏgak.

Kim Yangt'aek 金陽澤. "Chimun" 誌文 (A Funerary Eulogy). In *Wŏnnŭngji*.

Kojong kasang chonho okch'aengmun 高宗加上尊號玉冊文 (The Offering of Additional Title to Kojong). Ms. 1890. Changsŏgak.

Kukcho oryeŭi 國朝五禮儀 (Five Categories of Dynastic Rites). 1475. Kyujanggak.

Kukcho poch'ŏp 國朝譜牒 (Genealogical Album of the Royal House). 1931. Changsŏgak.

Kukcho sok oryeŭi 國朝續五禮儀 (Five Categories of Dynastic Rites, Continued). 1744. Kyujanggak.

Kwŏn Chŏngch'im 權正忱. *P'yŏngam sŏnsaeng munjip* 平菴先生文集 (Collected Literary

Bibliography

Writings of Master Kwŏn Chŏngch'im). 4 *ch'aek*. N.d. Kyujanggak.

Kyŏngjong ch'un'gung ilgi 景宗春宮日記 (Record of Crown Prince Kyŏngjong's Tutorial Office). 16 *ch'aek*. Ms. 1690–1720. Kyujanggak.

Kyŏngjong Taewang kukhyul tŭngnok 景宗大王國恤謄錄 (Record of King Kyŏngjong's Funeral). Ms. 1724. Changsŏgak.

Kyŏngmogung poyangch'ŏng ilgi 景慕宮輔養廳日記 (Record of the Guidance Office of Prince Sado). Ms. 1735. Kyujanggak.

Min Chinwŏn 閔鎮遠. *Tanam mallok* 丹巖漫錄 (Leisurely Jottings of Min Chinwŏn). 2 *ch'aek*. 1724–1776. Kyujanggak.

Min Iksu 閔翼洙. *Yŏhŭng Min Ssi kasŭng kiryak* 驪興閔氏家乘記略 (Record of the Min Family). 6 *ch'aek*. 1744. Changsŏgak.

Min Pyŏngsŭng 閔丙承. *Tanam sŏnsaeng yŏnbo* 丹巖先生年譜 (A Chronological Biography of Master Min Chinwŏn). 5 *ch'aek*. 1937. Changsŏgak.

Monyŏn kisa 某年記事 (Record of a Certain Year). N.d. Kuksa p'yŏnch'an wiwŏnhoe.

Munjo ikhwangje ch'usang chonho okch'aengmun 文祖翼皇帝追上尊號玉册文 (The Offering of a Posthumous Title to Munjo). Ms. 1883. Changsŏgak.

Musin yŏgok ch'uan 戊申逆獄推案 (Trial Record of the 1728 Rebels). 10 *ch'aek*. Ms. 1728–1729. Kyujanggak.

On'gung sasil 溫宮事實 (Factual Record of the Onyang Trip). 3 *ch'aek*. Ms. 1759. Kyujanggak.

Onhaeng ilgi 溫行日記 (Travel Record to Onyang). Ms. 1750. Kyujanggak.

Onhaeng tŭngnok 溫幸謄錄 (Record of Onyang Trip). Ms. 1717. Changsŏgak.

Pak Chonggyŏm 朴宗謙. *Hyŏn'gogi* 玄皋記 (Record of a Dark Mound). 2 *ch'aek*. Ms. N.d. Kyujanggak.

—— *Hyŏn'gu kisa* 玄駒記事 (Record of a Dark Donkey). Ms. N.d. Kyujanggak.

Pak Munsu 朴文秀, ed. *T'akchi chŏngnye* 度支定例 (Rules and Regulations of the Board of Taxation). 12 *ch'aek* (*ch'aek* 5, 7, and 12 are missing). 1749. Kyujanggak.

Pak Suwŏn 朴綏源. *Yŏho sŏnsaeng yŏnbo* 黎湖先生年譜 (A Chronological Biography of Master Pak Pilchu). 2 *ch'aek*. 1809–1906. Changsŏgak.

Pak Yŏngse 朴永世. *Mongwa sŏnsaeng silgi* 夢窩先生實記 (True Record of Master Kim Ch'angjip). N.d. Kyujanggak.

Ponggyo ŏmbyŏnnok 奉教嚴辨錄 (Record of Authoritative Judgment, Written Under Royal Order). Ms. 1762. Kyujanggak.

Sado Seja (or Changhŏn Seja) 思悼世子 (莊獻世子). *Nŭnghŏgwan man'go* 凌虛關漫稿 (Leisurely Writings of Prince Sado). 3 *ch'aek*. 1762. Changsŏgak.

Sado Seja sangjang tŭngnok 思悼世子喪葬謄錄 (Record of Prince Sado's Funeral). Ms. 1762. Changsŏgak.

Sajik ŭigwe 社稷儀軌 (Rituals Concerning the Altar of Grain and Land). N.d. Changsŏgak.

Sim Naksu 沈樂洙. *Ŭnp'a san'go* 恩坡散稿 (Scattered Manuscripts of Sim Naksu). Ms. N.d. Kyujanggak.

Song Inmyŏng 宋寅明, ed. *Kamnannok* 勘亂錄 (Investigative Report on the Rebellion). 4 *ch'aek*. 1729. Kyujanggak.

Song Siyŏl 宋時烈. *Toktae sŏrhwa* 獨對說話 (Report on the Solitary Audience). Ms. 1659. Kyujanggak.

Sŏ Myŏngŭng 徐命膺. "Haengjang" 行狀 (A Biography). In *Wŏnnŭngji*.

Sŏnŭi Wanghu kukhyul tŭngnok 宣懿王后國恤謄錄 (Record of Queen Sŏnŭi's Funeral). Ms. 1730. Changsŏgak.

297

Bibliography

Sŏnwŏn segye 璿源世系 (Genealogy of the Royal Family). Ms. 1900. Kyujanggak.

Sukpin Suyang Ch'oe Ssi myoji 淑嬪首陽崔氏墓誌 (A Biography of Lady Ch'oe on the Occasion of Her Burial). Ms. 1718. Changsŏgak.

Taech'ŏnnok 待闡錄 (The Record of Waiting for Clarification). 10 *ch'aek*. Ms. 1776–1800. Changsŏgak.

Ŭiyŏn ch'uan 義淵推案 (Trial Record of the Criminal Ŭiyŏn). In *Ch'uan kŭp kugan, ch'aek*, 132

Wangja karye tŭngnok 王子嘉禮謄錄 (Records of the Prince's Felicitous Ceremonies). Ms. 1703–1712. Changsŏgak.

Wangseson karye tŭngnok 王世孫嘉禮謄錄 (Records of the Grand Heir's Felicitous Ceremonies). Ms. 1752–1766. Changsŏgak.

Wŏn Kyŏngha 元景夏. *Ch'anghajip* 蒼霞集 (Collected Writings of Wŏn Kyŏngha). 5 *ch'aek*. N.d. Kyujanggak.

Wŏnnŭngji 元陵誌 (The Writings Composed on Yŏngjo's Funeral). Ms. 1910. Changsŏgak.

Yangjo hongyunnok 兩朝弘倫錄 (Records of Humane Rule of the Two Reigns). 4 *ch'aek*. Changsŏgak.

Yi Ch'ŏnbo 李天輔. *Chinamjip* 晉菴集 (Collected Writings of Yi Ch'ŏnbo). 4 *ch'aek*. 1762. Kyujanggak.

Yi Imyŏng 李頤命. *Sojaejip* 疎齋集 (Collected Writings of Yi Imyŏng). 7 *ch'aek*. N.d. Kyujanggak.

Yi Kwanghyŏn 李光鉉 et al., eds. *Imo ilgi* 壬午日記 (Records Concerning the Year 1762). Ms. N.d. Changsŏgak.

—— *Yi Kwanghyŏn ilgi* 李光鉉日記 (Yi Kwanghyŏn's Diary). In *Imo ilgi*.

Yi Minhwan 李民寏. *Ch'aekchung ilgi* 柵中日記 (A Record of Years in Captivity). In Yi Minhwan, *Chaamjip* 紫巖集 (Collected Writings of Yi Minhwan). 2 *ch'aek*. N.d. Kyujanggak.

Yi Tŏksu 李德壽 et al., eds. *Kyŏngmo haengjang* 景廟行狀 (A Biography of Kyŏngjong). Ms. 1732. Changsŏgak.

Yŏlsŏngjo kye kang ch'aekcha ch'aje 列聖朝繼講册子次第 (The List of Books Studied in the Royal Lectures of Successive Reigns). Ms. N.d. Kyujanggak.

Yŏngjo 英祖. *Ŏje chasŏng p'yŏn* 御製自省編 (A Royal Self-Reflection). 2 *ch'aek*. Ms. 1746. Changsŏgak.

—— *Ŏje chŏnghun* 御製政訓 (A Royal Instruction on Governance). Ms. 1749. Changsŏgak.

—— *Ŏje hoegap monyŏnsŏ si wŏllyang* 御製回甲暮年示元良 (A Royal Essay Written in the Sixtieth Year to Instruct the Crown Prince). Ms. 1754. Kyujanggak.

—— *Ŏje kogŭm yŏndae kwigam* 御製古今年代龜鑑 (Royal Mirror of Past and Present). Ms. 1757. Changsŏgak.

—— *Ŏje kyŏngse mundap* 御製警世問答 (Royal Questions and Answers on Cautioning the World). Ms. 1762. Changsŏgak.

—— *Ŏje kyŏngse mundap songnok* 御製警世問答續錄 (Royal Questions and Answers on Cautioning the World, Continued). Ms. 1763. Changsŏgak.

—— *Ŏje kyŏngse p'yŏn* 御製警世編 (A Royal Discourse on Cautioning the World). Ms. 1764. Changsŏgak.

—— *Ŏje paekhaengwŏn* 御製百行源 (A Royal Lecture on the Sources of Good Conduct). Ms. 1765. Changsŏgak.

—— *Ŏje p'youirok* 御製表義錄 (Record of Manifest Righteousness). 1764. Ms. Changsŏgak.

—— *Ŏje taehun* 御製大訓 (Great Instruction). 1755. Kyujanggak.

Bibliography

—— *Yŏngse ch'umorok* 永世追慕錄 (Record of Eternal Remembrance). 1764. Ms. Changsŏgak.

—— *Yŏngse sok ch'umorok* 永世續追慕錄 (Record of Eternal Remembrance, Continued). Ms. 1770. Changsŏgak.

Yŏngjo ch'usang okch'aengmun 英祖追上玉册文 (Offering of A Posthumous Title to Yŏngjo). Ms. 1784. Changsŏgak.

Yŏngjo tonggung ilgi 英祖東宮日記 (Record of Crown Prince Yŏngjo's Tutorial Office). 5 *ch'aek*. 1721–1724. Kyujanggak.

Yŏngjong Taewang sillokch'ŏng ŭigwe 英宗大王實錄廳儀軌 (Proceedings of the Compilation of the Veritable Record of King Yŏngjo's Reign). 2 *ch'aek*. Ms. 1776. Kyujanggak.

Yŏngmo kosa 英廟故事 (The Accounts of Yŏngjo's Reign). Ms. N.d. Kungnip tosŏgwan.

Yu Ch'ŏkki 兪拓基. *Chisujaejip* 知守齋集 (Collected Writings of Yu Ch'ŏkki). 8 *ch'aek*. 1787. Kyujanggak.

Yu Ŏnho 兪彥鎬. *Yŏnsŏk* 燕石 (False Jade). 13 *ch'aek*. 1775. Kyujanggak.

Yu Sukki 兪肅基. *Kyŏmsanjip* 兼山集 (Collected Writings of Yu Sukki). 10 *ch'aek*. 1775. Kyujanggak.

Yuksanggung sangch'aengin ŭi 毓祥宮上册印儀 (The Ritual of Offering a Title and a Seal to Lady Ch'oe). Ms. 1753. Changsŏgak.

Yun Kwangso 尹光紹. *Myŏngjae sŏnsaeng yŏnbo* 明齋先生年譜 (A Chronological Biography of Master Yun Chŭng). 3 *ch'aek*. 1749. Kyujanggak.

Works in Modern Editions (Including Modern Editions of Early Works)

Bendix, Reinhard. *Kings or People*. Berkeley and Los Angeles: University of California Press. 1978.

Ch'a Munsŏp 車文燮. "Imnan ihu ŭi yangyŏk kwa kyunyŏkpŏp ŭi sŏngnip" 壬亂以後의良役과均役法의成立 (The Establishment of the Commoner Military Service and the Equal Military Tax After the Imjin Wars). *Sahak yŏn'gu* 史學研究 (April 1961), 10:115–30; (July 1961), 11:83–146.

Changsŏgak tosŏ Han'gukp'an ch'ongmongnok 藏書閣圖書韓國版總目錄 (A Complete Catalogue of the Korean Books at the Changsŏgak). Seoul: Changsŏgak, 1972.

Ch'ien, Edward T. "Chiao Hung and the Revolt Against Ch'eng-Chu Orthodoxy." In de Bary and the Conference on Seventeenth-Century Chinese Thought, eds., *The Unfolding of Neo-Confucianism*. pp. 271–303. New York: Columbia University Press, 1975.

Ch'oe Chaesŏk 崔在錫. *Han'guk kajok chedosa yŏn'gu* 韓國家族制度史研究 (A Study in the History of the Korean Family System). Seoul: Ilchisa, 1983.

Ch'oe Honggi 崔弘基. *Han'guk hojŏk chedosa yŏn'gu* 韓國戶籍制度史研究 (A Study of the Korean Census Register System). Seoul: Seoul Taehakkyo ch'ulp'anbu, 1975.

Ch'oe Sŭnghŭi 崔承熙. *Chosŏn ch'ogi ŏn'gwan ŏllon yŏn'gu* 朝鮮初期言官言論研究 (A Study of the Censors and the Censorial Voice in the Early Yi Dynasty). Seoul: Seoul Taehakkyo ch'ulp'anbu, 1976.

Ch'oe Wan'gi 崔完基. "Yŏngjo t'angp'yŏngch'aek ŭi ch'anbannon kŏmt'o" 英祖蕩平策의贊反論檢討 (An Investigation Into the Ideology of Support and Opposition to Yŏngjo's Policy of Grand Harmony). *Chindan hakpo* 震檀學報 (Dec. 1983), 56:67–96.

Ch'ŏn Kwanu 千寬宇. *Han'guk t'oji chedosa* 韓國土地制度史 (A History of the Korean Land System). In *Han'guk munhwasa taegye*. 2:1381–1561.

Bibliography

Chŏn Pongdŏk 田鳳德. *Han'guk pŏpchesa yŏn'gu* 韓國法制史研究 (A History of the Korean Legal System). Seoul: Seoul Taehakkyo ch'ulp'anbu, 1968.

Chŏng Chedu 鄭齊斗. *Hagokchip* 霞谷集 (Collected Writings of Chŏng Chedu). Seoul: Minjok munhwa ch'ujinhoe, 1972.

Chŏng Kubok 鄭求福. "Pan'gye Yu Hyŏngwŏn ŭi sahoe kaehyŏk sasang" 磻溪柳馨遠의 社會改革思想 (Yu Hyŏngwŏn's Ideas on Social Reform). *Yŏksa hakpo* 歷史學報 (March 1970), 45:1–53.

Chŏng Manjo 鄭萬祚. "Yŏngjodae ch'oban ŭi t'angp'yŏngch'aek kwa t'angp'yŏngp'a ŭi hwaltong" 英祖代初半의蕩平策과蕩平派의活動 (The Policy and the Faction of Grand Harmony in the Early Years of Yŏngjo's Reign). *Chindan hakpo* 震檀學報 (Dec. 1983), 56:27–66.

Chŏng Sŏkchong 鄭奭鍾. *Chosŏn hugi sahoe pyŏndong yŏn'gu* 朝鮮後期社會變動研究 (A Study of the Social Changes in the Late Yi Dynasty). Seoul: Ilchogak, 1983.

Chŏng Tojŏn 鄭道傳. *Chosŏn kyŏnggukchŏn* 朝鮮經國典 (Statutes for the Governance of Chosŏn). In Chŏng Tojŏn, *Sambongjip*.

—— *Kyŏngje mun'gam* 經濟文鑑 (A Mirror for the Economic System). In Chŏng Tojŏn, *Sambongjip*.

—— *Sambongjip* 三峯集 (Collected Writings of Chŏng Tojŏn). Seoul: Kuksa p'yŏnch'an wiwŏnhoe, 1971.

Chŏng Yagyong 丁若鏞. *Chŏng Tasan chŏsŏ* 丁茶山全書 (Complete Works of Chŏng Yagyong). 3 vols. Seoul: Munhŏn p'yŏnch'an wiwŏnhoe, 1960.

Chŏngjo sillok 正祖實錄 (The Veritable Record of Chŏngjo's Reign). 54 *kwŏn*. In *Chosŏn wangjo sillok*, vols. 44–47.

Chosŏn wangjo sillok 朝鮮王朝實錄 (The Veritable Record of the Yi Dynasty). 48 vols. + index. Seoul: Kuksa p'yŏnch'an wiwŏnhoe, 1955–1963.

Chosŏn wangjo ŭi chesa 朝鮮王朝의祭祀 (Sacrifices of the Yi Royal House). Seoul: Munhwaje kwalliguk, 1967.

Chu Hsi 朱熹. *Hui-an hsien-sheng Chu Wen-kung wen-chi* 晦菴先生朱文公文集 (Collection of Literary Works by Chu Hsi). Kyoto: Chūbun shuppan-sha, 1977.

Chung Chai-sik. "Chŏng Tojŏn: 'Architect' of Yi Dynasty Government and Ideology." In de Bary and Haboush, eds., *The Rise of Neo-Confucianism in Korea*, pp. 59–88. New York: Columbia University Press, 1985.

Chŭngbo munhŏn pigo 增補文獻備考 (Encyclopedia, Enlarged and Supplemented). 3 vols. Seoul: Kojŏn kanhaenghoe, 1959.

Chungjong sillok 中宗實錄 (The Veritable Record of Chungjong's Reign). 105 *kwŏn*. In *Chosŏn wangjo sillok*, vols. 14–19.

Crawford, Robert. "Eunuch Power in the Ming Dynasty." *T'oung Pao* (1961), 49(3):115–48.

Dardess, John D. *Confucianism and Autocracy*. Berkeley and Los Angeles: University of California Press, 1983.

de Bary, Wm. Theodore. "A Reappraisal of Neo-Confucianism." In Arthur F. Wright, ed., *Studies in Chinese Thought*, pp. 81–111. Chicago: University of Chicago Press, 1953.

—— "Chinese Despotism and the Confucian Ideal." In John K. Fairbank, ed., *Chinese Thought and Institutions*, pp. 163–203. Chicago: University of Chicago Press, 1957.

—— *Neo-Confucian Orthodoxy and the Learning of the Mind-and-Heart*. New York: Columbia University Press, 1981.

Bibliography

Demiéville, Paul. "Chang Hsüeh-ch'eng and His Historiography." In W. G. Beasley and E. G. Pulleyblank, eds., *Historians of China and Japan*, pp. 167–85.

Deuchler, Martina. "Neo-Confucianism: The Impulse for Social Action in Early Yi Korea." *The Journal of Korean Studies* (1980), 2:71–111.

—— "Reject the False and Uphold the Straight: Attitudes Toward Heterodox Thought in Early Yi Korea." In de Bary and Haboush, eds., *The Rise of Neo-Confucianism in Korea*, pp. 375–410.

—— "The Tradition: Women During the Yi Dynasty." In Sandra Mattielli, ed., *Virtues in Conflict*, pp. 1–47. Seoul: Royal Asiatic Society, Korea Branch, 1977.

Fan Tsu-yü 范祖禹. *Fan t'ai-shih chi* 范太史集 (Collected Writings of the Great Teacher Fan Tsu-yü). Shanghai: Commerical Press, 1935.

Fisher, Carney T. "The Great Ritual Controversy in the Age of Ming Shih-tsung." *Society for the Study of Chinese Religions Bulletin* (Fall 1979), 7:71–87.

Fung Yulan. *A Study of Chinese Philosophy*. 2 vols. Trans. Derk Bodde. Princeton: Princeton University Press, 1952.

Haboush, JaHyun Kim. "Confucian Rhetoric and Ritual as Techniques of Political Dominance: Yŏngjo's Use of the Royal Lecture." *The Journal of Korean Studies* (1985), 5:39–62.

—— "The Education of the Yi Crown Prince: A Study in Confucian Pedagogy." In de Bary and Haboush, eds., *The Rise of Neo-Confucianism in Korea*, pp. 166–222.

—— "A Heritage of Kings: One Man's Monarchy in the Confucian World." Ph. D. diss., Columbia University, 1978.

—— "The *Sirhak* Movement of the Late Yi Dynasty." *Korean Culture* (Summer 1987), 8(2):22–27.

Han Yŏngu (Young-woo) 韓永愚. *Chosŏn chŏn'gi sahoe kyŏngje yŏn'gu* 朝鮮前期社會經濟研究 (The Early Yi Society and Economy). Seoul: Ŭryu munhwasa, 1983.

—— "Kija Worship in the Koryŏ and Early Yi Dynasties: A Cultural Symbol in the Relationship Between Korea and China." In de Bary and Haboush, eds., *The Rise of Neo-Confucianism in Korea*, pp. 349–74.

Han'guk munhwasa taegye 韓國文化史大系 (Compendium of Korean Cultural History). 7 vols. Seoul: Koryŏ Taehakkyo ch'ulp'anbu, 1964–1972.

Ho, Ping-ti. *The Ladder of Success in Imperial China*. New York: Columbia University Press, 1962.

Hong Taeyong 洪大容. *Tamhŏnsŏ* 湛軒書 (Writings of Hong Taeyong). 2 vols. Seoul: Kyŏngin munhwasa, 1969.

Hucker, Charles O. "Confucianism and the Chinese Censorial System." In David S. Nivison and Arthur F. Wright, eds., *Confucianism in Action*, pp. 182–208. Stanford: Stanford University Press, 1959.

Hwang Wŏn'gu 黃元九. "Sirhakp'a ŭi sahak iron" 實學派의史學理論 (The Historiography of the Practical Learning School). *Yŏnse nonch'ong* 延世論叢 (May 1970), 7:181–232.

Hyegyŏnggung Hong Ssi 惠慶宮洪氏, *Hanjungnok* 한중록 (A Journal Written in Leisure). Ed. Kim Tonguk. Seoul: Minjung sŏgwan, 1960.

Hyojong sillok 孝宗實錄 (The Veritable Record of Hyojong's Reign). 21 kwŏn. In *Chosŏn wangjo sillok*, vols. 35–36.

Hyŏn Sangyun 玄相允. *Chosŏn yuhaksa* 朝鮮儒學史 (A History of Confucianism in Korea). Seoul: Minjung sŏgwan, 1954.

Bibliography

Hyŏnjong kaesu sillok 顯宗改修實錄 (The Revised Veritable Record of Hyŏnjong's Reign). 23 *kwŏn*. In *Chosŏn wangjo sillok*, vols. 37–38.

Hyŏnjong sillok 顯宗實錄 (The Veritable Record of Hyŏnjong's Reign). 22 *kwŏn*. In *Chosŏn wangjo sillok*, vols. 36–37.

Inaba Iwakichi 稻葉岩吉. *Kōkaikun jidai no Man Sen kankei* 光海君時代の滿鮮關係 (The Manchu-Korean Relation During Kwanghae's Reign). Seoul: Osakayago shoten, 1933.

Injo sillok 仁祖實錄 (The Veritable Record of Injo's Reign). 50 *kwŏn*. In *Chosŏn wangjo sillok*, vols. 33–35.

Jüan Yüan 阮元, ed. *Shih-san-ching chu-su* 十三經注疏 (The Thirteen Classics with Commentaries). 2 vols. Taipei: Kai-ming shu-chü, 1959.

Kahn, Harold L. *Monarchy in the Emperor's Eyes*. Cambridge: Harvard University Press, 1971.

—— "The Politics of Filiality: Justification for Imperial Action in Eighteenth-Century China." *Journal of Asian Studies* (Feb. 1967), 26(2):197–203.

Kang, Hi-woong. *The Development of the Korean Ruling Class from Late Silla to Early Koryŏ*. Ann Arbor, Mich.: University Microfilms, 1974.

Kawashima, Fujiya. "The Local Gentry Association in Mid-Yi Dynasty Korea: A Preliminary Study of the Ch'angnyŏng Hyangan, 1600–1838." *The Journal of Korean Studies* (1980), 2:113–37.

Kim Sŏkhŭi and Pak Yongsuk. 金錫禧, 朴容淑. "18 segi nongch'on ŭi sahoe kujo" 18世紀農村의社會構造 (The Social Structure of Eighteenth-Century Rural Korea). *Pudae sahak* 釜大史學 (1979), 3:25–60.

Kim Tonguk 金東旭. *Yijo chŏn'gi poksik yŏn'gu* 李朝前期服飾研究 (A Study of Early Yi Dynasty Clothing and Costumes). Seoul: Han'guk yŏn'guwŏn, 1963.

—— "Yijo chung-hugi ŭi yŏbok kujo" 李朝中後期의女服構造 (The Structure of Women's Clothes During the Middle and Late Yi Dynasty). *Asea yŏsŏng yŏn'gu* 亞細亞女性研究 (Dec. 1964), 3:85–121.

Kim Yongdŏk 金龍德. "Kyujanggak ko" 奎章閣考 (On Kyujanggak). *Chungang Taehakkyo nonmunjip* 中央大學校論文集 (Dec. 1957), 2:223–38.

Kim Yongsŏp 金容燮. "Chosŏn hugi e issŏsŏ ŭi sinbunje ŭi tongyo wa nongji soyu" 朝鮮後期에있어서의身分制의動搖와農地所有 (The Disruption of the Social Status System and Land Tenure in the Late Yi Dynasty). In Kim Yongsŏp. *Chosŏn hugi nongŏpsa yŏn'gu*, pp. 394–444.

—— *Chosŏn hugi nongŏpsa yŏn'gu* 朝鮮後期農業史研究 (The Agrarian History of the Late Yi Dynasty). Seoul: Ilchogak, 1970.

—— "Sagungjangt'o ŭi sehukyŏngje wa kŭ sŏngjang" 司宮庄土의佃戶經濟와그成長 (Destitute Households and Their Growth on Palace Estates). In Kim Yongsŏp, *Chosŏn hugi nongŏpsa yŏn'gu*, pp. 155–64.

—— "Yangan ŭi yŏn'gu" 量案의研究 (A Study of Land Registers). In Kim Yongsŏp, *Chosŏn hugi nongŏpsa yŏn'gu*, pp. 135–55.

Kim Yongsuk 金用淑. "Sado Seja ŭi pigŭk kwa kŭŭi chŏngsin punsŏkhakchŏk koch'al" 思悼世子의悲劇과그의精神分析學的考察 (A Psychoanalytic Approach to the Tragedy of Prince Sado). *Kugŏ kungmunhak* 국어국문학 (1958), 19:3–52.

—— "Yijo kungjung p'ungsok ŭi yŏn'gu" 李朝宮中風俗의研究 (A Study of Yi Court Customs and Manners). In Kim Yongsuk, *Yijo yŏryu munhak mit kungjung p'ungsok ŭi yŏn'gu* 李朝女流文學및宮中風俗의研究 (Studies on Women Writers and Yi Court

Customs and Manners), pp. 279–499. Seoul: Sungmyŏng Taehakkyo ch'ulp'anbu, 1970.

Ku Suhun 具樹勳. *Isunnok* 二旬錄 (The Record of Two Decades). In *P'aerim*, 9:402–79.

Kukcho inmulchi 國朝人物志. Kwangnŭng, 1909.

Kwanghaegun ilgi 光海君日記 (The Veritable Record of Kwanghae's Reign). *T'aebaeksan pon* 太白山本 (Mt. T'aebaek ed.) 187 *kwŏn*. In *Chosŏn wangjo sillok*, vols. 26–31.

Kwangsan Kim Ssi Och'ŏn komunsŏ 光山金氏烏川古文書 (The Old Documents of the Och'ŏn Kwangsan Kim Family). Seoul: Han'guk chŏngsin munhwa yŏn'guwŏn, 1982.

Kwon, Yon-Ung. "The Royal Lecture of Early Yi Korea (1)." *Journal of Social Sciences and Humanities* (Dec. 1979), 50:62–107.

Kyŏngguk taejŏn 經國大典 (Great Statutes for the Governance of the State). 2 vols. Seoul: Pŏpchech'ŏ, 1962.

Kyŏngjong sillok 景宗實錄 (The Veritable Record of Kyŏngjong's Reign). 15 *kwŏn*. In *Chosŏn wangjo sillok*, vol. 41.

Ledyard, Gari. "Korean Travellers in China Over Four Hundred years, 1488–1877." *Occasional Papers on Korea* (1974), 2:1–42.

Lee, Peter H. *Songs of Flying Dragons*. Cambridge: Harvard University Press, 1974.

Legge, James. *The Chinese Classics*. 7 vols. Oxford: Clarendon Press, 1895.

Levenson, Joseph R. *Confucian China and Its Modern Fate: A Trilogy*. 3 vols. Berkeley and Los Angeles: University of California Press, 1968.

Liu, James T. C. "How Did a Neo-Confucian School Become the State Orthodoxy?" *Philosophy East and West* (1973), 23(4):484–505.

—— *Ou-yang Hsiu*. Stanford: Stanford University Press, 1967.

Maruyama Masao. *Studies in the Intellectual History of Tokugawa Japan*. Princeton: Princeton University Press, 1974.

McCune, G. M. "The Yi Dynasty Annals of Korea." *Transactions of the Korea Branch of the Royal Asiatic Society* (1929), 18:57–82.

Meng Tzu 孟子 (*Mencius*). 14 *chüan*. In *Shih-san-ching chu-su*.

Meskill, John. *Ch'oe Pu's Diary: A Record of Drifting Across the Sea*. Tuscon: University of Arizona Press, 1965.

Min Tugi 閔斗基. "*Yŏrha ilgi* ŭi iryŏn'gu" 「熱河日記」의 一研究 (A Study of the Jehol Diary). *Yŏksa hakpo* 歷史學報 (April 1963), 20:81–116.

Miura Kunio. "Orthodoxy and Heterodoxy in Seventeenth-Century Korea: Song Siyŏl and Yun Hyu." In de Bary and Haboush, eds., *The Rise of Neo-Confucianism in Korea*, pp. 411–44.

Munro, Donald. *The Concept of Man in Early China*. Stanford: Stanford University Press, 1969.

Nakamura Hidetaka 中村榮孝. "Chōsen Eisō no Chōseiin nikki kaishu jigyō" 朝鮮英祖の「承政院日記」改修事業 (Yŏngjo's Reconstruction Project of the Records of the Royal Secretariat). In *Nissen kankeishi no kenkyū* 日鮮関係史の研究 (Researches on Japanese-Korean Relations). 3:648–51. 3 vols. Tokyo: Yoshikawa kobunkan, 1965–1969.

Nivison, David S. "Ho-shen and His Accusers." In Nivison and Wright, eds., *Confucianism in Action*, pp. 209–43.

Nunome Chōfū 布目潮渢. "Minchō no shooseisaku to sono eikyō" 明朝の諸王政策とその影響 (The Policies on the Imperial Princes and Their Influence During the

Ming Dynasty). *Shigaku zasshi* 史學雜誌 (March 1944), 55(3):105–36; (April 1944), 55(4):274–311; (May 1944), 55(5):367–417.

Ou-yang Hsiu 歐陽修. *Ou-yang Yung-shu-chi* 歐陽永叔集 (Collected Writings of Ou-yang Hsiu). 3 vols. Shanghai: Shang-wu yin-shu-kuan, 1958.

P'aerim 稗林 (Miscellaneous Tales). 10 vols. Seoul: T'amgudang, 1969–1970.

Pak Chiwŏn 朴趾源. *Yŏnamjip* 燕巖集 (Collected Writings of Pak Chiwŏn). Seoul: Kyŏnghŭi ch'ulp'ansa, 1966.

Palais, James B. *Politics and Policy in Traditional Korea*. Cambridge: Harvard University Press, 1975.

Peterson, Mark. "Women without Sons." In Laurel Kendall and Mark Peterson, eds., *Korean Women*, pp. 33–44. New Haven: East Rock Press, 1983.

Peterson, Willard J. *Bitter Gourd*. New Haven: Yale University Press, 1979.

Pibyŏnsa tŭngnok 備邊司謄錄 (Records of the Border Defense Command). 28 vols. Seoul: Kuksa p'yŏnch'an wiwŏnhoe, 1959–1960.

Puan Kim Ssi Uban komunsŏ 扶安金氏愚磻古文書 (The Old Documents of the Uban Puan Kim Family). Seoul: Han'guk chŏngsin munhwa yŏn'guwŏn, 1983.

Sakai Tadao 酒井忠夫. *Chūgoku zensho no kenkyū* 中国善書の研究 (A Study of the Morality Books of China). Tokyo: Kokusho kankokai, 1972.

—— "Yi Yulgok and the Community Compact." In de Bary and Haboush, eds., *The Rise of Neo-Confucianism in Korea*, pp. 323–48.

Sejong sillok 世宗實錄 (The Veritable Record of Sejong's Reign). 163 *kwŏn*. In *Chosŏn wangjo sillok*, vols. 2–6.

Shikata Hiroshi 四方博. "Richō jinkō kansuru mibun kaikyubetsuteki kansatsu" 李朝人口に關する身分階級別的觀察 (Observations on the Status and Class of the Yi Dynasty Population). In *Chōsen keizai no kenkyū* 朝鮮經濟の研究 (Studies in the Korean Economy). 3:368–482. 3 vols. Seoul: Keijō teikoku Daigaku hogakukai, 1938.

Shin, Susan. "Land Tenure and the Agrarian Economy in Yi Dynasty Korea 1600–1800." Ph. D. diss., Harvard University, 1973.

—— "The Social Structure of Kŭmhwa County in the Late Seventeenth Century." *Occasional Papers on Korea* (April 1974), 1:9–35.

—— "Some Aspects of Landlord-Tenant Relations in Yi Dynasty Korea." *Occasional Papers on Korea* (June 1975), 3:49–88.

Shirokauer, Conrad M. "Chu Hsi's Political Career: A Study in Ambivalence." In Arthur F. Wright and Denis Twichett, eds., *Confucian Personalities*, pp. 162–88. Stanford: Stanford University Press.

Shryock, John K. *The Origin and Development of the State Cult of Confucius: An Introductory Study*. New York and London: The Century Co., 1932.

Shu-ching 書經 (Book of Documents). 20 *chüan*. In *Shih-san-ching chu-su*.

Sohn, Pow-key. *Social History of the Early Yi Dynasty 1392–1592: With Emphasis on the Functional Aspects of Governmental Structure*. Ann Arbor, Mich.: University Microfilms, 1963.

Sok taejŏn 續大典 (Great Statutes, Continued). Seoul: Pŏpchech'ŏ, 1965.

Song Chunho 宋俊浩, "Han'guk e issŏsŏ ŭi kagye kirok ŭi yŏksa wa kŭ ihae" 韓國에있어서의家系記錄의歷史와그理解 (A History of Family Genealogies in Korea). *Yŏksa hakpo* 歷史學報 (1980), 87:99–143.

—— *Yijo saengwŏn chinsa-si ŭi yŏn'gu* 李朝生員進士試의研究 (The Saengwŏn and Chinsa

Bibliography

Examinations of the Yi Dynasty). Seoul: Taehan min'guk kukhoe tosŏgwan, 1970.

Sŏng Nakhun 成樂勳. *Han'guk tangjaengsa* 韓國黨爭史 (A History of Factionalism in Korea). In *Han'guk munhwasa taegye*, 2 : 219–388.

Song Siyŏl 宋時烈. *Songja taejŏn* 宋子大全 (Compendium of Master Song Siyŏl's Works). 7 vols. Seoul: Kimun hakhoe, 1971.

Sŏngjong sillok 成宗實錄 (The Veritable Record of Sŏngjong's Reign). 297 *kwŏn*. In *Chosŏn wangjo sillok*, vols. 8–12.

Sŏnjo sillok 宣祖實錄 (The Veritable Record of Sŏnjo's Reign). 221 *kwŏn*. In *Chosŏn wangjo sillok*, vols. 21–25.

Sŏnjo sujŏng sillok 宣祖修正實錄 (The Revised Veritable Record of Sŏnjo's Reign). 42 *kwŏn*. In *Chosŏn wangjo sillok*, vol. 25.

Spence, Jonathan D. *Emperor of China*. New York: Knopf, 1974.

Ssu-ma Ch'ien 司馬遷. *Shih-chi* 史記 (Records of the Grand Historian). 10 vols. Hong Kong: Chung-hua shu-chü, 1969.

Struve, Lynn A. *The Southern Ming, 1644–1662*. New Haven: Yale University Press, 1984.

Sukchong sillok 肅宗實錄 (The Veritable Record of Sukchong's Reign). 65 *kwŏn*. In *Chosŏn wangjo sillok*, vols. 38–41.

Sŭngjŏngwŏn ilgi 承政院日記 (Records of the Royal Secretariat), 115 vols. Seoul: Kuksa p'yŏnch'an wiwŏnhoe, 1961–1970.

T'aejo sillok 太祖實錄 (The Veritable Record of T'aejo's Reign). 36 *kwŏn*. In *Chosŏn wangjo sillok*, vol. 1.

T'aejong sillok 太宗實錄 (The Veritable Record of T'aejong's Reign). 36 *kwŏn*. In *Chosŏn wangjo sillok*, vols. 1–2.

Taga Akigorō 多賀秋五郎. *Chūgoku kyōikushi* 中国教育史 (A History of Education in China). Tokyo: Kawasaki shoten, 1955.

Takahashi Tōru 高橋亨. "Richō jugakushi ni okeru shuriha shukiha no hattatsu" 李朝儒學史に於ける主理派主氣派の發達 (Development of the Schools of Principle and of Material Force in Yi Confucianism). In *Chōsen Shina bunka no kenkyū* 朝鮮支那文化の研究 (Studies in Korean and Chinese Cultures), pp. 141–281. Seoul: Keijō teikoku Daigaku hobungakukai, 1929.

Tongguk yŏji pigo 東國輿地備攷 (Guide to Korean Geography). Seoul: Seoul T'ukpyŏlsisa p'yŏnch'an wiwŏnhoe, 1956.

T'ongmun'gwanji 通文館志 (Diplomatic Documents of the Yi Dynasty). Tokyo: Kankoku chinsho kankōkai, 1907.

Wagner, Edward W. "The Ladder of Success in Yi Dynasty Korea." *Occasional Papers on Korea* (April 1974), 1 : 1–8.

—— *The Literati Purges: Political Conflict in Early Yi Korea*. Cambridge: Harvard University Press, 1974.

—— "Social Stratification in Seventeenth-Century Korea: Some Observations from a 1663 Seoul Census Register." *Occasional Papers on Korea* (April 1974), 1 : 39–54.

Waley, Arthur, tr. *The Book of Songs*. New York: Grove Press, 1960.

Wang Ch'ung-wu 王崇武. *Ming pen-chi chiao-chu* 明本記校注 (The Ming Chronological History, Edited with Commentaries). Shanghai: Kuo-li chung-yang yen-chiu li-shih yü-yen yen-chiu-so, 1945.

Wechsler, Howard J. *Offerings of Jade and Silk: Ritual and Symbol in the Legitimation of the T'ang Dynasty*. New Haven: Yale University Press, 1985.

Bibliography

Wills, John E., Jr. "Maritime China from Wang Chih to Shih Lang." In Jonathan D. Spence and John E. Wills, Jr., eds., *From Ming to Ching*, pp. 203–38. New Haven: Yale University Press, 1979.

Wright, Arthur F. "Sui Legitimation: Formal Procedures." Paper read at the Conference on Legitimation in Chinese Regimes, June 15–24, 1975, Asilomar, Calif. Mimeograph.

Wright, Mary C. *The Last Stand of Chinese Conservatism*. New York: Atheneum, 1966.

Wu, Silas H. L. *Communication and Imperial Control in China: Evolution of the Palace Memorial System, 1693–1735*. Cambridge: Harvard University Press, 1970.

Yang Lien-sheng. "Historical Notes on the Chinese World Order." In John K. Fairbank, ed., *The Chinese World Order: Traditional China's Foreign Relations*, pp. 20–33. Cambridge: Harvard University Press, 1968.

Yi Chae 李縡. *Samgwan'gi* 三官記 (Records of the Three Offices). In *P'aerim*, pp. 331–401.

Yi Ch'unhŭi 李春熙. *Yijo sowŏn mun'gogo* 李朝書院文庫考 (Library Holdings of Private Academies in the Yi Dynasty). Seoul: Taehan min'guk kukhoe tosŏgwan, 1969.

Yi Ik 李瀷. *Sŏngho sasŏl* 星湖僿說 (Insignificant Jottings of Yi Ik). 2 vols. Seoul: Kyŏnghŭi ch'ulp'ansa, 1967.

Yi Kibaek 李基白. *Han'guksa sillon* 韓國史新論 (A New History of Korea). Seoul: Ilchogak, 1972.

Yi Kŏnch'ang 李建昌. *Tangŭi t'ongnyak* 黨議通略 (A General History of Factional Debates). Trans. Yi Minsu. Seoul: Ŭryu munhwasa, 1971.

Yi Kwanggyu 李光奎. "Chosŏn wangjo sidae ŭi chaesan sangsok" 朝鮮王朝時代의財產相續 (Property Inheritance in the Yi Dynasty). *Han'guk hakpo* 韓國學報 (1976), 2(2):58–91.

Yi Kwangjwa 李光佐. *Un'gok silgi* 雲谷實紀 (True Record of Yi Kwangjwa). Seoul: Ch'ŏnggu munhwasa, 1972.

Yi Munjŏng 李聞政. *Sumunnok* 隨聞錄 (Hearsay and Rumors). In *P'aerim*, 9:206–330.

Yi Pŏmjik 李範稷. "Chosŏn chŏn'gi ŭi kyosaeng sinbun" 朝鮮初期의校生身分 (The Status of Students in the Public School System of the Early Yi Dynasty). *Han'guk saron* 韓國史論 (Aug. 1976), 3:321–57.

Yi Pyŏnghyu 李秉烋. *Chosŏn chŏn'gi Kiho sarimp'a yŏn'gu* 朝鮮前期畿湖士林派研究 (A Study of the Kiho Sarim Group in the Early Yi Dynasty). Seoul: Ilchogak, 1984.

Yi Sangbaek 李相佰 et al. *Han'guksa* 韓國史 (History of Korea). 7 vols. Seoul: Chindan hakhoe, 1959–1965.

Yi Sŏngmu 李成茂. *Chosŏn ch'ogi yangban yŏn'gu* 朝鮮初期兩班研究 (A Study of the Yangban of the Early Yi Dynasty). Seoul: Ilchogak, 1980.

—— "The Influence of Neo-Confucianism on Education and the Civil Service Examination System in Fourteenth- and Fifteenth-Century Korea." In de Bary and Haboush, eds., *The Rise of Neo-Confucianism in Korea*, pp. 135–60.

Yi Sugŏn 李樹健, ed. *Kyŏngbuk chibang komunsŏ chipsŏng* 慶北地方古文書集成 (A Collection of Old Documents in the Northern Kyŏngsang Province). Kyŏngbuk: Yŏngnam Taehakkyo minjok munhwasa yŏn'gu, 1981.

—— *Yŏngnam sarimp'a ŭi hyŏngsŏng* 嶺南士林派의形成 (The Formation of the Yŏngnam Sarim Group). Kyŏngbuk: Yŏngnam Taehakkyo ch'ulp'anbu, 1979.

Yi T'aejin 李泰鎮. "Sŏŏl ch'adaego" 庶孼差待考 (On Discriminatory Practices Against Concubines' Children). *Yŏksa hakpo* 歷史學報 (April 1965), 27:65–104.

Bibliography

Yi Ŭrho 李乙浩. *Tasan kyŏnghak sasang yŏn'gu* 茶山經學思想研究 (A Study on Chŏng Yagyong's Ideas of the Classics). Seoul: Ŭryu munhwasa, 1966.

Yi Usŏng 李佑成. ''Yijo hugi Kŭn'gi hakp'a e issŏsŏ ŭi chŏngt'ongnon ŭi chŏn'gae'' 李朝後期近畿學派에있어서의正統論의展開 (The Theory of Legitimacy Developed by the Kyŏnggi School in the Late Yi Dynasty). *Yŏksa hakpo* 歷史學報 (Aug. 1966), 31:174–79.

Yi Yulgok (or Yi I) 李栗谷 (李珥). *Sŏnghak chibyo* 聖學輯要 (An Essential Guide for the Learning of the Sage). In Yi Yulgok, *Yulgok chŏnsŏ*.

—— *Tongho mundap* 東湖問答 (Questions and Answers at the East Lake). In Yi Yulgok, *Yulgok chŏnsŏ*.

—— *Yi Yulgok chŏnsŏ* 栗谷全書 (Complete Works of Yi Yulgok). 2 vols. Seoul: Sŏnggyun'gwan Taehakkyo Tonga yŏn'guwŏn, 1961.

Yŏlsŏng ŏje 列聖御製 (The Writings of the Successive Kings). Seoul: Myŏngmundang, 1983.

Yŏngjo sillok 英祖實錄 (The Veritable Record of Yŏngjo's Reign). 127 *kwŏn*. In *Chosŏn wangjo sillok*, vols. 41–44.

Yu Hongnyŏl 柳洪烈. ''Chōsen ni okeru shoin no seiritsu (2)'' 朝鮮に於ける書院の成立 (The Establishment of Private Academies in Korea). *Seikyū gakusō* 靑丘學叢 (Oct. 1939), 30:63–116.

Yu Hyŏngwŏn 柳馨遠. *Pan'gye surok* 磻溪隨錄 (The Free Jottings of Yu Hyŏngwŏn). Seoul: Tongguk munhwasa, 1958.

Yun Changsŏp 尹張燮. *Han'guk kŏnch'uksa* 韓國建築史 (A History of Architecture in Korea). Seoul: Tongmyŏngsa, 1984.

Yun Chŭng 尹拯. *Myŏngjae sŏnsaeng yugo* 明齋先生遺稿 (Manuscripts Left by Yun Chŭng). 2 vols. Seoul: Kyŏngin munhwasa, 1973.

Yun Hyu 尹鑴. *Paekho chŏnsŏ* 白湖全書 (Complete Works of Yun Hyu). 3 vols. Taegu: Kyŏngbuk Taekakkyo ch'ulp'anbu, 1974.

INDEX

Index

China, as center of civilization, 261*n*86
Ch'ing dynasty, 24-25
Ch'ing T'ai-tsung, invasion of Korea, 24
Ching-yen (Classics Mat Lecture), 63
Chinsa, increase of, 90
Chinsa-si, 89-90; *see also* Civil examination
Cho Chaeho, 210; opposes tax reform, 111; summoned to palace, 214
Cho Chunghoe, 152-53, 219-20, 225, 252
Cho Hyŏnmyŏng, 56, 93, 111, 135, 155-56, 159-60; military tax reform, 103; concurrence about tax reform, 108-9; replaces Noron with Soron (1727), 135; trusted minister, 157; implementation of *Great Instruction*, 160; memorials of resignation, 161; resignation accepted, 163; reappointed to State Council, 164; cautions Sado to consult with Yŏngjo, 177; sacrifice given, 191; death, 195
Cho Munmyŏng, 129-32, 135-36
Cho T'aech'ae, 123
Cho T'aegu, posthumously adjudged a rebel, 188
Cho T'aeŏk, 135
Cho Tobin, 135
Cho Yŏngjin, 211
Cho Yujin, 214
Ch'oe (lady), 54; as *musuri*, 57-58; first appearance in *Sillok*, 58; death in 1718, 58-59; conferring of title Hwagyŏng, 59; elevation of status after 1739, 59-60; new titles conferred, 59-60; conferred titles, 62
Ch'oe Kyusŏ, 137
Ch'oe Sŏkhang, posthumously stripped of post, 188
Ch'oe Sukpin, *see* Ch'oe (lady)
Chŏk (primary wives), 57
Chŏlla Province, seditious activity, 136
Chŏng Chedu, 67, 170
Chŏng Chin'gyo, 94
Chŏng Hongsun, 113

Chŏng Hwiryang, 211-12, 223; tries to resign, 180
Chŏng Mongju, 48
Chŏng Sun'gŏm, 229
Chŏng Tojŏn, 15-16; as author of Yi T'aejo's edict, 11-12; role in creation of Prime Minister, 12
Ch'ŏnggwan (pure officials), 95, 270*n*36
Ch'onggyech'ŏng (General Defense Unit), 97-98
Chŏnghun (*Instructions on Rule*), 177
Chŏngjo (r. 1776-1800), 168, 201, 202; Yŏngjo fears for his safety, 209; summary of reign, 233
Ch'ŏngju: planned attack on, 137; taken by rebels, 138-39
Chongmyo (Yi Ancestral Temple), 36, 49
Chŏngsŏng (queen), 62, 174-75; death, 193, 196; relationship with Sado, 196; cited in *Sillok* account of Sado's death, 211
Ch'ŏngyŏn (princess), 218
Ch'ŏnjo (Court of Heaven), 24
Chŏnju Yi (royal clan), 18-19; restriction on office holding, 19; clan with largest number of *munkwa* passers, 93
Ch'ŏnmyŏng (Mandate of Heaven), 7, 21, 108
Ch'ŏnŭi sogam (*Illuminating Mirror of Righteousness*), 190-91
Chosŏn wangjo sillok, see Sillok
Chou Shih-tsung, 69
Chronicles of the Successive Rules, 131
Chu Hsi, 13, 88; memorial to Hsiao-tsung (emperor), 10; regarded as peak of human achievement, 25-26
Chu Hsi school, 23-24
Chu Tzu chia-li (*Family Ritual*, Chu Hsi), 13, 88
Chu-ko Liang, 48
Ch'unch'ugwan (Bureau of State Records), 245
Ch'ung-chen (emperor), 39; sexagesima sacrifice, 40; offering of

Index

Index

Hwap'yŏng (princess), 197; death, 164
Hwawŏn (princess), 167, 197, 200; attends Sado's parties, 203
Hwinyŏngjŏn, 211
Hyangan (local gentry associations), 13
Hyanggyo (country schools), 17
Hyangyak (community compacts), 13
Hyojang (prince), 80, 154, 202, 233; death of, 148
Hyojong (r. 1649-1659), 98; audience with Song Siyŏl, 19; hostage in Mukden, 24; emulated by Yŏngjo, 50-51; reform of military tax, 96
Hyŏnjong (r. 1659-1674), 24, 248; conscription system, 100
Hyŏnjong kaesu sillok, 248
Hyŏnjong sillok, 248
Hyulmin ŭi (Ceremony of Expressing Sympathy to the People), 106-8
Hyungnye, see Mourning rituals

Identification plaques, offense to Ch'ing, 45-46
Illuminating Mirror of Righteousness, 190-91
Ilsŏngnok, 277-78n6
Im Sŏng, 219-20; advises Sado, 212; tries to prevent Sado from hurting his head, 222; pleads with Yŏngjo for Sado, 223; feeds Sado through hole, 227-28; final years, 232
Im Tŏkche, 212, 219-20, 225-26; ordered beheaded, 226, banished, 229
Imjin Wars, inadequacy of conscription system, 97
Imo ilgi, 202, 253
In (humanity), 38
In'gyŏng (queen), served by Yŏngjo, 51
Inhyŏn (queen), served by Yŏngjo, 51; possible cause of death, 58
Injo (r. 1623-1649), 50, 131; ignores Manchu overtures, 23-24
Instruction on Rule, 177
Investitutes of Yi king, 21-22

Inwŏn (queen), 31, 51, 61, 182; served by Yŏngjo, 51-53; honorifics given by Yŏngjo, 52; protects Yŏngjo, 124; death, 196

Japan, invasion of Korea (1590s), 23
Journal Written in Leisure, A, 167, 173-73, 232; historiography, 254-55
Justice, and a public man, 133-34

Kang Chihwan, 50
Kang Hongnip, 260n74
K'ang-hsi (r. 1661-1722), 25; tours kingdom, 104
Kangwŏn Province, population distribution, 87
Karye (rites of happiness), 36
Kiho hakp'a (Kiho school of Confucian scholarship), 88
Kija, 22, 41; appealed to for authority, 27
Kija Chosŏn, 41
Killye (auspicious rites), 36
Kim Chaero, 43, 80, 95, 111, 113, 160; counsels Yŏngjo to be gentle with his son, 181
Kim Ch'angjip, 123; restoration of honor, 150
Kim Chu, 48
Kim Chunggi, 138-41
Kim Chungman, 137
Kim Hwajung, appointed as recorder, 219, 252
Kim Igon, 228
Kim Ilgyŏng, 126-27, 131; execution, 140; posthumously adjudged a rebel, 188
Kim Sangno, 79, 182, 193-94; criticizes Yŏngjo's behavior to Sado, 195
Kim Sangsaeng, 68-69
Kim Sŏngŭng, 55, 211; ordered to behead Yun Hye, 189-90
Kim Suhang, 101
Kim Sujŏng, 224
Kim Tonguk, 254

313

Index

Kim Yangt'aek, 222
Kim Yŏnghae, 138
Kingly Way, 14, 117-18
Knowledge: relation to morality, 26
Kojong (r. 1863-1907), 93
Komyŏng (investiture), 21-22
Kong (public welfare), 120
Kongsin (merit subjects), 14
Korea: as sole custodian of
   civilization, 2-3; invasion by
   Japanese (1590s), 23; military
   security, 23; referred to as
   barbarian nation, 47-48
Korean society, Confucianization of,
   12-13
Koryŏ dynasty, and Yi legitimacy, 48
Koryŏ regime (918-1392), compared to
   Yi dynasty, 12
Koryŏ T'aejo (r. 918-943), 48
Kuan Yü, 49
Kuan Yü shrine, 49
Kŭkhaeng ("a most reverential
   ceremony"), 55
Kŭmwiyŏng (Palace Defense Unit), 98
Kunnye (military rites), 36
Kwanghae (r. 1608-1623), 23, 32, 49,
   247; deposal, 260*n*74
Kwanjemyo (Kuan Yü shrine), 49
Kwŏn Chŏngch'im, 220, 225; final
   years, 232
Kyŏnggi Province unrest, 137
Kyŏngjong (r. 1720-1724), 30;
   factionalism of reign, 3; purported
   poisoning by Yŏngjo, 32; served by
   Yŏngjo, 51; military tax reform,
   102; relation to Yŏngjo, 124; cause
   of death, 160, cause of death
   announced, 162-63; resembles Sado,
   175
Kyŏngjong sillok, 248; compared to
   Kyŏngjong sujŏng sillok, 249
Kyŏngjong sujŏng sillok, 248; compared
   to *Kyŏngjong sillok*, 249
Kyŏngyŏn, *see* Royal Lecture
Kyŏngsang Province, population
   distribution, 87-88
Kyŏngsun (king), Yŏngjo sacrifice, 48

Kyunyŏkch'ŏng (Office of the Equal
   Military Tax), 112, 114

Ladies-in-waiting, 267*n*192
Land acquisition, by commoners, 89
Landholding tax, 112-13; and military
   tax reform, 109
Landholdings, 99
Lesser offerings, 36
Literacy, as factor in growth of
   yangban, 89
Literary licentiate examination, *see*
   Chinsa-si
Lo Hsiang-chih, 97
Local gentry associations, 13
Loving majesty, 59-60
Loving parent, title of Lady Ch'oe, 59
Lu Chung-lien, 61
Lu wo (*Thick grows that tarragon*), 183

Magnificent harmony, *see T'angp'yŏng*
Manchus, effect on Yi dynasty, 23-24
Mandate of Heaven, 7, 21, 108
Mandongmyo (shrine), 40
Mapa'e (identification plaques), 45-46
Marriage custom, 259*n*43
Marriages, uxorilocal, 13
Master of the *T'angp'yŏng* policy, 148
Medium offerings, 36
Mencius, 73
Merit subjects, 14
Meritocracy: in Yi dynasty, 12; as
   bureaucratic alternative, 15
Military examinations, *see Mukwa*
Military rites, 36
Military service, financial support of,
   96-97
Military tax: compromised, 112; result
   of reform, 113-14
Military tax reform, 3, 84-85; defeated
   in 1681, 101; in wake of rebellion of
   1728, 102-3; and epidemic of 1750,
   108-9; protest, 180

314

Index

Ŏje kyŏngse p'yŏn (A Royal Discourse
on Cautioning the World), 73
Ŏje paekhaengwŏn (A Royal Study on
the Sources of Good Conduct), 73
Ŏllo (Official Channel for Speech), 125
Ŏn'gwan (Speaking officials), 125
Onyang, trip by Sado, 200-1
Oryun (five relations), 13
Outline of Koryŏ History, An, 48
Ou-yang Hsiu, 121
Owi (Five Commanderies), 96
Ŏyŏngch'ŏng (Royal Commandery
Division), 98

Pak Ch'ansin, 138
Pak Munsu, 81, 103, 111, 135-36;
proponent of household tax, 110;
trusted minister, 157; biography,
158-59; and support of Soron, 162;
frustrated with Yŏngjo's abdication,
183; talks to Yŏngjo concerning
harshness to Sado, 187-88; death,
195
Pak P'ilchu: appointed Minister of
Personnel, 162; resigns as tutor, 173
Pak P'ilmong, 140
Pak P'irhyŏn, arrest, 140
Pak Sanap, 219, 252
Pak Tongjun, 150
Palace Defense Unit, 98
Palace Estates, 99
Palace Intrigue, 148
Pao (judge), 158
Patrilineality, importance in Yi
dynasty, 13
Penal codes, Yŏngjo's approach, 95-96
P'il, 270n51
Pingae, 199; beaten to death by Sado,
201
Pinnye (guest rites), 36
Pirates, 258n15
Pogwŏl chŏngo, 248, 249
Population distribution, in Yi dynasty,
87
Posters: anti-Yŏngjo, 149; rebellious,
161; on palace gate, 164
Primary wives, 57

Prince of Mournful Thought, 231
Principle, 27
Private academies, 17-18; number
reduced by Yŏngjo, 152
Private parent, 54
Public man, and justice, 133-34
Public office: attitude toward by
scholar-officials, 121
Public welfare, 120
Pure officials, 95, 270n36
Purge of 1721-22, 30-31, 126-27;
destruction of transcript, 160
Pyŏn Tŭngnyang, 219-20
P'yŏngyang, trip by Sado, 202
P'youirok, 231

Rebellion of 1728, 3, 136-42;
conducted by Soron, 102; effects on
Yŏngjo, 142-43; Kim Ilgyŏng
responsibility, 150
Rebels, interrogation, 140
Record of Manifest Righteousness
(P'youirok), 231
Record of Prince Sado's Tutorial Office
(Changhŏn Seja tonggung ilgi), 251
Records Concerning the year 1762 (Imo
ilgi), 202, 253
Records of Administration, see Sijŏnggi
Records of the Crown Prince Office,
168-69
Records of the Grand Historian (Shih-
chi), 61
Records of the Royal Secretariat, see
Sŭngjŏngwŏn ilgi
Red Turbans, 258n15
Regent, power of, 177
Restoration: meaning of term, 33-34;
invocation of spirit of Yŏngjo, 34;
by Yŏngjo and its implications, 76
Revenue, decrease resulting from tax
loopholes, 100
Righteous principle, importance to
Noron, 133
Rites of happiness, 36
Ritual, 36-39; five categories of, 36;
requiring king's presence, 37;
political aspects, 37-39

316

Index

Index

Index

exercise of power, 75; military tax reform, 101; and *t'angp'yŏng* policy, 118-19

Sukchong sillok, 248-49

Sumptuary laws, 76-77

Sung dynasty (960-1279), bureaucracy, 1

Sung Jen-tsung, 70

Sungdŏkchŏn, 47

Sunginjŏn, 47

Sŭngjŏngwŏn (Royal Secretariat), 20

Sŭngjŏngwŏn ilgi, 202, 245-46, 251, 252; on merits of tax reform, 110-11; partially destroyed, 168

Sungnyŏlchŏn, 47

Sungnyŏngjŏn, 47

Sungŭijŏn, 47

Sunjo (r. 1800-1834), 254

Suŏch'ŏng (Royal Castle Defense Unit), 98

Supplement to the Extension of the Great Learning (Ta-hsüeh yen-i pu), 47-48

Ta-hsüeh (Great Learning), 8-9, 66, 72

Ta-hsüeh yen-i pu, 47-48

Taebodan (altar), 40

Taehun, see Great Instruction

T'aejo, 131

Taesa (great offerings), 36

Taiwan, conquest by Ch'ing court (1683), 24

Tanjong (r. 1452-1455), 14

T'angp'yŏng, 117-19; becomes medium of repression, 232

T'angp'yŏng policy: central defense of, 143; declaration of, 129; enforcement, 157; and expectations for Sado, 171; as inhibitor for communication between Sado and Yŏngjo, 179; threatened by subjugations of rebels and publication of *Illuminating Mirror*, 190-91; threatens Noron self-image as moral beings, 134

T'angp'yŏngju (Master of the T'angp'yŏng policy), 148

Tan'gun, 47

Tanŭi (queen), served by Yŏngjo, 51

Tax exempt land, 99

Tax loopholes, 99-100

Tax reform, opposition, 111-12

Thick grows that tarragon, 183

T'ien-tzu (Son of Heaven), 20-21

Titles, purchase during Imjin Wars, 89

Tŏk, see Virtue

Toktae (solitary audience), 20

Tongin (faction), 20

Tongmyŏng (king), 47

Tradition: as continually evolving, 27-28

Tu Yen, 70

Twiju taewang (Great King of the Rice Chest), 167

Ŭijŏngbu (State Council), 12

Ŭiri (righteous principle), 133

Virtue, 38; and kingship, 7-8

Wagner, Edward, 16

Wan-li (emperor), 39; calligraphy published, 45; erection of permanent altar to, 40

Wang Yang-ming school, 23

Wangdo (Kingly Way), 15, 117-18

Wen (king), 106

Wen-ti (emperor), 56, 57, 176

Wen T'ien-hsiang, 48

Westerners (faction), *see* Sŏin

White dragon, in dream on night of Yŏngjo's birth, 76

Wild histories, 169

Wine, and Yŏngjo temperance, 79

Wine brewing, proscription of, 80

Wine law, violation of, 79

Wŏnja poyangch'ŏng (Guidance Office of the Primary Prince), 170

Wu San-kuei, rebellion 1673, 24

Wu-ti (emperor), 176

Index

Index

Ying-tsung (emperor), 56
Yongbi ŏch'ŏn'ga (*Songs of Flying Dragons*), 22, 23
Yŏngbin, *see* Yi (lady)
Yŏngjo: basis of pursuit of sage kingship, 2; political ethos of court, 3; relations with Sado, 4, 5; eschews factionalism, 20; difficulty of drawing symbols of authority from China, 26; and ancestral authority, 28; coronation ceremony of 1724, 29-30; coronation edict, 31; use of rituals, 36-38; acts of penance, 38; appeasement of acts of Heaven, 38-39; use of symbols of history and tradition, 39; use of Ming symbols, 43-44; reluctance to share Ming symbols, 46; respect for Ming, 46; campaign to establish Korea's noble origins, 47; uses of symbols, 47-49; reverence to T'aejo, 49-50; as mourner, 51; relation with mother, 53-54; clash with officials over serving Lady Ch'oe, 54-55; conflict with Song Inmyŏng over respect for mother Lady Ch'oe, 55-56; titles conferred, 59; authority sought through moral perfection, 60; absurd loyalty tests for officials, 61; additional titles in 1776, 62; mother honored, 62; role in Royal Lecture, 63-64; diligence in study, 66--67; self-depreciation at Royal Lecture, 67; as arbiter at Royal Lecture, 68; metamorphosis at Royal Lecture, 68; quoted in *Sodae*, 68-69; as arbiter and lecturer, 72; lecture on *Doctrine of the Mean*, 72; erudition and sage rule, 73; writings, 73-74; various works, 74; usefulness of moral image, 83; concessions to discontents, 92-93; increase in degree holders with undistinguished rural backgrounds, 93; attempts to subdue factionalism, 94; deals with discrimination against children of concubines, 94-95; lives outside palace, 104-5; abstention of overt use of power with commoners, 105; compensation for damage done to populace, 105; direct contact with people, 105-6; announcement to people about military tax reform, 109-10; sends gifts to commoners, 115; objective with *t'angp'yŏng*, 119-21; as cause of factional rift, 122-23; plot on life by Soron, 123; relation to Kyŏngjong, 124; problems with factional alliances, 124-25; attempts to avoid purges, 127-28; conversation with Min Chinwŏn, 129-32; orders mobilization of troops, 138; accused of Kyŏngjong's murder, 141; effects of rebellion of 1728, 142-43; attempts at factional cooperation, 143-44; hunger strike to stop factionalism, 145-46; ambivalence toward Soron, 147; assumes autocratic role, 151; equates his person to state, 152; tightens grip on official community, 152; surpresses censorial voice, 152-53; use of threat of abdication, 154, 157; first edict of abdication, 155; edict of abdication (1749), 164-65; execution of Sado, 166-69; chooses wife for Sado, 170-71; expectations for Sado, 172-73; difficulties with Sado, 173-74; relationship with Sado worsens, 175; transfers responsibilities to Sado, 178; rumors of Kyŏngjong's death, 182; talks of abdication, 183-84; rebuffs Sado's memorials, 184; teaches Sado filial piety, 186-87; criticizes Sado publicly, 187; dream concerning factions, 188; punishes Soron for rebellious posters, 188-89; challenged at *munkwa* examination, 189; attempts to behead Yun Hye, 189-90; defense against regicide, 190; demands written pledges renouncing factionalism, 191; refuses to acknowledge Sado's

Index

OTHER WORKS IN ASIAN
STUDIES SERIES

NEO-CONFUCIAN STUDIES

Instructions for Practical Living and Other Neo-Confucian Writings by
    Wang Yang-ming, tr. Wing-tsit Chan   1963
Reflections on Things at Hand: The Neo-Confucian Anthology, comp.
    Chu Hsi and Lü Tsu-ch'ien, tr. Wing-tsit Chan   1967
Self and Society in Ming Thought, by Wm. Theodore de Bary and the
    Conference on Ming Thought. Also in paperback ed.   1970
The Unfolding of Neo-Confucianism, by Wm. Theodore de Bary and the
    Conference on Seventeenth-Century Chinese Thought. Also in
    paperback ed.   1975
Principle and Practicality:Essays in Neo-Confucianism and Practical
    Learning, ed. Wm. Theodore de Bary and Irene Bloom. Also in
    paperback ed.   1979
The Syncretic Religion of Lin Chao-en, by Judith A. Berling   1980
The Renewal of Buddhism in China: Chu-hung and the Late Ming
    Synthesis, by Chün-fang Yü   1981
Neo-Confucian Orthodoxy and the Learning of the Mind-and-Heart, by
    Wm. Theodore de Bary   1981
Yüan Thought: Chinese Thought and Religion Under the Mongols, ed.
    Hok-lam Chan and Wm. Theodore de Bary   1982
The Liberal Tradition in China, by Wm. Theodore de Bary   1983
The Development and Decline of Chinese Cosmology, by John B.
    Henderson   1984
The Rise of Neo-Confucianism in Korea, ed. Wm. Theodore de Bary and
    JaHyun Kim Haboush   1985
Chiao Hung and the Restructuring of Neo-Confucianism in the Late Ming,
    by Edward T. Ch'ien   1985
Neo-Confucian Terms Explained: The *Pei-hsi tzu-i* by Ch'en Ch'un, ed.
    and trans. Wing-tsit Chan   1986
Knowledge Painfully Acquired: The *K'un-chih chi* by Lo Ch'in-shun, ed.
    and trans. Irene Bloom   1987
To Become a Sage: The Ten Diagrams on Sage Learning by Yi T'oegye, ed.
    and trans. Michael C. Kalton   1988

MODERN ASIAN LITERATURE SERIES

Modern Japanese Drama: An Anthology, ed. and tr. Ted T. Takaya. Also
    in paperback ed.   1979

Other Works in Asian Studies Series

TRANSLATIONS FROM THE ORIENTAL CLASSICS

Other Works in Asian Studies Series

The *Manyōshū*, Nippon Gakujutsu Shinkōkai edition. Paperback text
    edition.   1969
Records of the Historian: Chapters from the Shih chi of Ssu-ma Ch'ien.
    Paperback text edition, tr. Burton Watson.   1969
Cold Mountain: 100 Poems by the T'ang Poet Han-shan, tr. Burton
    Watson. Also in paperback ed.   1970
Twenty Plays of the Nō Theatre, ed. Donald Keene. Also in paperback ed.   1970
Chushingura: The Treasury of Loyal Retainers, tr. Donald Keene. Also in
    paperback ed.   1971
The Zen Master Hakuin: Selected Writings, tr. Philip B. Yampolsky   1971
*Chinese Rhyme-Prose: Poems in the Fu Form from the Han and Six
    Dynasties Periods,* tr. Burton Watson. Also in paperback ed.   1971
Kūkai: Major Works, tr. Yoshito S. Hakeda. Also in paperback ed.   1972
*The Old Man Who Does as He Pleases: Selections from the Poetry and
    Prose of Lu Yu,* tr. Burton Watson   1973
The Lion's Roar of Queen Śrīmālā, tr. Alex & Hideko Wayman   1974
*Courtier and Commoner in Ancient China: Selections from the History of
    the Former Han by Pan Ku,* tr. Burton Watson. Also in paperback ed.   1974
Japanese Literature in Chinese, vol. 1: *Poetry and Prose in Chinese by
    Japanese Writers of the Early Period,* tr. Burton Watson   1975
Japanese Literature in Chinese, vol. 2: *Poetry and Prose in Chinese by
    Japanese Writers of the Later Peiod,* tr. Burton Watson   1976
Scripture of the Lotus Blossom of the Fine Dharma, tr. Leon Hurvitz. Also
    in paperback ed.   1976
Love Song of the Dark Lord: Jayadeva's Gītagovinda, tr. Barbara Stoler
    Miller. Also in paperback ed. Cloth ed. includes critical text of the
    Sanskrit.   1977
Ryōkan: Zen Monk-Poet of Japan, tr. Burton Watson   1977
*Calming the Mind and Discerning the Real: From the Lam rim chen mo of
    Tson-kha-pa,* tr. Alex Wayman   1978
*The Hermit and the Love-Thief: Sanskirt Poems of Bhartrihari and
    Bilhana,* tr. Barbara Stoler Miller   1978
The Lute: Kao Ming's p'i-p'a chi, tr. Jean Mulligan. Also in paperback ed.   1980
*A Chronicle of Gods and Sovereigns: Jinnō Shōtōki of Kitabatake
    Chikafusa,* tr. H. Paul Varley   1980
Among the Flowers: The Hua-chien chi, tr. Lois Fusek   1982
Grass Hill: Poems and Prose by the Japanese Monk Gensei, tr. Burton
    Watson   1983
*Doctors, Diviners, and Magicians of Ancient China: Biographies of
    Fang-shih,* tr. Kenneth J. DeWoskin. Also in paperback ed.   1983
Theatre of Memory: The Plays of Kālidāsa, ed. Barbara Stoler Miller. Also
    in paperback ed.   1984
*The Columbia Book of Chinese Poetry: From Early Times to the Thirteenth
    Century,* ed. and tr. Burton Watson   1984
*Poems of Love and War: From the Eight Anthologies and the Ten Songs of
    Classical Tamil,* tr. A. K. Ramanujan. Also in paperback ed.   1985
The Columbia Book of Later Chinese Poetry, ed. and tr. Jonathan Chaves   1986

Other Works in Asian Studies Series

STUDIES IN ORIENTAL CULTURE

COMPANIONS TO ASIAN STUDIES

326

Other Works in Asian Studies Series

The Classic Chinese Novel: A Critical Introduction, by C. T. Hsia. Also in
    paperback ed.   1968
Chinese Lyricism: Shih Poetry from the Second to the Twelfth Century, tr.
    Burton Watson. Also in paperback ed.   1971
A Syllabus of Indian Civilization, by Leonard A. Gordon and Barbara
    Stoler Miller   1971
Twentieth-Century Chinese Stories, ed. C. T. Hsia and Joseph S. M. Lau.
    Also in paperback ed.   1971
A Syllabus of Chinese Civilization, by J. Mason Gentzler, 2d ed.   1972
A Syllabus of Japanese Civilization, by H. Paul Varley, 2d ed.   1972
An Introduction to Chinese Civilization, ed. John Meskill, with the
    assistance of J. Mason Gentzler   1973
An Introduction to Japanese Civilization, ed. Arthur E. Tiedemann   1974
A Guide to Oriental Classics, ed. Wm. Theodore de Bary and Ainslie T.
    Embree, 2d ed. Also in paperback ed.   1975
Ukifune: Love in the Tale of Genji, ed. Andrew Pekarik   1982

INTRODUCTION TO ORIENTAL CIVILIZATIONS
Wm. Theodore de Bary, Editor

Sources of Japanese Tradition 1958 Paperback ed., 2 vols., 1964
Sources of Indian Tradition 1958 Paperback ed., 2 vols., 1964
Sources of Chinese Tradition 1960 Paperback ed., 2 vols., 1964
Sources of Japanese Tradition 1958 Paperback ed., 2 vols., 1964
Sources of Indian Tradition 1958 Paperback ed., 2 vols., 1964
Sources of Chinese Tradition 1960 Paperback ed., 2 vols., 1964

IN THE NEO-CONFUCIAN WORLD, THE ideal of the sage king was that of an ordinary man whose extraordinary virtue made him supreme. Possessing concern, compassion, unfailing discernment, and undivided dedication to public welfare, he was, by his example, to lead men into a perfect order in which they lived in harmony with themselves and the moral universe. One of the most fascinating examples of Neo-Confucian sage kingship is that of Yŏngjo, the eighteenth-century Korean monarch who was one of that country's most illustrious yet most tragic rulers. In *A Heritage of Kings*, JaHyun Kim Haboush provides an outstanding introduction to traditional Korean culture through the story of Yŏngjo, and offers profound insights into the complex interplay between Confucian rhetoric and the politics of the Yi monarchy (1392-1910).

Haboush focuses on the deteriorating relationship between Yŏngjo, who ruled from 1724 to 1776, and his only son, Crown Prince Sado. She examines how Yŏngjo attempted to build his image as sage king and how he used it first to overcome the aftereffects of his predecessors' factional politics, and then to buttress his legitimacy and authority. Yŏngjo astutely sought and employed the appropriate rhetoric and themes in Confucian rule to help effect the policies he thought necessary. Among these approaches were the rhetoric of the ruler-father, which he used to implement military tax reform, and the theme of grand harmony, utilized to curb factionalism in his court.

As Haboush shows, the Confucian ruler possessed a dual character, as public figure and private man. For Yŏngjo, this duality is poignantly portrayed in his troubled relationship with his son Sado. Expected by his father to be at once a private son